Shakespeare and Continental Philosophy

Shakespeare and Continental Philosophy

Edited by Jennifer Ann Bates
and Richard Wilson

EDINBURGH
University Press

© editorial matter and organisation Jennifer Ann Bates and
Richard Wilson, 2014
© the chapters their several authors, 2014

Edinburgh University Press Ltd
The Tun - Holyrood Road, 12(2f) Jackson's Entry, Edinburgh EH8 8PJ

www.euppublishing.com

Typeset in 10.5/13 Adobe Sabon by
Servis Filmsetting Ltd, Stockport, Cheshire,
and printed and bound in Great Britain by
CPI Group (UK) Ltd, Croydon CR0 4YY

A CIP record for this book is available from the British Library

ISBN 978 0 7486 9494 5 (hardback)
ISBN 978 0 7486 9495 2 (webready PDF)
ISBN 978 0 7486 9559 1 (paperback)
ISBN 978 0 7486 9497 6 (epub)

The right of Jennifer Ann Bates and Richard Wilson
to be identified as Editor of this work has been
asserted in accordance with the Copyright,
Designs and Patents Act 1988, and the Copyright
and Related Rights Regulations 2003 (SI No. 2498).

Contents

Part Three: Damnable Iteration

Foreword

The essays collected in this volume testify to the ongoing appeal of Shakespeare as both dramatist and thinker. While their contents are varied – the essays here touch on a range of thinkers from Ibn Sīnā to Jean-Luc Marion – they explore the ways in which Shakespearean drama presents thought with powerful and, at times, sensuous objects for reflection. Shakespeare studies has begun to move towards philosophy again after a period of wariness: poststructuralism offered new ways of talking about subjectivity, discourse, and the language of these plays, but it made the sustained study of ideas in the plays problematic. The essays in this collection do not solve that problem, which grows out of a sense that the study of *concepts* in drama is a misnomer. Certain forms of poststructuralism and historicist criticism, for example, have questioned the diagrammatic power of concepts to bring persons, events or things into intelligible kinds of relation. That power is being tested anew by scholars and thinkers willing to stray back into the hinterland of ideas.

What is important about this collection of essays, aside from the insights advanced by the individual authors, is what it represents as an undertaking: a desire to count the benefits of our engagement with Shakespearean drama as *conceptual* ones, a process that deepens our understanding of basic notions such as art, forgiveness, tragedy, dreams or desire and asserts the ongoing claim of these concepts on life and thought. Continental philosophy is a powerful resource in this enterprise, powerful precisely because it recognises (and perhaps even demands) imaginative experience of the sort we have in the theatre as a source of productive thinking and reflection.

If, as the commonplace goes, all great artists are also thinkers, we might think of this collection as an exploration of the commonplace's three key terms: 'great', 'artist' and 'thinker'. Take any two of these names and apply them to an individual; the first two will often explain why that individual also deserves the third. Exploring this geometry and these questions is an admirable goal for a collection of essays on Shakespeare and Continental Philosophy, one that is accomplished in the pages that follow.

Michael Witmore
Washington DC, February 2012

Acknowledgements

We would like to thank our contributors, and the Edinburgh University Press, especially our editor Jackie Jones, for her support of the project. Thanks are also due to Jackie's staff, especially Ellie Bush and Dhara Patel for their help in putting this book into its published shape. We would also like to thank the Department of Philosophy, Duquesne University, (especially the Chair, Ronald Polansky) for generously covering reprint costs for Julia Lupton Reinhard's and Christopher Pye's articles.

'Levinas and Shakespeare' by Howard Caygill was first published in *Monokl*, 8–9 (2010), pp. 507–11; 'Contra Schmitt: Law, Aesthetics and Absolutism in Shakespeare's *The Winter's Tale*' by Christopher Pye was first published in *South Atlantic Quarterly*, 108:1 (2009), pp. 197–217; 'Arendt in Italy: Or, the Taming of the Shrew' by Julia Reinhard Lupton was first published in *Law, Culture and the Humanities*, 1:16 (2011); 'Ship of Fools: Foucault and the Shakespeareans' by Richard Wilson was first published in *English Studies*, 94:7 (2013), pp. 773–87; a longer version of 'Provoking Philosophy: Shakespeare, Johnson, Wittgenstein, Derrida' by Christopher Norris, first appeared in the *Journal of Literary Criticism*, 12:1–2 (2012), pp. 51–107 reprinted here with thanks to the editor Rajnath; 'Miracle Play' by Nicholas Royle was first published in *Oxford Literary Review*, 34 (2012), pp. 123–53. We are grateful to the publishers and editors for permission to reprint these essays, which appear here with minor revisions and corrections.

Notes on Contributors

Jennifer Ann Bates is Associate Professor of Philosophy at Duquesne University. She is the author of *Hegel's Theory of Imagination* (2004) and *Hegel and Shakespeare on Moral Imagination* (2010). She has published in the *Wallace Stevens Journal*, the *Journal for Environmental Ethics*, *Criticism*, *Philosophy Compass*, and most recently in the Special Issue 'Thinking with Shakespeare' of *Memoria di Shakespeare*.

Catherine Belsey is Research Professor in English at Swansea University. She is author of *Critical Practice* (1980, 2002), *A Very Short Introduction to Poststructuralism* (2002), *Culture and the Real* (2005) and *A Future for Criticism* (2011). Her other books include *Shakespeare and the Loss of Eden* (1999), *Why Shakespeare?* (2007) and *Shakespeare in Theory and Practice* (2008).

Edward S. Casey is Distinguished Professor of Philosophy at SUNY, Stony Brook. The immediate past president of the American Philosophical Association, Eastern Division, he is the author of a number of books and many articles. His dissertation was entitled 'Poetry and Ontology'. Among his major books are *Getting Back into Place* (2nd edn, 2009), *The Fate of Place* (1997), *Remembering* (2nd edn, 2000), and *Imagining* (2nd edn, 2000). His most recently published book is *The World at a Glance* (2007), a companion volume to which he is now completing to be titled *The World on Edge*.

Howard Caygill is Professor of Modern European Philosophy at Kingston University, London. He is author of *Levinas and the Political* (2002); *Walter Benjamin: The Colour of Experience* (1998); *A Kant Dictionary* (1995); *Art of Judgment* (1989). He has published many articles and book chapters on authors ranging from Momigliano to Kafka,

Benjamin, Levinas and Derrida, and on topics as diverse as history, political theology, memory, allegory, messianism and art.

Andrew Cutrofello is Professor of Philosophy at Loyola University Chicago. He received his doctorate from Northwestern University in 1989. He is the author of five books, including *All for Nothing: Hamlet's Negativity* (2014), *Continental Philosophy: A Contemporary Introduction* (2005), and *The Owl at Dawn: A Sequel to Hegel's* Phenomenology of Spirit (1995).

Bernard Freydberg is Emeritus Professor of Philosophy at Slippery Rock University and Scholar in Residence at Duquesne University. His latest two books are *The Thought of John Sallis: Phenomenology, Plato, Imagination* (Northwestern University Press, 2012) and *David Hume, Platonic Philosopher, Continental Ancestor* (2012). He is currently working on a book tentatively entitled *Under the Overwritten Palimpsest: Uncovering the Genesis of Modern Philosophy.*

Peter Holbrook is Professor of Shakespeare and English Renaissance Literature at the University of Queensland, Australia, and Director of the UQ Node of the ARC Centre of Excellence for the History of Emotions (Europe 1100–1800). He is the author of *Shakespeare's Individualism* (2010) and *Literature and Degree in Renaissance England: Nashe, Bourgeois Tragedy, Shakespeare* (1994), and co-editor, with David Bevington, of *The Politics of the Stuart Court Masque* (1998).

James A. Knapp is Associate Professor and Edward L. Surtz, S.J. Professor of English at Loyola University Chicago. He is the author of *Illustrating the Past in Early Modern England* (2003) and *Image Ethics in Shakespeare and Spenser* (2011). His work has appeared in *Shakespeare Quarterly*, *ELH*, *Criticism* and *Poetics Today* as well as a variety of essay collections.

Paul A. Kottman is Associate Professor of Comparative Literature at the New School for Social Research. He is the author of *A Politics of the Scene* (2008) and *Tragic Conditions in Shakespeare* (2009), as well as the editor of *Philosophers on Shakespeare* (2009). He is also the editor of a new book series, entitled *Square One: First Order Questions in the Humanities* (Stanford University Press). He is currently completing a book tentatively entitled, *Defying the Stars: Romantic Love as Human Freedom.*

Julia Reinhard Lupton is Professor of English and Comparative Literature at the University of California, Irvine, where she has taught since 1989. She is the author or co-author of four books on Shakespeare, most recently *Thinking with Shakespeare: Essays on Politics and Life* (2011). She is co-editor with Graham Hammill of *Political Theology in Early Modernity* (2012). Her current book project is entitled *Shakespeare Dwelling: Habitation, Hospitality, and Environments of Action*. She is a 2013–14 Guggenheim Fellow.

Christopher Norris is Distinguished Research Professor in Philosophy at the University of Cardiff, Wales, where he previously taught English Literature. He has written more than thirty books to date on aspects of philosophy and literary theory. His most recent publications are *Philosophy Outside-In: A Critique of Academic Reason* (2013) and *The Cardinal's Dog and Other Poems* (2013), a collection of verse-essays on philosophical, musical and literary themes, including one about Wittgenstein and Shakespeare, the topic of his chapter here.

Christopher Pye is Class of 1924 Professor of English at Williams College. He is the author of *The Regal Phantasm: Shakespeare and the Politics of Spectacle* (1990), *The Vanishing: Shakespeare, the Subject and Early Modern Culture* (2000), and *The Storm at Sea: Political Aesthetics in the Time of Shakespeare* (forthcoming). He is currently working on a history of distraction.

Nicholas Royle is Professor of English at the University of Sussex, England. He is author of numerous books, including *Telepathy and Literature: Essays on the Reading Mind* (1991), *The Uncanny* (2003), *How to Read Shakespeare* (2005), and *Veering: A Theory of Literature* (2011). He has also published a novel, *Quilt* (2010). He is an editor of the *Oxford Literary Review* and director of the Centre for Creative and Critical Thought at Sussex.

Tom Stern is a Lecturer in Philosophy and the Academic Director of European Social and Political Studies at University College London, where he has worked since getting his PhD from Cambridge University. His research interests include nineteenth-century German philosophy (especially Schopenhauer and Nietzsche) and aesthetics. His book, *Philosophy and Theatre* (2013), presents a series of philosophical topics, problems or questions which arise in relation to theatre.

Richard Wilson is the Sir Peter Hall Professor of Shakespeare Studies at Kingston University, London, and the author of *Will Power: Studies in Shakespearean Authority* (1993), *Secret Shakespeare: Essays on Theatre, Religion and Resistance* (2004), *Shakespeare in French Theory: King of Shadows* (2007), and *Free Will: Art and Power on Shakespeare's Stage* (2013). Previously Professor of English Literature at Cardiff University, he was until 2005 Professor of Renaissance Studies at Lancaster University. He has been a Visiting Professor of the Sorbonne Nouvelle (Paris III), and in 2011–12 was Distinguished Visiting Professor at the Sorbonne (Paris IV). His forthcoming book is a study of Shakespeare and globalisation: *Worldly Shakespeare: The Theatre of Our Good Will.*

Introduction

Richard Wilson

'It sometimes seems to me that the whole of philosophy is only a meditation of Shakespeare': Emmanuel Levinas's encomium testifies to the
centrality of the English writer's plays and poems in the European
philosophical tradition for which the Jewish thinker was exemplary.[1] In
Shakespeare and Continental Philosophy fifteen literary critics and philosophers consider why such a tribute could only come from a continental
philosopher. By doing so they also ask implicitly why this homage could
never have come from a philosopher working in the Anglo-American tradition. For a surprising paradox of the global reception of Shakespeare's
works has been the imperviousness of professional philosophy in Britain
and the United States towards these primary Western cultural icons, an
obtuseness so dense that when some academic philosopher from the
Cambridge of either country does reflect on them 'from a specifically
philosophical perspective', the assumption is that while we might 'feel
large themes are at work in the plays' – in the words of *Shakespeare's
Philosophy*, a 2006 book grandly subtitled, *Discovering the Meaning
Behind the Plays* – 'little attempt has been made to identify and articulate
these philosophical themes'.[2] One of the aims of the present collection
is to counter such obliviousness by contrasting Anglophone philosophical critiques with the richness of the engagement with the works
of Shakespeare sustained over three centuries by continental philosophy,
and with the interpretative opportunities that this engagement opens up
for contemporary philosophers and critics.

It seems all too apt that, although the earliest extant criticism of
Shakespeare we possess originated in the bedchamber of the father of
Anglo-Saxon empiricism, Sir Francis Bacon, this record of a country-
house performance of *Titus Andronicus* in 1596 was penned not by
the author of *The New Atlantis*, but by one of his French *mignons*, a
teenage musician named Jacques Petit.[3] England's premier philosopher,
who to the chagrin of authorship high-birthers believed theatre a mere

toy, left no comment on Shakespeare. A year after his protégé reported, however, that the play was 'all show and no substance', the voice of Baconian science was heard in a memorandum by one William Scott, a secretary in the Elizabethan defence ministry, who set the terms for the philosophical interrogation of these works when he complained that in *Richard II* he found only flashiness and confusion. In the style-manual he issued to his office, Scott singled out the history play as a caution against 'stuffing' a 'well conceited' brief with 'very idle' phraseology, and anathematised Shakespeare's 'piling of one phrase upon another' for obstructing the 'perspicuity when words are, as it were, thoroughly clear and transparent to convey the meaning to our understanding'. The bureaucrat's fetish for 'well-sorted usual words and fit and natural knitting of them' stands behind the regime of *The Complete Plain Words* in the civil service milieu of the TV comedy *Yes, Minister!* But his delusion that it is possible to communicate with zero-degree figuration, so that 'having no obscure ambiguous phrase, the reader proceeds without let or rub to understand what is delivered', also anticipated the 'ordinary language' ethos that prevented Wittgenstein from appreciating the Shakespeare productions at Keynes's Cambridge Arts Theatre:[4]

> When I hear the expression of admiration for Shakespeare by distinguished men, I can never rid myself of the suspicion that praising him has been the conventional thing to do . . . His pieces give me the impression of enormous 'sketches' rather than paintings; as though they had been 'dashed off' by someone who can permit himself 'anything', so to speak. And . . . I don't like it.[5]

How could two thinkers disagree as radically about something so central to our culture as Levinas and Wittgenstein did about Shakespeare? One answer *Shakespeare and Continental Philosophy* suggests is that this conflict over show and substance is simply the latest bout in what Plato was already calling 'the ancient quarrel between philosophy and poetry' when he banished plays and poets from his republic.[6] For if continental philosophy believes that 'literature thinks', being 'the form *par excellence* of the practice of language', as Jean-Jacques Lecercle puts it, that controversy focuses acutely on a theatre poet for whom, as Samuel Johnson famously regretted, equivocating wordplay 'was what luminous vapours are to the traveller . . . the fatal Cleopatra for which he lost the world'.[7] Indeed, introducing one of the best previous anthologies on the philosophical Shakespeare, John Joughin diagnoses the logical-positivist aversion precisely as an abjection of the uncanniness implied by the Doctor's pregnant metaphor, when he observes that these dramas 'are phantoms that resist critical appropriation', even as they 'constantly invite changing modes of theoretical analysis'. Thus, it is in hypothesising the 'hitherto unthought', and 'revealing the limits of our truth claims' in scenes that 'let wonder seem familiar' (*Much Ado*, 5.4.70), that Shakespeare remains, on this view, so *unheimlich* for analytic thinking; and one of the rare Anglo-American philosophers to hear the siren song agrees: 'What Wittgenstein senses in Shakespeare's language', Stanley Cavell infers, is the threat that 'chaos is come again' (*Othello*, 3.3.95).[8] Of course, these gendered reactions reflect male domination of the philosophical discipline. But they reveal too how the Shakespeare question is at the epicentre of philosophy's seismic rift with the aesthetic. For as Hugh Grady comments, 'In Shakespeare's age and our own, the aesthetic is a licensed discourse precisely because it is deemed to be in a special zone exempt from the truth claims implied by ordinary discourse.'[9]

When Anglophone philosophy does yoke Shakespeare to its ideals of truth and logic, it is as a realist, for whom the purpose of art is 'to hold the mirror up to nature' (*Hamlet*, 3.2.20).[10] Such is Hamlet's advice to the Players. But Hamlet is not Shakespeare; and nothing could be less like the Bardolatry of Harold Bloom, let alone of continental philosophy, than the argument in *Shakespeare's Philosophy* that 'he didn't *invent* humanity ... It was waiting to be discovered', so his genius consisted of 'submission to nature. He didn't impose his vision on reality. He told us how the world looks'.[11] Less naively mimetic has been the realism of the Chicago School that descends *via* Leo Strauss from the Nazi attorney Carl Schmitt. Allan Bloom's project, for instance, 'of making Shakespeare the theme of philosophic reflection', as 'the first philosopher of history', who portrayed 'human beings just as they are', was rooted in a Schmittian prioritising of politics over aesthetics, the existentialism spelled out in the lawyer's own *Hamlet or Hecuba*.[12] The force of this book lies in its claim that as there was no separation in a playhouse between players and playgoers, 'society too was on stage', and this anachronism substantiated the political theology of divine right. 'Hitler's Crown Jurist' thus de-Hamletised *Hamlet*, as a *presentation* of his Hobbesian maxim that 'Sovereign is he who decides on the exception', by grounding its plot in the Prince's 'sacred blood right'.[13] A 2009 English translation of Schmitt's decisionist critique therefore brought to a crunch the debate on whether Shakespearean theatre incarnated princely *presence*, or symbolised its transfer, as Ernst Kantorowicz and Jürgen Habermas countered, into a *representation* of the people.[14] Hans-Georg Gadamer liked to say that his generation of philosophers read the plays to escape militarism.[15] But how far did Shakespeare's 'language of power' assist the birth of a democratic public sphere, or remain – as Hazlitt sensed, and Eric Santner maintains, after Giorgio Agamben – 'on the arbitrary side', as the 'right-royal' exception of a 'lordly beast'?[16] This is one of the live issues that recur in *Shakespeare and Continental Philosophy*.

Between acting and action, as Simon Critchley and Jamieson Webster prove in their recent skit *The Hamlet Doctrine*, Shakespeare studies seem like an endless raking over of Plato's problem with democracy as a *theatrocracy* or society of spectacle.[17] For if the turn to political theology throws into relief how, as Stephen Greenblatt notes in *Shakespeare's Freedom*, it is a short step from these plays to the ironic vision of autonomy in Theodor Adorno's *Aesthetic Theory*, which starts with 'art's proud claim to absolute freedom' but ends in its entrapment, the idea of the Bard as a proto-theorist of the aesthetic remains thinkable for Kantians like Grady.[18] What continental philosophy does, then, is return us to Keats's notion of Shakespeare's 'negative capability' as a *great refusal* of determination, 'a medium of subjective spirit', in Adorno's formula, thrown back on itself.[19] For it is the *non-referentiality* of what Christine Buci-Glucksman calls this 'Tragedy of Shadows' that is usually felt to define its contiguity with postmodern 'thinking without a banister'.[20] Such was, for instance, the thrust of the anthology *Shakespeare and the Question of Theory* assembled by Geoffrey Hartman and Patricia Parker to illustrate how this drama's alertness to the 'mediacy of language, instability of meaning and radical uncertainty of interpretation' foreshadowed deconstructionism.[21] So it was no surprise that in Frank Kermode's *Shakespeare's Language* the power of the plays was likewise said to arise from an opacity that bewildered even Coleridge. For it is 'inconceivable that anybody at the Globe could have followed' the meaning, Kermode smiled, when it is as if Escher-like mental puzzles are being posed by 'metaphors that flash and disappear before we can consider them'.[22] And in his monumental tome *Shakespeare the Thinker*, intended to refute 'the post-Structuralist urge' that 'there is nothing outside the text', even the realist A.D. Nuttall concurred, when he closed with a salute to Shakespeare as 'the philosopher of human possibility' worthy of the messianism of Jacques Derrida:

> Of course he is not a consistent philosopher; he is a dramatist. But he shares with the major philosophers a knack of asking fundamental (sometimes very simple) questions. [And] because he will question anything, he treads on the toes of *later* theorists . . . He is fascinated by what could (just) be the case . . . Here indeed Shakespeare, though working with maximal intellectual power, finds no terminus to his thought.[23]

'I would like to become (alas it's pretty late) a "Shakespeare expert"': Derrida's dream of writing 'in the space or heritage of Shakespeare', because 'I know everything is in Shakespeare', might be Bardolatrous, but it does point to the continental philosophical terrain he imaged, *via* Paul Valéry's vision of a war-ravaged Europe as 'an immense terrace of Elsinore', to be nothing but Hamlet's graveyard.[24] So no wonder his *Specters of Marx* got short shrift from Marxists, for Derrida's theme there was that because the play's premonition of being 'acted over, / In states unborn and accents yet unknown' (*Julius*, 3.1.113–14) ghosted the Marxian theatricalisation of history in *The Eighteenth Brumaire of Louis Bonaparte*, it was '*Shakespeare qui genuit Hegel qui genuit Marx qui genuit Valéry*, and a few others', including Kant.[25] Yet by reducing Marxism to a skull that once 'had a tongue in it, and could sing' (*Hamlet*, 5.1.70), the theorist was simply pursuing the mad method of his 'hauntology', that 'one cannot speak of generations except on the condition of language', so taking seriously the anachrony of Marxists like Terry Eagleton, who love to jest that the Bard was 'certainly familiar with Hegel, Marx, Nietzsche, Freud, Wittgenstein, and Derrida' himself.[26] The phantasmic figure of Shakespeare as 'the greatest theoretician, who had obviously read Lacan, Brecht, and Artaud', might in fact be seen as a defining trope of poststructuralism, made accessible by Marjorie Garber's *Shakespeare's Ghost Writing*.[27] But long ago T.S. Eliot greeted the genial poet as *his own* 'affable familiar ghost' (Sonnet 86).[28] John D. Caputo designates this groundlessness Shakespearean 'hyper-reality'.[29] And it is in the genesis of such a genre of uncanny genealogy – 'a play of potence and impotence . . . out of proportion with other types of discourse, and sometimes even with all the rules of art', according to continental philosophy's reciprocal generosity – that the genius of these *untimely* texts abides.[30]

'Each of his plays is a complete philosophy of the passion whereof it treats': it was Johann Gottfried Herder, rhapsodising about this 'bard of northern man', who first interpreted Shakespeare as such a philosopher of time and being, whose drama 'aims at the totality of an *occurrence*', because 'the poet's space and time lie in the unfolding of his event'.[31] His characters' gibes that 'there was never yet philosopher / That could endure toothache' (*Much Ado*, 5.1.35–6) appear to bear this existentialism out. Thus, 'Hang up philosophy', exclaims Romeo, 'Unless philosophy can make a Juliet' (*Romeo*, 3.3.55–8). Shakespeare refers to 'the weeping philosopher' Heraclitus (*Merchant*, 1.2.42); alludes to Aristotle's 'moral philosophy' (*Troilus*, 2.2.166) as 'that part of philosophy . . . that treats of happiness' (*Shrew*, 1.1.19–20), and cites the 'heathen philosopher who when he had a desire to eat a grape, would open his lips when he put it into his mouth' (*As You*, 5.1.30–1). He has Brutus quote Epicurus for 'the rule of that philosophy' that the gods are indifferent to human affairs (*Julius*, 5.1.100); and Lear confuse his own 'noble philosopher' Edgar with the 'good Athenian' Socrates (*Lear*, 3.4.142–68). Finally, his entire half of *Timon of Athens*, with its literalisation of the Cynic Apemantus as a 'dog' (1.1.203), seems one extended exercise in the Lucianic turn of philosophy against philosophy.[32] So, what these allusions all have in common is the reflexiveness that allowed Herder to claim that 'Each play is History'.[33] Shakespeare, as is well known, quotes his contemporary Montaigne most of all. And what he evidently shared with the sceptical French thinker was the capacity that Herder saluted, and that is 'the beginning of modern hermeneutics', to stand outside thinking, and treat thought itself as a historical object:[34] 'They say miracles are past; and we have our philosophical persons to make modern and familiar things supernatural and causeless' (*All's Well*, 2.3.1–2).

A continental philosophical criticism finds in Shakespeare's 'aesthetic reversal of "free will"', to use Jacques Rancière's phrase, a virtual resistance to totalised meaning in the 'phantasma' (*Julius*, 2.1.65) of 'theoretic spaces for thought'.[35] Such metatheatre inspired Goethe's *Wilhelm Meister*. For spliced between a classical culture of imitation and the romantic cult of originality, Shakespearean drama appears to perform its own thesis, that if 'All the world's a stage / And all the men and women in it merely players' (*As You*, 2.7.138), with prescribed parts, yet 'every like is not the same' (*Julius*, 2.2.128): a notion of punning 'repetition as nonoriginary origin, repetition that moves forward'.[36] Marc Shell therefore traces philosophy's elective affinity with Shakespeare to the actor's Pyrrhic 'pause' (*Hamlet*, 2.2.467) that punctuates these texts; for is not all philosophy, he asks, what Gilles Deleuze called it: 'that which stutters'?[37] It is in this self-reflexive theatrical temporising, or '*contretemps* of ironic consciousness', at any rate, that the essays gathered here identify Shakespeare's *timeless* legacy to continental philosophy.[38] Thus, Paul Kottmann raises the curtain on the colloquium by showing how the Shakespearean fusion of the stage with 'the great globe itself' (*Tempest*, 4.1.153), the 'double theatrical self-awareness' that was Schmitt's starting point, ultimately works to erase its mimetic relation to the 'here and now', so fulfilling Hegel's axiom that the *telos* of art is to make itself 'a thing of the past', and 'Leave not a rack behind' (156).[39]

Shakespeare seems to regard the task of drama to be 'figuring out what drama should or could do', Kottmann quotes Herder as saying over 200 years ago. So, dissolving its charm apace, the end of this self-reflexiveness, he concludes, is that 'all the men and women' should *be* 'themselves' (*Tempest*, 5.1.32), as Prospero enjoins them, 'as free-determining agents in the world'. Jennifer Bates similarly seizes on

Shakespearean theatre's awareness that its time is 'out of joint' (*Hamlet*, 2.1.189) to spotlight its prefiguration of Kierkegaard's concept of the 'absolute, qualitative disjunction' of time for the 'existentially concrete' self. The oath-taking scenes in *Hamlet*, and in the philosopher's own theatricalised *Postscript*, constitute a 'double reflection' on the ghostliness of language and knowledge, Bates suggests, that works to shake those who understand the irony out of their 'un-decided "to be or not to be"' (3.1.58). Such a knowing actor's 'readiness' (5.2.160), before Time's capricious 'power / To o'erthrow' logic, truth and law (*Winter's Tale*, 4.1.7–8), is also the theme of Tom Stern's discussion of Schopenhauer's lifelong obsession with Shakespeare's ruling topos of the *mundus theatrum*, the aesthetic of 'the world as a play' that inspired the pessimistic philosopher's *ethic* of resigned compassion towards 'A stage where every man must play a part', and that 'a sad one' (*Merchant*, 1.1.78–9).

'Ripeness is all': the pathos of Shakespearean metadrama, with its Baroque reflection that because 'Men must endure / Their going hence even as their coming hither' (*Lear*, 5.2.9–10), 'The best in this kind are but shadows' (*Dream*, 5.1.208), frames Peter Holbrook's response to Nietzsche's belief that 'only as an aesthetic phenomenon' is existence justified. To the author of *Beyond Good and Evil*, Shakespeare offered a worldliness like Montaigne's, Holbrook suggests, through which to revel in the human comedy as a dance to the music of time in which 'all things are enamoured'. Nietzsche's Dionysian Shakespeare, drunk on 'an orgy of power', would acquire fascistic regalia in Germany's occultist Stefan George *kreis*.[40] But James Knapp instead aligns Nietzsche's 'Dionysian wisdom' with the 'desacralisation' that results from the *perspective* of an anamorphic drama such as *Richard II*: that the performance of 'earthly power' proceeds 'As in a theatre' (5.2.23). This recuperation harks back to Kantorowicz's intuition that in rehearsing the mystical doctrine of 'the King's Two Bodies' Shakespeare honours our human need for enabling fictions, a self-consciousness concerning the creativity of symbolic forms that Knapp recognises, via the Catholic phenomenology of Jean-Luc Marion, in Richard's dying benediction on the syncopated music that has maddened him as 'a sign of love' (5.5.65).[41]

The essays in the first part of this collection all agree that 'The play's the thing' (*Hamlet*, 2.2.581) 'to render the whole system of political theology', as Knapp puts it, 'an object for contemplation'. In the second part, however, Andrew Cutrofello turns to a tragedy that intrigues philosophers in its denigration of the play as a 'pageant to keep us in false gaze' (*Othello*, 1.3.18). Cavell, in particular, has allegorised the murder of Desdemona in terms of Cartesian scepticism's 'annihilation of the other'.[42] Othello's theatrical 'capacity for figuration' is a displacement of his sexual impotence, on this view; an interpretation derided by Shakespeareans for ignoring the fact that the scenario is a 'ghastly play within the play' stage-managed by Iago, and for typifying how 'the philosophical model can blot out the literary work'.[43] Cutrofello enters this interdisciplinary spat to qualify Cavell's Nietzscheanism with Bertrand Russell's observation that the truth about her 'could only be self-evident to Desdemona'. And if Cavell's misreadings serve as a lesson in the dangers of the philosophical appropriation of Shakespeare, Edward Casey reaffirms that this stage inhabits a boundary zone of 'seeming', like the mirror in Merleau-Ponty's phenomenology, which positively demands we step like this 'between imagination and reality'. That liminal *bor de mer*, into which the blind Gloucester plunges in *King Lear*, is indeed the void that prompted Levinas to claim that all philosophy is an extended meditation on Shakespeare.

Levinas's reverence for Shakespeare as a 'fabricator of nothingness', who shows how the Pascalian 'night is long that never finds the day' (*Macbeth*, 4.3.242), is here dated by Howard Caygill to the philosopher's suffering whilst a Jewish prisoner of war, and seen as a repudiation not only of Heidegger's Hitlerian 'being-for-death', but of Walter Benjamin's divination in these mourning works of 'Christian sparks'.[44] For François Lyotard, too, it was the disavowal of any sovereignty that would master nothingness, by science, spirituality, or suicide, that affiliated Shakespeare with the Wandering Jew as a prophet of the Shoah.[45] Thus, if Descartes' *cogito* is traceable to Hamlet's self, so too can Shakespeare's groundless potentiality be discerned in what Coleridge considered Spinoza's 'majesty of openness'.[46] This 'Jewish Shakespeare' could not be more at odds, therefore, with Schmittian mythologising of the sovereign decision as a miracle triumphing precisely over 'nothingness'.[47] But Christopher Pye contends that Schmitt's cooption of Shakespeare as a mystagogue of sacral kingship is mocked by the preposterousness of a drama like *The Winter's Tale*, which sends sovereign being back to the abyss it had abjected, figured by 'that wide gap' of Time (4.1.7) in which Leontes learns his power is indeed 'coactive' with 'nothing' (1.2.140). This 'foul gap' (4.4.195), into which the old Lord exits *'pursued by a bear'* (SD, 3.3.57), is the political 'caesura that opens the possibility of the aesthetic'; but Julia Lupton adds that is also the *aporia* that divides *bios*, or the human, from *zoē*, its others, in the work of Hannah Arendt. The Italian philosopher Roberto Esposito has annexed Arendt's project for a political personhood to his Deleuzean programme of 'becoming animal'; an appropriation Lupton finds already finessed, however, in *The Taming of the Shrew*, where, after

Petruchio's animalising biopolitics, Kate's infamous last words about being at home in her world acquire a civic gravity worthy of the author of *The Human Condition*.

The opportunity to convert Kate's homily on obedience into a manifesto for the weak power of a 'master-mistress' (Sonnet 20) springs from current brooding on Shakespeare's dramatisation of Pindar's paradox, beloved by Hölderlin and Heidegger, that 'where danger threatens / That which saves also grows'.[48] Such a *détournement* was the surprise in the late lectures of Michel Foucault; and Richard Wilson opens the third part of this volume relating how the theorist of biopolitics recoiled from Derrida's deconstruction of his idealisation of madness as 'a tear in the fabric of the world', depicted in the Ship of Fools, by analysing the Ubu-like irrationality *within* 'the hollow crown' of Shakespeare's king (*Richard II*, 3.2.158–9). Foucault's revelation that in these plays power performs such grotesque tricks 'As make the angels weep' (*Measure*, 2.2.124) foretold alarm over the intimacy of the sovereign and the beast. That sovereignty is founded in violence and unreason is thus the burden of Catherine Belsey's explication of the Sonnets as practising 'deconstruction *avant la lettre*' by withholding meaning from the object of their love and hate. Foucault decried deconstruction for the 'sovereignty that allows it to indefinitely re-say the text'.[49] And Belsey detects a like passive aggression in Shakespeare's 'love with menaces', which by eliding 'one angel in another's hell' (Sonnet 144), enacts Lyotard's dictum that 'to speak is to fight'.[50] The radical passivity of the 'sovereign creature' (*Antony*, 5.2.80) is the antinomy Bernard Freydberg similarly identifies in *Coriolanus*, where Rome's sovereignty hinges, however, not on speech, but on the 'gracious silence' (2.1.162) of Virgilia, the protagonist's 'idle housewife' (1.3.66), who figures as 'a sort of gap' in the text, like Rancière's 'mute speech', yet who, by keeping to her 'threshold' (70), in this tragedy of liminality, marks the 'awesome power' of the Shakespearean resolve that 'silence shall be most my glory . . . being dumb' (Sonnet 83).[51]

In Delmore Schwartz's poem on *Coriolanus*, cited by Freydberg, the best response to the tragedy is the rage of Beethoven as he 'hammered and stammered'. That was also the fantasy of Thomas Mann, whose *Doctor Faustus* offered a paradigm for a continental philosophical critique by ascribing Nietzsche's mania to the Shakespearean *aporia* that 'Light seeking light doth light of light beguile' (*Love's*, 1.1.77), then imaging Beethoven stuttering in 'mad abstraction' at this fix.[52] The novelist noticed how plays in which 'good wits must be jangling' (2.1.224) make a song and dance of the crisis of iteration when actors 'throttle their practised accents' (*Dream*, 5.1.97). That perseveration is the 'negative capability' Christopher Norris prizes, in contrasting Wittgenstein's antipathy to Shakespeare with Derrida's mimetic rapport. For where Wittgenstein deplored language that 'goes on holiday', Derrida relished the 'deviant performative' of such an interregnum. The playwright and poststructuralist suffered similar hostility, Norris recounts, for an inventiveness so 'inextricably perplexed', as Johnson lamented, that it demands 'more than humanity possesses'.

'There are more things in heaven and earth ... Than are dreamt of in your philosophy', insists Shakespeare's philosophical Prince (1.5.168). It is in the dimension of the supernatural that *Shakespeare and Continental Philosophy* therefore concludes, when Nicholas Royle likens Shakespeare's 'damnable iteration' (*1 Henry IV*, 1.2.80) to that of a miracle play. Royle is here truly beside himself in wonder at the uncanniness of what Derrida calls 'the Thing Shakespeare'; but also in two minds as to whether what the philosopher does is not also 'beyond the human'.[53] Schmitt deployed the same wonder to conscript Shakespeare to the 'most high miracle' (*Tempest*, 5.1.177) of an originary power; but Derrida's Shakespeare entails 'thinking wonder otherwise, as without single origin'. The most difficult task, the philosopher warned us at the end, 'would be to dissociate *unconditionality* from sovereignty' in such a way.[54] But in Royle's *envoi* that difficulty is eased by Shakespeare, when he renders his sovereign 'might' a contingency, by an everlasting *attendance* on the performance of the other: 'When my cue comes, call me, and I will answer' (*Dream*, 4.1.196).

Notes

1. Emmanuel Levinas, *Time and the Other*, trans. Richard Cohen (Pittsburgh: Duquesne University Press, 1987), p. 72.
2. Colin McGinn, *Shakespeare's Philosophy: Discovering the Meaning Behind the Plays* (New York: Harper Collins, 2006), p. 1.
3. Gustav Ungerer, 'An Unrecorded Elizabethan Performance of *Titus Andronicus*', *Shakespeare Survey*, 14 (1961), pp. 102–9.
4. Sir Ernest Gowers, *The Complete Plain Words* (London: Her Majesty's Stationery Office, 1954); William Scott, unpublished mss., quoted in Stanley Wells, 'By the Placing of his Words', *Times Literary Supplement*, 26 September 2003, 14–15.
5. Ludwig Wittgenstein, *Culture and Value*, trans. Peter Winch (Oxford: Blackwell, 1980), pp. 48 and 83.
6. Plato, *Republic*, trans. Robin Waterfield (Oxford: Oxford University Press, 1993), p. 361.
7. Jean-Jacques Lecercle, 'Mutuality and Challenges in Literature, Theory and the Philosophy of Language', *The European English Messenger*,

20:2 (2011), pp. 59–66, here 62; Samuel Johnson, *Johnson: The Critical Heritage*, ed. James Boulton (London: Routledge, 1971), p. 169.

8. John Joughin, 'Introduction', *Philosophical Shakespeares* (London: Routledge, 2000), pp. 3–5; Stanley Cavell, 'Foreword', ibid., p. xiv.

9. Hugh Grady, *Shakespeare and Impure Aesthetics* (Cambridge: Cambridge University Press, 2009), p. 29.

10. McGinn, *Shakespeare's Philosophy*, p. 142, n. 2.

11. Ibid., pp. 203–4; Harold Bloom, *Shakespeare: The Invention of the Human* (New York: Riverhead, 1998).

12. Allan Bloom, *Shakespeare's Politics* (Chicago: University of Chicago Press, 1981), p. 3; *Shakespeare on Love and Friendship* (Chicago: University of Chicago Press, 2000), pp. 1 and 29.

13. Carl Schmitt, *Hamlet or Hecuba: The Intrusion of the Time Into the Play*, trans. David Pan and Jennifer Rust (New York: Telos, 2011), pp. 39 and 56; *Political Theology: Four Chapters on the Concept of Sovereignty*, trans. George Schwab (Chicago: University of Chicago Press, 1985), p. 5.

14. Ernst Kantorowicz, *The King's Two Bodies: A Study in Medieval Political Theology* (Princeton: Princeton University Press, 1957), pp. 24–41; Jürgen Habermas, *The Structural Transformation of the Public Sphere*, trans. Thomas Burger and Frederick Lawrence (Cambridge: Polity Press, 1989), pp. 12–14, 38–40 and passim. For an influential riff on this theme, see David Scott Kastan, 'Proud Majesty Made a Subject: Shakespeare and Spectacle of Rule', *Shakespeare Quarterly*, 37 (1986), pp. 460–75.

15. Hans-Georg Gadamer, *A Century of Philosophy: A Conversation with Riccardo Dottori* (London: Continuum, 2003), pp. 77 and 79.

16. Eric Santner, *The Royal Remains: The People's Two Bodies and the Endgames of Sovereignty* (Chicago: University of Chicago Press, 2011); Giorgio Agamben, *Homo Sacer: Sovereign Power and Bare Life*, trans. Daniel Heller-Roazen (Stanford: Stanford University Press, 1998); *The State of Exception*, trans. Kevin Attell (Chicago: Chicago University Press, 2005); William Hazlitt, 'Coriolanus', in *The Characters of Shakespeare's Plays* (Cambridge: Cambridge University Press, 1955), p. 59. For an important elaboration of Hazlitt, see Richard Helgerson, *Forms of Nationhood: The Elizabethan Writing of England* (Chicago: Chicago University Press, 1992), p. 244.

17. Simon Critchley and Jamieson Webster, *The Hamlet Doctrine* (Chicago: University of Chicago Press, 2013), p. 15.

18. Stephen Greenblatt, *Shakespeare's Freedom* (Chicago: University of Chicago Press, 2010), p. 96; Grady, *Shakespeare and Impure Aesthetics*, pp. 41–2.

19. John Keats, *The Complete Poems and Selected Letters of John Keats*, ed. Edward Hirsch (New York: Random House, 2001), p. 492; Theodor Adorno, *Notes to Literature*, trans. Shierry Weber Nicholsen (2 vols, New York: Columbia University Press, 1991), vol. 1, p. 42.

20. Christine Buci-Glucksmann, *Tragique de l'ombre: Shakespeare et la maniérisme* (Paris: Gallilée, 1990); 'thinking without a banister': Hannah Arendt quoted in Tracy Strong, *Politics Without Vision: Thinking Without a Banister in the Twentieth Century* (Chicago: University of Chicago Press, 2012).

21. Patricia Parker, 'Introduction', in Patricia Parker and Geoffrey Hartman (eds), *Shakespeare and the Question of Theory* (London: Methuen, 1985), p. viii.

22. Frank Kermode, *Shakespeare's Language* (London: Allen Lane, 2004), pp. 5, 16 and 254.

23. A.D. Nuttall, *Shakespeare the Thinker* (New Haven: Yale University Press, 2007), pp. 381–2.

24. Jacques Derrida, 'This Strange Institution Called Literature', trans. Geoffrey Bennington and Rachel Bowlby, in *Acts of Literature*, ed. Derek Attridge (London: Routledge, 1992), p. 67.

25. Paul Valéry, 'La crise de l'esprit', in *Oeuvres* (Paris: Gallimard, Bibliotheque de la Pléiade, 1957), vol. 1, p. 993; Jacques Derrida, *Specters of Marx: The State of the Debt, the Work of Mourning, and the New International*, trans. Peggy Kamuf (London: Routledge, 1994), pp. 4–5.

26. Ibid., p. 9; Terry Eagleton, *William Shakespeare* (Oxford: Basil Blackwell, 1986), pp. ix–x.

27. Daniel Mesguich, 'The Book to Come in the Theatre', *Sub-Stance*, 18/19 (1977), p. 118; Marjorie Garber, *Shakespeare's Ghost Writing: Literature as Uncanny Causality* (London: Methuen, 1987).

28. T.S. Eliot, 'Little Gidding', *The Complete Poems and Plays* (London: 1969), p. 193.

29. John D. Caputo, 'Foreword: Of Hyper-Reality', in Ewan Fernie (ed.), *Spiritual Shakespeares* (London: Routledge, 2005), pp. xvi–xix.

30. Jacques Derrida, *Points. . . Interviews, 1974–1994*, ed. Elizabeth Weber, trans. Peggy Kamuf (Stanford: Stanford University Press, 1995), pp. 149–50.

31. Johann Gottfried Herder, *Briefe*, ed. Wilhelm Dobbek and Günter Arnold (Weimar: Böhlaus Nachfolger, 1977–2004), vol. 1, pp. 270–1; *Shakespeare*, trans. and ed. Gregory Moore (Princeton: Princeton University Press, 2008), pp. xviii, 31–3, and 56.

32. See Galena Hashhozheva, '*Timon of Athens* and the Wilderness of the City', in Christina Wald and Felix Sprang (eds), *Shakespeare and the City: The Negotiation of Urban Spaces in Shakespeare's Plays* (Weimar: Deutsche Shakespeare-Gesellschaft, 2010), pp. 3–19.

33. Herder, Shakespeare, p. 62.

34. Kristin Gjesdal, 'Shakespeare's Hermeneutic Legacy: Herder on Modern Drama and the Challenge of Cultural Prejudice', *Shakespeare Quarterly*, 64:1 (2013), pp. 60–9, here 69.

35. Jacques Rancière, *Mute Speech*, trans. James Swenson (New York: Columbia University Press, 2011), p. 120; Thomas Betterridge, *Shakespearean Fantasy and Politics* (Hatfield: University of Hertfordshire Press, 2005), p. 201.

36. John D. Caputo, *Radical Hermeneutics: Repetition, Deconstruction, and the Hermeneutic Project* (Bloomington: Indiana University Press, 1987), p. 139.

37. Marc Shell, *Stutter* (Cambridge, MA: Harvard University Press, 2005), pp. 39–40 and 169–200; Gilles Deleuze and Félix Guattari, *What is Philosophy?*, trans. Hugh Tomlinson and Graham Burchill (New York: Columbia University Press, 1994), p. 69.

38. Jacques Derrida, 'Aphorism Countertime', trans. Nicholas Royle, in *Acts of Literature*, p. 431.

39. G.W.F. Hegel, *Lectures on Fine Art*, trans. T.M. Knox (2 vols, Oxford: Clarendon Press, 1975), vol. 1, p. 31.
40. Stefan Zweig, *Confusion*, trans. Anthea Bell (London: Pushkin Press, 2002), p. 28. For the influence of Shakespeare on the George *kreis*, see Robert Norton, *Secret Germany: Stefan George and His Circle* (Ithaca: Cornell University Press, 2002), pp. 270–1, 337–8 and passim.
41. See Victoria Kahn, 'Political Theology and Fiction in *The King's Two Bodies*', *Representations*, 106 (2009), 79–81.
42. Stanley Cavell, *Philosophy the Day After Tomorrow* (Cambridge, MA: Harvard University Press, 2005), p. 150.
43. Stanley Cavell, *Disowning Knowledge in Six Plays of Shakespeare* (Cambridge: Cambridge University Press, 2003), p. 135; Anne Barton, *Shakespeare and the Idea of the Play* (London: Chatto & Windus, 1962), p. 185; Brian Vickers, *Appropriating Shakespeare: Contemporary Critical Quarrels* (New Haven: Yale University Press, 1993), p. 310.
44. Levinas, *Time and the Other*, p. 72; Walter Benjamin, *The Origin of German Tragic Drama*, trans. John Osborne (London: Verso, 1998), p. 158.
45. François Lyotard, 'Jewish Oedipus', in *Driftworks*, trans. Roger McKeon (New York: Semiotext(e), 1984), pp. 20–31.
46. Samuel Taylor Coleridge, *Collected Letters: Volume 4: 1815–19*, ed. Earl Leslie Griggs (Oxford: Oxford University Press, 2000), p. 548. See Margherita Pascucci, *Philosophical Readings of Shakespeare: 'Thou Art the Thing Itself'* (New York: Palgrave Macmillan, 2013), Chap. 5.
47. Schmitt, *Political Theology*, pp. 31–2.
48. Friedrich Hölderlin, 'Patmos', *Selected Poems and Fragments*, trans. Michael Hamburger (London: Penguin, 1998), p. 231. For the relevance of Hölderlin's lines to the plays, see Ian Ward, *Shakespeare and the Legal Imagination* (London: Butterworths, 1999), p. 193.
49. Michel Foucault, 'My Body, This Paper, This Fire: Appendix to the 1972 Edition', in Michel Foucault, *History of Madness*, trans. Jonathan Murphy and Jean Khalfa (London: Routledge, 2006), p. 573.
50. Jean-François Lyotard, *The Postmodern Condition: A Report on Knowledge*, trans. Geoffrey Bennington and Brian Massumi (Manchester: Manchester University Press, 1984), p. 10.
51. Rancière, *Mute Speech*, trans. James Swenson (New York: Columbia University Press, 2011).
52. Thomas Mann, *Doctor Faustus: The Life of the German Composer Adrian Leverkühn as Told by a Friend*, trans. John E. Woods (New York: Vintage, 1997), p. 63.
53. Derrida, 'This Strange Institution Called Literature', p. 22.
54. Jacques Derrida, *Cosmopolitanism and Forgiveness*, trans. Mark Dooley and Michael Hughes (London: Routledge, 2002), p. 59.

Part One

The Play's the Thing

Chapter 1

'The Charm Dissolves Apace': Shakespeare and the Self-dissolution of Drama

Paul A. Kottman

Everything I will try to say in this chapter will, I believe, make a bit more sense if I begin with a few words about G.W.F. Hegel's reflections on the fate of art.

According to Hegel, artistic practices are ways that we try to evaluate and make sense of our lives, of our world, of the claims of nature upon us, and of what we do (or might do) and say with one another. Art is not the only way we do this, of course; there is also mythology, religion, education, science or philosophy. Artistic practices are distinctive, however, in that their sense-making potential is tied to the way they work with and through specific media – stone, paint, sound, or speech – and to the way in which artistic transformations of these media reflect socio-historical transformations in our overall self-understanding.

In Hegel's account, the development of artistic practices – that is, of historically shifting, context-specific needs for different arts (e.g. the need for pyramids in Egypt, for classical sculpture in Greece, or for painting in Christian Europe), as well as internal developments within those arts (from symbolic to classical to romantic, for example, or from epic to lyric) – presents an ongoing and increasing de-naturalisation or spiritualisation of our self-understanding. According to Hegel, the more that we see ourselves as – or teach ourselves that we are – free and self-determining subjects, the less we are dependent upon, or needful of, artistic expressions that work with natural or sensible media in order to understand ourselves, and our world. The twist in Hegel's story is that sensuous, representational artistic practices *are* (or 'were') a primary way we teach ourselves this lesson – because by transforming natural material in modes that we can regard as free from material or instrumental needs, we express our own liberation and, in this way, *become* free. 'Art by means of its representations', says Hegel, 'while remaining within the sensuous sphere, liberates man at the same time from the power of sensuousness.'[1] And in another famous passage, Hegel says that art allows us to 'strip the external world of its inflexible foreignness and to enjoy in the shape of things only an external realization of [ourselves]'.[2] This – and the self-understanding to which this enjoyment leads – is the heart of our past and present 'need' for art, according to Hegel. And once this lesson is absorbed – that is, once we see ourselves as liberated from nature, inasmuch as the terms of our self-understanding no longer depend upon, and are no longer limited by, something out there called Nature or God or the One or whatever – we find ourselves less needful of the sensuous representational works by which we taught ourselves this lesson. Art, we are told, 'lifts' us 'with gentle hands out of and above imprisonment in nature'.[3] Coming to understand ourselves as free and self-determining thus entails (and perhaps even requires) a diminishing need to make sensuous, representational artworks, even as it entails a heightened need for philosophical reflection on our (past) need for sensuous representation. This is what Hegel means when, famously, he claims – 'art, considered in its highest vocation, is and remains for us a thing of the past'. (As others have pointed out, Hegel's argument is not that art has come to an end, but rather that we can outlive, culturally, our need for sensuous, representational art as a deeply essential mode of self-understanding.[4])

Furthermore, for Hegel, this ongoing de-naturalisation unfolds (or has unfolded) through an increased awareness *within* artistic practices *of* artistic practices as medium-specific. So, for instance, classical architecture manifests a higher awareness of its own status as architecture – of itself as a freestanding, artificial, material construction – than does symbolic architecture. ('The peculiarity of Greek architecture', writes Hegel in a typical formulation, is that by fluting and other means 'it gives shape to . . . supporting *as such* and therefore employs the column as the fundamental element in the purposiveness of architecture'.[5]) Similarly, as Robert Pippin has convincingly argued, the deepening self-reflexivity of modernist and abstract painting – paintings about painting as such – might be understood to fall within the purview of the overall narrative that Hegel offers.[6] Perhaps the easiest way to see the point here is to consider how artworks – once they no longer need to be about this or that content out there (a material purpose, an animal quarry, a god, a bit of shared history) – are freed up to determine *for themselves* their own content. And this freeing up is perhaps most clearly manifested when artworks start to be about themselves. Self-reflexive artworks and practices undeniably assert the autonomy of human artistry.

Now – to move closer to our topic here – thinking along these lines also led Hegel himself, at the end of his *Lectures on Fine Art*, to consider dramatic poetry as 'the highest stage of poetry and of art generally' because 'in contrast to the other perceptible materials, stone, wood, color and notes, speech is alone the element worthy of the expression of spirit'.[7] Dramatic poetry is, for Hegel, inherently more self-reflexive than sculpture, painting or architecture because its medium – namely, speech – is from the start spiritual, human, de-naturalised. Hence, drama is already freer than the other arts when it comes to choosing its content.

A quick way of grasping the stakes of Hegel's high regard for dramatic poetry is to recall his idiosyncratic (for a German writer of his period) disinterest in natural beauty, his assertion that 'the beauty of art is *higher* than the beauty of nature'.[8] (Recall, for instance, Hegel's blunt declaration that in landscape painting 'the work of spirit acquires a higher rank than the mere natural landscape'; or, similarly, his provocative assertion that Titian, Dürer and others have painted portraits that are 'more like the individual than the actual individual himself'.[9]) Only in being transformed artistically do natural materials (stone, sound, color and so on) acquire a specific meaning for us.[10] In Hegel's view, nature and natural materials are in and of themselves – as the philosopher of history, Hayden White, once quipped to me, as we gazed upon a choice piece of California real estate – boring, lacking a plot.[11] Northrop Frye expressed the same thought about drama when he wrote that dramatic poetry fully 'belongs to the world man constructs, not to the [natural] world he sees; to his home, not his environment'.[12]

If artistic practices are medium-specific modes of self-understanding, goes the thinking here, then what medium could be more adequate to our reflexive self-understanding than that which, so to speak, we know to be ours from the get-go? Not elements ripped from an indifferent domain of nature (sound, color, hard materials like stone or marble), in other words – but rather what Giambattista Vico described in terms of 'poetic wisdom': elements of culture and history, words and deeds, social principles and passionate aims, conflicts between individual characters. Because such elements are the 'stuff' of poetry, and in a special way of dramatic poetry, to work in the dramatic arts entails a degree of self-awareness (as a historical being or 'people') that is probably missing, say, from most symbolic sculpture. This is not to say that Hegel did not also emphasise the importance of theatrical representation: 'drama . . . imperatively needs a sensuous presentation, and this can only be given artistically by actual performance in the theater'.[13] But what matters in such passages is a larger point: namely, that dramatic poetry could only (that is, *historically* could only) present and develop a 'complete and specific action' by means of theatrical-sensuous representation – that is, by becoming something other than epic or narrative or lyric. The importance of the theatre as distinct from, though historically linked to, dramatic poetry lies, for Hegel, in its making possible the historical development and presentation of a complete and specific action. It is not that theatricality or the stage is 'important' as such, independent of this larger history of the art of what he calls dramatic poetry. Hegel's primary focus, after all, is not on the theatre but on dramatic poetry – though he cannot focus on the latter in the historical way he wants without attending to the importance of theatrical presentation. The larger point, that is, remains the 'spiritual need' to which dramatic poetry responds – to develop a presentation of human actions for the sake of our self-understanding.[14]

Moreover – à propos of our topic here – we will do well to remember not only that Hegel ranks dramatic poetry as the highest (the most prevalently spiritual) artistic practice, but also the fact that he thought among modern dramatists 'you will scarcely find any . . . who can be compared with Shakespeare'.[15]

And so, although Hegel does not say so explicitly, we can nevertheless infer – from the perspective of my highly condensed account here – that Shakespeare's pre-eminence in Hegel's account of the history of human artistic development should have something to do with Shakespeare's heightened degree of self-reflexivity, his dramatic presentation of drama *as such* and of the sort of self-understanding it affords.[16] Or, at least, I want to assert such an inference as my opening gambit in this short chapter.

*

Now, of course, self-reflexivity (or self-referential theatricality) abounds in other pre- or non-Shakespearean dramatic works and practices – for example, in the formal composition of the Chorus in Greek Tragedy, or the self-referential character of gestures and costumes in Japanese Noh, Kyogen or Kabuki. (Not to mention in the architectonics and choreographic practices of various types of world drama, whether or not such dramas are scripted.) Likewise – to scoot closer to Shakespeare's original context – it is by now a scholarly truism to note that sixteenth- and seventeenth-century English drama was comprised of a set of highly self-conscious artistic practices, in which a dramatic work's standing as 'theatre' was reflexively presented in both the composition and the performance itself.[17] In light of all this, the highly self-conscious nature of so much Shakespearean drama – the play-within-the play of *Hamlet*, the Chorus of *Henry V*, Rosalind's epilogue in *As You Like It* and so forth – can seem, simply, of a piece with so much self-awareness in the dramatic practices of various periods and regions, above all his own native context.

At the same time, one of the distinguishing features of sixteenth- and seventeenth-century European dramatic practices – and, especially, of Shakespeare's work – is a double theatrical self-awareness: namely, a certain *historical* self-awareness of their own presentation of theatrical self-reflexivity as such vis-à-vis earlier self-reflexive dramatic practices, in addition to self-referentiality vis-à-vis their own works. In other words, early modern European (English but also Spanish, French and Italian) dramatists not only presented and composed dramas that referred back to themselves as such; they also showed a keen awareness of earlier dramatic practices *as having been self-reflexive and self-aware*, as well as of the metaphorical status of theatrical space (especially with regard to the image of the 'world stage' or *theatrum mundi*) in classical antiquity and beyond – and they were, furthermore, particularly adept at invoking an awareness of this history *as* a particular form of self-reflexive theatre.[18] When, for example, at the outset of Shakespeare's *The Merchant of Venice* (1596), Antonio sighs –

> I hold the world but as the world, Gratiano
> A stage, where every man must play a part,
> And mine a sad one. (*Merchant*, 1.1.77–9)

– he is manifesting not only an immediate reflection on the present context of the utterance, but also a refined self-awareness of a long and varied history of comparing the world to the stage.

Elsewhere, I have argued that what distinguishes the early modern English theatre (and above all Shakespeare) in this regard is the way in which it erodes the representational difference between world and stage, purposefully accomplishing a 'literalisation' of what had been an ancient, philosophical metaphor.[19]

Here, however, I would like to take a different approach by suggesting that the self-reflexivity of Shakespearean drama manifests a lessening need for the material-site-specific context of the playhouse, for the concrete practice of what we now call 'theatricality' – to the point of accomplishing a self-dissolution of drama as a sensuous, material representational practice.[20] (By using scare quotes, I mean to leave open the possibility that what I am about to say does not pertain exclusively to Shakespeare – that it expresses something about modernist drama since, at least, the early modern period – though I will try to say why I think it does pertain to Shakespeare in a special way.)

Such a claim is bound to raise the hackles of (or, more likely these days, to simply be ignored by) cultural-materialist scholars of early modern drama – not to mention those invested in the ongoing practical work of staging Shakespeare's plays. Which is to say, also, that this claim will need further explaining and defending. But, before I begin the explanation and defence, let me once again try to state the thesis in the plainest terms possible: The self-reflexive character of Shakespearean drama – both its manifest awareness of past, self-reflexive dramatic practices *and* its own self-referential character (the so-called 'meta-theatricality' of Shakespeare) – portends the historical self-dissolution of drama as a sensuous, representational artistic practice.

Even more plainly: Shakespeare – perhaps the world's pre-eminent dramatist – stages, from within his drama, the self-dissolution of our *need* for the sensuous, material representation of human actions in order to understand ourselves as actors, as free self-determining agents in the world.[21]

Put yet another way: the depiction of our lessening need for sensuous representational drama becomes, itself, a primary task of Shakespearean drama – as if being a dramatist, for Shakespeare, means making the historical disappearance of the conditions under which traditional (sensuous, representational) forms of drama matter into the very stuff of a dramatic work.

Moreover, *this* kind of dramatic self-reflexivity demands something not required, I think, of analogous modernist movements in the other arts – the abstract expressionism of Pollock, say, or the music of John Cage – inasmuch as the Shakespearean self-dissolution of drama cannot fall back on its own sensuous medium (paint, canvas, instrument) in order to thematise its own expressive material capacities. Because speaking and doing – the 'material' of drama – is already de-naturalised, Shakespeare cannot expose the expressive capacities of speech and action in the same way that Pollack can drip paint, or that Cage can pluck a piano string. Part of my effort here, then, is also to suggest that Shakespearean drama offers an alternative future for modernism to the one presented in recent philosophical work on modernist painting.[22] Precisely because Shakespeare's artistic horizons are less limited than other modernist movements – his dramatic work is not nearly as restricted (not nearly as precious, some might say) as Cage's or Pollock's – it is to Shakespeare's radical modernism that we might turn to find a more capacious future for art (and, hence, for philosophical reflection on art) beyond both its sensuous and its representational form.

These are, at any rate, my primary arguments here.

*

Let me now proceed, first, by discussing the dissolution of sensuousness in drama – the materiality of its being performed for eyes and ears – before turning, second, to the dissolution of its representational, mimetic character in Shakespeare.

Perhaps the simplest way to begin defending my claim with regard to the self-dissolution of sensuous materiality in drama is by noting that, since at least Aristotle's *Poetics*, dramatic works have been understood to be graspable apart from – at a minimum – the sensuousness of their material performance. Here we can recall, for instance, Aristotle's well-known assertion that plot (*mythos*), rather than diction or spectacle (*opsis*), is the soul of tragedy – and that, furthermore, 'the plot [of a tragedy] should be so structured that, even without seeing it performed, the person . . . experiences horror and pity at what comes about'.[23] For Aristotle, tragedies are gripping quite apart from their reliance on sensuous representation – indeed, for the author of the *Poetics*, it is enough to recall to mind a tragic *mythos* in order to be moved by it.

If the thought that dramas matter – grip us, move us, offer an occasion for self-understanding and reflection – independent of their material performance is not new, then of course we still need to consider *why*, after all, Greek tragedies were performed in such a highly ritualised, formalised, choreographed manner in such precise, concrete, specially constructed settings.[24] Aristotle may have thought the performance relatively unnecessary with respect to the plot Sophocles composed, but, obviously, Sophocles himself had written for the Greek stage and its peculiar material conventions. And if the fifth-century BCE Athenians felt a *need* for the sensuous representation of tragedies (masks, choruses, ritualised festivals and so on) then this deep need still requires explaining in the context of my claim about Shakespeare – if, that is, we are going to understand what it means that Shakespeare stages the self-dissolution of our 'highest need' for the sensuous representation of human actions.

At the risk of oversimplification – and just for the sake of generating the discussion – my rough and ready understanding of the deep Athenian need for the sensuous representation of tragedies goes like this. Unlike epic, which offered occasions for self-understanding (of human life, of our place with respect to nature, of our natality and mortality and so forth) through idealised uttered representations of *past* actions – hence, the central role famously played by Mnemosyne and her daughters the Muses in the performance of Homeric epic – tragedy expanded occasions for self-understanding by bringing us 'into the presence' of these same idealised representations, so that we might watch the protagonists suffer before our eyes (not just our ears) in the theatre. Hence, these heroes, legends or divinities had to appear not only in the material form of the audible 'once upon a time' as in Homer, but also in the flesh, 'here and now', before us: history made sensuously present because both audible and visible.

Of course, that we are still dealing with a historical world that could understand itself only in heroic terms is manifest in the idealised aesthetic portrayal of the tragic mask, not to mention in the ritualised structure the tragic festival itself. In other words, because the tragic hero represented shared concerns and occasioned new collective self-understandings on the part of the Athenians (as Jean-Pierre Vernant and Pierre Vidal-Naquet have so elegantly demonstrated), an idealised material representation of the hero on stage was both possible and required.[25] This social-historical need for the particular formal innovations of classical drama at the sensuous, material level can thus be explained by a continued dependence on normative idealised representations of human life (namely, tragic-heroic figures) coupled with the expansion of that representation from the imagistic and narrative into the 'here-and-now' of the stage and its scenic, spatial-temporal representation of actions.

But – and this is the turn that leads to Aristotle's insight – once dramas were actually performed in Athens, *once tragedy became a self-consciously ritual activity*, it became clear that what was being sensuously represented were not only the idealised representations of human life (characters like Oedipus, say, to stick with Aristotle's favorite example) but the *actions themselves* of these figures – their words, their gestures, their individual deeds. And furthermore, once it became clear that tragedies represented human *actions* – that tragedies were sensuous representations *of* an action and its consequences for the agent and his world (*mimeseos praxis* to use Aristotle's famous definition of tragedy)[26] – then the specific power of drama with respect to the other arts (image, narrative, dance) was seen to lie, significantly, *not* in its status as sensuous performance (*mousike*) but rather in its capacity to yield understanding about what it is for human beings to act, a philosophical understanding in light of which the poetic mimesis of action becomes philosophically defensible, as in Aristotle's own account. (That tragic drama – as the representation of action – yields a special understanding not available elsewhere was, of course, central to Aristotle's defense of tragedy in the face of Plato's criticism of tragic drama. Note: Aristotle did not defend tragedy as sensuous presentation [*mousike*] against Plato's attack; his defense of tragedy lay in his view of tragedy as yielding an understanding of an action in light of its unintended consequences.)

And once it was recognised that the chief accomplishment of the sensuous performance was, at bottom, a new understanding of human *praxis* through its mimetic representation, the tragic drama ended up *by means of its ritualised sensuous performance* obviating – in Aristotle's own view – the need for that very sensuous performance. That this obviation was not only Aristotle's idiosyncratic opinion is, of course, borne out by the historical fact that performances of tragic dramas were well on the wane in Athens by the time Aristotle composed the *Poetics*.

In light of all this, it could be said that the self-dissolution of the *sensuous* material performance of drama belongs, already, to its classical milieu as a formal artistic practice.

Classical drama *lends itself to this self-dissolution* inasmuch as it succeeds in bringing what it represents – human actions – to the understanding. The understanding, as it were, takes over for our eyes and ears – hence, again, Aristotle's claims about the ability of a tragic *mythos* to move us independently of its sensuous performance.

The same self-dissolution does not, I would argue, apply to the other arts in their classical forms: epic narrative still requires the spoken word if it is to represent *the past* (that is, the temporal distance between the speaker and that of which he speaks) – so the fate of epic narration is, as Walter Benjamin aptly suggested, tied to a tradition in which the physical act of speaking is capable of transmitting historical experience.[27] Similarly, the performance of music obviously requires the hearing of sound; images require light and surfaces.[28] Drama alone among the classical fine arts emerges as a practice that tends towards self-dissolution because the medium of its artifice – the here-and-now performance of human words and deeds – invariably evacuates the here-and-now, leaving behind only an *ex post facto* practical understanding of the deeds that have been represented. (It would be important to consider drama's special significance for Greek philosophy's own self-authorisation in light of drama's distinctiveness in this regard.)

Thus, by sensuously representing human beings in action, drama obviates the need for the sensuousness of that very representation. *This obviation is nothing less than the temporality of the performance of drama itself* – its resistance to sensuous reification, its dependence on a shared here-and-now context, its inevitable vanishing at the end of the play, its iterability, its retrospective fulfillment in the understanding or collective judgement (*phronesis*) that the performance occasions.[29] Drama is intrinsically self-dissolving as a sensuous practice – both as a historical-artistic practice and at the level of each individual performance.

*

The first remnant of this dissolution of the sensuous performance of drama would seem to be the stand-alone dramatic work or poetic product that survives – that has a life beyond – its individual performances. In the ancient world, we need only think of the way in which Aristotle's notion of a poetic product – namely, the *mythos* that the poet fabricates – became the locus of interest, exerting an immense influence over literary history and the treatment of uniquely literary works. For modern Shakespeareans, this remnant is most obviously the script or literary text that stands at the centre of the English canon – although corollary remnants can be found in the way that certain performances, once recorded or otherwise reified, can come to stand as artworks in their own right.

So, at first blush, it would appear that the self-dissolution of the sensuous performance does not necessarily entail the dissolution of the dramatic work as *representation* – as belonging, say, to an aesthetic domain of art-objects set apart from the real life of subjects. (Indeed, for Aristotle, the *mythos* – the imitation of a significant action – was more fundamentally mimetic than was the sensuousness of the optics or the diction. And, working under the long shadow cast by Aristotle, scholars in Literature departments have long been studying the texts of Shakespeare's plays as textual artifacts, free from their sensuous performance as drama.) In short, it would appear that the representational character of drama has proven more durable and essential than its sensuousness as visible or audible performance – and, more importantly, has proven that drama can survive as poetic *representation* without needing its sensuous context in dramatic practices.

On closer inspection, however, we should see that the mimetic-representational status of the dramatic-poetic work is tightly bound up with the distance between spectacle and spectator that belongs to the sensuous performance of representational works of drama – whether of Attic tragedy or Shakespeare or other dramatists. The sensuous character of the performance – hearing and seeing of actors in a here-and-now context – corresponds to the way the dramatic work comes to be perceived as a mimetic or aesthetic work. I sensuously perceive the performer and the role *as performer and role* – I sensuously experience the drama *as dramatic art*, in other words – inasmuch as I also recognise *through the sensuous performance* that I am watching a mimetic performance (a performer's representation of Hamlet the aesthetic creation, not Hamlet himself).[30] In short, it turns out not to be so clear that a dramatic work (as distinct, say, from a novelistic or lyric or narrative work) would ever have been grasped as mimetic (as aesthetic) were it not sensuously performed – even as, at the same time, the literary-mimetic-aesthetic status of the dramatic work (as plot, as script, as text) springs from the perception of its having an existence *apart from* its sensuous presentation before an audience.

So we are left with a kind of chiasmus with respect to the sensuous, representational status of drama – such that the sensuous performance of a dramatic work continues, even after the classical era, to be bound up with its status as a mimetic artwork, and vice versa. If the dramatic work were not reifiable as a representational artwork (a plot, a story, a script) – as belonging to the domain of aesthetics – then nothing would assure us that what we watch is just a fiction and not really history itself unfolding before our eyes. At the same time, without the sensuous experience of watching something we take to be somehow unreal, we would probably have no concept of a reified dramatic artwork.[31]

Here, then, we trip upon the traditional (and thorny) question of what we are doing when we ritually enact a dramatic work as *representational*, as an aesthetic object, that stands apart from our own actions and lives. (Remember, for instance, Plato's worry – in the Tenth book of the *Republic* – that tragedies are not so distant from us after all, that they affectively worm their way into our psychic and somatic lives.[32] Plato had a point, after all: If we were to go through life weeping and grieving the way we do when we watch tragedies, then our capacity to carry out ordinary, desirable lives would be diminished. It was in part to respond to Plato's worry that Aristotle insisted on the significance of tragic drama as *mimetic* – inasmuch as tragedy might thereby afford an experience that in 'real life' would be impossible and hence provide a necessary outlet for feelings and affects that cannot be, and ought not be, felt in the same way in 'real life'.[33]) Aristotle's answer to this question, at any rate, is well known: Because we *need* feelings of fear and pity in order to understand our social or existential predicament we need a 'safe place' (the theatre) to experience these feelings without having to 'really' go through the predicaments themselves. The relief of *catharsis* is feeling fear and pity without having to suffer their empirical consequences, and without having to feel 'real' shame for feeling the way we do.

All of these familiar Aristotelian thoughts can also be gathered up as follows: The sensuous performance of a representational work before an audience – spectators watching or hearing actors perform a drama on stage (or screen) – is precisely what *assures* us of the 'safe' distance between the representation and what is represented. Inasmuch as we see and hear actors act a drama, to invoke Stanley Cavell's framing of the same problem, we feel free not to intervene – we feel assured that what we are seeing and watching is not the thing itself, and therefore requires no active participation on our part.[34]

Thus, our sensuous perception of the drama as drama goes hand in hand with our grasp of the drama as *mimetic* or *representational*. It turns out that the two cannot be separated. Hence, the sensuous self-dissolution of the theatre – to which, as I have already suggested,

Aristotle and the classical theatre already pointed – necessarily begs as well the question of the fate of drama as representational or aesthetic.

*

This brings me to the problem that will occupy me through the rest of this chapter. If, as I am arguing, the fate of drama as *sensuous perfor-mance* is necessarily tied to the fate of drama as *mimetic* – that is, to the representation of actions that are safely at a distance from the rest of us – then the self-dissolution of drama as sensuous performance (which I described in section 3 above) ought to entail, or come to be seen as, a self-dissolution of drama as mimetic.

I want to propose that we regard Shakespeare's drama as bearing out this inevitability.

Before defending this proposition, a few clarifications must be made to avoid confusion. First, let me make clear that I am discussing the fate of *drama* as it appears in Shakespeare. (Inasmuch as Shakespeare's plays are understood to constitute a *literary-aesthetic* artifact – poetry or nar-rative, say – the question of Shakespeare's relation to the fate of dramatic practices simply gets shoved to the side, or begged, without being ade-quately addressed. As if Shakespeare's status as literary-aesthetic artifact secretly required, as its disavowed precondition, that Shakespeare's role in the fate of dramatic practices not be seen as mattering to the achieve-ment of that status.[35])

Second, and to repeat a point I made earlier, I am not suggesting that we no longer (or no longer should) engage in the sensuous representa-tion of dramatic works after Shakespeare. Rather, I am suggesting that Shakespeare's drama reveals – that Shakespeare depicts, from within the practice of dramatic art – our diminishing need for the sensuous, repre-sentational practice of drama as an essential mode of our collective self-understanding. (Clearly, we still 'need' to perform Shakespeare for other perfectly valid educational, cultural, economic, personal or professional reasons, and I do not wish to claim otherwise.[36])

Let me now build outward from this last point. I argued at the outset that we might understand Shakespeare's place in the history of dramatic practices – and in the history of artistic practices generally – in light of the self-reflexive character of his drama: both Shakespeare's historical reflection on prior dramatic practices (including, perhaps especially, his own) and the self-referential character of his individual works, with respect to their own portrayal of themselves as 'dramatic'. I now want to try to explain both why and how the special self-reflexive character of Shakespearean drama shows – from inside its own dramatic practices – the dissolution of our need for sensuous, representational drama.

First, the 'why'. And here I need to simply to make an assertion: drama becomes more self-reflexive the more it realises that it cannot adequately capture or express an idealised picture of any particular aspect of human-historical experience (let alone of our existence as a whole).

The less that the ambition of furnishing an idealised representation of some feature of human existence is felt to drive the making of a drama, the more that drama is able to – the more it *must* (however inadequately) – reflect on its own status as a dramatic work, in light of those diminished idealising ambitions. Conversely, the more that a dramatic practice understands itself to aspire to the idealised representation of some fundamental aspect of human experience – the way, say, that death is represented in *Oedipus at Colonus*, or sexual obsession in *Antony and Cleopatra* – the less that drama will be able to reflect explicitly on its own status as drama, on its own idealising ambitions. In short: *If no idealised dramatic representation can capture or express a shared feature of human existence, then the task of drama must involve expressively reflecting on its failure to offer such an idealised representation.*

Corollary to this suggestion is the following: Self-reflexivity in drama (and in artistic practices generally) is a reflection on the prior ambition of art to furnish an adequate or idealised picture of some aspect of human life; self-reflexive art thus presupposes that prior ambition – and the failure to achieve it – as critical to its own capacity for self-reflection, and not just as a mistake to be disowned. (Hence: Shakespeare's own attempts at representing something fundamental in human existence – for instance, over-riding passions, like murderousness in *Othello*, sexual obsession in *Antony and Cleopatra*, ambition in *Macbeth* – are part and parcel of what I am calling his self-reflexive dramatic practice; even though, by the same token, these idealising plays or moments are among his least self-reflexively dramatic.)

A simpler way of putting all this is to note that modern drama knows, less and less, just what exactly it is supposed to depict or represent, and why. If Aeschylus and Sophocles had, at least, some sense of what the appropriate purview of tragedy was – the relation between family life and city life, or the struggle between ancient religious beliefs and (then) contemporary political values – then Shakespeare and modern dramatists have far fewer productive limitations. Even though Shakespeare of course continued to represent historically significant figures (Princes, Kings, Generals) as well as apparently 'universal' concerns (death, family life, sexual desire) he nevertheless leaves us with no sense that he knew, finally, just what exactly he was supposed to show us about any of these things. And this is why, after all, we see Shakespeare as possessed (as *needing* to be possessed) of far more imaginative energy than, say, Sophocles. Indeed, Shakespeare continually expands his dramatic vision to include whores, merchants, beggars, children, spirits and so on in a seemingly infinite variety of worldly contexts – to the point that we (modern directors and actors) must also imaginatively *choose* how, where and in what way to perform multifarious 'Shakespearean' works which seem suitable to so many domains and, hence, representative of no single, particular viewpoint on human life.

All of which is to say that Shakespeare did not regard being a dramatist as an activity that could be fixed or governed by taking for granted what a drama should do, should depict, should accomplish. Instead, he seemed to regard the task of drama – as Johann Gottfried Herder observed about Shakespeare over 200 years ago – to involve figuring out what, exactly, drama should or could do. Hence, the sense of ongoing revisions in Shakespeare – the feeling that *Cymbeline* and *The Winter's Tale* re-visit *Othello* and *King Lear*; that each new comedy is a self-critical vision of its predecessor. Think, too, of the way that Hamlet's inability to furnish an answer to his own rhetorical question – 'What's Hecuba to him, or he to Hecuba, that he should weep for her?' (*Hamlet*, 2.2.536) – necessitates and prompts Hamlet's reflection not on his or our connection to the events of the Iliad, but on the dramatically self-reflexive question of whether the sensuous performance of a mimetic action can (still) grip an audience in a meaningful way. In sum: Shakespeare challenges us to understand drama – *his* drama – not as responding to given facts of human existence (desire, or mortality) or to a historical situation (Henry V's invasion of France, or the fate of the Roman republic), but as responding to the fact that *there are no givens that govern our dramatic activity, and hence the task of drama must be in part to come to terms with our self-determination, with our relative freedom from given authorities that might determine or make sense of what we do and say with one another.*

The special self-reflexivity of Shakespearean drama is, under this light, an expression of the self-determining, self-authorising character of our experience as subjects – as human beings who feel 'freed' from the determinacy of nature and history. If we sense that Shakespeare represents us, then, it is because he does not simply 'represent' our lives; he refuses to capture or offer an idealised version of (modern) human beings. He presents us to ourselves – our self-determination as actors in the world – through the erosion of a mediating representational distance between the play and that which it depicts.[37]

✳

How, then, does the special self-reflexive character of Shakespearean drama show – from inside its own dramatic practices – the dissolution of our need for sensuous, representational drama?

Here one could continue to invoke a great many moments from the Shakespearean corpus. But because its conclusion now seems to us indicative of Shakespeare's (the artist's) own self-reflexive 'leave-taking' of drama – let me close with a few words about *The Tempest* (1610–11), in light of what I have said in the previous sections of this chapter. (By 'leave-taking' I do not at all mean to imply that Shakespeare-the-artist meant to leave drama or art *behind*; rather, as I hope I have been making clear throughout, I see a self-dissolution of drama that is accomplished from *within* and *by* Shakespearean drama. I see this self-dissolution at work in virtually the entire Shakespearean corpus, and so I see *The Tempest* not as closing or transcending drama, but as a culminating achievement of Shakespeare's dramatic self-reflexivity – his drama's attempt at self-transcendence from within its own sphere, to borrow Hegel's turn of phrase.[38])

In the first section, recall, I invoked Hegel's claim about the way in which the history of art presents an ongoing and increasing de-naturalisation or 'spiritualisation' of our self-understanding. If Hegel is right, then we are less and less dependent upon – less needful of – artistic expressions that work with the given-ness of 'natural' or sensible media in order to understand ourselves, and our world. Does not Prospero's 'art' – not simply as a fictional device (since, I want to claim, Prospero is not simply a fictional character) but also as a reflective presentation of the dramatic arts – express this de-naturalisation, the denial of nature's claims upon us? And does not the Tempest itself depict this humanisation or 'spiritualisation' (to use Hegel's parlance) of the seeming indifference of nature's elements – wind, water and air? Recall Prospero's own words:

> I have bedimm'd
> The noontide sun, call'd forth the mutinous winds,
> And 'twixt the green sea and the azur'd vault
> Set roaring war: to the dread rattling thunder
> Have I given fire, and rifted Jove's stout oak
> With his own bolt; the strong-bas'd promontory
> Have I made shake, and by the spurs pluck'd up
> The pine and cedar: graves at my command
> Have wak'd their sleepers, op'd forth, and let 'em forth
> By my so potent Art . . . (*Tempest*, 5.1.41–50)

Moreover, Shakespeare's dramatic interest – I mean, his interest in Prospero's 'art' and in the achievement of our de-naturalisation as a dramatically motivational predicament – lies in the manifestly social-historical (human) consequences of this 'art', in the 'spiritual' stakes of our de-naturalisation. As if the very experience of natural elements – the storm, the waves – was to be regarded as an artistic accomplishment. At any rate, the significance of Prospero's art is obviously not to be found in the frothy waves he whips up but – as Miranda, and the rest of us find out – in the stirring social consequences that follow upon the roaring storm. Indeed, even those on the ship feel that their fate lies not in the sublime indifference of the roaring waves to the king's command, but in the autonomous capacities of their own hands – inebriated as they are ('We are merely cheated of our lives by drunkards' [*Tempest*, 1.1.55]).

Second, the unravelling of art's purpose requires, from Prospero, a highly self-aware choreography of happenings on the island: individuals are brought into carefully arranged contact, as if on cue (Miranda and Ferdinand); the most refined spectacular techniques of the era (Masques and so forth) are pressed into the service of filling the island with sights and sounds – spirits, trances, somnolence, charms – so that we might see others in the grip of the same sensuous display that commands our attention.

Why this exhibition of sensuousness 'theatricality'? It is difficult not to see these displays as self-reflexively presenting the sensuous capacities of drama in order to show – importantly – the relative freedom of drama with respect to other material media. Drama can *contain* music without being reducible to a musical performance, can *contain* dance without being confused with an occasion to move one's body about, can *contain* spectacles of all sorts without being thereby reducible to mere show. Moreover, drama can purposefully *show* this containment – and, hence, supersession – of other media as essential to its *own* specifically expressive power. Which is, of course, just what Prospero demonstrates. And all of this – whatever else it might mean in the context of *The Tempest* (and it is not at all clear what *else* the demonstrations from Act 4, Scene 1 are 'about') – can be taken as a self-conscious presentation of various components of dramatic practices that would normally escape our special attention, that we might otherwise pass over as simply part of the proceedings at a playhouse. Prospero, however, does not let us pass over these elements un-attentively – 'No tongue! All eyes! Be silent' (4.1.59).

To what 'end' are we asked to be thus attentive to the elements of drama, its constitutive de-naturalisation? Simply so that we might perceive the special sensuous power of the theatre – its *containment* and *supersession* of other arts, its 'spell' as Prospero calls it – and its eventual self-dissolution at Prospero's own command. 'Well done! Avoid; no more!' (4.1.142).

Were this all, however, we would not be sure that Prospero himself sees matters as we do – we would not be sure that the self-dissolution of the drama were his (or the play's) *purpose*. As if to erase all doubts, Shakespeare has Prospero address his own activity, in order to underscore that the fulfillment of his drama lies in its foretold dissolution:

> Our revels now are ended. These our actors,
> As I foretold you, were all spirits and
> Are melted into air, into thin air . . . (4.1.148–50)

I cannot be the first to hear in Prospero's lines not only a description of the limits of dramatic revels, but also a *reflective stance* on the significance of those limits. (Ferdinand and Miranda themselves give voice to this same perception – 'This is strange: your father's in some passion that works him strongly' [4.1.143–4].) At any rate, Prospero leaves no doubt about his reflective stance on the revels' end when he continues:

> And, like the baseless fabric of this vision,
> The cloud-capp'd towers, the gorgeous palaces,
> The solemn temples, the great globe itself,
> Ye all which it inherit, shall dissolve
> And, like this insubstantial pageant faded,
> Leave not a rack behind. (4.1.151–6)

And once this *reflective* stance – 'if revels end it is because *we* end' – comes into view, we see that our condition was not fully captured or represented by the spatial-temporal limitations of drama. Rather, by virtue of the self-reflexive presentation of drama's sensuous-representational *limitations* – and by virtue of our reflective stance on these limitations – we gain a perspective on what we were struggling all along to see more clearly: ourselves.

> We are such stuff
> As dreams are made on, and our little life
> Is rounded with a sleep. (4.1.156–8)

If 'we are such stuff as dreams are made on' (and we can think here, too, of Puck's address at the close of *A Midsummer Night's Dream*) then is it not because our imaginative capacities as free self-determining beings refuse the limitations of sensuous, material representation?

At the same time, if the sensuousness of the representation is to be truly *self-dissolving* – and not just a further display of aesthetic autonomy (of Prospero's artistic power) – then this self-dissolution cannot itself be aesthetically accomplished, cannot be merely offered as the self-conscious 'representation' of a play coming to its close. (Shakespeare is not just rehearsing, in other words, the standard Elizabethan-Jacobean 'epilogue' about a play's ending.)

Instead, sensuous representational artistry as such must be disavowed, revels ended – first of all by the artist, who drowns his book and staff.

> *Now my charms are all o'erthrown,*
> *And what strength I have's mine own.* (*Tempest*, Epilogue, 1–2)

Thus, the challenge is: How is artistry to be dissolved *by the artist himself*? How can drama transcend itself, from within its own sphere?

To address this challenge, several moments seem to be required.[39] First, the artist must risk appearing otherwise than as an artist. It is not (yet) a matter of the artist's disappearance, pure and simple, but rather of a risk that the artist takes – namely, appearing otherwise than as an artist. Certain trappings have to be jettisoned.

> . . . I'll break my staff,
> Bury it certain fathoms in the earth,
> And deeper than did ever plummet sound
> I'll drown my book. (*Tempest*, 5.1.54–7)

This is not only a matter of trading one guise for another, nor is it merely that the artist is undergoing a shift within himself. Rather, and this is the second requirement, it must be seen that the risk he has taken, in appearing otherwise than as an artist, *also* means that the way things stand for others, too, changes. It would not be enough for the artist to appear as otherwise than an artist if everyone persisted in their assumption or belief or stupor – if everyone were still held, as it were, by the enduring effects of art's spell. The spell also must dissolve – so that we, too, might see how things between us really stand now.

> . . . The charm dissolves apace;
> And as the morning steals upon the night,
> Melting the darkness, so their rising senses
> Begin to chase the ignorant fumes that mantle
> Their clearer reason . . . (*Tempest*, 5.1.64–8)

Third, to truly risk appearing to others as otherwise than an artist – if it is to be a risk and not merely a further demonstration of artistry – requires the recognition that letting go of art (if it is a real 'letting go') cannot itself be artfully accomplished. To appear as otherwise than an artist therefore could not be accomplished by an artist – lest that 'appearance' be taken for another demonstration of artistry. Only a human being could appear as otherwise than as an artist.

And finally – as if Shakespeare's drama, *as if all of drama*, had been a preparation for this moment – a human being stands forth, and steps away from the 'art' he made and from what that art itself wrought.

> *Now my charms are all o'erthrown,*
> *And what strength I have's mine own*
> *Which is most faint . . . (Tempest*, Epilogue, 1–3)

But even at this point, another moment is still required. The sensuous-mimetic distance between what we see and our own lives must dissolve. *We* must acknowledge that Prospero is not just a 'fictional character', that the 'island' is not a safely distant aesthetic domain . . .

> *I must be here confin'd by you*
> *. . . Let me not*
> *. . . dwell*
> *In this bare island by your spell;*
> *But release me from my bands*
> *With the help of your good hands . . . (Tempest*, Epilogue, 4–10)

. . . hence, that we are no longer acquitted from the obligation to inter-vene.

Nothing is sacred in Shakespeare's drama – not even its own status as dramatic art.

Drama as sensuous representation dissolves the moment it wants something other than passivity from *us* – when it asks us not to represent ourselves, but to become ourselves.

Notes

1. G.W.F. Hegel, *Lectures on Fine Art*, trans. T.M. Knox (Oxford: Clarendon University Press, 1975), vol. 1, p. 49.
2. Ibid., p. 31.
3. Ibid., p. 49.
4. So, this is not to say that there are not other ongoing critical needs for sensuous, representational art – only that these needs are now less essential to our deepest efforts at self-understanding, what Hegel calls 'the deepest interests of mankind, and the most comprehensive truths of spirit [*Geist*]' (ibid., p. 7). For more on this point, see, as a start, the discussions of Hegel – and the debates over this pronouncement – in Dieter Heinrich, 'Art and Philosophy of Art Today: Reflections with Reference to Hegel', in R. Amacher and V. Lange (eds), *New Perspectives in German Literary Criticism*, trans. D. Wilson et al. (Princeton: Princeton University Press, 1979), pp. 107–33; Arthur Danto, *The Philosophical Disenfranchisement of Art* (New York: Columbia University Press, 1986), especially pp. 81–115; Stephen Houlgate, 'Hegel and the "End" of Art', *Owl of Minerva*, 29:1 (1997), pp. 1–19; Gregg Horowitz, *Sustaining Loss: Art and Mournful*

Life (Stanford: Stanford University Press, 2001); Eva Geulen, *The End of Art: Readings in a Rumor After Hegel*, trans. James McFarland (Stanford: Stanford University Press, 2006), especially Chapter 2.

5. G.W.F. Hegel, *Lectures on Fine Art*, trans. T.M. Knox (Oxford: Clarendon University Press, 1975), vol. 2, p. 666, my emphasis.

6. I realise, of course, that I am skipping over a number of important questions – for example, those having to do with the differences between the fates of classical and romantic art in Hegel's account. But I think my overall point about denaturalisation as self-reflexivity can stand, for the moment, without tackling those questions. On this point, I am following Robert Pippin, 'What was Abstract Art? (From the Point of View of Hegel)', *Critical Inquiry*, 29 (2002), pp. 1–24.

7. G.W.F. Hegel, 'Dramatic Poetry', in Paul A. Kottman (ed.), *Philosophers on Shakespeare* (Stanford: Stanford University Press, 2009), p. 57.

8. Hegel, *Lectures on Fine Art*, vol. 1, p. 2. On this point see Pippin, 'What was Abstract Art?', p. 9.

9. Hegel, *Lectures on Fine Art*, vol. 1, p. 29; vol. 2, pp. 866–7.

10. At a minimum, a bit of nature-wrought-into-art expresses the capacity of stone, sound or color to transmit meaning for a particular community and its practices. Art, as Hegel puts it, creates a reality that is 'besouled' ('für sich beseelt') – by which, as Robert Pippin aptly states, Hegel does not mean that human freedom re-enchants the world through artistic means but rather that art 'elevates us above the need for [the] enchantment [of the natural world]'. See Hegel, *Lectures on Fine Art*, vol. 2, p. 834, and Pippin, 'What was Abstract Art?', p. 8.

11. Hegel's way of putting it is to say that nature is 'spiritless'.

12. Northrop Frye, *The Educated Imagination* (Canadian Broadcasting Corporation, 1963), p. 8.

13. Hegel, *Lectures on Fine Art*, vol. 2, p. 1192, English translation modified. The German reads: 'einer vollständig sinnlichen Darstellung, welche sie kunstgemäß erst durch die wirkliche theatralische Exekution erhält'.

14. The same goes for the other passages from the *Lectures* in which Hegel refers to 'actual theatrical production' as the 'touchstone' for dramatic poetry (see, for instance, ibid., p. 1184). True, Hegel thinks a dramatist must keep the stage and the "demands of dramatic liveliness" in view. Otherwise, he's not a dramatist but some other kind of artist. (And of course Hegel writes in the 1820s as an avid theatregoer himself!) Still, the larger issue remains *why* dramatic art places these demands – *why* sensuous presentation is required. And the answer, again, seems to have to do with a historical-*geistig* need to present a 'complete and specific action' both 'subjectively' (as in lyric) and 'objectively' (as in epic). The only way that human beings had, historically in ancient Greece say, to get both 'subjective' and 'objective' views at once was to do something theatrical. However, while the fate of dramatic poetry is doubtless linked to its having needed to become theatrical it is not clear that – for Hegel, or in general – dramatic poetry must remain theatrical, or must always remain a matter of sensuous representation on stage. Or at least it is not clear that Hegel's emphasis on theatrical representation is anything other than a historical claim – a claim about the historical necessity of a certain artistic mode. Given the historical

narrative-cast of the Lectures as a whole, I doubt that there is any ahistorical claim about the need for theatricality being advanced here.

15. Ibid., p. 1228.

16. Shakespeare's pre-eminence in Hegel's account – the fact, for instance, that Hegel's discussion of Shakespeare comes at the culmination of his Lectures on Fine Art – would, of course, require some qualification. Hegel also seems to claim that Greek art is more fulfilled *as art* than modern art, and his high regard for Sophocles seems of a piece with that view. 'There is', however, as Pippin notes, 'another sense in which he claims that the ethical life behind Shakespeare's presentation and the kind of self-awareness visible in Hamlet, say, does represent an advance or moment of progress'. Robert Pippin, *The Persistence of Subjectivity: On the Kantian Aftermath* (Cambridge: Cambridge University Press, 2005), p. 84, n. 12. See, further, the discussion of Hegel and Shakespeare in Henry and Anne Paolucci, *Hegelian Literary Perspectives* (Smyrna, DE: Griffon House [reprinted], 2002).

17. The scholarship that treats this topic is extensive. An astute, philosophically informed place to start is Anne Barton's classic study, *Shakespeare and the Idea of the Play* (New York: Greenwood [reprint], 1977). Barton points out that, with very few exceptions, the discursive comparison of the world with the stage is not uttered in what we might call an explicitly dramatic context until the middle of the sixteenth century, when the theatre began to acquire its modern, secularised form in London. She lists moments from Greek New Comedy and the Roman comedies of Plautus, which were among the first to be rediscovered by the early English dramatists, as exceptions to this. See pp. 60–1.

18. There would be more to say about Spanish, Italian or French dramas in this regard. See, as a start, Louise George Clubb's study of theatregrams in *Italian Drama in Shakespeare's Time* (New Haven: Yale University Press, 1989).

19. See the Epilogue, 'The World Stage', in Paul A. Kottman, *A Politics of the Scene* (Stanford: Stanford University Press, 2008).

20. By 'theatricality' I mean what Henry Turner has described as 'the clusters of techniques, objects, bodies, conventions, signs, and other significant elements that characterized early modern performance and that extended beyond the public theatres to public entertainments and spectacles of all types, from the Tudor period to the Restoration'. I cite from his remarks at Rutgers University in December 2011 at the conference, 'Early Modern Theatricality in the 21st Century'. See http://earlymoderntheatricality.com.

21. Again, this does not mean that we now have no need for drama, Shakespearean or other – just that this need is no longer deeply essential to our own self-understanding as free and self-determining. I would even suggest that Shakespeare's pre-eminence among modern dramatists – for Hegel, for German philosophy and for most of us – is connected to his modernist reflexivity as an artist, to his artistic response to the challenge of making art after its 'highest' vocation has ended. I realise, of course, that stating matters thus might seem anachronistic – given that Hegel's pronouncement postdates Shakespeare by more than two centuries. But given the extent to which Hegel himself grappled with Shakespearean drama

from his earliest writings to his Berlin lectures on art, there is certainly a basis for considering Shakespeare as a necessary touchstone for later developments in Hegel's aesthetic philosophy. (Incidentally, by 'earliest writings' I mean not only the remarks on Shakespeare's *Macbeth* from Hegel's 'Spirit of Christianity and its Fate' but also the very earliest document of Hegel's to have come down to us – a rewriting of Shakespeare's *Julius Caesar*, composed when Hegel was a teenager. See *Miscellaneous Writings of G.W.F. Hegel*, ed. Jon Stewart [Evanston: Northwestern University Press, 2002].)

22. I am thinking of accounts of modernist painting that, albeit in diverging ways, defend a future for modernist painting on the basis of art's reflection on its material medium. See, as two instances of this, the defences of painting and modernist art given by Yves-Alain Bois, *Painting as Model* (Cambridge, MA: MIT Press, 1990), especially pp. 229–44; and J.M. Bernstein, *Against Voluptuous Bodies: Late Modernism and the Meaning of Painting* (Stanford: Stanford University Press, 2006).

23. See Aristotle, *Poetics*, trans. Stephen Halliwell (Chapel Hill: University of North Carolina Press, 1987), 1453b1–4.

24. For a discussion of affective response to tragedy as arbiter of communal self-understanding, see my *Tragic Conditions in Shakespeare* (Baltimore: Johns Hopkins University Press, 2009), p. 6 and passim.

25. The real protagonist of tragedy, notes Vernant in a well-known thesis, is the city, its values, attitudes and modes of thought. Jean-Pierre Vernant and Pierre Vidal-Naquet, *Myth and Tragedy*, trans. Janet Lloyd (New York: Zone Books, 1990), 35 and passim.

26. *Mimeseos* is the genitive of *mimesis*, indicating that the representation 'belongs' to the action, not the reverse.

27. Cf. Walter Benjamin, 'The Storyteller', in *Selected Writings*, vol. 3 (Cambridge, MA: Harvard University Press, 2002).

28. Unless one sees in the Pythagorean (or Platonic) conception of music as an invisible *harmonia* (a 'harmony of the spheres') a similar philosophical self-dissolution of the sensuousness of music. See the discussion in Adriana Cavarero, *For More Than One Voice: Toward a Philosophy of Vocal Expression* (Stanford: Stanford University Press, 2005). But here philosophy would silence music from the outside, in mute opposition to its sonority – whereas I am arguing, pace Aristotle, that drama is self-dissolving and this historical self-dissolution is noted by, but not enacted by, philosophy.

29. It is this last element, especially, that distinguishes the performance of spoken drama from the acoustics of music in classical accounts like Aristotle's.

30. Recall that, for Aristotle, the sensuous perception of a mimetic work *as mimetic* requires and entails perceiving the sensuous material as something more than sensuous material; namely, perceiving that it is mimetic. Hence, the 'pleasure' afforded in understanding that a given sensuous presentation is mimetic is different from the pleasure taken in the mere sensuousness itself (pretty colors or sounds). Think of the pleasure taken by very young children in seeing that yellow and brown combine to represent a giraffe, rather than present just the prettiness of yellow and brown.

31. We might still, of course, have the concept of a literary or poetic document or text, or of some other reification – but it would not be a work of

drama, a specifically *dramatic* artwork. For a fuller discussion of this same problem, see Chapter 6, 'Memory, Mimesis, Tragedy: The Scene Before Philosophy', of my *A Politics of the Scene* (Stanford: Stanford University Press, 2008).

32. Remember that Plato's real concern with tragedy was not just part of his general worry about mimetic artists, but a specific concern about tragedy's capacity to exacerbate grief, psychic pain and its attendant displays.

33. I am thinking, for instance, of Aristotle's famous observation that we take pleasure in seeing represented in tragedies that which would cause pain were it seen in real life.

34. See Cavell's discussion of Aristotle as offering a theory of tragedy that establishes the aesthetic domain as 'a context in which I am to do nothing'. Stanley Cavell, 'The Avoidance of Love', in *Disowning Knowledge in Seven Plays of Shakespeare* (Cambridge: Cambridge University Press, 2003), p. 91.

35. This disavowal has been the topic of probing work done by William B. Worthen, in *Shakespeare and the Force of Modern Performance* (Cambridge: Cambridge University Press, 2002), *Print and the Poetics of Modern Drama* (Cambridge: Cambridge University Press, 2006), and *Drama Between Poetry and Performance* (New York: Wiley-Blackwell, 2010).

36. For instance, I think we continue to need Shakespeare (or the theatre generally) to do important work for, and by, the imagination (what the Chorus in *Henry V* calls our 'imaginary forces'). I am thinking, especially, of the way in which reading or performing Shakespeare can, from a young age, 'educate the imagination' (to use Northrop Frye's felicitous phrase) or cultivate emotional sensibility to, and practical judgements about, intractably difficult human predicaments. This is a deeply important cultural need, surely, and one that Shakespeare and great literature meet better, probably, than any other human product.

37. For more on the dissolution of mimetic distance in Shakespeare, see my *Tragic Conditions in Shakespeare*, especially pp. 18–20.

38. Hegel predicted that post-Romantic art would entail 'the self-transcendence of art but within its own sphere and in the form of art itself'. Hegel, *Lectures on Fine Art*, vol. 1, p. 80. (Cited in Pippin, *The Persistence of Subjectivity*, p. 306.) As I indicated in note 16 above, I see Shakespeare as post-Romantic in Hegel's sense – and I tend to think that Hegel himself saw Shakespeare as his contemporary, too.

39. Here I am echoing the conclusion offered in the final pages of my *Tragic Conditions in Shakespeare*.

Chapter 2

Hamlet and Kierkegaard on Outwitting Recollection

Jennifer Ann Bates

Many articles have teased out links between these two Danish melancholics.[1] I am interested, first, in the fact that Kierkegaard thinks that Shakespeare's plays in general deal with terrible collisions, but not with deep, religious ones,[2] and second, that there are parallels in Kierkegaard's and Hamlet's view of themselves as having to set right the joint of time.

I discuss *Hamlet* together with Kierkegaard's pseudonymously authored *Concluding Unscientific Postscript*.[3] I refer to the pseudonym – Climacus – as the author.[4] My theme is the grave plot common to *Hamlet* and the *Postscript*.

Introduction: The Task of Remembering

'Adieu, adieu, Hamlet. Remember me' (1.5.91). With these words, Hamlet's ghostly father returns to a restless grave. So begins Hamlet's vocation to set time right in Denmark.

In the *Postscript*, Johannes Climacus has an analogous experience, in a graveyard with a buried father. It is an experience that starts his vocation to set time right in Denmark. The *Postscript* itself unearths, from Climacus's previously published *Philosophical Fragments*, the task of remembering the moment when the Divine Father appeared as man – the Christian Incarnation.

For Climacus, as for Hamlet, the task of remembering 'the Father' also means restoring what it means to conceive being. Unlike for Hamlet, for Climacus this task requires a leap of faith beyond *human* conception. Remembering Christianity means: remembering primordial genesis.

But for both Hamlet and Climacus, to merely recollect is to forget to be. Let us begin with this similarity.

The Structure of the Grave Plot

Hamlet and the *Postscript* are each efforts to make what I call 'vertical determinism' into the flow of becoming. Vertical determinism is a given 'plot' of history, a broken joint of time that will not develop beyond its formal constraints. It is a plot that has a social and ethical (and in the case of the *Postscript*, an apparently religious) continuity; but the plot keeps returning to itself in mortal repetitions.

The central image in both *Hamlet* and the *Postscript* is therefore that of a grave out of which and into which things rise and fall back. The task for Hamlet and Climacus is to make the plot into a moment of genuine embodiment that becomes, has actual, forward movement.

For Climacus, this is a Christian task. It is arrived at by inwardis-ing, when the subject, divested of objectivity, leaps into relation with the paradox of the incarnation. The forward movement is then a becoming-actual: a repetition of spiritual life. Another of Kierkegaard's pseudonyms, Anti-Climacus, makes this clear in his opening remarks to *Sickness Unto Death*: there is no use in bringing Lazareth back from the dead if he is just going to die all over again: the key is to bring him back from the death of spirit.[5]

According to Climacus, this requires of the individual not just self-annihilation before the negative, but a leap of faith before the positive paradox. Therein lies the all-important 'Offence' of Christianity.[6]

By contrast, Hamlet's 'to be or not to be' concerns self-annihilation in suicide. This gives rise to a superstitious 'rub', not the Christian 'Offense'. Nonetheless, this difference between Climacus and Hamlet is hard to maintain. As I will show, there are other ways in which Hamlet engages the problem 'to be or not to be'; and Climacus's Christian plot has ironic complexities which draw it into the plot of Hamlet. Let us begin with the overlap between Hamlet and Climacus.

Recollection as Forgetting to Exist in Denmark's Castle, Church and Hegelian Philosophy

Gertrude: You false Danish dogs. (4.5.110)

Hamlet: One may smile and smile and be a villain.
At least I am sure it may be so in Denmark. (1.5.109–10)

The central problem with the plot given to Hamlet and the plot given to Climacus is that, in their Denmarks, recollection means forgetting to exist. Hamlet's and Climacus's task, announced to them each by a ghostly figure, is to outwit recollection.

Hamlet's Given Plot: Recollection as Forgetting to Exist

In *Hamlet*, time is 'out of joint'. The plot repeats one structure: an antecedent ground out of which events, ghostlike, arise and return. Everything is a consequence of what occurred before the opening scene. A ghost tells us what happened – Claudius murdered him and married his queen. The ghost makes it clear that any future action is to be in response to those crimes. As the player king says: 'Purpose is but the slave to memory' (3.2.170).

The spuriousness of this grave vertical determinism is expressed in the words of Claudius:

> My words fly up, my thoughts remain below.
> Words without thoughts never to heaven go. (3.3.97–8)

Everything growing up in the play is pulled down: witness young Ophelia's garland-strewn drowning.[7] Scattering flowers on Ophelia's grave, Queen Gertrude says:

> I had hoped thou shouldst have been my Hamlet's wife.
> I thought thy bride-bed to have decked, sweet maid,
> And not t' have strewed thy grave. (5.1.227–9)

Into Ophelia's grave jump Laertes and Hamlet, just hours before they too will be buried. Yorick's skull pulls Hamlet into memories; there is the pit of the king's ear, into which poison is poured – a 'forged process' by which the 'whole ear of Denmark / [is] Rankly abused' (1.5.36–8). There is also the swearing above the stage, echoed and elicited by the ghost 'beneath the stage' (1.5.152, 157, 163, 182). Finally, there is Fortinbras's battle over a plot of land – a plot that becomes the soldiers' grave. Indeed, the Fortinbras sub-plot is a metonymy of the entire play: *Hamlet* is about the 'shocks / that flesh is heir to' (3.1.64–5); the suffering we endure in our plot of time.

A Kierkegaardian – for example, his pseudonym Taciturnus – might wonder: If Hamlet had had deeper plots – those of Christian subjectivity and despair – would those religious depths have given him the possibility of changing his plot, of changing its mortal repetitions of rising and falling, into eternal becoming? This question is not so easy to answer.

Let us take a closer look at how vertical determinism – this inability to get out of the grave of the past – is at work in our other Denmark.

Climacus's Given Plot: Recollection as Forgetting to Exist

Time is 'out of joint'.[8] In the *Postscript*, Climacus writes that 'people in our day have forgotten what it means *to exist*, and what *inwardness* is . . . the misunderstanding between speculative thought and Christianity could be explained by that'.[9] The word 'forget' occurs on almost every other page of the book. Climacus's correction for such forgetting is that 'The subjective thinker's task is to *understand himself in existence*.'[10]

According to Climacus, at the deepest level of subjectivity, there is the possibility of the subject's possible relation to the Incarnate God.[11] The absurdity of the eternal being finite transforms theoretical knowing into subjective decision: in choosing, one becomes. All other forms of thought are non-actual; they are recollections without the movement of becoming. Such recollections are either imaginative reconstructions of the past, or, worse, speculative reconstructions about those imagined recollections. Speculation is the worst form of recollection because it is the furthest thing from existence; it is pure thought about the past.

For Climacus, therefore, the recluse who does not act is better than the speculative thinker for whom every experience in life is recollected knowledge: 'the recluse's pathos-filled lack of actuality is far preferable to the comic lack of actuality of the pure thinker, and the recluse's passionate forgetfulness that takes the whole world away is far preferable to the comic distraction of the world-historical thinker who forgets himself'.[12] Although this passage is not said of Hamlet, it very well could have been. From it we can conclude that for Climacus, Hamlet is better than Hegel.[13] Reclusive Hamlet, even when not acting, is more ethical than Hegel because he does not forget himself in the pure recollection of thinking. (If there is a figure for the Speculative Professor in the play, it would be Polonius.)

For Climacus, recollection of objective history is quantitative. *Subjective* certainty involves 'the absolute, qualitative disjunction'.[14] This disjunction does not create an abstract, known self. Rather, it creates the most existentially concrete one.[15] To remember to exist is to remember that embodied time is this absolute, qualitative disjunction. This joint of time in Climacus's account is the place in history and in our selves where the infinite and the finite are, paradoxically, joined. Theoretical comprehension of this is the experience of encountering paradox (the incommensurability of the infinite being in a finite body). Practical experience of this is the leap of faith.

The realisation that time is out of joint is the realisation that the everyday temporal order does not realise this distinction. That realisation is the first step towards properly understanding time's dis-joint as the paradox; it opens up the possibility of willing by virtue of the absurd, in offense to reason – a repetition of the incarnate Moment. Not realising sin means continuing recollection: a repetition of time being out of joint.

Recollection as Forgetting to Exist in Hamlet: Take(s) Two

Hamlet's task from the beginning is to restore time's flow. But the weight of recollection – like the flowers of remembrance on sinking Ophelia's dress – is the drench of consequence: it pulls everything into the grave. Hamlet's despair about this is itself a sinking, even as he tries to transcend it.

For Hamlet, Claudius's claim to the throne is an objective history which, to use Climacus's language, is merely quantitatively real. Claudius's *realpolitik* is to view his coronation as the proper order of things.[16] For Hamlet, this is a false ordering of time. More importantly, this ordering obfuscates the subjective, ethical responsibility that makes a person's tasks *qualitatively* real. This forgetful recollection has the appearance of a linear flow of time – the passage of generations and entitlements. But the plot reveals this flow to be the vertical determinism of a grave yielding up deathly consequences.

Hamlet's despair is shaped by the absence of the qualitative disjunc-tion; it is shaped most profoundly by this absence in his mother. The king and court have forgotten to exist; but far worse, Hamlet's mother has forgotten Hamlet's father.

For Hamlet, as for Climacus, the greatest problem with forgetting oneself is not in the gross sins of, say, murder, but rather in the failure to remember the 'Father' and the effect that such forgetting has on the past as origin of the present.

Gertrude has not sinned in the gross sense: she is faultless of Claudius's crime of murder. Her crime, in Hamlet's eyes, is that she has forgotten Hamlet senior. She has instead re-collected a king who is not the one she loved and with whom she bore young Hamlet. The depth of transgression here is precisely that she continues in the flow of things without taking the time to mourn. Time is out of joint even as it appears to move forward.

Hamlet alone notices that time is moving over a gaping grave and that conception itself is at stake. His chastisement of Ophelia, while appear-ing to delve into the religious, is just an elaboration of this. If true of his mother's marriage and conception (of thoughts and children), then by extension it must be true that all marriages and all conceptions (of thoughts and children) are abortive: like the events in the play these conceptions ignore the grave of sin out of which they spring. Existence is improperly conceived (3.1.94–147).

What is all-important for Hamlet is that Gertrude remember his father: witness how he tries to make her remember, using a picture of him (3.4.52). Gertrude's forgetting opens a pit of despair for Hamlet; the absence of her grief raises the spectre that Hamlet is the spawn of lust, a spiritual bastard. Hamlet falls into the absence of his mother's desire (for him). Time is out of joint, and Gertrude is 'Th' imperial join-tress' (1.2.9).

Hamlet must set time's joint in two ways: he must solve the existential corruption of the court and of the 'original scene'.[17] This is his task, 'to understand himself in existence'.[18]

It is not hard to transpose this onto the *Postscript*: Climacus's Gertrude is the Church. Is Climacus's angst more profound because it goes beyond *human* conception? Or is Climacus's angst, at its deepest, still inside a grave plot?

Kierkegaard's Pseudonym 'Taciturnus' on the Failure of Hamlet to Exist

Kierkegaard discusses *Hamlet* for two pages, in *Stages on Life's Way*, through his pseudonym Frater Taciturnus.[19] For Taciturnus, the play has no good reason for getting on with its plot; all the variations Taciturnus makes up to explain the plot's progression, fail to do so. Taciturnus attempts to explain how the plot could have made sense religiously or aesthetically. He wants it to be a religious plot, but then it would not have been able to be communicated aesthetically; he does not want the play to be a bad one about a secular ditherer. So on the one hand, the drama of *Hamlet* is not religious enough, and if it were, it would not be able to be a drama; on the other, if it is not a question of religious colli-sions underlying Hamlet's angst, then what, asks Taciturnus, is holding Hamlet back?[20]

I think that Taciturnus's turns and returns are reflections of the play's intentional plot – a plot that resists becoming and that makes its being questionable. I think this because the plot of *Hamlet* deals not just with relative contradictions, but also with the *absolute* contradiction of 'to be or not to be'.

The issue for both *Hamlet* and the *Postscript* is the either/or of exist-ence: to be or not to be. That dialectic cannot 'progress'; to be is an existential choice. It is a becoming that is an entering into actuality, not a movement towards an objective goal.

To Be or Not to Be: An 'Absolute Contradiction'

In his journals, Kierkegaard writes:

> Verily, we do not need Hegel, to tell us that *relative* contradictions can be mediated . . . [but] personality will protest in all eternity against the proposition that *absolute* contradictions can be mediated . . . It will repeat its immortal dilemma through all eternity: 'to be or not to be, that is the question'.[21]

The plots of *Hamlet* and the *Postscript* each find their deepest collision in Hamlet's words 'to be or not to be'. In both texts, this phrase expresses three things that defy becoming: a despairing self-annihilation; the duplicitous (either/or) status of a ghost (especially the ghost of the Father); and third, a knowing that is only a seeming. In this third sense, the phrase 'to be or not to be' gapes wider than its literal meaning, in that 'to be' in the sense of *existing* is opposed to 'not to be' in the sense of a knowing that is only a seeming.[22]

The question 'To be or not to be', understood in these three senses (despair, the Father's ghostly duplicity, and seeming), is the grave plot shared by Hamlet and Climacus. Their task is to communicate absolute contradiction to Denmark (Gertrude/the Church); their problem is that the absolute contradiction manifests in these three duplicitous ways.

To delve deeper into this, let us return to the grave scenes that inaugurate Hamlet's and Climacus's vocations. In these scenes, spiritual suicide, ghostly calls to remember and seeming-knowledge are all present. Remarkably, both scenes involve oath-taking as a means of inscribing the ghostly call to remember. Let me begin with these oaths.

Remembering 'to be' Through Oath-Taking: The 'Swear!' Scenes in *Hamlet* and the *Postscript*

Oaths are plots to remember. Hamlet takes an oath, Climacus rejects taking an oath. The larger issue here is the role of aesthetics as a means (for remembering) to be.

The first of three oaths taken in *Hamlet* is about remembering. Hamlet writes his oath to the ghost, in his 'tables' or college notebook:

> My tables,
> My tables – meet it is I set it down
> That one may smile and smile and be a villain.
> At least I'm sure it may be so in Denmark
> [*He writes*]

So, uncle, there you are,
Now to my word:
It is 'Adieu, adieu, remember me.'
I have sworn't. (1.5.107)

It is soon after this that Hamlet says:

The time is out of joint.
O cursed spite
That ever I was born to set it right! (1.5.189–90)

With these words, the grave plot is established.

The second oath is about *not* progressing with a narrative: 'Never make known what you have seen tonight' (1.5.147) and 'Never speak of this that you have seen, Swear by my sword' (1.5.155–6). The swearing is itself interrupted by the 'old mole' 'under the stage'. The interred ruptures forth: 'Swear' (1.5.157, 164, 182).

All this swearing is inverted and repeated at the end of the play when Hamlet makes Horatio swear that he *will* tell everyone everything. That is the third oath.

Now to Climacus. Climacus's discussion of taking oaths occurs immediately following his narration of the graveyard scene – the scene that establishes *his* plot.[23] Let us give that scene its due.

Two hundred pages into the *Postscript*, Climacus decides to narrate how he came to his vocation to write the *Fragments* and the *Postscript*. He recounts himself sitting in a graveyard, unseen, near a new grave. At the grave, a grandfather advises his grandson against the waywardness of the boy's buried father. Climacus writes:

Although only a spectator and a witness, I was deeply affected . . . But I felt no urge to rush forward and emotionally express my sympathy to the old man, assuring him with tears and quivering voice that I would never forget this scene, or perhaps even beseeching him to put me under oath. Only for rash [*overilede*] people, barren clouds, and bursts of passing showers [*Ilinger*] is nothing more precipitous [*ilsom*] than to take an oath, because, being unable to keep it, they must keep on taking it. In my opinion, 'to want never to forget this impression' is different from saying once in a solemn moment, 'I will never forget this.' . . . if one never forgets it, the solemnity with which it was said does not seem so important, since the sustained solemnity with which one day by day keeps oneself from forgetting it is a truer solemnity . . . Inwardness of spirit is indeed always like a stranger and foreigner in a body – why, then, gesticulations?[24]

Climacus then cites Shakespeare's Brutus in *Julius Caesar*: 'No, not an oath . . . let priests and cowards and rogues, marrowless oldsters and crushed souls swear . . . but do not weaken the quiet strength of our purpose, our inner invincible fire, by thinking that our cause, our performance, needs an oath.'[25]

So for Climacus, an oath is too much in the moment and too much in the body. It is a plot that is supposed to give rise to the spiritual work of remembering, but one that, really, prevents spiritual work; it prevents the subjective labour of sustaining the integrity of the remembrance over time. Oaths do not do the work of remaining self-same against the 'shocks that flesh is heir to'.

The *proper* place of remembering is one's inward commitment, the 'sustained solemnity with which one day by day keeps oneself from forgetting'.[26]

Now let us trace the three forms of the question 'to be or not to be' in Climacus's experience.

Despair

We can see that for Climacus, an oath is an instance of the more general failure of Christendom. That failure consists in kneeling before objective approximations of the truth (of incarnation) instead of doing the work of the subject in time (in order to properly understand incarnation). Like the pastor's speeches or the inattentive Christian habits of Denmark's church-goers, taking oaths is recollecting as forgetting. An oath is an existential failure; a plot that goes nowhere. A grave plot indeed. This is the pit of Climacus's despair.

An oath is the *broken* joint of time because it does not preserve or repeat the *qualitative disjuncture* of time.

It is not just Christendom that is oath-like. For Climacus, speculative knowing is another of these 'approximations'.[27] Speculative knowing is given as the source of the wayward son's downfall. 'The august old man's pain over losing his son, not only through death but, as he understood it, even more terribly through speculative thought, moved me deeply . . .' This becomes for Climacus a 'decisive summons' to figure out why speculative thought deviates from the truth in such a spiritually deadening way.[28]

Ghostly Existence

Like Hamlet, Climacus has a ghostly reminder: 'My studies . . . now became more definitely organized, but the old gentleman's august figure always hovered before my thoughts every time I wanted to transform my deliberations into learned knowledge.'[29]

It finally dawns on Climacus 'that the deviation of speculative thought

. . . [is that,] because of much knowledge people have entirely forgotten what it means to exist and what inwardness is'.[30]

Climacus rejects oaths and, for similar reasons, speculative knowing. Climacus thinks that a kind of ghost – the august figure of the old man – is a better device for remembering to exist than knowledge is.

Here, the 'Father' is a ghost in the mind of a pseudonymous author.

Seeming/Knowing

Like oaths, language and knowledge are media – ghosts of existence. Climacus concludes that only *indirect* communication can be used to accomplish his task; only double reflection, the ironic use of mediation, gives rise to enough ambiguity to shake a subject out of entrenchment in recollections. 'Every word must go through the process of double reflection.'[31]

Double reflection is ghost-like with a twist: something that is doubly reflected expresses the un-decided 'to be or not to be' in such a way as to point out the absolute contradiction itself.

Double Reflection

Double reflection is Kierkegaard's self-conscious use of pseudonyms and imaginative constructions. It is *double* reflection since for Kierkegaard reality – because of original sin – is always already an imagined, recollected construction, rather than being in time. Ironic use of imaginative constructions means that one knows them as such and strives, through them, to express original becoming. This doubling-up is not Hegelian speculation: the latter, for Climacus, is twice removed from the actual. In double reflection, one is striving to be the joint of time in which infinite possibility encounters finite embodiment in a free (rather than a gravely determined) way.

Each of Kierkegaard's pseudonyms is his doubly reflected ghost – each represents the aesthetic contradiction of being an author: in *words*, Kierkegaard both is and is not. His pseudonymous voices rise from beneath the stage; his Climacus asks us to remember the Christian primordial scene, to not forget the qualitative joint in time in which the spirit is conceived – i.e., in which the Word is made flesh.

Through the either/or of a pseudonym being and not being Kierkegaard, Kierkegaard pressures us to experience a gap in representation and to see ourselves as choosers in face of an incommensurability. Double reflection is Kierkegaard's way of outwitting recollection and setting right the joint of time.

A problem remains. Whether it is the play *Hamlet* or an aesthetic representation of the Divine, what is *staged* in experience is a ghostly 'to be or not to be'. For those not 'in' on double reflection, what is on the stage is a tragedy of self-annihilating despair, ghostly existence and seeming-knowing. Once staged, the Father is a ghost and His call to action is a thought about action. Objectivity makes subjectivity into seeming-knowledge. For the faithful, the doubly reflected Father is the *Holy* Ghost, but for the non-believer, He is a monster with three heads. It is this that Kierkegaard tries to catch in his Mousetraps of double reflection. He drives out the devil by the power of the devil.[32]

Double reflection is a conscientious use of ghosts to evoke something beyond appearance. It is therefore not surprising – albeit tantalising for us – that Kierkegaard, *citing Hamlet*, writes in *his* 'tables' the following defence of what is beyond the ordinary:

> German philosophy, because of its addiction to Hegelian logic and metaphysics, proclaims that 'there is nothing new under the sun', whereas the motto of the 'new Danish philosophy' [i.e., Kierkegaard's] must be, in the words of Hamlet, 'There are more things in heaven and earth than are dreamt of in your philosophy.'[33]

Conclusion

Hamlet: 'What's Hecuba to him, or he to Hecuba?' (2.2.536)

What's Hamlet to Climacus, or Climacus to Hamlet, or either of these ghosts to us? Climacus evokes Hamlet in another way: he urges his readers to be, in their prayers, diligent like the actor who 'devoted all his ability and his entire life to continued study of the role of Hamlet'.[34]

Climacus's message here is not that, in prayer, one should strive to be like the guy (the actor) who strives to be like the guy (Hamlet) who strives to get out of his plot and fails. Rather, the truth, I assume, is the same here as for the player in *Hamlet* who acts out Aeneas' tale to Dido about the death of Priam (2.2.425ff): the point is not to be Aeneas or Dido or Hecuba or Priam or, for that matter, Hamlet or Jesus. In prayer as in acting, one ought to continuously strive to be; this indicates that one is not equivalent to one's given plot and that that non-equivalence is salutary.

Climacus's advice here reveals that one is always already in the paradox of one's subjectivity being deeper than one's staged self; the paradox that reflections of identity can only ever capture approximations of subjective becoming.

The recluse can err by being only *passively* aware of this paradox. This is why, from a 'Climacus' standpoint, we should not strive to be Hamlet himself. For Hamlet, the defining moment of the play *arrives*: Hamlet does not make it happen. Hamlet's ultimate view is, passively, that 'the readiness is all' (5.2.160).

Hamlet had tried to reach beyond his passivity by swearing an oath to remember. But if Climacus is right about oaths, Hamlet was destined from then on to get nowhere.[35]

Hamlet's oath is supposed to support *doing* something – taking revenge. But an oath transforms the doing into a knowing, and the time of action into a plot about time rather than a plot that becomes in time. The structure is repeated at the end of the play: Horatio's agreement to tell all is an entrenchment in recollection.[36] Indeed, the entire play, like these oaths, resists genuine becoming.

The play *Hamlet* is the plot of entrenched commitment. That is why it is tragic: Hamlet never gets his mother back; at his death, his conception – his birth and his life, are recollections. His last wish is to be recollected. The play is theatre, *theoria*: it is about knowledge of the truth about existence, not about existing.[37] Absolute contradiction in Hamlet is not conceived through a leap of faith into a plot that he chooses.

For Climacus, the recluse's awareness is necessary but not sufficient. We cannot be only audiences or poets or even knowing readers: we must also be choosers and actors.[38] But merely choosing 'to be' means not-knowing: choosing and not-knowing produce the existentialist's rub, the fear and trembling about our plot.[39]

For the leap of faith to bring eternal salvation there must be faith in a God beneath the stage. But since one cannot *know* grace, one can only strive to continuously remember to live that other plot – the plot of the Holy Ghost, the 'sacred history' of contemporaneity with Christ.[40] To exist, we must conceive by virtue of the absurd.

Faith is objective uncertainty. What *is* certain for Climacus is that staged oath-taking does not bring salvation.[41]

A person can come to properly remember the joint of time either through grace, or as a result of encountering someone or some text which uses double reflection – that mnemonic device of Incarnation. Either way, for the Christian, true being in time is a revelation coming from (there having been) a god-man.

If grace results from faith, then, unlike the tragic play *Hamlet*, Christian existentialism *does* exit the grave plot. It does, even if such faith can only ever appear in theory as the plot of a ghost – a ghost who, in the absence of faith, looks like a depressing, dubiously present, only apparently real thing rising out of a grave.

But like the *Tragedy of Hamlet*, that Climacusian plot cannot be seen to progress. It cannot because there is no objective goal in double reflection or in inward leaping.

The *Tragedy of Hamlet* and the *Postscript* are, therefore, spectres of existentialism. Whether either spectre is, at bottom, a divine voice calling us to remember the joint of time as primordial becoming is for the reader to decide.

Notes

1. Richard Kearney, 'Kierkegaard on Hamlet: Between Art and Religion', in Elsebet Jegstrup (ed.), *The New Kierkegaard* (Bloomington: Indiana University Press, 2004); Denis de Rougemont, 'Kierkegaard and Hamlet: Two Danish Princes', *The Anchor Review*, 1 (1955), pp. 109–27; James E. Ruoff, 'Kierkegaard and Shakespeare', *Comparative Literature*, 20 (1968), pp. 343–54. Rougemount, with appropriate self-irony and circumspection, outlines the remarkable parallels between the lives of Hamlet and Kierkegaard.

2. For example, there is the Christian collision between the finite and the infinite, a hallmark of the 'sickness unto death'. Søren Kierkegaard, *Sickness Unto Death*, ed. and trans. Howard V. Hong and Edna H. Hong (Princeton: Princeton University Press, 1980), p. 8. 'Unlike many modern scholars, he read Shakespeare's plays as dramatizations of life, not as religious allegories, and in Shakespeare's plays he came face to face with himself, not with God' (Ruoff, 'Kierkegaard and Shakespeare', p. 354). Ruoff claims that for Kierkegaard 'tragedy and Christianity are irreconcilable . . . Shakespeare offers us a pellucid, frightening glimpse of the truth of our worldly existence, but that glimpse provides no hint of the eternal vistas beyond the range of earthly life. Like Santayana, Kierkegaard concluded that "Shakespeare himself seems to have shrunk back from the genuinely religious collisions. Perhaps these can only be expressed in the language of the gods. And this language no man can speak . . ." [Kierkegaard, *Sickness Unto Death*]' (ibid.). In *Stages on Life's Way*, Kierkegaard's pseudonym Frater Taciturnus discusses difficulties in viewing *Hamlet* as a religious play. See *Stages on Life's Way*, ed. and trans. Howard V. Hong and Edna H. Hong (Princeton: Princeton University Press, 1988), pp. 452–4. I discuss this below.

3. Shakespeare, 'The Tragedy of Hamlet, Prince of Denmark', Stephen Greenblatt (general ed.), Walter Cohen, Jean E. Howard, Katherine Eisaman Maus (eds), in *The Norton Shakespeare: Based on the Oxford Edition* (New York, London: W.W. Norton and Company, 1997), pp. 1659–1759. Søren Kierkegaard, *Concluding Unscientific Postscript to Philosophical Fragments*, vol. 1, ed. and trans. Howard V. Hong and Edna H. Hong (Princeton: Princeton University Press, 1992), henceforth CUP.

An early version of this chapter was originally presented on the panel 'Hamlet and Continental Philosophy' organised by Andrew Cutrofello, at the SPEP (Society for Phenomenology and Existential Philosophy), Montreal, Canada, 4–6 November 2010.

4. This is in deference to Kierkegaard's explicit request that we do so with his pseudonyms (CUP 627).

5. Kierkegaard, *Sickness Unto Death*, pp. 7–8.

6. 'How does the paradox emerge? By placing the eternal, essential truth together with existing . . . The eternal truth has come into existence in time. That is the paradox. If the subject just mentioned was prevented by sin from taking himself back into eternity, now he is not to concern himself with this, because now the eternal essential truth is not behind him but has come in front of him by existing itself or by having existed, so that if the individual, existing, does not lay hold of the truth in existence, he will never have it.

Existence can never be accentuated more sharply than it has been here. The fraud of speculative thought in wanting to recollect itself out of existence has been made impossible . . .

When the eternal truth relates itself to an existing person, it becomes the paradox . . . the more risk, the more faith; the more objective reliability, the less inwardness . . . When the paradox itself is the paradox, it thrusts away by virtue of the absurd, and the corresponding passion of inwardness is faith' (CUP 209).

7. Ophelia: 'There's Rosemary, that's for remembrance. Pray, love, remember' (4.5.173–4).

8. '. . . if the lofty wisdom can explain everything else but cannot answer a simple question, one surely sees that the world is out of joint' (CUP 120).

9. CUP 249.

10. CUP 351.

11. See Chapter II, 'Subjective Truth, Inwardness: Truth is Subjectivity' (CUP 189ff).

12. CUP 320.

13. For Climacus, religious ethics requires that one *not* forget oneself: 'It can be entirely proper for a thinker *qua* thinker to think humanity in general, but *qua* existing individual he is forbidden by ethics to forget himself, to forget that he is an existing human being' (CUP 343–4, author's note).

14. CUP 350.

15. 'The subjective thinker, therefore has with intellectual passion the absolute disjunction as belonging to existence, but he has it as the final decision that prevents everything from ending in a quantifying . . . The subjective thinker, therefore, has also esthetic passion and ethical passion, whereby concretion is gained' (CUP 350).

16. See too Claudius's advice to Hamlet about sons losing fathers who in their day lost their fathers (1.2.86–106).

17. Stanley Cavell's claim that Hamlet's melancholia stems from the trauma of the original scene is, in this sense, true. See Stanley Cavell, 'Hamlet's Burden of Proof', in *Disowning Knowledge in Seven Plays of Shakespeare* (Cambridge: Cambridge University Press, 1987), pp. 179–91.

18. CUP 351.

19. Kierkegaard, *Stages on Life's Way*, pp. 452–4. The question that opens Taciturnus's discussion of the play is Börne's comment that '*Hamlet* is a Christian Tragedy' (see ibid., p. 737, n. 525).
20. See Kearney, 'Kierkegaard on Hamlet' for another discussion of Taciturnus. Kearney suggests that Kierkegaard is Derridean *avant le temps*.
21. Kierkegaard, *Journals*, p. 74 (14 June 1834), as cited in Ruoff, 'Kierkegaard and Shakespeare', p. 347, my italics.
22. This is central, as of Hamlet's first words to his mother: 'Seems, madam? Nay, it is. I know not "seems"' (1.2.76).
23. CUP 236–42.
24. CUP 239–40.
25. CUP 239–40.
26. CUP 239.
27. The assertion that any objective knowledge of Christianity is mere approximation is found throughout the CUP, especially Part One.
28. CUP 241. 'This, then, was my resolution. I have not spoken about it to anyone at all, and I am sure that my landlady has detected no change in me . . .' jabs Climacus, again, at the falseness of posturing (ibid.).
29. CUP 241.
30. CUP 242.
31. CUP 250. See also 242ff.
32. 'A poet is not an apostle; he drives out devils only by the power of the devil.' Søren Kierkegaard, *Fear and Trembling*, ed. and trans. Howard V. Hong and Edna H. Hong (Princeton: Princeton University Press, 1983), p. 61. The expression is biblical (Mark, 3:15–22).
33. Kierkegaard, *Journals*, p. 74, as cited in Ruoff, 'Kierkegaard and Shakespeare', pp. 347–8. According to Climacus, Hegel's *Geist*, unlike a doubly reflected ghost, is empty: ironically, 'Pure thinking is a phantom' (CUP 316).
34. Climacus: 'To pray is also an action. Ah, in this regard, Luther was indeed a tried and tested man, and he is supposed to have said that never in his life had he even once prayed so fervently that, while praying, some disturbing thought did not intrude. So one could almost think that to pray is just as difficult as to play the role of Hamlet, of which the greatest actor is supposed to have said that only once had he been close to playing it well; nevertheless he would devote all his ability and his entire life to continued study of this role. Should not praying be almost as important and significant?' (CUP 163).
35. Hamlet does use the indirect communication of the 'Mousetrap' play to outwit Claudius's recollections, but Hamlet does not outwit the grave plot of the play.
36. I discuss this from a Hegelian point of view in *Hegel and Shakespeare on Moral Imagination* (Albany: SUNY, 2010): Hamlet is, at his death, perversely, a *successful* Unhappy Consciousness: he has divested himself of his changeableness and sublated himself completely into an unchanging narrative. From a Hegelian point of view, this is of course, a very undesirable condition – a dialectically recursive one-sidedness.
37. Even the final scene, in which Hamlet acts vengefully, lies inside the recollected form of revenge: it is not an existentially defined moment of decision

and action. The extent to which it appears to be action is swallowed in Horatio's narrative recollection. In *Hegel and Shakespeare on Moral Imagination*, I argue that this is tragic for the audience unless we penetrate the reasoned necessity in the play. But Climacus would never let the play be 'reasoned' into knowledge: knowledge is forgetting-recollection, not inward, subjective relating to the absolute contradiction that is existence.

38. 'To exist is an art' (CUP 351).
39. 'If objective uncertainty is the primary characteristic of a genuine vocation, acceptance of the unlikely is its necessary consequence'. Rougemont, 'Kierkegaard and Hamlet: Two Danish Princes', p. 126.
40. 'Thus every human being is able to become contemporary only with the time in which he is living – and then with one more, with Christ's life upon earth, for Christ's life upon earth, the sacred history, stands alone by itself, outside history.' Søren Kierkegaard, *Practice in Christianity*, ed. and trans. Howard V. Hong and Edna H. Hong (Princeton: Princeton University Press, 1991), p. 64.
41. A non-Kierkegaardian Hegelian would reply: we must keep in mind the absolute contradiction that being and nothing are dialectically inseparable and interpret this over time; remember to exist and also remember the ethical advances that we have made as a result of existential self-interpretations.

Chapter 3

Schopenhauer's Shakespeare: The Genius on the World Stage

Tom Stern

Schopenhauer's deep admiration for Shakespeare dated back to his youth and continued throughout his life. After a performance at Drury Lane, the adolescent future-philosopher was already noting down deviations from the text in a performance of Richard III. Shakespeare's name would appear in Schopenhauer's diaries, throughout his published works and in his conversations with others. In his various books, we find references to 22 Shakespeare plays – from all different genres and from the most famous to the least. A contemporary recalled him hurling the 'angriest' bits of Shakespeare at his adversaries.[1] Upon his sister's death, he wrote to her closest friend, consoling her with (carefully edited) lines from Sonnet 71.[2] Having spent some unhappy months at school in England, Schopenhauer's English was good enough not only to read Shakespeare in the original, but to offer philological speculations on Hamlet's soliloquy or to compare English with German translations.[3] A remark in Schopenhauer's masterpiece – *The World as Will and Representation* – sums up his view: Shakespeare stands 'at the head of the poets'.[4] But what, for Schopenhauer, is the significance of that? And how does it suggest that we think about Shakespeare?

A frequent occurrence in Schopenhauer's prose is the use of Shakespeare as an authority figure, who prefigures, in various quotations, thoughts to which Schopenhauer's philosophy gave a clear expression, a conceptual formulation and a metaphysical underpinning. Now, plucking lines from Shakespeare's plays and throwing them down in support of speculative philosophical claims does no favours to either philosophy or literature. That sort of activity has come in for justifiable criticism, both from philosophers and from literary scholars. As for the former: since Plato, it has seemed appropriate to ask why a talent for writing very good plays should amount to anything more than that: it doesn't seem to offer theoretical or practical wisdom and there's no reason why it should. When Socrates challenges the playwrights and rhapsodes to justify themselves in philosophical debate, they come up magnificently short. As he penned the line, 'cowards father cowards' (*Cymbeline*, 4.2), Shakespeare probably wasn't (contra Schopenhauer) offering a gendered theory of inherited traits according to which the character is passed down by the male parent only.[5] But, even if he did, the theory is still just as wrong as if Schopenhauer alone had proposed it.

There is also hostility from the literary side, too. Evidently, the statements, remarks and words of wisdom to which Schopenhauer appeals are taken from the mouths of characters in plays – characters to whom Schopenhauer frequently does not refer. Their lines often have a dramatic purpose in mind which, when removed, can damage our appreciation of his literary skill, not to mention rob us of the context needed, one might suppose, to understand what the characters are getting at.[6] Hence, in context, Belarius says 'cowards father cowards' and it arises from his knowledge that he stole away Cymbeline's sons, who do not know their noble origin. (In many respects, as it happens, the character of the sons seems remarkably unlike the character of their royal father.) Yet Schopenhauer doesn't mention Belarius, instead presenting directly the words of the great Shakespeare.

I mention these two powerful, well-known problems, because one purpose I have here is to defend Schopenhauer against them – at least against the simple versions sketched above. After all, he warns quite explicitly against boiling plays or poems down to simple truths or philosophical arguments, dismissing this as 'unworthy and absurd'.[7] Indeed, he reports, with mockery, the story of the mathematician who attends a Racine play and asks: 'what does that prove?'[8] Similarly, playwrights need not and should not steep themselves in philosophy: Schiller, well-versed in Kant, wrote worse plays than Shakespeare, who had nothing approaching a philosophical training.[9] And if, on occasions, Schopenhauer fails to associate a quotation with a character, on other occasions he offers extended analysis of particular characters in Shakespeare's plays, placing their actions firmly within a dramatic context.[10]

What, then, does the self-proclaimed head of the philosophers see in the head of the poets? What, for Schopenhauer, is Shakespeare's significance? And how does Schopenhauer's account of Shakespeare stand up to scrutiny? To answer these questions, we must begin with (1) Schopenhauer's philosophy in general and (2) his aesthetics in particular. Then we can look at where, in general, Schopenhauer locates Shakespeare's particular talents – (3) in his treatment of character throughout his dramatic works and (4) within each genre. Finally, (5) we look closely at Schopenhauer's account of *Hamlet*: as the 'most perfect masterpiece', in the 'most sublime form of poetry' (tragedy) by the foremost poet, *Hamlet* is analysed by Schopenhauer both in terms of its generic features and in more specific terms.

Schopenhauer's Worldview

The mechanics of Schopenhauer's worldview are relatively well-known and may be offered here in the briefest summary. (Those who are familiar with it will appreciate my obligation to set it out for those who are not – and are welcome to skip to section 3.) Following Kant's division between the noumenal and phenomenal worlds, Schopenhauer held that time, space and causation were functions of our mode of representation, not a feature of things as they are in themselves. But, in several ways, Schopenhauer thought that he could extend and perfect the Kantian project. Lacking space and time, the world as it is in itself – as opposed to the world as it is represented by us to ourselves – consequently lacks at least two extremely important features that we take for granted in daily life. The first of these is change, the concept of which makes no sense without the concept of time. The second is individuation – that there are separate or distinct things, like different people or objects: one cannot conceive of 'separateness' or 'individuality' without the notions of time and space. So beyond the apparent world (of representation) – a world of change and individuation – there lies another world which is both unchanging and singular. More important still – and yet further from Kant – Schopenhauer claimed to be able to identify the characteristic feature of the time-less, space-less world as it is in itself: it is 'will'.

The will manifests itself in many different ways in the world of representation. But for our purposes, two distinct manifestation are worthy of comment. First, in our experience of desire; second, via character and 'Ideas'. First: being essentially will, we are the kinds of beings who will always want things and chase after them. Our mistaken but in-built belief is that getting the object of our desire will satisfy us. In fact, if we are lucky enough to get what we want, the will merely generates a new desire. Schopenhauer frequently characterises us as trapped between lack (when we don't have what we want) and boredom (when we do).

Second, the will, for Schopenhauer, is 'objectified' in all things – not just in things, like humans, who 'desire' in a straightforward, everyday sense. Once properly understood, it can be shown to be active in all objects to different degrees and to an increasing degree in inanimate objects, plants, animals and humans. The will therefore also functions as a quasi-scientific explanatory concept: it sheds light on gravity, on the attraction between two magnets, on the breeding habits of birds, on animal physiology. Schopenhauer's pre-Darwinist thought allows for a strict division between permanent plant and animal species. The will is objectified in 'Ideas' or quasi-Platonic forms of each species or type, which determine what that species essentially is. Corresponding to all pieces of copper, all crocuses and all cats, then, there is the Idea of copper, crocus and cat, respectively, to which the individual instantiations correspond. In some respects, real-world instantiations will be found wanting in comparison with the pure Ideas, but they will certainly correspond in some sense, for that correspondence is what makes them what they are. The Ideas, Schopenhauer tells us, are – like the will itself – beyond space and time, therefore fixed and unchanging – and as fixed and unchanging Ideas, they are more suitable and appropriate objects of reflection than their ephemeral counterparts in time and space, which, as he puts it, 'obscure' the Ideas.[11] Figuratively, then, Ideas are 'between' the everyday objects and the will as thing-in-itself.

When it comes to human beings, there is an Idea of mankind as a species; but what sets us apart from other beings is that the will is also objectified in each of us in virtue of our 'character' – which is different for each human being, but which, as will, is also beyond space and time, hence also unchanging. The character of an animal just is the Idea of that animal's species; human beings have both the character of the species and also an individual character.[12] This is used by Schopenhauer to explain why (supposedly) any potato plant will behave in exactly the same way in the same circumstances, but one cannot say the same for two human beings: all potato plants have the same character, but no two humans have the same character.[13]

Humans also have an intellect – the ability to think about the world they find themselves in. Naively, we might suppose that our intellects control our desires – that we first of all think about how things are and then choose what we want accordingly. But for Schopenhauer this gets things exactly wrong: the intellect is basically the tool of the will (desires and character). It can investigate and understand the world, to be sure, but it does this to aid the will better in shaping its desires and choosing what the individual does next. The intellect is like a group of imperial advisors, set a particular task or challenge and charged with submitting a proposed plan of action to the emperor (the will). The advisors do the work to prepare the plan, but it is the emperor who always sets the terms of enquiry (as everyday desires, for example) and has the final say from the comfort of his throne (as the intelligible character). The point of this rough analogy is to emphasise the psychological fact, ever present in Schopenhauer, that we can decide to do whatever we want to for all sorts of good reasons – eat healthily, work hard – but this 'decision' sometimes is and sometimes isn't carried through. The will has the final say. It is important that he speaks of 'the will' as making decisions about what 'we' do, such that from our point of view it may as well be the will of another person which chooses. Everyday life is a kind of bondage.

Art and the Genius

The role of art in general in this Schopenhauerian picture is to 'unhook', as it were, the intellect from the will. Aesthetic experience is disinterested or detached, so the aesthetic observer contemplates the objects presented to her in a desire-free or will-less manner. This detachment offers us two distinct advantages relating to the two elements of the will, outlined above. First of all, the unhooked intellect is free from the everyday condition of constant willing, boredom, frustration, bondage and alienation. This, we are told, is pleasurable in itself. Second, though, the absence of a master for the intellect somehow frees it to contemplate in the absence of time and space. Crucially, then, this allows for a potentially unmediated access to the Ideas which are also beyond time and space – hence for more profound contemplation.[14] Now, the first of these advantages is available in all aesthetic experience – that is what aesthetic experience is. And in the respite of aesthetic experience, I am more clearly able to appreciate my former, will-governed condition and reflect upon its drawbacks. But the second advantage will depend on the type of art and also on the skill of the artist: what I 'see' in my state of aesthetic detachment is the artist's product. In aesthetic experience, 'the perceived individual thing is raised to the Idea of its species' – so it really matters which individual things are presented.[15] Continuing our analogy: the emperor's advisors are now free to contemplate the world without the emperor setting the terms of inquiry. What they contemplate is, in part, the influence that the emperor had upon them and, in part, new terms of inquiry set by the benign figure of the artist. The idea that art provides desire-free contemplation has certainly proved appealing to some; but we might have reason to doubt it: still-life paintings that make us hungry, or the long-standing, traditional fear of the dangerously seductive power of the actress certainly suggest otherwise. Schopenhauer's claim that aesthetic experience occurs beyond space and time is also hard to square with the appreciation of a theatrical performance, which obviously unfolds over time and in a particularly place.

The experience of the spectator is made possible by the genius – the creator of the artwork – whose talents are explained using the apparatus we have just outlined. A genius is fortunate enough that his intellect is simply too powerful for his will: analogously, the imperial advisors are simply so smart and efficient that – whatever orders they are given – they still have plenty of free time left over to devote to thinking about the world as they wish. What the genius can do, therefore, is (as Schopenhauer says of Shakespeare) 'run his eye over the world' in a manner that the ordinary individual could only access in aesthetic experience – the kind of experience produced, of course, by the genius himself.[16] Just as dock leaves grow near nettles, so wherever we find the term 'genius' in Schopenhauer, we can be sure to find 'Shakespeare' somewhere nearby.

The connection between the way the genius sees the world and the way the spectator experiences the play can hardly be missed. For when the spectator sees the play, she finds her intellect freed from the clutches of her will – and this, indeed, is the state of the genius without the aid of art.[17] The works produced by the genius are not merely 'fictions', where that is to be understood as something that is made up; they are readings off the Ideas of the genius's world – readings which contain as much valuable insight and information as any survey or study and which can therefore be used to back up the theories of the philosophers.[18] This, in part, is Schopenhauer's answer to the first of the criticisms we began with. Using the material from the products of genius is reliable, since that material emerges from an intellectually heightened understanding of the world. It is perfectly safe to use Ophelia as a case study for a theory of madness, because Shakespeare's intellect gave him deeper insight.[19]

To view the world 'as a play', therefore, is to view it more soberly and in a sense more accurately than to view it as we normally do in day-to-day life. This connects with Schopenhauer's frequent use of the world-stage metaphor in relation to the world of representation – 'the great drama of life', as he puts it, or the great spectacle (*Schauspiel*), in which the actors are simply the puppets of the will.[20] The genius has stepped away from the endless cycle of willing that motivates the world-drama, becoming the 'one living actor among the puppets'.[21] In this re-telling of the cave myth, the enlightened one is no longer the one who stops watching the drama (as Plato would have it), but rather the one who *starts* watching it – in other words, he realises that he has until now been an actor and from now on must become a spectator.

Drama and Character

Schopenhauer places drama – and modern tragedy in particular – at the forefront of literary arts. Once the will has been removed from the picture, the depictions and subjects offered up to the intellect for contemplation are of paramount importance. Drama shows the interactions between human beings – the 'highest' grade of the will's objectification – hence revealing the 'Idea of mankind'.[22] (Architecture, by comparison, only presents us with the Ideas associated with material and force.) One typical dramatic offering – available in all forms of drama (as Schopenhauer sees it) – relates to the notion of character. Aesthetic experience enables will-free contemplation of what lies behind the world of appearances; in the case of human beings, as we have seen, that is not merely our character as a species, but also each of our unique, unchanging, individual characters. In literature in general, the writer creates 'significant characters' and places them in situations in which their properties become 'peculiarly and strikingly visible'.[23] And what plays can do, better than anything else, is character.

'Character', of course, can mean many different things – an everyday meaning is a person's typical dispositions or tendencies. But, unlike Schopenhauer, most of us think that a person can, on occasions, act 'uncharacteristically'. What I've so far been calling 'character' in Schopenhauer's philosophy really consists of two parts: the 'intelligible character' is what lies behind the world of appearances and is permanent, timeless and unchanging. The 'empirical character' refers to the various ways in which the intelligible character manifests itself in the world – through the various actions of individuals in space and time. Your empirical character must, of course, correspond to your intelligible character, so, for Schopenhauer, 'uncharacteristic' actions are not *really* uncharacteristic, just new revelations about fixed character in different circumstances. Needless to say, the 'characters' in a play – the ones typically listed at the start of the text – are none of these things. I'll call these the 'dramatic characters'.

Schopenhauer seems to follow Aristotle in holding that plays are no place for character development in the everyday sense (compared, say, to epics).[24] For Aristotle, this is a practical consideration about the art form: the allotted time for the drama is simply insufficient for the personalities of the dramatic characters to develop in any profound way, so drama presents fixed types clashing with one another. The characters of Antigone and Creon do not really change during the course of *Antigone*, though they may come to certain realisations about what it *means* to be the characters they already are. Similarly, Oedipus remains proud, self-sufficient and self-important – it's just that at the beginning he takes those characteristics into the hunt for the polluter of Thebes and at the end he uses them to respond to his terrible discovery of who that polluter is.

Aristotle's view is consistent with the idea that, in real life, character is not unchanging: of course, there are those who behave inconsistently or uncharacteristically – they just make for bad plays. For
Schopenhauer, though, the practical requirements of a good play lead
to a distinct philosophical advantage. After all, fixity of (intelligible)
character – in his particular sense – is a central plank of his philosophy
and the drama is the form of art *par excellence* for exploring human
relations in the context of dramatic characters whose 'characters' are
unchanging. It is no surprise, therefore, that Shakespeare stands at the
summit of the poets in virtue of his character portrayal. He is the best,
because he 'shows [best] how the will conducts itself under the influence
of motives and of reflection'; to do so, one must present the 'actions
and sufferings' of 'rational beings, whose character is individual'.[25]
Elsewhere, in expounding his claim that one's actions are produced not
by the intellect but by specific desires combined with 'the inborn and
unalterable character', Schopenhauer does not hesitate to claim that
'Shakespeare's dramas as a rule afford us the best illustration of the
truth in question.'[26]

Two clarifications of Schopenhauer's position are required at this
stage. First, the appeal to fixity of character can make it seem as
though Schopenhauer takes a very rigid, blinkered critical view of
Shakespeare's plays: after all, don't plenty of his characters change and
develop, learn and look with scorn upon their former selves? Can we
compare Gloucester the boasting, hasty oaf at the start of *King Lear*
with the blind, pitiful figure who is brought to the imaginary cliff face?
Or Prince Hal with Henry V? Yet these criticisms underestimate the
subtlety of Schopenhauer's view with its emphasis on revealing character under different circumstances: it's not that people never change,
it's that, as the circumstances change, so do the kinds of things that
people do – but this is merely their (fixed) character expressing itself
in different ways. To borrow one of his analogies, it might help to
think about the 'character' of water.[27] You would never be able to tell,
simply from looking at the liquid in your glass, that it could be part of
a tsunami, a whirlpool, a glacier or that it may have helped to carve
out mountains and valleys. The water in your glass can do all of these
things (under the right circumstances); but, of course, there are plenty
of things it can't do, like write poetry or turn into wine on command.
For Schopenhauer, a person's character is fixed like the 'character' of
water: it will certainly do very different things under different circumstances, but nonetheless, first, it will always do the same thing under
the same circumstances (under 'tsunami' conditions it will become a
tsunami) and, second, there are certain things that are quite impossible

for it. This, then, is how he would explain the apparent objections given above: Prince Hal and King Henry V are different in the way that the waterfall and the glacier are different: the same character placed under different circumstances.

Shakespeare's talent, he thinks, is for knowing how to vary the circumstances under which the characters are placed, showing their innate potential without ever asking them to do the impossible. Variety of actions in the context of fixity of character (if that is how we understand Gloucester and Hal) is therefore not only possible but desirable. The laidback Hal who is at ease in the local tavern reveals the same character as the chirpy King Henry who can trade insults with the French envoy; but the latter has been placed in completely different circumstances from the former. Schopenhauer's explicit examples of this are relatively brief, but one character he looks at in detail is the figure of the Earl of Northumberland throughout Richard II and the two parts of Henry IV.[28] Northumberland is placed in a variety of situations, serving different masters and chasing different goals, yet he always reveals his character with consistency: he plots first against Richard II in favour of Bolingbroke, mocking Richard and arranging for the decapitation of the deposed king's supporters; then he plots against Bolingbroke (now Henry IV), though failing to show up for battle and losing his son in the subsequent fight; finally, he seeks revenge for his son's death, only to fail to show up once more, at the crucial moment. What we are seeing, Schopenhauer suggests, is the character of Northumberland sketched out in a variety of different circumstances: fundamentally treacherous and cowardly, he'll plot, he'll make cutting remarks, he'll play the silver-tongued negotiator and boast about his warrior-like activities, but he won't turn this into action, even if it means abandoning his own son or the possibility of avenging his son's death.

Second, we must be clear what is and is not made available through the drama to the will-free spectator. Fixity of character in varied conditions is what makes for the 'revelation of the Idea of mankind' in poetry.[29] Each of us, as discussed, corresponds to the Idea of mankind, but also corresponds to a particular, fixed character; Shakespeare, through his dramas, offers the opportunity for reflection on both. Yet, to state the obvious, the dramatic characters presented in Shakespeare's dramas can have no corresponding *intelligible* character beyond space and time for us to access through aesthetic experience – they are *made up*. So we cannot, through watching Hamlet on stage, be offered direct access to Hamlet's intelligible character. Of course, we can see mimetic representations of Hamlet's (fictional) empirical character, which show the kind of consistency that we would find in everyday life; but, *ex hypothesi*, the empirical characters depicted on stage cannot be *more* consistent than those we meet on the street. Instead, Schopenhauer suggests that the characters presented on stage are more helpful than those we meet everyday because the characters in question are 'significant' or 'momentous' (*bedeutsam*), as are the situations in which they find themselves clashing.[30] It is almost as though Shakespeare, looking at the world as a genius, simply plucks out from nature the most 'significant' characters he meets in real life, gives them new names and places them in those circumstance in which they turn, as it were, from ponds into waterfalls.[31] Schopenhauer does not give us a thorough account of what makes a character and clash 'significant' (beyond the circular claim that it reveals more about the Idea of mankind), but it is suggested via his remarks on tragedy, which we discuss shortly.

Even with these clarifications set out, Schopenhauer's view leaves him open to other, opposing concerns. For one thing, if the changes that occur in a Hal or a Gloucester serve to reinforce Schopenhauer's view of character, then we might ask what sort of character changes might *fail* to count as an instance of fixity of character. Obviously, he thinks such a 'contradiction' is possible in lesser poets than Shakespeare: but, for any two apparently contradictory actions, one could always argue that some change of circumstances has revealed a new side to the fixed character that was always already there.[32] (This, of course, is a challenge to Schopenhauer's view of character in general.) More importantly for our purposes, if placing dramatic characters in ever-new situations to shine new light on their fixed characters is the sign of effective literary art, then theatre seems *less* suitable than a novel or an epic as a means to do so. Tolstoy can place Pierre, Andrey and Natasha in more and more varied situations than Shakespeare can Hal, thus revealing (on Schopenhauer's line) more aspects of their fixed characters. It is telling, for instance, that the Earl of Northumberland – the character most extensively discussed by Schopenhauer in this regard – features in three consecutive plays and hence has more time to develop. Shakespeare may be particularly efficient at character portrayal, but it's not clear why the efficient playwright should outweigh the comprehensive novelist.

Tragedy, Comedy, History

While Shakespeare's skill as a portrayer of character in this sense is on display in all of his plays, Schopenhauer places tragedy at the forefront of dramatic art. All dramas offer the opportunity to reflect on character, but tragedies portray characters dealing with horrible events and therefore more accurately reflect our lives than do other forms of drama: 'the peculiar effect of the tragedy rests ultimately on the fact that it shakes that inborn error [i.e. 'that we exist in order to be happy'], since it furnishes a vivid illustration of the frustration of human effort and of the vanity of this whole existence in a great and striking example'.[33] This alone accounts for why aesthetic contemplation of tragedy is superior. But the best tragedies, he thinks, offer to their audiences not merely the horrors of life, but an exemplary instance of resignation in the face of those horrors: the hero comes to a realisation that his will-based activities are futile and he resigns himself to his fate, often death.[34]

Resignation plays a part in two further grounds for preferring tragedy. First, aesthetic experience at a tragedy is counted by Schopenhauer as a case of the 'sublime', which he defines as the aesthetic contemplation of what would, under normal circumstances, amount to a threat to the will. The aesthetic contemplation of a desert, for example, is an instance of the sublime, because a real desert carries the threat of starvation.[35] But a resignation-tragedy is the ultimate instance of the sublime, in that resignation is the lasting and deliberate destruction of all willing (not merely the accidental and passing threat from the desert). Given that the experience of the sublime is structured by the significance of the threat to the will, resignation-tragedy is maximally sublime.

Second, as some commentators have suggested, Schopenhauer may further be hoping that the experience of being freed from the will for the duration of the performance could lead to a desire to be freed from it on a more permanent basis, through what he calls the ethics of resignation. While the will encourages us to think of ourselves (erroneously) as separate and competing individuals who can be made happy by the fulfilment of specific desires, the ethical man recognises, implicitly or explicitly, that we are all one and the correct attitude to others is one of compassion – literally, because when one suffers we all suffer. The ethical stance, then, is an ascetic one which denies the will of the individual and is resigned to suffering the fate of all. The aesthetic experience of the spectator matches, more or less, the resigned, will-less attitude of the ethical individual. This is supposed to correspond to the resigned attitude of the tragic hero, who – after struggling with the hand he has been dealt – comes to accept it with a certain grace.[36] It would be a mistake, though, to imagine that all characters must come to such recognition or that a depiction of a character who refuses to abandon the will would be a slight on the playwright's art: indeed, Schopenhauer specifically praises Shakespeare's depiction of a character who steadfastly refuses to negate his will and is depicted as suffering horribly as a result – this, for Schopenhauer, is the fate of Cardinal Beaufort in 2 Henry VI.[37]

In that the tragedy is meant to be a kind of universal experience reflecting something about what happens to us all, it is important, Schopenhauer thinks, to pay attention to the narrative structure, in particular to how and why the principal tragic characters are broken. In his analysis, this occurs in one of three ways.[38] First, the tragic hero is undone by the wickedness of another; second, the tragic hero suffers terrible misfortune (i.e. a *particular* piece of unusually bad luck, rather than the general sorts of misfortunes that Schopenhauer quite obviously thinks are unavoidable in a human life and which tragedies must show); third, the tragic events occur simply through the (presumably non-wicked) attitudes and characters of the main persons involved. Shakespeare's plays are invoked to exemplify all of these different types: Iago, Richard III and, curiously enough, Shylock are named as wicked characters who bring about tragic conclusions.[39] Romeo suffers on account of an accident: the message that doesn't arrive on time. Hamlet's relations to Ophelia and Laertes are offered as tentative cases of the third variety. The third category is superior, since the misfortunes to which we all ultimately fall victim are not really a matter of the wickedness of others, nor do they result from the 'bad luck' of *Romeo and Juliet*: our misfortunes, overall, stem simply from the sorts of beings we are.

But while Schopenhauer's view of tragedy has entered the canon of tragic theories, less attention has been paid to the place he allows for comedy. If comedy is characterised by the fulfilment of desires in the end, then obviously the subject-matter would be inappropriate for a good Schopenhauerian. Certainly, Schopenhauer wryly notes that the curtain had better come down quickly on the happy couple at the end, because what happens next – their long marriage – can be far from amusing. But inasmuch as a comedy shows us individuals failing to get what they want on a daily basis, it does contain some element of truth. So it is that stock comic characters are so frequently characterised by a desire – for the girl, for the money, for glory, to avoid battle and so on – and we laugh as their goals eludes them. To the person who could look at an individual life as a drama, it would appear as the comic frustration of desire on a daily basis, formed into an overarching tragedy, as each of us ultimately fails to get those things we most want.[40] And, ultimately, the 'thoughtful contemplator' can see that the human frailties on display at the comedy reflect a form of life which, though apparently affirmed, is 'something that really had better not be'.[41]

In terms of Shakespeare's plays, this leaves an obvious gap for the histories. When Immanuel Kant imagined taking a view of world history, he spoke of the disgust we might feel when looking out at the 'world-stage'. Kant is considering a very particular question: whether human beings can make meaningful progress over the generations or whether we are doomed to repeat the same mistakes over and over again. The latter is sad to contemplate, of course, but the former is troubling too, since it would imply that only those at the end of history, as it were, would get to enjoy the painful labour of their predecessors.[42] For Schopenhauer, though, there is no question of meaningful historical progress. The spectator who beholds the world-stage will see a repetition of the same basic scenarios, just with different languages and costumes. The essential or fundamental characteristics of human beings are on display at all times.[43] Historians are therefore either providing material of merely antiquarian interest or they are subject to a false view, according to which it *really* or deeply matters when and where you are born. In making this claim, Schopenhauer echoes and amplifies Aristotle's preference for drama over history: the former can say what sorts of things happen in general, whereas the latter is stuck with the specifics of what has happened. To this he adds that a historical record, where it is attempting to report historical fact, can only ever be partial and incomplete, probably largely false in places – whereas a well-made philosophical argument can guarantee its own truth, as can the product of artistic genius which is, in his peculiar phrase, 'half a priori'.[44] It would be an 'abasement' for a gifted thinker to get caught up in one particular place or time.[45]

Could the prevalence and success of Shakespeare's history plays pose a challenge to Schopenhauer's view? Predictably, Schopenhauer's Shakespeare ignores the history. The 'history plays' are not historical at all: instead, Shakespeare replaces Romans with perfect Englishmen and lets them get on with it.[46] The fact that the historical depictions take place primarily in the form of (constructed) speeches also takes Shakespeare's dramas further from the sorts of narrative histories to which Schopenhauer objects. As for Shakespeare's English history plays, Schopenhauer locates the success of these, as in the other plays, with the exploration of character and the mapping out of motivations and conflicts; all antiquarian historical material is either removed or irrelevant.[47]

Schopenhauer's *Hamlet*

Of all the works by Shakespeare, Schopenhauer hardly takes a controversial line in declaring *Hamlet* to be the greatest – a 'most perfect masterpiece'.[48] But once we have Schopenhauer's philosophical outlook in place, we can begin to understand why. This includes the general features of *Hamlet* as an exemplary work of art, drama and tragedy. *Hamlet* is also an exemplary kind of tragedy for Schopenhauer, both in terms of Hamlet's final resignation and in terms of the plot structure. As for resignation, think of Hamlet's final description of death as 'felicity' (uttered to Horatio, trying to end his own life). To Hamlet and Horatio, we might be tempted to add Ophelia's likely suicide – a qualified resignation, as discussed below. As for plot structure, it is such that Hamlet's tragic fate is brought about not by anybody's evil doings, or by bad luck, but simply by the clash of characters involved – at least, Schopenhauer suggests, with regard to Ophelia and Laertes. (Presumably, this makes room for the nefarious deeds of Claudius or the bad luck of killing Polonius and the way his death echoes across the play.) The tone of Schopenhauer's remarks on this interpretation is speculative, as well it might be: after all, Hamlet is brought into conflict with Laertes (at least) because he has rashly murdered Laertes's father – an act that doesn't seem to trouble him all that much.

The combination of resignation and plot structure lend *Hamlet* significant status as a will-denying play of the right kind. Speaking of *Hamlet* as the supreme example, Schopenhauer can write that 'if knowledge reaches the point where the vanity of all willing and striving dawns on it and the will consequently abolishes itself, it is then that the drama becomes really tragic and hence truly sublime and attains its real purpose'.[49] But in addition to its status as exemplary resignation-tragedy, there are also specific features of *Hamlet* which – though Schopenhauer does not draw them altogether in one place to offer a 'reading' as such – give us a glimpse of why he finds this play so important.

Hamlet's Soliloquy

One frequent point of reference in Schopenhauer's praise for *Hamlet* lies in Hamlet's soliloquy in which (on Schopenhauer's understanding) Hamlet straightforwardly expresses the view that it would be better to be dead than alive and that the dreams of the dead are the only thing keeping him from killing himself.[50] The unbridled pessimism of Schopenhauer's philosophy certainly lends itself to the conclusion that one might be better off dead than alive and Schopenhauer seeks to defend suicides against the claim that they are cowardly or criminal. But, in one of his less convincing arguments, he nonetheless maintains that suicide isn't an appropriate action, on the metaphysical grounds that it isn't a true denial of the will, in comparison with genuine asceticism.[51]

The argument is that suicide is an *act of willing* in which only the appearance is annihilated. It therefore offers a denial only of the world as representation, not as will; from the more real, eternal, changeless will, it offers no true escape. Hence it is better to stay alive and actively deny the will (in saint-like asceticism) than to choose an easy and ultimately ineffectual get-out by way of suicide. The argument seems weak, not least because the same could be said of the ascetic: namely that his attempt to evade the clutches of the will cannot be successful because he is will all along – surely just as much as the suicide is – so asceticism might be said to offer no true escape either.[52]

Nonetheless, Schopenhauer finds an echo of his thought on life and suicide via Hamlet's reflections. Hamlet seeks to escape the cruelty of the world. But he doesn't choose suicide, due to some kind of inkling that the world as he knows it isn't all that there is: a return to apparent nothingness would not rule out a 'dream' of the dead. Hamlet is in a particularly good place to contemplate life after death in a more literal sense than that suggested by Schopenhauer's philosophy, since he has recently been visited by the ghost of his dead father. So one thought Hamlet might have is that he, Hamlet the individual, might continue to exist, to dream, and to haunt Bernado. But this more prosaic afterlife isn't what concerns Schopenhauer. Instead, the 'dream' has a certain figurative significance in Schopenhauer's writing – a characteristic way of describing the world of representation as opposed to the world as will.[53] (This explains, for example, Schopenhauer's admiration for the speech about dreams in *The Tempest* or Calderón's *Life is a Dream*.[54]) In expressing the thought that there could be some 'dreaming' after death, Hamlet connects us with Schopenhauer's concerns about suicide: that the death of the apparent individual does nothing to negate the thing in itself – the will – and indeed acts in accordance with it; in Schopenhauer's chosen terms, the suicide destroys one particular dream, but the dreamer remains the same and goes on producing other dreams instead (the world of representation).[55]

The Character of Horatio

Hamlet, of course, meets his death in the end. Horatio, eager to follow him, is asked by Hamlet to stay and tell Hamlet's story – an interface between what went on at Elsinore and the rest of the world.[56] As we have seen, the ultimate poetic achievement rests not merely in correct character portrayal, but in choosing 'significant' characters to portray and in placing them in the appropriate situations. The place of Horatio in *Hamlet* is one of the many puzzles offered up by the play. Amongst his many noteworthy features may be counted: his presumed invention by Shakespeare; his presence in both the opening and closing scenes; his tendency to be on stage a great deal without saying or doing anything; the curious absence and even the apparent inconsistency of biographical details. Interestingly, for an invention on the part of the author, Horatio performs next to no plot-related function – certainly nothing that could not be replaced by a Bernado or a nameless messenger – and he is remarkably less active or engaged than those around him. Yet, while playing no active part, Horatio frequently functions as a witness – of the ghost at the start, of the king's reaction to the play in the middle, of Hamlet's affairs once the action is done. Without him, our experience of the play would surely be different.[57]

Schopenhauer's concern with Horatio relates to these characteristics – he seems drawn to Horatio as a sort of ethical-aesthetic onlooker. Sometimes Schopenhauer suggests that Horatio, as a 'noble character', simply subordinates his own desires to those of the people around him, having implicitly recognised the insignificance and suspect nature of his individual desire.[58] Elsewhere, in his discussion of what he calls the 'ethical sublime' character, Schopenhauer brings Horatio in as an example of one who contemplates men 'in a purely objective way', regardless of his own direct interest: 'He will contemplate their happiness without feeling envy, recognise their good qualities without desiring closer associations with them, perceive the beauty of women without hankering after them. His personal happiness or unhappiness will not violently affect him.'[59]

Schopenhauer develops the idea of Horatio as 'a knower rather than a sufferer' from Hamlet's speech, offered to his friend in Act 3, Scene 2, in which Hamlet describes Horatio as 'one, in suffering all, that suffers nothing': he is 'not a pipe for fortune's finger to sound what stop she please'. Hamlet's praise for Horatio as having a temperament that is beyond the reaches of fortune might well be taken to be a suggestion that Horatio holds to a Stoic philosophy. But instead of identifying him with any particular philosophical position (and, indeed, Schopenhauer is elsewhere highly critical of the Stoics), Schopenhauer suggests that in the figure of Horatio we find the echo of both the spectator and the genius – both of whom have been freed to some extent from the clutches of the will. In the case of the 'ethical sublime' type, it is an attitude towards others born not from an excess of intellect but from a lack of attraction to the kinds of objects that would typically draw one into the world of representation and misleading desire. On that understanding, Horatio's lack of action – and more particularly, his lack of any apparent desire – is central to his significance. Unlike Hamlet, Horatio doesn't seem to *want* anything in particular. As Hamlet moves towards his state of resignation of the will, he is accompanied – often silently – by one who is already there.

What Horatio offers the spectator, therefore, is a link between what has been achieved by Hamlet in his resignation before death, what has been achieved (temporarily) in the spectator's own aesthetic experience and what it would be like to be in something like that state on a more permanent basis. Horatio, on my understanding of Schopenhauer, amounts to a crucial interface between the subject matter of the play and the aesthetic experience of the spectator. Hence, when Hamlet asks Horatio to stay behind and tell his story, Schopenhauer can read this in the light of Horatio's function to connect what the audience experiences in their will-free contemplation with what Horatio – as an ethical-sublime character – can experience in general. What makes *Hamlet* stand out among tragedies – at least when one looks at Schopenhauer's discussions of the play – is not the move from will to renunciation on the part of the tragic hero (though that is of course important), but rather the presence, all along, of a character who is already removed from the clutches of the will and who remains, after the hero's downfall, as a kind of bridge between the aesthetic experience of the tragedy and the ethical life of the rest of the world.

As with Schopenhauer's reading of the soliloquy, it is easy to imagine a critical response to the reading of Horatio just outlined. Much depends, after all, on taking Hamlet's description of Horatio's kindness and selflessness as a general description of Horatio's attitude to the world. That may well be *Hamlet's* view, given Horatio's devotion to him. But one might question whether Horatio is putting all others before himself (as a compassionate ascetic) or whether he merely puts *Hamlet's* needs before his own as a loyal friend. If Horatio were really so detached and disinterested, would he be ready to end his own life when Hamlet dies? One might look to Horatio, then, as a model of *philia* – the love between friends – rather than a model of *agape* – the compassion towards all which Schopenhauer so values.

In emphasising the 'vanity of all willing' as exposed in *Hamlet*, Schopenhauer touches on one traditional problem in the play, namely Hamlet's apparent indecision and its psychological causes – an interpretative line that was already well under way with Coleridge, although Schopenhauer makes no explicit mention of it. Of course, Hamlet is indecisive in a sense – for whatever reason, he doesn't act when he has the chance. But the crux of the tragedy, on a Schopenhauerian reading, can hardly be Hamlet's *failure* to act, since not acting – the ultimate vanity of doing anything at all – is precisely what Hamlet is supposed to learn during the course of the drama. Instead, the arc of the narrative leads us from a particular individual failing to act (and tormenting himself over it) to his comprehension, aided by Horatio's presence, that acting in itself is futile and that not-acting is a kind of relief.[60] Hamlet's reluctance to act might even be seen as an early recognition of the fruitlessness of any attempts to fulfil desires.

Notes

1. David Cartwright, *Schopenhauer: A Biography* (Cambridge: Cambridge University Press, 2010), p. 282.
2. Ibid., p. 464.
3. Arthur Schopenhauer, *Parerga and Paralipomena*, trans. E.F.J. Payne (Oxford: Oxford University Press, 2000), vol. II, pp. 445 and 437 (henceforth PP). References will give volume and section or chapter number unless otherwise stated. Page numbers refer to this edition.
4. Arthur Schopenhauer, *The World as Will and Representation*, trans. E.F.J. Payne (New York: Dover, 1969), vol. II, ch. 23 (henceforth WWR). References to WWR give volume and section or chapter unless otherwise stated. Page numbers refer to this edition.
5. Cf. WWR II 43, p. 519.
6. On the relationship, in general, between such 'words of wisdom' and the plays from which they are taken, see Tom Stern, *Philosophy and Theatre* (New York: Routledge, 2013), pp. 48–54.
7. WWR I 34, also II 34.
8. WWR I 36.
9. PP II 49.
10. See below for discussions of Horatio or the Earl of Northumberland.
11. WWR I 34.
12. WWR I 45.
13. WWR I 23–4.
14. WWR I 42–3.
15. WWR I 38.
16. PP II 49. Schopenhauer thought that only men could be geniuses and produced a variety of pseudo-justifications for this claim. It would be misleading to refer to the Schopenhauerian genius with anything other than the masculine pronoun. See WWR II 31.
17. WWR I 36. Or, at least, this is what happens to the genius as long as he is being a genius: presumably Shakespeare wanted things occasionally just like the rest of us – indeed, Schopenhauer feels the need to explain Shakespeare's marriage. See WWR II 44.
18. WWR I 36, 45.
19. WWR I 36.
20. WWR I 52.
21. WWR II 31.
22. WWR I 43; I 51. All literature reveals the Idea of mankind – drama, Schopenhauer thinks, does it best.

23. WWR I 51.
24. See e.g. Aristotle, *Poetics*, 54a.
25. WWR II 23.
26. PP II 118; see also PP I 5, p. 452.
27. See WWR I 26.
28. PP II 118, pp. 230–6.
29. WWR I 51, p. 251.
30. WWR I 51, p. 251.
31. WWR I 51, p. 253.
32. WWR I 51, p. 252.
33. WWR II 49.
34. Tragedy is certainly possible without resignation; indeed, this, Schopenhauer thinks, was lacking in ancient tragedy.
35. WWR I 39.
36. Hence the list of tragic heroes who supposedly embody this notion – see WWR I 253–5.
37. WWR I 395.
38. WWR I 51.
39. Shylock is curious for a number of reasons: first, *The Merchant of Venice* is not strictly a tragedy; second, Shylock – though he has plenty of faults – is not obviously wicked in the mould of Richard or Iago.
40. See WWR I 58; II 37.
41. WWR II 37.
42. See Immanuel Kant, *Political Writings*, trans. H.B. Nisbet, ed. H.S. Reiss (Cambridge: Cambridge University Press, 1991), 'Idea for a universal history with a cosmopolitan purpose', p. 44.
43. WWR II 38.
44. See WWR I 51, also WWR I 45.
45. So Schopenhauer said of himself, at least. See Cartwright, *Schopenhauer: A Biography*, p. 361.
46. WWR II 37.
47. PP II 49, p. 67.
48. WWR II 34.
49. PP II, p. 600.
50. WWR I 324; PP II 13.
51. WWR I 69; PP II 13.
52. Schopenhauer does not exactly explore this objection, at least in his published works. But see the exchange of letters with Becker, discussed in Cartwright, *Schopenhauer: A Biography*, pp. 509–11, in which he makes some concessions. Dale Jacquette offers a limited defence of Schopenhauer, using some of his obscure remarks about being and willing, but even so concludes that Schopenhauer's argument is unsatisfactory. See 'Schopenhauer on Death', in Christopher Janaway (ed.), *The Cambridge Companion to Schopenhauer* (Cambridge: Cambridge University Press, 1999), pp. 293–317.
53. WWR II 41.
54. WWR I 17.
55. See WWR II 41.
56. WWR I, pp. 253–5.

57. For some of these ideas, and a more thorough investigation of Horatio, see J. Halverson, 'The Importance of Horatio', *Hamlet Studies*, 16 (1994), pp. 57–70.
58. PP II 165, pp. 315–16.
59. WWR I 39, p. 206.
60. Ethical actions taken out of pity might form one exception, but that exception threatens to bring an inconsistency into Schopenhauer's account of tragedy. See Sebastian Gardner, 'Tragedy, Morality and Metaphysics', in S. Gardner and J.L. Bermúdez (eds), *Art and Morality* (London: Routledge, 2003), pp. 218–59.

Chapter 4

Nietzsche's Shakespeare

Peter Holbrook

Nietzsche had a profound kinship with Shakespeare because he was fundamentally a *dramatic* thinker, apprehending the world through notions of character and action. For Nietzsche, and, I will suggest, for Shakespeare, ideas and values were never abstract propositions, the truth or falsehood of which was logically or empirically testable. Rather they were elements of a particular life – attractive or repellent, inspiring or miserable.

Nietzsche's mind worked through contrasts: Shakespeare is brought into relation with figures, past and present, who fascinate, trouble, or enliven him, or all at once. Often his observations are biographical – he must understand human life psychologically: what does an action or idea mean for the person doing or holding it? Nietzsche was 'an old psychologist'.[1] Shakespeare the man is his focus: if you want to understand the works, he suggests, you need to know how they made up a particular life.

Nietzsche breaks completely with the nineteenth-century sentimental view of Shakespeare as a serene and lofty sage. His Shakespeare is a tortured, divided figure. Of *Julius Caesar*, he writes that

> Twice in the tragedy [Shakespeare] introduced a poet, and twice he poured such impatient and ultimate contempt upon him that it sounds like a cry – like the cry of self-contempt ... even Brutus loses patience when the poet enters – conceited, pathetic, obtrusive, as poets usually are – as a being who appears to be bursting with possibilities of greatness, even moral greatness, although in the philosophy of deed and life he rarely attains even a passable integrity.[2]

Why would Shakespeare have experienced self-contempt? The answer lies in how Nietzsche conceives of art. To be an artist, he tells us, is to trade in illusions – dream images making existence bearable by steering our minds away from a meaningless and chaotic reality. Art's '*good* will to appearance' offsets what we know about the actual conditions of human life, '*Honesty*' about which 'would lead to nausea and suicide'.[3] Lesser artists mistake their fantasies for reality. But an artist of integrity, like Shakespeare, *knows* he is lying – and hence suffers from a certain contempt for himself. Note that Shakespeare is understood in this passage as a flesh-and-blood being rather than the impersonal vehicle of a philosophy to be evaluated without reference to the life out of which it springs. On the contrary, Shakespeare is conceived dramatically, as a *persona*, or character.

In *Ecce Homo*, his prankish review of his writings written towards the end of his sane existence, Nietzsche painted another picture of Shakespeare: 'Shakespeare is the most poignant reading I know' he declared:

> how much suffering does it take for somebody to need to play the clown! . . . And just to confess, I have an instinctive certainty that Lord Bacon was the author, the self-torturer of animals who is behind this uncanniest type of literature . . .[4]

Not very promising – and of a piece with Nietzsche's own snobbish fantasy that he descended from Polish nobility. In fact Nietzsche's mob-baiting was an early, and unfortunate, way in which he was discussed in relation to Shakespeare. The Danish critic Georg Brandes casted Nietzsche as a champion of 'aristocratic radicalism'[5] – a characterisation Nietzsche approved ('the cleverest thing I have yet read about myself'[6]). Brandes was a liberal but noted Shakespeare's 'contempt for the judgment of the masses' and 'anti-democratic' bias[7] – an inaccurate view reproduced by the great twentieth-century commentator on Nietzsche, Walter Kaufmann.[8]

Such judgements highlight a larger problem in the way the philosophically minded sometimes cast Shakespeare as the expounder of various propositions 'illustrated' in the plays. Nothing could be further from the way Nietzsche approaches Shakespeare; and we too should not treat Shakespeare as a 'thinker' in this sense. Focusing on Shakespeare *as a person* – tormented, ambivalent, passionate – forbids our seeing his works as 'philosophical' in the bland sense of 'objective', 'universal', 'systematic', etc. Yes, Nietzsche's understanding of Shakespeare as harbouring a secret self-contempt is based partly on his suspicion that the theatre, as a site of mob-rule, is unworthy of the efforts of a great poet: 'theatre', he wrote, with Wagner in mind, 'is a rebellion of the masses, a plebiscite *against* good taste'.[9] Elsewhere he observes that Shakespeare's plays 'contain entirely serious ideas in a polished form, but are for that reason too remote and subtle for the theatre public'.[10] In *Nietzsche contra Wagner* he exclaims:

What is the theatre to *me*? The cramps of its moral ecstasies that satisfy the 'people' – and who isn't 'the people'! The whole hocus pocus of gestures of the actor! – You will guess that I am essentially anti-theatrical, that I regard the theatre, this art of the masses *par excellence*, with the same deep contempt from the bottom of my soul that every artist today will feel.[11]

But none of this should obscure the larger point that drama is the ground of Nietzsche's philosophy – that he represents thought dramatically. Nietzsche pursued what he called 'the *hidden* history of the philosophers, the psychology of its greatest names',[12] declaring that: 'I have gradually come to realize what every great philosophy so far has been: a confession of faith on the part of its author, and a type of involuntary and unself-conscious memoir.'[13] Thought expresses character.

Shakespeare, it seems to me, understands thought this way too. Consider his clever villains Iago and Edmund. Both are masters of what Eugen Fink (in relation to Nietzsche) called the explanation *ab inferiori*.[14] Both are biological reductionists. Love is 'merely a lust of the blood' to Iago;[15] Desdemona no better than other women ('The wine she drinks is made of grapes' [*Othello*, 2.1.254–5]). Edmund's 'goddess' is 'Nature' (*King Lear*, 1.2.1). But all of these truth-claims, Shakespeare makes clear, are only expressions of who Iago and Edmund are *as people* – are ideas that help them act; and Albany in *King Lear* might be addressing Iago when he avers that 'Wisdom and goodness to the vile seem vile' (4.2.39). Shakespeare is giving us not philosophy but *dramatisations of* philosophy. There is, for example, a deep irony in Iago's and Edmund's theoretical insistence on human agency and freedom – ''Tis in ourselves that we are thus or thus' (*Othello*, 1.3.322–3); 'This is the excellent foppery of the world . . . as if we were villains on necessity' (*King Lear*, 1.2.121, 124–5) – since both are so evidently in the dark as to what is driving them on towards their respective atrocities. These two putative philosophers of free will are helpless before passions neither controls or is even aware of (hatred of his father, perhaps, in Edmund's case; goodness knows what in Iago's).

To repeat, then: Shakespeare is not for Nietzsche an abstract, doctrinal thinker. 'I distrust all systematizers', wrote Nietzsche, 'and avoid them. The will to a system is a lack of integrity.'[16] Nietzsche did not avoid Shakespeare and did not attribute to him 'lack of integrity'. We should heed Nietzsche's words here, resist the temptation to treat Shakespeare as a system-builder.

Nietzsche's engagement with the theatre goes well beyond Shakespeare. An early notebook entry sums up the argument of *The Birth of Tragedy*: 'At that time', Nietzsche wrote,

> I believed that from the aesthetic point of view the world was a drama and meant as such by its author, but that as a moral phenomenon it was a *fraud*: therefore I came to the conclusion that the world could be justified only as an aesthetic phenomenon.[17]

The key point is that *Nietzsche wants us to think of the world dramatically not morally.* This is what lies behind the famous words of *The Birth of Tragedy,* that 'only as an *aesthetic phenomenon* is existence and the world eternally *justified*'.[18] The notion that art makes life bearable can sound shabby, implying that art lies. Of course there are kinds of art (Nietzsche does not disparage these necessarily) that do simply transport us into a delightful never-never land of frivolity. But Nietzsche's claim that 'the world [is] a drama' is a profound defence of art. For what art invites us to do is look at human life *as a play* – an unfolding, complex, yet unified, *action*. It is not that art simply prettifies life, though it does that too – as Nietzsche wrote:

> Art makes the sight of life bearable by laying over it the veil of unclear thinking . . . It is supposed to *conceal* or *reinterpret* everything ugly, those painful, dreadful, disgusting things which, all efforts not withstanding, in accord with the origin of human nature again and again insist on breaking forth.[19]

But *how* does art reinterpret ugliness? By understanding human life as a play, in which nothing is dispensable and everything is interesting and contributes to the whole.

Everything in Nietzsche comes back to the question of life. What enhances living? How can we be more joyful, creative? Which of our ideas and values will make life on earth more zestful, which depress and enervate us? In *The Birth of Tragedy* Nietzsche proposed '*to look at science through the prism of the artist, but also to look at art through the prism of life*'.[20] Art evaluates science (or knowledge), but in turn is judged by life itself. The challenge is to find what will help us live with gusto in the face of what we know to be true.

Some art has an escapist nature, and this has its place. But the danger is that, in so far as art is seen to be obviously falsifying, it will be less effective as a tonic. It may distract us for a while, but, in the end, reality – unjust, illogical, meaningless – awaits us. 'Do you know what "the world" is to me?', asked Nietzsche: 'a monster of force, without beginning, without end, . . . self-creating, . . . self-destroying, . . . beyond good and evil, without goal.'[21] Art seduces us to life in spite of our knowledge that the universe is chaotic, knowledge that could easily bring us to our knees. But art that included as much reality as was compatible with the perception of form and beauty – that inspired us while also acknowledging the world as a scene of irrational creation and destruction – would be all the stronger as a cure. Greek tragedy achieved this synthesis: in it 'passing away appears equally dignified and worthy of reverence as coming into being'.[22] Tragedy made the suffering and transience of human life interesting, exciting and alluring. Rather than denying the existence of the painful qualities of life, Greek tragedy reflected these back under a heightened glow, the Greek pantheon being human life glamorised: 'The Greeks are the artists of *life*; they have their gods in order to be able to live, not in order to alienate themselves from life.'[23] Greek tragedy was, for Nietzsche, a *strong* illusion because its celebration of life was predicated on unflinching recognition of suffering. 'The only satisfactory theodicy', Nietzsche declared, was that in which the gods 'justify the life of men by living it themselves'.[24]

The belief that it is 'only as an *aesthetic phenomenon* [that] existence and the world [are] eternally *justified*' is basic to Nietzsche. The problem is how to live after one knows the truth – a topic addressed in Nietzsche's wholly original account of *Hamlet*, which tries to solve the traditional difficulty of Hamlet's 'delay' (why the hero does not proceed instantly to dispatch the villainous Claudius). For Nietzsche,

> Dionysiac man is similar to Hamlet: both have gazed into the true essence of things, they have *acquired knowledge* and they find action repulsive, for their actions can do nothing to change the eternal essence of things; they regard it as laughable or shameful that they should be expected to set to rights a world so out of joint. Knowledge kills action; action requires one to be shrouded in a veil of illusion – this is the lesson of Hamlet, not that cheap wisdom about Jack the Dreamer who does not get around to acting because he reflects too much, out of an excess of possibilities, as it were. No, it is not reflection, it is true knowledge, insight into the terrible truth, which outweighs every motive for action, both in the case of Hamlet, and in that of Dionysiac man.[25]

The problem – as always for Nietzsche – is nihilism. Absence of a higher order renders all action futile. 'Knowledge kills action', says Nietzsche: truth is inimical to life, dries up the springs from which action flows. Nietzsche admires what he sees as Shakespeare's realism, his refusal to lie: Shakespeare's Hamlet acknowledges the truth about life.

What is central for Nietzsche, and for Shakespeare, too, I suggest, is the desire not to contain existence solely within a moral framework. Nietzsche tried to shock his contemporaries out of narrowly moralistic attitudes, which he felt damaged our capacity to relish life. And what countered morality was drama, because the dramatist is, ultimately, less concerned with whether an action is moral than with whether it is interesting and exciting. For Nietzsche, humanity needed to look at life with the eyes of the dramatist rather than with those of the parson or philosopher. We should stop scrutinising life for evidence of moral goodness or rationality – qualities always in short supply – and instead examine it for memorable character and engrossing action.

Nietzsche declared of the Homeric gods that

> What speaks out of them is a religion of life, not one of duty or asceticism or spirituality. All these figures breathe the triumph of existence, a luxuriant vitality accompanies their cult. They do not make demands; all that exists is deified in them, regardless of whether it is good or evil.[26]

Countenancing evil and suffering as part of 'the triumph of life' – as a reason to want more, not less, life – is a prominent thread in all Nietzsche's work, part of his conviction that 'Nothing in existence should be excluded, nothing is dispensable.'[27] The same notion is articulated in the myth of the Eternal Return proposed in *Thus Spoke Zarathustra*: 'Have you ever said Yes to a single joy?', asks Zarathustra:

> O my friends, then you said Yes too to *all* woe. All things are entangled, ensnared, enamored; if ever you wanted one thing twice, if ever you said, 'You please me, happiness! Abide, moment!' then you wanted *all* back.[28]

Nietzsche's conviction that 'all things are . . . enamored' is a monism; also a metaphysical foundation for tolerance. You cannot have any good thing in existence without everything else enchained with it. All things imply each other; picking the darker from the lighter threads will rend the garment. As First Lord puts it in *All's Well That Ends Well*, 'The web of our life is of a mingled yarn, good and ill together. Our virtues would be proud if our faults whipped them not, and our crimes would despair if they were not cherished by our virtues' (4.3.70–3). What Shakespeare articulates in a moral-religious idiom Nietzsche expresses in a naturalistic one: we should tolerate and sometimes applaud our vices because they are inseparable from what we value. But this broadminded outlook Nietzsche attributes especially to the dramatist, whose concern is above all for compelling characters and involving stories. Here is Nietzsche's tongue-in-cheek account of '*the morality of the stage*':

> Whoever thinks that Shakespeare's theatre has a moral effect, and that the sight of Macbeth irresistibly repels one from the evil of ambition, is in error: and he is again in error if he thinks Shakespeare himself felt as he feels. He who is really possessed by raging ambition beholds this its image with *joy*; and if the hero perishes by his passion this is precisely the sharpest spice in the hot draught of this joy. Can the poet have felt otherwise? How royally, and not at all like a rogue, does his ambitious man pursue his course from the moment of his great crime! . . . Do you suppose that Tristan and Isolde are preaching *against* adultery when they both perish by it? This would be to stand the poets on their head: they, and especially Shakespeare, are enamoured of the passions as such and not least of their death-welcoming moods

. . . The tragic poet . . . cries [out]: 'it is the stimulant of stimulants, this exciting, changing, dangerous, gloomy and often sun-drenched existence! It is an
adventure to live . . .' – He speaks thus out of a restless, vigorous age which is
half-drunk and stupefied by its excess of blood and energy – out of a wickeder
age than ours is: which is why we need first to *adjust* and *justify* the goal of a
Shakespearean drama, that is to say, not to understand it.[29]

Nietzsche objected to all attempts to 'adjust' and 'justify' Shakespearean
tragedy by moralising it (he was especially exasperated by the German
Shakespeare critic Georg Gottfried Gervinus's focus on poetic justice[30]).
In this he was restating, in a different key, what other critics had noticed
before him – Samuel Johnson, for instance, for whom Shakespeare's
'first defect' was 'that to which may be imputed most of the evil in
books or in men. He sacrifices virtue to convenience, and is so much
more careful to please than to instruct, that he seems to write without
any moral purpose.'[31] Both Nietzsche and Johnson notice Shakespeare's
indifference to the convention that fictional works should reward the
virtuous and punish the vicious. Nietzsche's understanding of the
'morality of the stage' might bear comparison to William Hazlitt's in his
Characters of Shakespeare's Plays (1817). In his essay on *Coriolanus*,
Hazlitt argued that poetry was drawn towards power: the imagination
was 'an exaggerating . . . faculty' that 'give[s] the greatest possible effect
to a favourite object'.[32] Since human beings are attracted to power, the
dramatic imagination, in plays like *Coriolanus*, duly exalts it.

'Morality *negates* life', wrote Nietzsche.[33] It is erroneous to suppose
that Nietzsche had no regard for moral heroism, that he was unmoved
by virtue or holiness, that cruelty and malice did not perturb him. But
he did worry that a *purely* moral outlook on life left too much out –
risked turning us into those 'Despisers of life' Zarathustra deplores.[34]
'The wisest men in every age have reached the same conclusion about
life', Nietzsche wrote elsewhere: '*it's no good* . . .'.[35] Nietzsche was
right, I believe, to attribute some such critical perspective on morality to
Shakespeare. As I have argued elsewhere,[36] Shakespeare seems intrigued
by the idea that there are certain persons whose charisma transforms
vices into virtues – hence the ability of Antony and Cleopatra to turn
debauchery into something noble. As Enobarbus tells us of Cleopatra,

> . . . vilest things
> Become themselves in her, that the holy priests
> Bless her when she is riggish [i.e., lustful]. (2.2.248–50)

The notion figures prominently in the Sonnets: 'Whence hast thou this
becoming of things ill[?]' Shakespeare asks the Dark Lady in Sonnet
150 – how is it, that is, that she makes a defect (vice) attractive? We

might adduce here too Sonnets 95 and 96, in which the dazzling Young Man 'mak[es] faults graces that to [him] resort' (Sonnet 96). When moral find-faults criticise him, 'Making lascivious comments on [his] sport', his very name frustrates their malice: 'Naming [his] name', claims Shakespeare, 'blesses an ill report'; his beauty 'all things turns to fair' (Sonnet 95).

To say that morality could turn us against life might seem implausible until one thinks of a play like Shakespeare's *Timon of Athens*, a text important to the great Shakespeare scholar, and Nietzschean, G. Wilson Knight. In *Christ and Nietzsche: An Essay in Poetic Wisdom*, Knight found in the 'diverse energies of Renaissance literature' an anticipation of Nietzsche's attack on morality and 'insincerity'.[37] As Knight understood it, Christ, St Paul, Luther, Shakespeare, and Nietzsche were as one in their disdain for 'legal morality';[38] like Jesus, both Nietzsche and Shakespeare challenged 'the very basis of ethical judgment' and were enemies of the 'pharasaic . . . filming over of vital energies'.[39] The challenge was to integrate these energies into a more generous understanding of the good; and it is in Zarathustra and Shakespeare that Knight finds the needed synthesis.[40] Nietzsche's mistake was to misread the New Testament as endorsing conventional, rule-bound morality; actually Christ and Zarathustra were both taboo-breakers and creators.[41] For Knight, summarising Nietzsche, 'the basic instincts must be assimilated rather than rejected'; and the 'interrelation of good and evil . . . seen . . . positively'.[42] As he comments elsewhere: 'A just interpretation of Shakespeare's art will inevitably thrill to, and may seem in danger of approving, essences which are, or appear, evil.'[43]

Nietzsche's critique of morality is adumbrated in *Timon*, a play portraying a dizzying descent from exalted moral idealism into misanthropic despair. Timon, his steward Flavius tells us, is someone 'undone by goodness' (4.2.39). Literally this is true: Timon's excessive generosity to his fair-weather friends has brought him to ruin. But he is 'undone by goodness' in another sense, too, for the destructive psychological reflex Timon undergoes – idealism to cynicism – is one Nietzsche warns against. To suppose humanity better than it can be is to guarantee disappointment. Once the world has failed to measure up to Timon's strictures the only conclusion can be that

> . . . All's obliquy;
> There's nothing level in our cursed natures
> But direct villainy. (4.3.18–20)

Yet arguably it is not the world that is crooked here so much as the measuring stick used; and what is missing in Timon is that quality of integration that, overall, Knight located in Shakespeare – that balance, or moderation, that enables one to approve the world without being deluded about it. 'The middle of humanity thou never knewest, but the extremity of both ends' (4.3.305–6), Apemantus points out to Timon. The hero's nihilism ('My long sickness / Of health and living' [5.1.185–6]) is the product of misguided idealism; and Timon's goodness succeeds only in turning the earth into the 'sterile promontory' Hamlet speaks of in a similar mood (*Hamlet*, 2.2.300): now, for Timon, 'Nothing brings . . . all things' (*Timon*, 5.1.187).

Nietzsche admires Shakespeare, as he does other artists, for the poet's willingness to affirm the world as it is. So many philosophers, he points out, have cast a pall of self-hatred over the passions, depicting them as evil and insisting we live up to a wholly unreal, self-lacerating image of ourselves as rationally directed free agents: 'Hatred of the "world"', Nietzsche writes,

> a curse on the passions, fear of beauty and sensuality, a Beyond, invented in order better to defame the Here-and-Now, fundamentally a desire for nothingness, for the end, for rest, for the 'Sabbath of Sabbaths'.[44]

– all of these idealistic manias, he argues, have made earth a hell. And the cure for such madness is art. The artists

> greatly encourage the *high value accorded the passions* and have always done so; they also, to be sure, glorify the fearful amends one must make for these same passions, the death, maiming and voluntary banishment following on outbursts of revenge, the resignation of the broken heart. In any event, they keep awake our curiosity regarding the passions, as though to say: 'experience without passion is nothing at all'.[45]

Elsewhere he asserts that 'Artists constantly *glorify* – they do nothing else.'[46] Shakespeare is a key figure in Nietzsche's belief that art helps us incorporate the passions into a more complete, forgiving, and manageable conception of human life. Shakespeare is a champion of the passions and of sensual liberation.

Nietzsche admired Shakespeare's honesty about his own passions, evident in, he thought, the Sonnets:

> *To think a thing evil means to make it evil.* – the passions become evil and malicious if they are regarded as evil and malicious. Thus Christianity has succeeded in transforming Eros and Aphrodite – great powers capable of idealisation – into diabolical kobolds and phantoms by means of the torments it introduces into the consciences of believers whenever they are excited sexually. Is it not dreadful to make necessary and regularly occurring sensations into a source of inner misery, and in this way to want to make inner misery a necessary and regularly recurring phenomenon *in every*

human being! In addition to which it remains a misery kept secret and thus more deeply rooted: for not everyone possesses the courage of Shakespeare to confess his Christian gloominess on this point in the way he did in his Sonnets.[47]

Shakespeare is valuable for his openness about his sexual life (including his anxiety about sex). And it is true, I think, that the Sonnets are indeed a remarkable document in this respect – presented on their title page as the work of an actual, knowable man and showing, in explicit detail, the viscissitudes of sexual desire. Shakespeare's frankness about his failure to live up to an ideal of purity is, for Nietzsche, itself helpful – as I think it was too, and irrespective of whether the Sonnets were authorised for publication or not (we know they were circulated among Shakespeare's friends). Nietzsche finds in Shakespeare a typically modern struggle between a pagan assent to the passions and a Christian guilt about them. But he also feels that Shakespeare is especially, and as a result of his own character, drawn to the passions. In *Daybreak* he considers the case of men subject to what he calls 'intellectual spasms'. They 'long', he says, 'to dissolve into something "*outside*"'.[48] And he claims that 'Shakespeare . . . is satisfied only with being dissolved into images of the most passionate life.'[49] Similarly, in one of the notebooks Shakespeare is identified with a Romantic predilection for the passions: where Aeschylus's mind works in terms of 'static, sculpturesque groups', Shakespeare's is focused on 'tremendously moving passions'.[50]

Shakespeare's endorsement of the passions makes him an ally in Nietzsche's campaign against the view that the most valuable aspect of human beings is their reason; and, indeed, Nietzsche's deep cynicism about reason – or, rather, about the claims made on reason's behalf – is an aspect of his philosophy that can strike us not only as important in itself but as decidedly Shakespearean. Consider as a small instance of this theme the status of reason in *The Two Gentlemen of Verona*. Proteus believes himself in love with Julia, but when his friend Valentine (who has formerly scoffed at love) finds himself head over heels in love with Sylvia, Proteus immediately follows suit. In thinking over his conversion to Sylvia Proteus admits the weakness of reason:

> Even as one heat another heat expels,
> Or as one nail by strength drives out another,
> So the remembrance of my former love
> Is by a newer object quite forgotten.
> Is it mine eye, or Valentine's praise,
> Her true perfection, or my false transgression
> That makes me, reasonless, to reason thus? (2.4.190–6)

And he concludes this meditation with the helpless vow that

> If I can check my erring love, I will;
> If not, to compass her I'll use my skill. (2.4.211–2)

Proteus's account of what has happened to him (and he must stand in here for a whole tribe of giddy Shakespearean lovers) chimes with Nietzsche's own physiological account of the passions: here one force ('the nail') or sensation ('heat') drives out another: choice, will, freedom have nothing to do with it. When Proteus attempts to rape Silvia the play takes a scandalously relaxed view of the matter, Valentine at once forgiving him. As in other plays, desire trumps morality, simply because it is all-powerful. (We might think here of Richard III's seduction of the Lady Anne in his play, or Cressida's change of heart in hers: in each case a sudden and inexplicable re-routing of desire occurs.) 'O most potential love!' declares the ruined woman of Shakespeare's *A Lover's Complaint*, 'For thou art all, and all things else are thine' (line 266). Love in that poem is slavery, the bewitchment exerted by an irresistible young man's 'charmed power' over a 'maid' (lines 146, 5). It is an old story, and the maid was warned about the young man's duplicity before she fell: 'But, ah, who ever shunned by precedent', she laments, 'The destined ill she must herself assay?' (lines 156–7). What is extraordinary, however, is the poem's conclusion, in which the maid confesses that should she have her time over again, and knowing what she now knows about her deceiver, he 'Would yet again betray the fore-betrayed, / And new pervert a reconciled maid!' (lines 328–9). So much for reason: even the awareness that this specious youth means to 'maim' her (line 312) would not stop her from submitting to him again.

'The irrationality of a thing', declared Nietzsche, 'is no argument against its existence, rather a condition of it.'[51] Again and again Nietzsche focuses our attention, not unlike Shakespeare, on how reason is the least impressive thing about us. 'It is not our folly which makes me laugh', wrote Nietzsche's hero Montaigne – of whom Nietzsche noted that Shakespeare was his 'best reader'[52] – 'it is our wisdom'.[53] For Nietzsche – as for Shakespeare, I believe – 'Below every thought lies an affect'; and 'thoughts', Nietzsche goes on, 'are *signs* of a play and struggle of the affects: they are always connected to their hidden roots'.[54] Ideas, for Nietzsche, are 'the shadows of our sensations – always darker, emptier, simpler'.[55] The view that human beings are the playthings of rival drives, now one, now another, that they have, ultimately, no choice in the question of who they are, is, I think, a fundamentally Shakespearean insight as well – and one available to Shakespeare within his own culture, as Nietzsche observed: 'All deeper men – Luther, Augustine, Paul come to mind – agree that our morality and its events do not coincide with our *conscious will* – in short, that an explanation in terms of having goals *is insufficient*.'[56] Shakespeare's characters, like many of the people appearing in Montaigne's essays, are often portrayed as acting out of the most obscure motives. Obviously the *rational* thing for Shylock to do is accept the sum offered by the court. Instead he demands his pound of flesh, the quest for which is, he admits, 'A losing suit' (*Merchant*, 4.1.62). The interesting thing is that Shylock's own account of his conduct in his long speech in Act 4, Scene 1, forgoes any claim to reasonableness. He acts as he does because of who he is: it is his 'humor' (4.1.43), which is as opaque to explanation (and as irresistible) as the factors that make one man unable to endure the sight of a roasted pig which has had its mouth opened, another man incapable of abiding the sight of a rat or cat, another unable to listen to a bagpipe without urinating (4.1.44–62).

'This is no answer', retorts Bassanio to Shylock (4.1.63), and neither is it. Whatever explanations Shylock offers elsewhere for his hatred of Antonio, Shakespeare is at this moment intrigued by the possibility that human beings act out of motives indecipherable to themselves: there is 'no firm reason', 'no reason' (4.1.53, 59), for any of the aversions listed in Shylock's speech, no way one can 'answer' for them – give a rational account of them. Blind desire (or 'affection'), which commands our feelings (or 'passion'), simply 'sways' those feelings according to what *it* (not *I*, we should note) 'likes or loathes' (4.1.50–2). Deliberate 'choice' has little to do with it: Shylock's use of the word in his speech (at 4.1.40) is merely a way of speaking. The truth is that Shylock is driven, willy-nilly, on this course of action – right up until another affect, fear, drives out his former one.

'He is a thinker', writes Nietzsche in *The Gay Science*: 'that means he knows how to make things simpler than they are'.[57] Neither Nietzsche nor Shakespeare logicises existence – holds that reason is the most important human faculty or that life is fully open to understanding. Nietzsche regularly targets the attempt to make of human existence something more comprehensible than it actually is. This, too, is fundamentally in the spirit of Shakespearean drama, which affirms that reality is complex and nuanced, that motives are often deeply perplexing even to those most convinced of their own (seeming) purposes, and that there is something frighteningly (or joyously) arbitrary and contingent about human life. Shakespeare (and literature generally, I submit) trades in this shadowy realm of the ambiguous, the half-true, the puzzling, the difficult and conditional. Why do Hamlet, Lear, Iago, Timon, Leontes, Cordelia, or any number of other Shakespearean characters, including those from the comedies, act the way they do? Shakespeare almost never opts to explain what he can complicate, enlighten when he can render more obscure. Nietzsche respected the opacity of Shakespearean characterisation – what we might call Shakespeare's lack of theoretical or philosophical clarity – on the grounds that conceptual rigour, the separating out of this from that, is so often a barrier to a truer and richer perception. 'Shakespeare', Nietzsche wrote,

> reflected a great deal on the passions and from his temperament probably had very intimate access to many of them (dramatists are in general some-what wicked men). But, unlike Montaigne, he was incapable of discoursing on them; instead of which he placed observations *about* the passions into the mouths of impassioned characters: a practice which, though counter to nature, makes his plays so full of ideas they make all others seem empty and can easily arouse in us a repugnance to them.[58]

Shakespeare, then, doesn't give us a treatise on the passions but pictures of actual people experiencing and expressing emotion. It is because Shakespeare does *not* explain that he is such a reliable guide to human life. Nietzsche's regard for what is indistinct and shifting in experience makes him, I think, a pre-eminently literary philosopher. And his respect for the unanalysable and riddling in human nature has an important ethical pay-off – namely, a disposition towards tolerance and forgive-ness. Tolerance's enemy is unconditional thinking, the refusal to accept that all things imply one another: 'An unspeakable amount of painful-ness', Nietzsche wrote, 'arrogance, harshness, estrangement, frigidity has entered into human feelings because we think we see opposites instead of transitions.'[59] Shakespeare, it seems to me, regularly pictures human life in terms of transitions rather than opposites.

Nietzsche's conviction that humanity is fundamentally mysterious, that untheoretical artists have done a better job than philosophers of grasping the reality of human life, underlies his esteem for Shakespeare. 'Man is very well defended against himself', Nietzsche observed, 'against being reconnoitred and besieged by himself, he is usually able to per-ceive of himself only his outer walls. The actual fortress is inaccessible, even invisible to him, unless his friends and enemies play the traitor and conduct him in by a secret path.'[60] Nietzsche here anticipates Freud – but is himself anticipated by Shakespeare, not least in the play Nietzsche felt to be Shakespeare's masterpiece, *Julius Caesar*. 'The most beautiful thing I can say in praise of Shakespeare', Nietzsche said,

> is this: he believed in Brutus and didn't cast a speck of suspicion on this type of virtue! To him he devoted his best tragedy – it is still called by the wrong name – to him and to the most dreadful epitome of lofty morality. Independence of soul! That's what's at stake here! No sacrifice could be too

great for that: one has to be capable of sacrificing even one's dearest friend for it, even if he should be the most marvelous human being, the ornament of the world, the genius without peer – if one loves freedom as the freedom of great souls and *this* freedom is endangered because of him: that is what Shakespeare must have felt![61]

Recall that in the play Cassius in effect acts as Brutus's therapist, bringing to awareness concealed desires: 'Into what dangers would you lead me, Cassius', asks Brutus, 'That you would have me seek into myself / For that which is not in me?' (1.2.63–5). And Cassius replies:

> . . . good Brutus, be prepared to hear;
> And since you know you cannot see yourself
> So well as by reflection, I, your glass,
> Will modestly discover to yourself
> That of yourself which you yet know not of. (1.2.66–70)

Nietzsche was moved by Brutus's 'independence of soul', his act of self-overcoming in detaching himself from someone he loved, Caesar, in order to attain freedom from an idol. But the key point is that what is most important to us is frequently what is most hidden, and that it is the dramatist, cleaving tightly to action and experience, who shows this to be so.

To see the world dramatically, as Nietzsche wanted us to, is to refuse to theoreticise it, which is an evasion. It is also to affirm it. Nietzsche deeply mistrusted the sort of man Portia derided as 'the weeping philosopher' (*Merchant*, 1.2.47–8) – the kind who 'hears merry tales and smiles not' (1.2.46–7), and who seems to regret the world as an error. Wisdom generally, and especially sad wisdom, is suspect, Gratiano advises Antonio:

> Why should a man whose blood is warm within
> Sit like his grandsire cut in alabaster?
> Sleep when he wakes, and creep into the jaundice
> By being peevish? I tell thee what, Antonio –
> I love thee, and 'tis my love that speaks –
> There are a sort of men whose visages
> Do cream and mantle like a standing pond,
> And do a willful stillness entertain
> With purpose to be dressed in an opinion
> Of wisdom, gravity, profound conceit,
> As who should say, 'I am Sir Oracle,
> And when I ope my lips let no dog bark!' (1.1.83–94)

There is a good argument to be made that both Shakespeare and Nietzsche hold to an essentially comic, rather than tragic, understanding of existence – comedy born out of the spirit of tragedy, as it were. As Zarathustra says: 'I . . . believe only in a god who could dance. And when I saw my devil I found him serious, thorough, profound, and solemn: it was the spirit of gravity – through him all things fall.'[62] The essential thing is to be able to affirm existence. And that is, to return to my earlier theme, what any great dramatist does. As Nietzsche put it, the great founders of moralities and religions are like dramatic characters on the stage of human life:

> What is the meaning of these heroes on this stage? . . . They . . . promote the life of the species *by promoting the faith in life.* 'Life is worth living', each of them shouts, 'there is something to life . . .' Every time 'the hero' appeared on stage, something new was attained . . . Life and I and you and all of us became *interesting* to ourselves once again for a while.[63]

To look at the world, and all the men and women in it, as a stage, is above all to find it interesting, with strongly defined characters and fascinating action. Moreover, and to repeat, nothing can be taken away without marring the total effect. Would *King Lear* be the great play it is if Cordelia had relented at its opening? But if you think *Lear* is a supreme work of art then you have to accept each and every one of its contents. And you have to assent to their necessity: everything in the play had to happen as it does, or it would not be what it is. It is the same with our world, Nietzsche urges: affirming rather than cursing it involves accepting that it could not have been different – each character in it has had to follow his or her script. Wishing things otherwise is nonsensical.

The '*Irreligiosity of artists*' is something Nietzsche took for granted,[64] and there does indeed, to my mind at least, appear something irreligious about the way Shakespeare depicts the world (though it might be noted that Nietzsche simply ignores that ancient Christian theodicy that holds that the world, for all its faults, is the *best possible world* a Creator could come up with – a Creator, that is, who valued the very things Nietzsche does: freedom, adventure, risk, glamour, experience). There are many examples of this *joyful* wisdom in Shakespeare that one might close with, but the astonishingly beautiful description of the 'fierce vanities' of the Field of the Cloth of Gold, the famous meeting between Francis I and Henry VIII, in Shakespeare's and Fletcher's play on the Tudor monarch, will suffice (*The Famous History of the Life of King Henry the Eighth*, 1.1.54). Norfolk tells us that not to have been present at the meeting was to have 'lost / The view of earthly glory':

> Men might say,
> Till this time pomp was single, but now married
> To one above itself. Each following day

Became the next day's master, till the last
Made former wonders its. Today the French,
All clinquant, all in gold, like heathen gods,
Shone down the English; and tomorrow they
Made Britain India – every man that stood
Showed like a mine. (1.1.12–22)

One feels the language struggling to keep up with this magnificent scene, as each wonder is topped by another, and as the two kings ('suns – / For so they phrase 'em') engage in feats of arms going 'beyond thought's compass' (1.1.33–4, 36). This is indeed an ideal picture of 'heathen gods' – but there is actually, of course, nothing unearthly about it. It is, in fact, the engineered 'great sport' of the ambitious 'spiderlike' (1.1.47, 62) church politician Wolsey. But the human, all-too-human origin of the festivities ought not (we hear Nietzsche counselling us) detract from our delight in the spectacle. What else did you expect? What other world did you hope to live in?

Notes

1. Friedrich Nietzsche, *Twilight of the Idols, or How to Philosophize with a Hammer* (1888), in *The Anti-Christ, Ecce Homo, Twilight of the Idols, and Other Writings*, ed. Aaron Ridley, trans. Judith Norman (Cambridge: Cambridge University Press, 2005), p. 155.
2. Friedrich Nietzsche, *The Gay Science* (1882), ed. Bernard Williams, trans. Josefine Nauckhoff (Cambridge: Cambridge University Press, 2001), p. 94.
3. Ibid., p. 104.
4. Friedrich Nietzsche, *Ecce Homo: How to Become What you Are* (1888), in *The Anti-Christ and Other Writings*, pp. 92–3.
5. George Brandes, *Friedrich Nietzsche* (1909), trans. A.G. Chater (London: William Heinemann, 1915), p. 1.
6. Quoted in ibid., p. 1, n. 1.
7. George Brandes, *William Shakespeare: A Critical Study* (1898), vol. 1 (2 vols), trans. William Archer and Diana White (New York: Frederick Ungar, 1963), p. 133.
8. For Kaufmann, Shakespeare's 'un-Christian', 'tragic world view' goes hand-in-hand with 'a profound contempt for the mass of men'. See Walter Kaufmann, *From Shakespeare to Existentialism: An Original Study* (Princeton: Princeton University Press, 1959), pp. 5, 14, 12; generally pp. 1–24.
9. Friedrich Nietzsche, *The Case of Wagner: A Musician's Problem* (1888), in *The Anti-Christ and Other Writings*, p. 256.
10. Friedrich Nietzsche, *Human, All Too Human: A Book for Free Spirits* (1878), trans. R.J. Hollingdale (Cambridge: Cambridge University Press, 1996), p. 91.

11. Friedrich Nietzsche, *Nietzsche contra Wagner: From the Files of a Psychologist* (1888), in *The Anti-Christ and Other Writings*, p. 267.

12. Nietzsche, *Ecce Homo*, p. 72.

13. Friedrich Nietzsche, *Beyond Good and Evil: Prelude to a Philosophy of the Future* (1886), ed. Rolf-Peter Horstmann, trans. Judith Norman (Cambridge: Cambridge University Press, 2001), p. 8.

14. Eugen Fink, *Nietzsche's Philosophy* (1960), trans. Goetz Richter (London: Continuum, 2003), p. 47.

15. William Shakespeare, *Othello, the Moor of Venice*, in *The Complete Works of William Shakespeare*, ed. David Bevington, 6th edn (New York: Pearson Longman, 2009), 1.3.337. Subsequent references to Shakespeare are to this edition, and in the text.

16. Nietzsche, *Twilight of the Idols*, p. 159.

17. Friedrich Nietzsche, *Writings from the Early Notebooks*, ed. Raymond Geuss and Alexander Nehamas, trans. Ladislaus Löb (Cambridge: Cambridge University Press, 2009), p. 238.

18. Friedrich Nietzsche, *The Birth of Tragedy* (1872), in *The Birth of Tragedy and Other Writings*, ed. Raymond Geuss and Ronald Speirs, trans. Roland Speirs (Cambridge: Cambridge University Press, 1999), p. 33.

19. Nietzsche, *Human, All Too Human*, pp. 82, 255.

20. Nietzsche, *The Birth of Tragedy*, p. 5.

21. Friedrich Nietzsche, *Writings from the Late Notebooks*, ed. Rüdiger Bittner, trans. Kate Sturge (Cambridge: Cambridge University Press, 2003), p. 38.

22. Nietzsche, *Early Notebooks*, p. 51.

23. Ibid., p. 23.

24. Nietzsche, *The Birth of Tragedy*, p. 24.

25. Ibid., p. 40.

26. Friedrich Nietzsche, *The Dionysiac World View* (1870), in *The Birth of Tragedy and Other Writings*, p. 124.

27. Nietzsche, *Ecce Homo*, p. 109.

28. Friedrich Nietzsche, *Thus Spoke Zarathustra: A Book for None and All* (1883–85), trans. Walter Kaufmann (London and New York: Penguin, 1978), p. 323.

29. Friedrich Nietzsche, *Daybreak: Thoughts on the Prejudices of Morality* (1881), ed. Maudemarie Clark and Brian Leiter, trans. R.J. Hollingdale (Cambridge: Cambridge University Press, 1997), pp. 243–4.

30. See Nietzsche, *The Birth of Tragedy*, p. 106.

31. Samuel Johnson, 'Preface to Shakespeare' (1755), in *The Works of Samuel Johnson*, vol. 7, ed. Arthur Sherbo (New Haven: Yale University Press, 1968), p. 71.

32. William Hazlitt, *Selected Writings*, ed. Jon Cook (Oxford: Oxford University Press, 1991), p. 345.

33. Nietzsche, *The Case of Wagner*, p. 233.

34. Nietzsche, *Thus Spoke Zarathustra*, p. 13.

35. Nietzsche, *Twilight of the Idols*, p. 162.

36. Peter Holbrook, *Shakespeare's Individualism* (Cambridge: Cambridge University Press, 2010).

37. G. Wilson Knight, *Christ and Nietzsche: An Essay in Poetic Wisdom* (London and New York: Staples Press, 1948), pp. 158–9.
38. Ibid., p. 31.
39. Ibid., pp. 165, 208.
40. Ibid., pp. 219–21.
41. Ibid., p. 215.
42. G. Wilson Knight, *Neglected Powers: Essays on Nineteenth and Twentieth Century Literature* (London: Routledge & Kegan Paul, 1971), pp. 172, 179.
43. G. Wilson Knight, *Shakespeare and Religion: Essays of Forty Years* (New York: Clarion, 1967), p. 209.
44. Nietzsche, *The Birth of Tragedy*, p. 9.
45. Nietzsche, *Human, All Too Human*, p. 198.
46. Nietzsche, *The Gay Science*, p. 86.
47. Nietzsche, *Daybreak*, p. 45.
48. Ibid., p. 221.
49. Ibid.
50. Friedrich Nietzsche, *Unpublished Writings from the Period of* Unfashionable Observations, trans. Richard T. Gray (Stanford: Stanford University Press, 1999), p. 102.
51. Nietzsche, *Human, All Too Human*, p. 182.
52. Nietzsche, *Untimely Meditations* (1873–76), ed. Daniel Breazeale, trans. R.J. Hollingdale (Cambridge: Cambridge University Press, 1997), p. 207.
53. Michel de Montaigne, *The Complete Essays*, trans. M.A. Screech (London: Penguin, 1991), p. 928.
54. Nietzsche, *Late Notebooks*, p. 60.
55. Nietzsche, *The Gay Science*, p. 137.
56. Nietzsche, *Late Notebooks*, p. 59.
57. Nietzsche, *The Gay Science*, p. 139.
58. Nietzsche, *Human, All Too Human*, p. 91.
59. Ibid., p. 326.
60. Ibid., pp. 179–80.
61. Nietzsche, *The Gay Science*, pp. 93–4.
62. Nietzsche, *Thus Spoke Zarathustra*, p. 41.
63. Nietzsche, *The Gay Science*, pp. 28–9.
64. Nietzsche, *Human, All Too Human*, p. 68.

Chapter 5

Richard II's Silent, Tortured Soul

James A. Knapp

Just after his deposition in *Richard II*, Shakespeare's 'poet king' famously calls for a mirror in perhaps his most performative poetic gesture of the play. When Bolingbroke humours him by having an attendant produce the glass, Richard laments that the image offered in the mirror fails to reflect the depth of his sorrow:

> Hath sorrow struck
> So many blows upon this face of mine
> And made no deeper wounds? (4.1.278–9)[1]

In apparent disgust at its failure to register his grief, Richard casts the mirror down dramatically reenacting the deposition itself – his divine authority represented in the majestic image, 'the pompous body' of the king 'cracked in an hundred shivers' (4.1.251, 290). Unfazed, the usurping Bolingbroke belittles the 'moral' of Richard's high drama – 'see how quickly my sorrow hath destroyed my face' – with his observation that in breaking the glass Richard has only played with appearances: 'The shadow of your sorrow hath destroyed / The shadow of your face' (293–4).[2]

In Richard's response, Shakespeare offers what appears to be a characteristic gesture towards interiority. The newly deposed king – the simply mortal Richard – agrees with Henry, 'the silent king', that the face reflected in the mirror

> And these external manners of laments
> Are merely shadows to the unseen grief
> That swells with silence in the tortured soul. (297–8)

The use of analogy – 'shadows to' – rather than empirical description – 'shadows of' – emphasises the immaterial nature of Richard's grief.[3] But Richard's insistence that his 'grief lies all within', confuses the use of analogy with a material metaphor, begging the question: within *where*? It is tempting to identify in Richard's lines evidence of a modern form of subjectivity, one that anticipates Cartesian dualism. But the form of his analogy complicates the matter: his external laments are to his 'unseen grief' as shadows are to material things. The analogy places special pressure on the material: material things block light to cause shadows, and though shadows have no substance, they indicate an unseen material substance presumably accessible to sense from another perspective (e.g. when not looking at the shadow but the object producing it). Richard's 'unseen grief / That swells with silence in the tortured soul' is thus 'the substance' that creates the 'external manner of laments', the insubstantial shadows of his grief, though the only access to that substance is through the 'insubstantial' materiality of his external laments.[4] When Shakespeare would return to this idea at the beginning of *Hamlet*, he would sever the connection between the prince's interior grief 'which passeth show' and the 'trappings and the suits of woe', that are mere 'actions that a man might play' (1.2.84–6). For Richard the distinction is less clear, as he envisions his 'unseen grief' in sensuous terms. Richard's grief points less to the emergent interiority of modern subjectivity some find in *Hamlet* than to a difficult immateriality, the no*thing* that will finally release his suffering body at the end of the play, captured in his later lament that he, and indeed all men, 'with nothing shall be pleased till he be eased / with being nothing' (5.5.40–1).

In this chapter, I examine how Shakespeare stages Richard's struggle to read in his experience with the material world its immaterial other: the absent, divine, and conceptual, but also the *self*. Taking as a starting point Nietzsche's account of art arising from the productive opposition of Apollinian and Dionysian forces in *The Birth of Tragedy*, I then turn to phenomenology to explore how Shakespeare establishes the relationship between the material and immaterial in phenomenological rather than metaphysical (especially Cartesian) terms. In particular, I draw on Jean-Luc Marion's concept of givenness, especially as it relates to what he calls saturated phenomena. Attending to Richard's engagement with the world through the lens of phenomenology enables a reading that locates the play's dramatic power in its portrayal of Richard's tragedy as a consequence of his confrontation with the impossibility of metaphysical self-knowledge rather than a result of his political failures as they relate to the historical concerns of the sixteenth century.

History or Tragedy?

Due to the historical subject matter it treats – the ostensible origin of the devastating Wars of the Roses – scholars have often considered the play

as an Elizabethan answer to the question: 'What caused Richard's fall?'
In the past century, the range of critical explanations for Richard's fall
include E.M.W. Tillyard's 'Tudor myth' of history, Ernst Kantorowicz's
influential discussion of the medieval doctrine of the King's Two Bodies
and, more recently, the new historicist readings of Stephen Greenblatt,
Phyllis Rackin and others that depict Shakespeare's Richard as an
emblem of Elizabethan national trauma, recovery and nostalgia. Such
readings make it possible to view all of Shakespeare's historical plays
as stemming from the ideological collapse of a medieval form of political theology based on divine right, and the desire for either the system's
rehabilitation – Hal's willingness to 'pay the debt [he] never promised'
(*1 Henry IV*, 1.2.203) – or an alternative. In an important sense, then,
Shakespeare's histories are *about* political theology, and in particular
they are about the Elizabethan need to shore up the coherence of divine
right monarchy in relation to the facts of a national history that would
seem to call that concept into question.[5]

In addition to historical concerns, the question 'What caused Richard's
fall?' also raises the issue of the play's genre.[6] Though early commentators recognised tragic elements in the play, they largely denied that it
succeeded in producing a genuinely tragic effect due in large part to its
reliance on historical events. Samuel Johnson would conclude that the
play fails 'to affect the passions, or enlarge the understanding'.[7] Such
early critical assessments of the play, as John Halverson notes, did not
prevent a great many critics from arguing that we find in Richard something like the 'psychological complexity and development and . . . deep
awareness of the human condition' that we find in *Lear*.[8] The argument
for this version of Richard reaches its height in Jan Kott's claim that
'Just before being hurled into the abyss, the deposed king reaches the
greatness of Lear.'[9] To accept that Richard is a tragic hero in the mould
of Lear and Hamlet, requires that we take Richard's self-indulgent
poetics of suffering seriously, as the pathos of a man truly coming into
an awareness of his reality before our eyes. Halverson takes consider-
able care to point out that such a reading would need the support of
evidence for Richard's psychological complexity and awareness of the
human condition that is difficult to find in the text of the play. Richard's
tragedy may be a tragedy of history, but it is not, according to this view,
a human tragedy.

Convinced that the play does allow for a reading of Richard's fall as
a human tragedy, apart from any investment in the historical debates of
the age, I will suggest an alternative reading focused on Shakespeare's
exploration of Richard's material expression and immaterial experience of grief.[10] Beginning with Nietzsche's emphasis on lyric and choric

understanding in *The Birth of Tragedy*, I will turn to a reading of *Richard II* as a meditation on the collapse of the medieval scholastic (largely Aristotelian) account of grief and its consequences for early modern ethical subjectivity that points to a more modern, though still emergent, understanding of phenomenality itself.

Richard II and *The Birth of Tragedy*

As early as Walter Pater's reflections on the play's powerful lyricism, critics have noted the poetic character of Shakespeare's title character. In this section, I explore the philosophical implications of the distinction between the play's intelligible content – it's political, historical, or ideological content – and its aesthetic power – specifically its ability to catalyse an experience with the phenomenal world and onto-theology that exceeds conventional understanding. Nietzsche's theory of tragedy dramatically stages the distinction between drama as a guide to understanding and drama as a guide to living. I find the distinction useful, for attempts to account for the play's elaboration of political theology focus on its ability to make both the promise and the liability of divine right monarchy manifest to the understanding – to render the whole system of early modern political theology an object for contemplation.[11] Similarly, to find in Richard a tragic hero awakened to an understanding of the human condition is to bring the play under the power of the understanding, to make sense of a series of events that may make no sense. On the other hand, to focus on the play's aesthetic power as tragedy in Nietzsche's sense is to consider the play's emphasis on the individual's experience of that system and its relation to one's sense of being that can only be produced through art; it is to accept our experience of the play as another experience in our lives.

Nietzsche opens *The Birth of Tragedy* with the sweeping statement that 'the continuous development of art is bound up with the Apollinian and Dionysian duality'.[12] He then elaborates by tracing that development to its roots in Greek tragedy, locating the power of attic tragedy in the productive tension between these two impulses: the Apollinian towards the form of sculpture and dream as coherent vision, and ultimately abstraction; the Dionysian towards music, the incoherence of drunkenness, and ultimately the ecstatic physicality of nature, of human being embodied. The impulse towards the Apollinian is at its heart the impulse to make sense of the world, to make it conform to the understanding; the Dionysian always haunts this fragile truce with experience, as it beckons to the meaningless and absurd reality of existence always kept at bay by the order offered in the coherence of the Apollinian dream. The opposition is captured early on in Nietzsche's discussion of the Dionysian folk wisdom of Silenus in response to King Midas's question of what is best in the world for man: 'What is best of all is utterly beyond your reach: not to be born, not to *be*, to be *nothing*. But the second best for you is – to die soon.'[13] Nietzsche contrasts this impossible Dionysian wisdom to the Apollinian alternative offered in the figure of the Homeric hero: 'to die soon is worst of all for them, the next worst – to die at all'.[14] While the Dionysian truth is incomprehensible on its own terms, the Apollinian dream relies on a naive fiction; the Apollinian triumphs over 'an abysmal and terrifying view of the world and the keenest susceptibility to suffering through recourse to the most forceful and pleasurable illusions'.[15] The miracle of attic tragedy for Nietzsche is its ability to bring the real power of Dionysian recognition before our conscious apprehension through the Apollinian 'genius' of coherence, structure and calm. The crucial point is that this can be achieved only as a result of the productive tension that exists between the two forces.

When we first meet Richard, we meet a king who seems to be firmly immersed in the comforting illusion of divine right monarchy. In assuring Mowbray that he will be an impartial judge, Richard stresses his divinity in concrete terms:

> Now by my sceptre's awe I make a vow
> Such neighbour-nearness to our sacred blood
> Should nothing privilege him, nor partialize
> The unstooping firmness of my upright soul. (1.1.118–21)

Richard's authority here relies on a fine balance of the immaterial and the material – his 'sceptre's awe', 'sacred blood' and 'upright soul'. The power of the divine illusion – 'the unstooping firmness of [Richard's] upright soul' – effectively abnegates Richard of responsibility in the situation. His 'vow' is guaranteed by the awe wrought by his sceptre rather than his own personal integrity; he will not be partial to Bolingbroke because his character is fixed, defined by his soul's 'unstooping firmness'.

It is precisely this freedom from personal responsibility, underwritten by the providential view of history, that allows Richard to leave the precarious political situation to a higher power, 'Since we cannot atone you, we shall see / Justice design the victor's chivalry' (1.1.202–3). Richard's confidence in his divinity here appears to coincide with that of the more practical members of the ruling class depicted in the play. For example, Gaunt defends his refusal to revenge Gloucester's death by referring to the conceptual logic of divine right monarchy:

God's is the quarrel; For God's substitute,
His deputy anointed in his sight,
Hath caused his death; the which if wrongfully,
Let heaven revenge, for I may never lift
An angry arm against his minister. (1.2.37–41)

Gaunt's impulse is to follow the rules – his obedience is to the system. This is true of Bolingbroke and Mowbray as well, as we find each willing to place their fate in God's hands according to the logic of trial by combat. Yet Richard's unwillingness to accept the outcome of the trial is only our first clue that his belief in divine justice, and by extension his own divinely anointed position on earth, is not what it appears to be.

In preventing the combat, Richard rejects the providential outcome and opts instead for the politically expedient path. He acts on the knowledge that either outcome would reflect poorly on his political authority. This detail makes it difficult to argue that Richard's tragedy is a result of his eventual recognition that his sacred and mortal bodies are dissoluble.[16] It also ironises his bombastic speeches about the inviolable nature of his divine right, thus making him a poor defender of medieval political theology against the encroaching Machiavellianism of Bolingbroke. The Richard who returns from Ireland is famous for what appears to be an audacious, but sincerely felt, fantasy of divine right monarchy. The king himself recognises that his invocation to the earth to rise up against the rebel forces in defence of his divine authority will be met with disbelief:

Mock not my senseless conjuration, lords
This earth shall have a feeling, and these stones
Prove armed soldiers, ere her native king
Shall falter under foul rebellion's arms. (3.2.23–6)

His subsequent defence of his passivity takes the form of an extended metaphor of the king as the sun, a conventional use of the sun-symbol that leads up to what appears to be a self-assured defence of his divine authority:

Not all the water in the rough rude sea
Can wash the balm off an anointed king;
The breath of worldly men cannot depose
The deputy elected by the Lord.
For every man that Bolingbroke hath pressed
To lift shrewed steel against our golden crown,
God for his Richard hath in heavenly pay
A glorious angel. Then, if angels fight,
Weak men must fall, for heaven still guards the right. (3.2.54–62)

As memorable as this rallying cry for divine right monarchy is, Richard can't possibly believe what he is saying here.[17] Like his call for the earth to rise up in his defence, Richard's appeal to heaven is performative and self-consciously ironic. Immediately after this speech the king learns of further defections to the rebel side, prompting him to additional poetic musings: 'But now the blood of twenty thousand men / Did triumph in my face, and they are fled' (3.2.72–3). When Aumerle urges him to lead – 'Comfort my liege. Remember who you are', Richard's response is comic:

> I had forgot myself. Am I not king?
> Awake, thou sluggard majesty, thou sleep'st!
> Is not the king's name forty thousand names?
> Arm, arm, my name! A puny subject strikes
> At thy great glory. (3.2.79–82)

Can we really imagine that this is an introspective speech, that Richard has 'forgot' *himself* and then suddenly remembered *who he really was*? The reference to 'myself' is certainly not the 'self' that we identify with the modern subject. Rather, we stand witness to Richard's poetic performances, his lyric attempts to capture the proper response a king might have to the news of his impending loss – to approximate his lyric conception to the experience at hand. First believing that his favourites have joined the rebels, Richard responds with rage, 'O villains, vipers damned without redemption!' (124), only to turn melancholy at the clarification that they had been executed: 'Of comfort no man speak!' (3.2.140). This second slip into despair introduces his wonderful speech on the mortality of kings, a moment that appears to mark in Richard a growing awareness of the distinction between his mortal and sacred body:

> Throw away respect,
> Tradition, form, and ceremonious duty,
> For you have but mistook me all the while.
> I live with bread, like you; feel want,
> Taste grief, need friends. Subjected thus,
> How can you say to me I am a king? (3.2.168–73)

The temptation to identify this passage with Richard's sudden realisation of his mortality is understandable.[18] Richard's nod to common humanity calls to mind the great speeches on the subject that Shakespeare would later write for Shylock and Lear. We might imagine that, like Lear, his recognition of the monarchical illusion renders him a common man.[19] But this would be to impose on the play a reading of Richard's development from confident monarch to humble everyman that the text does not support.

Rather, what Richard seems to be doing at such moments is avoiding the kind of self-reflection that would put him face to face with the terrifying reality of his existence that Nietzsche identifies with Dionysian wisdom. Instead of reflecting on his inward soul or the reality of the political threat, Richard opts to hide behind the 'forceful and pleasurable illusions' of his lyric imagination: the anointed king defeating a rebel army first with the aid of the animated earth itself, then an army of angels, and finally – in the most abstracted fantasy – the power of his own name. These fantasies are all powerfully realised in his performative language. Richard, as the poet king, tries on different linguistic masks in the hopes of keeping the more absurd reality of his existence at bay. For the knowledge that haunts his self-understanding is not only that he is a man, like any other, clothed in the majesty of a king. What seems to worry Richard is that his only escape from his particular tragic life is beyond his reach – what is best for man according to Silenus's Dionysian wisdom: to not have been born, to not be, to be *nothing*. This is an impossibility that haunts Richard's speeches to the end of the play. His resignation that he will 'pine away' at Flint Castle (3.2.205), and weak request that Bolingbroke 'give [him] leave to go' 'so I were from your sights' (4.1.303, 305), pale in comparison to his continued, and emotionally charged, exploration of non-existence. If Richard does not gain knowledge of himself as a subject, he does seem to try; his many efforts to create for himself another self in language nevertheless lead him to the unfortunate conclusion that that his existence is irreversible:

> O God, O God, that e'er this tongue of mine,
> That laid the sentence of dread banishment
> On yon proud man, should take it off again
> With words of sooth! O, that I were as great
> As my grief, or lesser than my name,
> Or that I could forget what I have been,
> Or not remember what I must be now! (3.3.132–7)

Deposition as (anti-) Reversal

The impossibility of reversal is especially important to what follows, as critics have long viewed the deposition scene as an inverted ritual.[20] To find Richard's inner self by heeding the king's plea, in Act 3, to 'throw away respect, / Tradition, form and ceremonious duty' – thus revealing the mortal man who lives 'with bread' – would be to simply substitute one of Richard's poetic illusions for another: the divinely anointed monarch for the common mortal man. But Richard is aware that this divestment of monarchical ornament cannot change the fact that he is the king, just as he knows that Bolingbroke must reject his request to 'Give Richard leave to live till Richard die' (3.3.173).[21]

Considering Richard's awareness of the situation he faces, it is difficult to view the deposition scene as anything but political performance, for all involved. As many critics have noted, the highly ceremonial character of the scene recalls the opening scenes of the play in which Richard presides over the dispute between Mowbray and Bolingbroke. But the event of the deposition is of a different magnitude. Gary Kuchar highlights the theological implications of the scene as part of a process of desacralisation at work in the play: 'the dividing asunder of divine narrative from lived history'.[22] In the early scenes, Richard's understanding of events does not penetrate any deeper than the level of signification: Bolingbroke's banishment signifies his transgression of monarchical authority; it has no reality for Richard, who is willing to reduce the sentence by four years with a word, 'such is the breath of kings' (1.3.208). That Richard's word, 'the breath of kings', makes the world, suggests that the substance of things proceeds from Richard to the world, rather than the other way around.[23] The deposition represents the utter failure of this system of representation and, by extension, of Richard's entire world. One would imagine that this would mark the moment of tragic recognition, that, having lost everything, Richard will finally recognise his existential condition, and despair. But at this point in the play, Richard can only see such a failure through the language of his former illusions, as a negation of his monarchical fantasy. While his repeated claim that in losing his crown he becomes 'nothing' might otherwise indicate an existential crisis, an encounter with the abyss, Richard's use of 'nothing' is not radical but contingent, a matter of negation rather than non-existence: he is 'not king' rather than 'no thing'. Though he claims to fear what is to come, which he figures poetically as his descent into nothingness, what he actually says betrays his increasing awareness that no matter how often he lays linguistic claim to nothingness, he is able to come no closer to an understanding of what that could possibly mean. This is the awful truth of Silenus: that it is already too late.

For Nietzsche, the truly Dionysian man resembles Hamlet, 'both have once looked truly into the essence of things, they have gained knowledge, and nausea inhibits action; for their action could not change anything in the eternal nature of things . . . Knowledge kills action; action requires the veils of illusion.'[24] In this way, Shakespeare's characterisation of Richard does look forward to _Hamlet_, but not in the sense of a tragic reflection on the emerging awareness of an inner self. While Richard's passivity does seem to be a result of this recognition of powerlessness

– that his fall and Bolingbroke's rise are inevitable, 'What must the king do now? Must he submit?' (3.3.142) – his return to action in the deposition scene highlights his unwillingness to abandon the most absurd 'veils of illusion'. Richard's command, 'Give me the crown', forcefully introduces the following display of ceremony and ritual throughout which Richard is in complete control. His command of the power of ceremonial speech eclipses Bolingbroke's weak attempts to legitimate the proceedings by eliciting Richard's consent: 'I thought you had been willing to resign', and then more directly, 'Are you contented to resign the crown?' (4.1.179, 190). We know by this point that Bolingbroke understands the importance of ceremony, as he has revealed his intentions earlier to York and Northumberland:

> Fetch hither Richard, that in common view
> He may surrender. So we shall proceed
> Without suspicion. (4.1.146–8)

But his is a concern for the utility of ceremony for political purposes – the appearance of legitimacy – whereas Richard's insistence on unmasking ritual power as illusion derives from a concern with something beyond or intrinsic to earthly power, something more like an understanding of the system itself.

His emphasis on grief throughout the scene might be taken as a sign of remorse or regret, as the first evidence of contrition on the part of a failed monarch. The scene is dominated by the language of sorrow: Richard's tears first filling his bucket in the image of the well, then washing away the balm of the anointed king, and finally, obscuring his ability to see the articles of treason he is meant to read aloud before the assembly. Yet, his fascination with his grief is saturated with the language of material experience, betraying his obsession with its location and claim to reality, a claim that might provide him with hope that something other than his own soaring rhetoric can redeem him.

Before turning explicitly to the nature of Richard's experience with grief, it is important to look at the play's earlier meditation on the subject in the remarkable exchange between the queen and Bushy in 2.2:

> *Bushy:* Madam, your majesty is too much sad.
>   You promised when you parted with the King
>   To lay aside life-harming heaviness
>   And entertain a cheerful disposition.
>
> *Queen:* To please the King I did; to please myself
>   I cannot do it. Yet I know no cause
>   Why I should welcome such a guest as grief,

Save bidding farewell to so sweet a guest
As my sweet Richard. Yet again methinks
Some unborn sorrow, ripe in fortune's womb,
Is coming towards me; and my inward soul
With nothing trembles. At some thing it grieves,
More than with parting from my lord the king. (2.2.1–13)[25]

As theatrical foreshadowing, the queen's grief anticipates the news of Bolingbroke's increasing power and the inevitability of Richard's fall. But the terms in which she considers her experience of sorrow are particularly important when contrasted with Richard's meditation on grief. Scott McMillin identifies this scene as the first indication of the play's 'strange meditation on "nothing", a meditation which surfaces in patches of difficult writing about the "eye" or the "I"'.[26] He goes on to suggest that the passage emphasises something like feminine intuition: 'the weeping Queen's intuition about the approach of disaster [is right]. Through her tears she sees the truth.'[27]

For the present purpose I am interested in considering the queen's reflection on her grief as an example of the play's exploration of the relationship between the material and the immaterial. Specifically, her identification of the source of her grief as both 'nothing' and 'some thing' reveals her faith in an Aristotelian 'inward sense' like that described by the medieval Islamic philosopher Avicenna (Ibn Sīnā), whose significant influence on medieval scholastic thought – and especially the relation of the immaterial and material – is evident in Aquinas.[28] As Marina Paola Banchetti-Robino explains,

> Perception, for Ibn Sīnā, occurs when common sense receives sensible forms, that is, form without matter. This account of perception is directly inherited from Aristotle, for whom the reception of form without matter was interpreted by the Scholastics as 'intentional in-existence'. Once the form without matter has been received by common sense, the imaginative faculty retains these sensible forms. Thus, the estimative faculty receives intentions on the basis of the sensible forms, or form without matter, that are received by common sense and that are retained by the imagination. This, then, establishes the dependence of the faculty of estimation, or of intentionality, on sense perception. '[F]or all five senses, the reception of form without matter is interpreted as making the perceiver become like the form of the thing perceived ... Although the form is received stripped of its original matter, the abstraction from matter in sense-perception is not so complete as in the estimative faculty or in the intellect.'[29]

This remarkable conception of the inward sense helps explain the paradox of the queen's palpable experience arising from nothing – the fact that the queen's inward soul 'trembles' at nothing. The queen's sensitivity to inward perception is precisely what Richard lacks in the deposition scene; his only recourse to his grief is through the material changes he can experience sensually.

In a misguided attempt to placate the queen, Bushy fails to understand the relationship between inward and external sense. For Bushy, all is a matter of appearance, as he employs two different optical comparisons in his attempt – somewhat confusedly – to convince her that she misperceives her own grief:

> Each substance of a grief hath twenty shadows,
> Which shows like grief itself, but is not so;
> For sorrow's eye, glazed with blinding tears,
> Divides one thing entire to many objects;
> Like perspectives, which rightly gazed upon
> Show nothing but confusion, eyed awry
> Distinguish form: so your sweet majesty,
> Looking awry upon your lord's departure,
> Find shapes of grief, more than himself, to wail;
> Which, look'd on as it is, is nought but shadows
> Of what it is not. Then, thrice-gracious queen,
> More than your lord's departure weep not: more's not seen;
> Or if it be, 'tis with false sorrow's eye,
> Which for things true weeps things imaginary. (2.2.14–27)[30]

In the context of the scene's immediate action, the unsuspecting Bushy can only see Richard's departure from the queen for what it is, a temporary separation. Though the ominous reality of the Irish war as prelude to Bolingbroke's usurpation would have been on the minds of everyone in the audience, having not yet seen any external threat, Bushy attributes the queen's trepidation to the power of imagination. But the queen's acceptance of the intuition of her inward soul relies in part on the physical change in her body that she is unable to ignore:

> It may be so; but yet my inward soul
> Persuades me it is otherwise. Howe'er it be,
> I cannot but be sad; so heavy sad
> As, though on thinking on no thought I think,
> Makes me with heavy nothing faint and shrink. (2.2.28–32)[31]

Avicenna's account of the role of the inward sense in perception sheds light on the queen's puzzling experience by highlighting the concept of intention:

> There are some faculties of internal perception which perceive the form of the sensed things, and others which perceive the 'intention' thereof . . . The distinction between the perception of the form and that of the intention is that the form is what is perceived both by the inner soul and the external sense; but the external sense perceives it first and then transmits it to the soul, as for

example, when the sheep perceives the form of the wolf, i.e., its shape, form, and colour . . . As for the intention, it is a thing which the soul perceives from the sensed object without its previously having been perceived by the external sense . . . Now, what is first perceived by the sense and then by the internal faculties is the form, while what only the internal faculties perceive without the external sense is the intention.[32]

Reading with this account of the inward sense in mind, it is possible to see that the queen's 'heavy nothing' is properly understood to be an *immaterial substance*: 'no thing' that the external senses can perceive, but 'some thing at which [her soul quite reasonably] grieves'. According to Aquinas, Avicenna 'reaches the conclusion that one thing can legitimately exist in the spirit and be missing from external objects'.[33] This conclusion, which would play an important role in the ongoing debates over the nature of the soul as an immaterial substance into the early modern period, also explains how apperception and understanding – here something like intuition and intention – are related in the queen's experience of a mental state like grief that can arise from non-sensible stimuli.

The flatterer, Bushy, serves as the queen's foil in the scene, arguing that her elaborate explanation of grief born of nothing, ''Tis nothing but conceit' (2.2.33). In her response, ''Tis nothing less: conceit is still derived / From some forefather grief' (2.2.34), the queen identifies Bushy's dismissal of her experience with an Aristotelian understanding of imagination, that all ideas require a phantasm (or image) – that all conceits are based on something. Her grief, on the other hand, arises from an inward perception like that in Ibn Sīnā that is in turn made sensuously available to the outward senses: 'with heavy nothing I faint and shrink'. Bushy's account is the reverse: he seeks to give a name to her sadness by drawing on the plausible explanations gleaned from past experience. The queen laments the lack of precedent; unlike Bushy's conceit, 'derived from some forefather grief', the queen's:

> is not so,
> For nothing hath begot my something grief;
> Or something hath the nothing that I grieve:
> 'Tis in reversion that I do possess;
> But what it is, that is not yet known; what
> I cannot name; 'tis nameless woe, I wot. (2.2.35–40)[34]

The queen's perception is potential rather than actual at this point, though as McMillin and others have noted, the queen's woe does not remain nameless for long. The external guarantee comes in the form of Green's entrance with the news of Bolingbroke's landing at

Ravenspurgh, which immediately follows this speech. Yet before Green enters, the queen's inward sense impresses upon her inward soul a perception of the world not available to the outward sense.

For the present reading, the scene establishes the queen and her inward sense as a kind of chorus for the play, a fact that is of special importance when considering it in light of Nietzsche's understanding of tragedy.[35] Against the unrealistic flattery of Richard's favourites – Bushy's attempt to placate the queen with false hope – the queen's sincere fear of an unknown future threat leads to her grief, an understandable and more realistic response than Bushy's to the historical events at hand. Returning to the deposition scene, we find Richard faced with a similar evasion of reality in Bolingbroke's attempt to placate the doomed king with a pretty illusion: his effort to maintain the absurd fiction that Richard is content to resign the crown. Just before the inverted ritual of the deposition, Richard responds to Bolingbroke's question 'Are you contented to resign the crown?' with the iconic existential pun: 'Ay, no; no, ay; for I must nothing be' (4.1.202). Yet, unlike the queen, Richard is not responding to an intuition of the events to come, born of his inward sense; he is voicing his reluctance to give up the externally visible trappings of kingship. This becomes clear in the inverted ritual that follows: 'I give this heavy weight from off my head / And this unwieldy sceptre from my hand', and so on. Richard 'unkings' himself through a series of linguistic acts of negation, poetic fantasies in which the material signs of his kingship are de-materialised through the power of language, culminating in an utterance fully dependent on the materiality of language itself: '"God save King Henry", unkinged Richard says' (4.1.210).

The politically meaningful ritual of the deposition, in which Richard is in fact divested of his monarchical authority, leads up to the mirror scene, a theatrical echo, that Richard orchestrates as a substitute for the official 'paperwork' that would legitimise the transfer of power. Despite Northumberland's repeated insistence that Richard 'Read o'er this paper' to 'satisfy the Commons', the fallen king claims he can read truth elsewhere:

> They shall be satisfied. I'll read enough
> When they do see the very book indeed
> Where all my sins are writ, and that's myself. (4.1.263–5)

Richard ostensibly offers to go much further than simply admitting his guilt here: he promises to display his inward soul to all present.[36] Taking Richard at his word, what we are about to witness is the material manifestation of his contrite soul reflected in his face. He will reveal before all present 'a traitor with the rest' brought low by his own 'soul's consent'. No longer able to entertain the fiction of his earlier majesty, of the 'unstooping firmness of his upright soul', he will now face reality. The mirror scene that follows is thus all the more surprising for its utter failure as both political drama and tragic catharsis. The glass in which he hopes to see his soul's sorrow reflected in his face yields no such satisfaction. Where the queen 'faints' under the weight of her 'nothing' grief, Richard cannot see the material impression of his imagined sorrow:

> O flattering glass,
> Like to my followers in prosperity,
> Thou dost beguile me. (4.1.281–2)

Far from intuitive, the 'substance' of his experience must be learned, and in fact he thanks Bolingbroke for teaching him:

> I thank thee, King,
> For thy great bounty, that not only giv'st
> Me cause to wail, but teachest me the way
> How to lament the cause. (4.1.300–3)

This Richard does not appear to have changed in anything but the register of his poetic presentation. The supposedly assured Richard of the play's early scenes grounded his sense of self in discursive fictions of divine providence that the king himself was unwilling to trust in practice. Having exhausted the language of divine right, Richard now (unconvincingly) tries on the language introduced by the queen in 2.2 and implicitly repeated by Bolingbroke in his reference to the 'shadow' of Richard's grief. If Richard is to learn anything about his *self*, if we are to witness any form of tragic recognition, we must look to the final scene in the prison and his remarkable extended soliloquy on materiality and time.

Music as Saturated Phenomena

Finally alone, Richard meditates one last time on the theme of representation, and specifically on the ability of language to capture his experience of lived reality in time: 'I have been studying how I may compare / This prison where I live unto the world' (5.5.1–2). Richard's comparison of his prison cell to the world suggests the further comparison of the body (embodied, material existence) to a prison of the soul. The comparison appears to be Neo-Platonic: Richard hopes that by comparing his internment in prison to the freedom of the outside world he will come closer to an understanding of the relationship between mortal embodiment and the freedom of the soul's eternal salvation. But try as he might to make the comparison, he 'cannot do it' (5.5.5). Though Richard vows to 'hammer it out' we get the sense that he has finally reached the limits of his lyric sensibility. He remains stuck in the thrall of the powerful illusions of his own language:

> Sometimes am I king;
> Then treason makes me wish myself a beggar,
> And so I am. Then crushing penury
> Persuades me I was better when a king;
> Then am I kinged again, and by and by
> Think that I am unkinged by Bolingbroke,
> And straight am nothing. (5.5.32–8)

It is this flight of narrative fancy that brings him to his darkest observation, and what appears to be the tragic moral of the play:

> But whate'er I be,
> Nor I, nor any man that but man is,
> With nothing shall be pleased till he be eased
> With being nothing. (5.5.38–41)

Richard's stark conclusion represents the king at his most overtly existential, even nihilist.[37] Yet at the very moment when he contemplates non-being as essential truth, when he comes closest to recognising Silenus's wisdom, he is interrupted by music.[38]

It is here that I would like to turn to Marion's theory of givenness and the saturated phenomenon. Broadly speaking, Marion's philosophy is an attempt to account for the experience of Revelation in phenomenological terms.[39] Although, as a Catholic phenomenologist Marion's interest in Revelation is explicitly theological, in his philosophical work he seeks to extend the special case of Revelation to the whole of phenomenality and the phenomenal experience of revelation in general. In this sense, Marion hopes to include in his phenomenological project both the miraculous form of Revelation found in an example like Christ's Transfiguration as well as the mundane form of revelation suggested by the word's root, to 'reveal'.[40] In particular, Marion's philosophical interest is in returning to the relationship between intuition and intention in classical phenomenology (and especially Kant and Husserl) as a way of elucidating a theory of 'givenness' that moves beyond Heidegger's turn to Being and Levinas's emphasis on the Other.[41] By focusing on the notion of givenness in phenomenology, Marion elevates the nature of the given itself over that which is given to: for example, Husserl's transcendental ego, the receiving subject, conscious being, the other, and so on. Thinking givenness itself, Marion argues, would allow phenomenological analysis to consider experience that falls outside certain limitations evident in Husserl's initial formulation of phenomenology, specifically the limitations imposed by intention on intuition. For Husserl, intuition cannot exceed intention; the intention of the subject towards the object marks the limit to which the subject's intuition – or apprehension of the given – is confined.[42]

Marion is particularly interested in questioning why phenomenology cannot accommodate an experience in which intuition exceeds intention. The role of intuition in the philosophical tradition sheds important light on Marion's project and its potential relevance to early modern thought and to the present discussion of Shakespeare. As Jaakko Hintikka explains:

> the primary sense of intuition in Husserl is basically the pre-Kantian one. Intuition is not a special capacity of the human mind. Intuitiveness is simply a label for immediate knowledge of any sort. This immediately (intuitively?) explains the central role of *Anschauungen* in Husserl's overall phenomenological enterprise. This enterprise involved tracing back our conceptual world to its sources in immediate experience . . . The identification of the intuitive with what is immediately given to me means that intuition is simply a generic term for the stopping-points of the [phenomenological] reductions. It is the medium in which things are given to me. It is a collective term for the given.[43]

Hintikka highlights two aspects of Husserl's notion of intuition that are relevant to the present discussion. First, the idea that Husserl essentially recovered a pre-Kantian notion of intuition allows us to trace the concerns of phenomenology to their roots in early modern thought, specifically in so far as the early moderns were reassessing the Aristotelian, specifically scholastic, Thomist account of experience and revelation. If we are to follow Hintikka, Husserl's use of the term *Anschauung* (usually translated 'intuition') to designate 'immediate knowledge of any sort . . . a collective term for the given' helps trace the origins of phenomenology to the Aristotelian phantasma (appearing to the mind) and its appropriation in medieval scholastic philosophy as *intuito*.[44] Second, Hintikka's account draws attention to the centrality of 'the given' in Husserlian phenomenology, the feature that most interests Marion.

In *Richard II*, we have a striking example of the intertwining of phantasm and intuition in the form of the queen's foreboding feeling that 'Some unborn sorrow, ripe in fortune's womb, / Is coming towards' her. Though the queen can see no external cause, she feels it both mentally and physically in the image of childbearing and childbirth: 'my inward soul / With nothing trembles' and 'Makes me with heavy nothing faint and shrink'.[45] The queen's experience here seems to oscillate between a medieval form of Avicennian, physicalised intuition that co-opted the

Aristotelian figure of the phantasm as the conduit between the sensible and the intelligible, and a Thomist defence of the immateriality of the soul.[46] It is important here to contrast the queen's meditation on impending grief with Richard's. Whereas the queen identifies her consciousness of her grief as originating in her 'inward soul', Richard has to be reminded (by Bolingbroke) that this is where he should be looking. Rather than learning Bolingbroke's lesson on 'how to lament the cause' and looking into the recesses of his 'inward soul' to find his 'unseen grief', Richard begins with his 'brain': 'My brain I'll prove the female to my soul, / My soul the father' (5.5.6–7). Unlike the queen, whose 'inward soul' trembles in contemplation of nothing, Richard cannot think without a conceit. Even as he tries to imagine how his immaterial soul could become the source of a new understanding of his self, he turns to the most material of images: his soul as 'father' to his 'female' brain. This conceit leads him to imagine something like a forcible assault of soul on body – his male soul fathering 'breeding thoughts' in his female brain.

Richard's elaborate final image of himself transformed into a mechanical time-piece marks his reification as a material thing, symbolic of his failure to recognise himself as having anything like an internal, immaterial soul. In the process, he does appear to make a Cartesian move, attempting to 'think away' the material world in order to get a purer understanding of his self. Importantly, the music plays throughout the soliloquy. The music is the one thing that exceeds Richard's lyric comprehension, shaking him back to the jail cell from his fantastic metaphysical conceit as Bolingbroke's 'jack of the clock': 'This music mads me. Let it sound no more' (5.5.61). But he cannot will the music away; its effect on him is confusing:

> Yet blessing on his heart that gives it me
> For 'tis a sign of love, and love to Richard
> Is a strange brooch in this all hating world. (5.5.64–6)

Up to this point, Richard has been able to find language adequate to his immediate experience of the world; his intuition has not posed a threat to his intention. But this moment is different. Richard's confusion here reflects Nietzsche's claim that 'Language can never adequately render the cosmic symbolism of music, because music stands in symbolic relation to the primordial contradiction and primordial pain in the heart of the primal unity, and thereby symbolizes a sphere which is beyond and prior to all phenomena.'[47] For Nietzsche the 'primordial contradiction' is too much to experience, it leads to nausea, to fainting, which can only be held off by the imagination, by a return to illusion. But for Marion such an event marked by excess is 'saturated', overflowing intuition, and leading to revelation: 'Determining the saturated phenomenon as irregardable amounts to imagining the possibility that it imposes itself on sight with such an excess of intuition that it can no longer be reduced to the conditions of experience (objecthood), therefore to the I that sets them.'[48] When faced with such an irregardable experience, one that foregrounds the conditions of experience themselves, the question of the limits of experience – the question that has preoccupied Richard throughout the play – becomes irrelevant. Here, that which is given to experience is given as 'pure givenness, precisely because it no longer discerns any objectifiable given therein'.[49] Marion uses the example of music:

> It falls to music, or rather to listening to music, to provide privileged occurrences of this sense of the phenomenon . . . A memory of previous performances no doubt allows me to identify the melody more quickly and to assess the orchestral ensemble, but it does not allow me to abolish the arising, therefore the event. The music offers the very movement of its coming forward, its effect on me who receives it without producing it, in short, its arising without real content. Consequently, it comes upon me in such a way that it affects me directly as pure givenness mediated by almost no objectifiable given, and therefore imposes upon me an actuality immediately its own . . . Let me name this phenomenological extremity where the coming forward exceeds what comes forward a *paradox*.[50]

Likewise Richard's reaction to the music seems to rise from his inability to contain it conceptually: though he recalls that music is known to cure madness, in his case he fears the opposite. Despite his negative reaction, Richard accepts its gift as a sign of love. And contemplating this gift, Richard comes face to face with a paradox: love in 'this all hating world'. Though he still seeks to materialise the experience, calling it a 'strange brooch', Richard's momentary contemplation of the gift of music brings him the closest he will come to a revelation of the immaterial, through the excess of intuition that Marion identifies with the saturated phenomenon. In wishing a blessing on the 'heart that gives it me' Richard momentarily opens himself to the possibility of the other person outside the prison of language. It occurs, phenomenologically speaking, in Richard's experience with the temporality of the music, at the only moment in the play when he is alone, when the music impinges upon his experience, distracting him from his linguistic conceit. To this point Richard has consistently tried to impose his consciousness on the world, to render meaningful the objects of his intentional consciousness. But that may not be the subject Shakespeare gives us in Richard's experience with the music. As Marion argues, if the 'subject' is defined as constituting objects, then it can only objectify the Other (Descartes, perhaps Sartre) or appresent him in ordinary inter-objectivity and therefore miss him as such (Husserl). If by contrast, he accomplishes this purely by his own self-resolution, he comes only across the Other according to his own-for-the-Other, without joining with him (Heidegger). It's entirely different with the gifted: defined as he who receives and receives himself from the given, he can receive, according to the ordinary procedures of givenness (no predetermined horizon, no a priori principle, no constitution), among other givens . . .[51]

Only alone and presented with the ephemeral temporality of music can Richard experience the phenomenal world in its plenitude, unpopulated by the objects of his imaginative mind – the world given to his experience in the name of love ('a blessing on the heart that gives it me!'). In this solitary space, and only for a moment, Richard is '[no] longer concern[ed with] intersubjectivity or interobjectivity, but inter-givenness'.[52] Marion calls 'intergivenness' one of the most 'advanced developments' of phenomenology, and that which opens philosophy to the concept of love by allowing for the revelation of the Other 'in his unsubstitutible particularity'.[53]

Of all Shakespeare's tragic heroes, Richard is quite possibly the one we would least expect to recognise givenness in Marion's sense. And yet the king's surprising reception of the gift of music in the final moments of his life is crucial to the play's aesthetic power. The moment is fleeting. In the lines that follow, and even as he finally takes action against his murderers and gives up his life, Richard falls back on the ineffectual poetic conceits he rehearsed through the play – first condemning his horse for treason and then urging his soul to ascend to heaven while his 'gross flesh sinks downward, here to die' (5.5.112). Though Richard's final defiance of his would-be assassins fails to raise him up to the level of the tragic hero, his ability, albeit momentarily, to receive the gift of love and accept its paradox may help explain the feeling that in his depiction of Richard's fall Shakespeare offered us something more than an exploration of history or tragedy as the deserved end of a weak monarch or the consequences of a blindness to self-knowledge.

Notes

1. Unless otherwise indicated, references to Shakespeare follow *The Norton Shakespeare*, ed. Stephen Greenblatt, Walter Cohen, Jean E. Howard and Katherine Eisaman Maus (New York: Norton, 1997).
2. The scene has attracted a mountain of critical attention. For some of the studies that share my interests here, see in particular, Scott McMillin,

'Shakespeare's *Richard II*: Eyes of Sorrow, Eyes of Desire', *Shakespeare Quarterly*, 35 (1984), pp. 40–52; Ernst H. Kantorowicz, *The King's Two Bodies: A Study in Medieval Political Theology* (1957; Princeton: Princeton University Press, 1997); Christopher Pye, *The Regal Phantasm: Shakespeare and the Politics of Spectacle* (London: Routledge, 1990); Philip Lorenz, 'Christall Mirrors: Analogy and Onto-Theology in Shakespeare and Francisco Suarez', *Religion and Literature*, 38 (2006), pp. 101–19; and Gary Kuchar, *The Poetry of Religious Sorrow in Early Modern England* (Cambridge: Cambridge University Press, 2008), pp. 31–77.

3. On analogy in the play see, Lorenz, 'Christall Mirrors', pp. 108–19.
4. Richard's conclusion, 'There lies the substance' (line 300), further complicates an already difficult negotiation between the material and immaterial, as the line could be read to suggest that the soul is substance and that the grief is thus embodied in the substance of the soul; or, Richard could mean that the substance of his speech lies in recognising the distinction between his immaterial grief and the visible laments that can never truly represent it.
5. The revival of *Richard II* in support of the Earl of Essex's ill-fated rebellion is only the most overt reminder during Shakespeare's career of the importance of representation in maintaining monarchical legitimacy. Even Leeds Barroll in an essay questioning the connection between the Essex revolt and the play admits: 'That Richard II was a suggestive subject in these years is, I think, beyond debate'. See his 'A New History for Shakespeare and His Time', in Kirby Farrell (ed.), *Critical Essays of Shakespeare's Richard II* (New York: G.K. Hall, 1999), p. 105.
6. When the play first appeared in quarto in 1597, it bore the title *The Tragedy of King Richard the Second*. A quarter century later, the Folio identified the play with the more neutral title, *The Life and Death of King Richard II*.
7. Johnson quoted in Harold Bloom (ed.), *William Shakespeare's Richard II: Modern Critical Interpretations* (New York: Chelsea House, 1988), p. 4. Some 35 years later Charles Dibdin would repeat the claim, suggesting that, 'we cannot trace in it his usual force, either as to the characters or the language'. Quoted in Charles Forker (ed.), *Richard II: Shakespeare The Critical Tradition* (Cambridge: Cambridge University Press, 1998), p. 90.
8. John Halverson, 'The Lamentable Comedy of *Richard II*', in Farrell (ed.), *Critical Essays*, p. 262.
9. Kott quoted in ibid., p. 263. Of course most critics are not willing to go this far. Though Ruth Nevo also compares Richard to Lear, hers is a qualified comparison: at the end of the play, she argues, Richard is 'reduced to something as near as the impure tragedy of the histories will get to unaccommodated man', but his resistance to the murderers 'is the simplest kind of catharsis'. See Ruth Nevo, 'The Genre of *Richard II*', in Bloom (ed.), *Critical Interpretations*, p. 35.
10. I would like to stress that my argument is that the power of the play does not require an *investment* in the historical issues with which it engages. This is not to suggest that the play does not require some knowledge of these same historical issues.
11. This is in keeping with the Elizabethan belief that the proper use of history was instruction.

12. Friedrich Nietzsche, *The Birth of Tragedy and The Case of Wagner*, trans. Walter Kaufmann (New York: Vintage, 1967), p. 33.
13. Ibid., p. 42, emphasis original. The story is related by Plutarch, and Kaufmann notes the repetition in Sophocles, *Oedipus at Colonus*.
14. Ibid., p. 43.
15. Ibid.
16. See Kantorowicz, *The King's Two Bodies*.
17. In his early edition of the play Nahum Tate gave this speech to Carlisle, rendering it, in Forker's terms, a 'choric expression of royalist orthodoxy', rather than a reflection on Richard's belief in divine right. See Forker (ed.), *Richard II*, p. 3.
18. See, for example, Dorothea Kehler, 'King of Tears: Mortality in *Richard II*', *Rocky Mountain Review of Language and Literature*, 39:1 (1985), pp. 7–18.
19. This was Pater's sense of the play, and of Shakespeare's historical kings generally: 'Shakespeare's kings are not, nor are meant to be, great men: rather, little or quite ordinary humanity, thrust upon greatness, with those pathetic results, the natural self-pity of the weak heightened in them into irresistible appeal as the net result of their royal prerogative.' Quoted in Forker (ed.), *Richard II*, p. 298.
20. Pater calls the mirror scene an 'inverted rite'; the king 'perform[s] a mock undoing of precisely what cannot be un-done: the anointing that made him a sacred king'. Quoted in Kantorowicz, *The King's Two Bodies*, p. 36.
21. His handling of the murder of Gloucester and its consequences indicates that he is aware of the political reality that Northumberland must explain to the queen in response to her plea for Bolingbroke to spare Richard's life: 'That were some love, but little policy' (5.2.84).
22. Kuchar, *Religious Sorrow*, p. 61.
23. Kuchar argues that Richard 'begins the play presuming a continuity between word and thing, intention and substance, [but] he ends it by recognizing an irremediable gap between them' (ibid., p. 59). I agree with Kuchar's initial premise, but come to a different conclusion about the resolution of the play.
24. Nietzsche, *Birth of Tragedy*, p. 60.
25. The Oxford editors follow the less authoritative Folio reading in this passage, changing 'with' to 'at' in line 12. I follow the Riverside edition here.
26. McMillin, 'Eyes of Desire', p. 40.
27. Ibid., p. 42. Also see Kuchar, *Religious Sorrow*, on the play's depiction of tears as representative of the tradition of religious sorrow. The queen's ability to see truth through tears is clearly an example of this tradition. However, as I will discuss below, Shakespeare contrasts the queen's tears to Richard's in the deposition scene.
28. Avicenna's medical works continued to be used as textbooks in Europe through the end of the sixteenth century. On the inward sense see Daniel Heller-Roazen, *The Inner Touch: Archaeology of a Sensation* (New York: Zone, 2009): 'Avicenna cast the inner power not only as the foundation of all the senses but also as their center, the point from which they all "emanated", engendered in the shared procession from a primary power' (p. 154).

29. Marina Paola Banchetti-Robino, 'Ibn Sīnā and Husserl on Intention and Intentionality', *Philosophy East and West*, 54 (2004), p. 74. The quote within the quote is Richard Sorabji, 'From Aristotle to Brentano: The Development of the Concept of Intentionality', in Henry Blumenthal and Howard Robinson (eds), *Aristotle and the Later Tradition*, Oxford Studies in Ancient Philosophy, Supplementary volume (Oxford: Clarendon Press, 1991), p. 236. Banchetti-Robino concludes that the unique theory has its roots in Avicenna's medical training: 'Therefore, since it can be shown that, for Ibn Sīnā, there is a physiological element to the reception and retention of the sensible forms of external objects, one would have to conclude that intentionality has, ultimately, physiological origins' (p. 74).

30. See Pye, Ernest B. Gilman, *The Curious Perspective: Literary and Pictorial Wit in the Seventeeth Century* (New Haven: Yale University Press, 1978), and McMillin on this passage.

31. The Oxford emendation and punctuation are again inferior here. I follow the Riverside, based on the quartos.

32. Ibn Sīnā, *Kitab al-Najat*, quoted in Banchetti-Robino, 'Ibn Sīnā and Husserl', p. 72.

33. Aquinas, quoted in ibid.

34. For a discussion of the temporal quality of the legal term 'reversion' and its relation to substance, see Bradin Cormac, 'Shakespeare Possessed: Legal Affect and the Time of Holding', in Paul Raffield and Gary Watt (eds), *Shakespeare and the Law* (Oxford and Portland, OR: Hart Publishing, 2008), pp. 83–100.

35. Nietzsche identified the origins of tragedy with the musicality of the dithyrambic chorus.

36. For the relation of this performance to one of James's before parliament, see Lorenz, 'Christall Mirrors', pp. 102–3.

37. Harold Bloom identifies this line as 'the earliest Shakespearean litany of nihilism, predating *Much Ado About Nothing* and prophesying Hamlet, Iago, and Leontes'. Harold Bloom, *Shakespeare: The Invention of the Human* (New York: Riverhead Books, 1998), p. 269. See Kirby Farrell, 'Introduction: Play, Death, and History', in Farrell (ed.), *Critical Essays*', pp. 1–22.

38. Here Nietzsche might identify the moment when art, that 'saving sorceress' appears in the form of the 'satyr chorus of the dithyramb' (*Birth of Tragedy*, p. 60). In Francis Golffing's translation, the role of the dithyramb is to 'turn his fits of nausea into imaginations with which it is possible to live' (p. 52). On the importance of the music see Richard Altick, 'Symphonic Imagery in *Richard II*', in Paul M. Cubeta (ed.), *Twentieth Century Interpretations of Richard II* (Englewood Cliffs, NJ: Prentice Hall, 1971), pp. 66–81; and Pieter D. Williams, 'Music, Time and Tears in *Richard II*', *The American Benedictine Review*, 22:4 (1971), pp. 472–85.

39. Marion develops his theory of saturated phenomena in *Being Given: Toward a Phenomenology of Givenness*, trans. Jeffrey L. Kosky (Stanford: Stanford University Press, 2002) and *In Excess: Studies of Saturated Phenomenon*, trans. Robyn Horner and Vincent Berraud (New York: Fordham University Press, 2004). In *Being Given* he writes that 'the very concept of Revelation belongs by right to phenomenality' (p. 5). His project

is a radical development in phenomenology considering that his work seeks both a return to a grounding of phenomenological inquiry in the things themselves and a call to move beyond a Husserlian conception of the limits of phenomenological engagement with the object.

40. See Merold Westphal, 'Saturated Phenomenon as Transfiguration', *Journal of Philosophy and Scripture*, 1 (2003), pp. 26–8.
41. Heidegger turned attention from the experience of phenomenal objects in general to the experience of being, whereas Levinas questioned the turn to being and urged a turn to the experience of the other.
42. In Banchetti-Robino's explanation: 'Husserl tells us that all consciousness is necessarily actionally 'directed' towards an 'object'. In other words, all consciousness is necessarily consciousness of something. It is this peculiarity of mental processes that is known as intentionality' ('Ibn Sīnā and Husserl', p. 76).
43. Jaakko Hintikka, 'The Notion of Intuition in Husserl', *Revue Internationale de Philosophie*, 224 (2003), pp. 173–4.
44. The notion of the phantasm was extremely muddled in early modern England. Though attributed to Aristotle, the phantasm was used inconsistently, often without any indication of an external stimulus, as most modern Aristotle scholars believe the term was originally intended. The phantasma (most often translated as 'image') was associated with the faculty of the imagination (an equally complex and unsettled category in early modern England), but wasn't always identical with it. Shakespeare uses the term 'phantasma' only once, in *Julius Caesar*:

> Between the acting of a dreadful thing
> And the first motion, all the interim is
> Like a phantasma or a hideous dream.
> The genius and the mortal instruments
> Are then in counsel; and the state of man,
> Like to a little kingdom, suffers then
> The nature of an insurrection. (2.1.63–9)

Editors often gloss the term in this passage as 'hallucination', but it is more accurate to understand the early modern phantasm as an intermediary. It is the medium through which the rational soul interacts with the material body, and by extension the world. For Aristotle the intermediary was a product of perception, and thus external to the soul: 'if one perceived nothing one would learn and understand nothing . . . whenever one is contemplating, it is some image that one is contemplating' (*De Anima*, 210). The word translated as 'image' here is 'phantasma'. The externality of the phantasma was called into question by early modern thinkers who, having inherited the term from the complex and often contradictory medieval philosophical tradition (both scholastic and Islamic), hoped to clarify the relationship between the immaterial (and thus eternal) soul and the extended, material body. I am suggesting that Shakespeare drew on the rich and confused swirl of thought surrounding this moment of transition in his exploration of perception, images, illusions, imagination, thought and nothingness.
45. See McMillin's excellent discussion in his 'Eyes of Desire' of the theme of childbirth here and elsewhere in the play.

46. Aquinas's theory of the soul is complex, as it includes both a material and an immaterial mode of being (based on the idea that the soul can be both a subsistent and an inherent form depending on its mode of being). This theory relies on the immateriality of intellection in Aquinas, one that draws on his argument that sense cognition and intellectual cognition (cognition in the brain and cognition in the soul) have a different relation to materiality and immateriality. See Gyula Klima, 'Aquinas's Proofs of the Immateriality of the Intellect from the Universality of Human Thought', *Proceedings of the Society for Medieval Logic and Metaphysics*, 1 (2001), pp. 19–28, and Mortimer J. Adler, 'Sense Cognition: Aristotle vs. Aquinas', *The New Scholasticism*, 42 (1968), pp. 578–91.
47. Nietzsche, *Birth of Tragedy*, p. 55.
48. Marion, *Being Given*, p. 215.
49. Ibid., p. 216.
50. Ibid.
51. Ibid., p. 323.
52. Ibid.
53. Ibid., pp. 323–4.

Part Two

That Wide Gap

Chapter 6

Is Othello Jealous? Coleridge and Russell contra Wittgenstein and Cavell

Andrew Cutrofello

The word 'cuckold' appears in seventeen of Shakespeare's plays (eighteen if we count *As You Like It*'s 'cuckoldy' [3.2.82]), while the fear of being cuckolded is alluded to in most, if not all, of the others. Many of Shakespeare's plots revolve around the threat of marital infidelity, including those of *Much Ado About Nothing*, *The Merry Wives of Windsor*, *Troilus and Cressida*, *Othello*, *The Winter's Tale*, and *Cymbeline*. In each of these plays a male lover comes to believe, usually falsely, that his partner has been unfaithful to him.[1] Collectively, they might be characterised as dramas of male jealousy. But is 'jealousy' the right word? Coleridge thought it was a mistake to regard Othello as jealous. In his Table Talk he is reported to have said,

> I do not think there is any jealousy, properly so called, in the character of Othello. There is no predisposition to suspicion . . . Desdemona very truly told Emilia that he was not jealous, that is, of a jealous habit, and he says so as truly of himself. Iago's suggestions, you see, are quite new to him; they do not correspond with anything of a like nature previously in his mind.[2]

Coleridge contrasts Othello with Leontes, the patently jealous lover of *The Winter's Tale*. Leontes has no Iago. If anyone deceives him, it is Leontes himself. His jealousy predisposes him to invent grounds for suspicion about Hermione. According to Coleridge, Othello is not at all like Leontes. Other critics, including Stanley Cavell, have felt differently. If Othello weren't prone to suspicion in the first place, they argue, he would have responded differently to Iago's insinuations. Consider the different ways in which Page and Ford respond to similar promptings in *The Merry Wives of Windsor*. When Pistol and Nym inform them that Falstaff has sent amorous proposals to their wives, Page simply refuses to believe that his wife would have an affair, but Ford is not so sure about his. While insisting, 'I do not misdoubt my wife', he immediately adds, 'A man may be too confident' (2.1.185–7).[3] This second reflection may be characterised as 'one thought too many', to borrow a relevant phrase from Bernard Williams. Williams observes that a man who doesn't spontaneously rush to rescue his wife from perceived harm but first considers whether doing so is consistent with his moral principles is guilty of having 'one thought too many'.[4] Ford's 'one thought too many' consists in the consideration that a man's wife ought to be defended against a charge of infidelity only if she is truly faithful to her husband. From here it is a short step to wondering whether Mistress Ford deserves to be defended. Does Othello, like Ford, have one thought too many? Or is he simply a victim of Iago's cunning, a more sorely tested double of Page?

When Iago seeks to elicit Othello's jealousy by allegedly warning him against it ('O, beware, my lord, of jealousy!'; 'Good God, the souls of all my tribe defend / From jealousy!' [3.3.165, 175–6]), Othello replies:

> Why? Why is this?
> Think'st thou I'ld make a life of jealousy?
> To follow still the changes of the moon
> With fresh suspicions? No! to be once in doubt
> Is once to be resolv'd. Exchange me for a goat,
> When I shall turn the business of my soul
> To such exsufflicate and blown surmises,
> Matching thy inference. (3.3.176–83)

> No, Iago,
> I'll see before I doubt; when I doubt, prove;
> And on this proof, there is no more but this –
> Away at once with love or jealousy! (3.3.189–92)

Othello forswears jealousy not by ruling out the possibility of Desdemona's infidelity, but by refusing to linger in the uncertainty that is jealousy's breeding ground should any ground for doubt about her fidelity ever arise. This might seem to be a Ford-like attitude to take, but since only empirical evidence could provide Othello with a ground for doubt it is closer to that of Page. Unlike Ford, Othello doesn't have one thought too many. *Pace* Coleridge, he isn't prone to suspicion, though he is susceptible to doubt. Iago perceives this. What he exploits isn't Othello's jealousy but his potential scepticism – his predisposition not to suspicion but to doubt.

To suggest that there is a difference between jealousy and scepticism is to question Cavell's interpretation of the play. Cavell takes jealousy and scepticism to be two sides of the same psychic coin. Contra Coleridge, he argues that Othello is jealous, and that his jealousy 'allegorizes (or recognizes)' 'what philosophy knows as doubt'.[5] On this interpretation, any way in which Iago exploits Othello's predisposition to doubt is a way in which he exploits Othello's jealousy. Cavell bases his interpretation partly on a reading of *Othello* and partly on a reading of Descartes' *Meditations*. In his First Meditation, Descartes professes to have good provisional reasons for distrusting the evidence of his senses. For all he knows, he could be mistaken in thinking that the world has the empirical characteristics that it seems to have. Perhaps he is being deceived by an all-powerful evil genius. Eventually, he resolves his doubts by purporting to prove that he himself exists as a thinking thing, and that there is a benevolent God who guarantees the truth of his clear and distinct perceptions. Such, at any rate, is Descartes' official story. Cavell questions Descartes' true motivations and the significance of his professed solution to the problem of scepticism. Why, Cavell wonders, would anyone doubt the existence of the world in the first place? Why would anyone doubt the existence of other people? Perhaps, Cavell conjectures, to avenge an obscure and indistinct injury: 'skepticism's "doubt" is motivated not by (not even where it is expressed as) a (misguided) intellectual scrupulousness but by a (displaced) denial, a self-consuming disappointment that seeks world-consuming revenge'.[6] Descartes smothers the world as Othello smothers Desdemona. Conversely, Othello smothers Desdemona as Descartes smothers the world. According to Cavell, what troubles Othello isn't uncertainty as to whether Desdemona exists; on the contrary, he is troubled by the certainty that she does exist: 'Nothing could be more certain to Othello than that Desdemona exists . . . is separate from him; other. This is precisely the possibility that tortures him.'[7] Cavell concludes that what makes Othello susceptible to Iago's deception is that he is unconsciously looking for a pretext for killing her. If this is jealousy, then the nature of jealousy – like that of scepticism – must be reconceived. Something like scepticism underlies Othello's jealousy, while something like jealousy underlies Descartes' scepticism. Less paradoxically, scepticism and jealousy are two forms of the same psychological complex, namely, an inability to tolerate someone else's independent existence. Departing from the letter of the play, Cavell speculates that Othello's complex was activated when he and Desdemona consummated their marriage – that is, when, in closest possible physical proximity, he was forced to acknowledge that the living Desdemona was not, and never could be, an extension of himself. The tragedy to which he eventually succumbs is rooted not in Iago's dishonesty, but in his own disavowal of his dim awareness that Iago's allegations must be false. As Cavell puts it, Othello is '*trying* . . . to believe' Iago.[8] Like Descartes' imaginary evil genius, Iago provides Othello with a mere pretext for spinning his own semi-delusional fantasy. Hence the psychological distance between Othello and Leontes is not as wide as Coleridge presumed. On the contrary, it seems they suffer from exactly the same pathological complex.

Fascinating as this interpretation is, it has the curious effect of removing Othello from his play and consigning him, like Descartes, to a heated room – as if the play were, literally, a closet drama. By reducing Iago to a mere pretext for Othello's solitary meditations, Cavell minimises, if not altogether eliminates, Iago's agency. Equally important, he overlooks the fact that Shakespeare represents Iago himself as a jealous husband who is bent on infecting Othello with the same self-destructive passion. The fact that the play contains more than one character who experiences doubts about his partner's fidelity (three, if we count Bianca) gives it a dramatic complexity that goes beyond the solitary Cartesian model. Factoring in Iago's agency doesn't necessarily undermine Cavell's fundamental insight, namely, that there is a deep connection between jealousy and scepticism, but it might require us to revise our understanding of that connection.

Cavell's views about scepticism are based on those of Wittgenstein. As Cavell interprets him, Wittgenstein thinks that scepticism about the existence of other people is a permanent possibility in human relations, one that calls not for refutation but for a special type of acknowledgement. To cope with the threat of scepticism, we must learn to acknowledge others as others. Acknowledgement is not the same thing as knowledge. Epistemically modest, acknowledgement involves shifting from thinking *about* someone or something to conversing *with* someone or something. Cavell's Wittgensteinian response to the problem of scepticism runs counter to that of Bertrand Russell. Russell's conception of the problem is based on his distinction between knowledge by acquaintance and knowledge by description. Knowledge by acquaintance is direct and incorrigible; it is the kind of knowledge we are supposed to have about our own mental states. Knowledge by description is indirect and corrigible; it is what we rely upon when we aren't in a position to be directly acquainted with something, such as the contents of other people's minds.[9] Russell gives the example of Othello's relationship to Desdemona's love for Cassio:

> When Othello believes that Desdemona loves Cassio, the corresponding fact, if his belief were true, would be 'Desdemona's love for Cassio'. This would be a fact with which no one could have acquaintance except Desdemona; hence in the sense of self-evidence that we are considering, the truth that Desdemona loves Cassio (if it were a truth) could only be self-evident to Desdemona.[10]

Since Othello cannot be acquainted with the quality of Desdemona's feelings, he can never be certain whether or not she loves Cassio. His lack of certainty is his potential for scepticism. Like Wittgenstein, however, Cavell resists Russell's idea that each of us has 'privileged access' to our own mental states. If scepticism about the contents of other people's minds remains a permanent possibility, it is not because each of us has a private mental theatre. Othello may be uncertain about whether or not Desdemona loves Cassio, but he isn't uncertain for the reason Russell alleges. His scepticism is rooted not in his lack of direct acquaintance with Desdemona's feelings, but in his inability to deal with the plain fact that she has feelings. As we have seen, it is Othello's certainty that Desdemona has feelings that Cavell takes to be the basis of his 'sceptical' jealousy. There are, however, two problems with Cavell's Wittgensteinian interpretation of the play. First, it overlooks the manner in which Iago exploits Othello's realisation that he can never be directly acquainted with the contents of Desdemona's heart. Second, it displaces onto Othello a jealousy that is properly Iago's.

The first sign of Iago's jealousy occurs in his report to Roderigo that Othello has given the lieutenancy – literally, the placeholdership – to Cassio rather than to Iago. Cassio has the place that Iago wishes he had. In this sense Iago might be described as envious rather than jealous, but envy and jealousy are close cousins, always being about placeholders of one sort or another. At the end of Act I we learn that Iago fears that Othello has taken his place in Emilia's bed. In 2.1 he expresses the same fear about Cassio. Coleridge, who evidently couldn't believe that anyone in the play was jealous, characterises these purported explanations as 'the motive-hunting of motiveless malignity'.[11] In agreement with Coleridge, R.B. Heilman found it significant that in Iago's statement –

> I hate the Moor,
> *And* it is thought abroad that 'twixt my sheets
> H'as done my office. (1.3.386–8, my italics)

– 'the hate is prior, and a motive is then discovered'.[12] On Heilman's reading, 'And it is thought abroad . . .' is one thought too many. But if Iago suffers from a jealousy that is intrinsically pathological, we should expect it to manifest itself in precisely this way. More than any other character in the play, he keenly feels his existential separation from other people. His sense of occupying a place apart from others takes the form of an extreme egoism, a propensity for lying, and a tendency to worry that someone else has taken his place. Far from professing too many motives for any one of them to be credible, they are all so many symptoms of a single pathology.

Iago says he isn't certain whether Othello or Cassio has slept with Emilia, but that despite or because of his uncertainty he will treat his suspicion '*as if* for surety' (1.3.390, my italics). In a similar vein, Othello demands that Iago resolve his doubts about Desdemona:

> Make me to see't; or (at the least) so prove it
> That the probation bear no hinge nor loop
> To hang a doubt on. (3.3.364–6)

Support for Cavell's idea that Othello doesn't really believe Iago's accusations could be found in the suggestion that Othello's need for epistemic closure makes him just as willing as Iago to conflate psychological conviction with demonstrable certainty.[13] But there is a difference between the suspicion that Iago treats as surety and the doubt that Othello is led by Iago to want to treat as certainty.

Iago begins his deception by exploiting Othello's awareness that he is not directly acquainted with the contents of Iago's mind:

> *Iago*: My noble lord –
> *Oth*:   What dost thou say, Iago?
> *Iago*: Did Michael Cassio, when you woo'd my lady,
>   Know of your love?
> *Oth*:   He did, from first to last. Why dost thou ask?
> *Iago*: But for a satisfaction of my thought,
>   No further harm. (3.3.93–8)

This cunning speech act operates on Othello's mind like an 'inception' in the sense in which this term is used in Christopher Nolan's eponymous film. The problem faced by Nolan's Dom Cobb (Leonardo DiCaprio) is to make a rich magnate's heir accept an idea that he would ordinarily reject. Cobb solves this problem by 'incepting' the idea, that is, by implanting it in the victim's mind in such a way as to make him believe that he is its author. Iago faces a similar problem. Othello would never believe Iago's bald assertion that he thinks Desdemona loves Cassio. On the contrary, he would just as swiftly dispatch Iago as A.C. Bradley thought Hamlet would have done had he found himself in Othello's shoes.[14] Accordingly, what Iago does is to implant the idea in Othello's mind that Iago is hiding his thoughts from Othello. He does this in such a way as to make Othello think it is his own idea that Iago is hiding his thoughts. The irony, of course, is that Iago really is hiding his thoughts from Othello, no more so than when he 'confesses' to thinking that Desdemona loves Cassio. At this moment in the play, Othello believes that he has the equivalent of direct access to the contents of Iago's mind, making him prone to trust Iago's subsequent assertions. He is simultaneously made painfully aware of the fact that he doesn't have direct access to the contents of Desdemona's heart. Iago is now in a position to transform Othello's scepticism into something like jealousy by allegedly warning him against it:

> O beware, my lord, of jealousy!
> It is the green-ey'd monster which doth mock
> The meat it feeds on. (3.3.165–7)

Cavell is right to point out that Iago's 'rumoring' isn't a sufficient, or, for that matter, efficient, cause of Othello's jealousy: 'What specifically for me is at stake epistemologically in the allegory of Othello and Desdemona is my finding that Othello's radical, consuming doubt is not *caused by* Iago's rumoring.'[15] Analogously, Descartes doesn't begin to doubt *because* an evil genius sows the seeds of suspicion in his mind; rather, he *invents* the hypothesis of an evil genius for the sake of extending (or, *pace* Cavell, pretending to extend) his incipient doubt. In a similar way, Cavell's Othello effectively 'invents' Iago, much as Hamlet is sometimes said to invent or project the Ghost.[16] As an alternative explanation, Cavell could appeal to Malebranche's conception of an *occasioning* cause. Iago's actual (not merely projected) remarks would provide an occasion on which Othello does something to himself. This interpretation would have the advantage of making Othello less gullible than he might otherwise appear to be. Some directors break up the temptation scene (3.3) into a series of separate conversations, the idea being to mitigate Othello's apparent naivety by slowing down his gulling. Since Cavell's Othello isn't really gulled at all, this problem disappears, but at the cost of raising another, namely, that Iago's cleverness now appears to be irrelevant. Had he in fact baldly stated that Desdemona was sleeping with Cassio, he should have provided Othello with just as convenient a pretext as he does through his sophisticated conniving. Iago's diabolical wit would be as wasted on Othello as is Touchstone's 'good wit' on Audrey in *As You Like It* (3.3.13). This problem is avoided once we recognise that there is more to the causality of an inception than the providing of a mere occasion. An inception involves the conveyance of an idea, coupled with the occlusion of that conveyance. By downplaying Iago's agency, Cavell effectively succumbs to Iago's occlusion of his inception no less than does Othello. The apparent swiftness of Othello's gulling can be accounted for on the basis of the catalytic character of an inception: once the conveyance of an idea has been occluded, the idea can be immediately taken on as one's own. The rest is stage management: Iago must provide Othello with ocular and audible evidence that seems to corroborate the thought that Othello 'forced' Iago to reveal.

Without Iago's inception and stage management, we have no play – or, rather, we have *The Winter's Tale*. Despite the presence of Mamillius, the scene in which Leontes engenders his jealousy really does have the form of a Cartesian 'closet' drama. Both *The Winter's Tale* and the *Meditations* culminate not in tragic loss, but in a recovery of the world through divine or magical intervention. Such a recovery is denied to Othello not because he is incapable of it but because Iago prevents it. Othello's scepticism would never have been transformed into jealousy or quasi-jealousy had it not been for Iago's intervention. In this respect, Othello is closer to Claudio in *Much Ado About Nothing* than he is to Leontes. Claudio would never have doubted Hero's fidelity were it not for the crude deception perpetrated by Don John the Bastard. From a long way off, the insufficiently clear and distinct Margaret looks just like Hero. The fact that Claudio is so readily taken in by this 'palpable device' is hardly to his moral or intellectual credit. Nevertheless, his belief in Hero's infidelity has some kind of justification, whereas Leontes' belief about Hermione's infidelity is entirely delusional. The difference between warranted and delusional jealousy is nicely analysed by Freud, who describes the case of a jealous husband whose belief that his wife was having an affair with another man – a belief expressed by the judgement 'She loves him' – was derived neither from empirical evidence nor from plausible testimony but from an unconscious deformation of the *warranted* judgement, '*I* love him.' The belief 'She loves him' was unwarranted not in the sense that there was only *bad* evidence to support it, but in the sense that it wasn't motivated by evidence of any sort. Once adopted, delusional beliefs are both unverifiable and unfalsifiable; they can only be therapeutically deconstructed.[17] Claudio's belief in Hero's infidelity isn't delusional because it is based on evidence of some sort. We fault him for failing to recognise that the evidence hardly amounts to proof, ocular or otherwise, and for his lack of trust in Hero. Yet we recognise that his jealousy has some sort of epistemic trigger. Leontes needs no such trigger. There are psychological *causes* for his suspicions about Hermione, but no *reasons* to support them.

Othello stands in between these extremes. He resembles Claudio in so far as he is deceived, but the manner of his deception (Iago's inception) is far more subtle. The truly gullible Claudio doesn't need much more than Don John's rumoring to make him think that Hero is unfaithful. Although he doesn't accept that rumoring entirely at face value, the fact that he is willing to put it to the test (like Ford) shows that his trust in Hero is less than absolute. Othello needs more than rumoring to activate his scepticism, but once it has been activated it takes on the character of delusional jealousy. In this respect he resembles Leontes. Emilia, the play's great theorist of delusional jealousy, observes that 'jealous souls'

> are not ever jealous for the cause,
> But jealious for they're jealious. It is a monster
> Begot upon itself, born on itself. (3.4.159–62)

Emilia also understands how an inception works. She suspects that Othello has been 'abus'd by some most villainous knave, / Some base notorious knave, some scurvy fellow' (4.2.139–40).

The scurvy Iago assures Othello that he could never be directly acquainted with Desdemona's affair with Cassio because she is too discreet. To Othello's demand for ocular proof, Iago replies, 'It is impossible you should see this' (3.3.402). Iago intends Othello to take this to mean that Desdemona is sufficiently cunning that she would never let her husband witness her illicit outward behaviour. On a second level, of which Othello is necessarily unaware since he lacks direct acquaintance with the contents of Iago's mind, Iago's remark is ironic because he knows that it is impossible for Othello to see something that isn't actually happening. On yet another level, of which Iago himself might be unaware, his remark reveals what it is that plagues all jealous lovers *including Iago himself*, namely, that there is always *something* with which they cannot be directly acquainted. Shakespeare makes it abundantly clear that Iago is suffering no less than Othello; indeed, Iago is trying as hard as he can to displace his own suffering onto Othello:

> I do suspect the lusty Moor
> Hath leap'd into my seat; the thought whereof
> Doth (like a poisonous mineral) gnaw my inwards;
> And nothing can or shall content my soul
> Till I am even'd with him, wife for wife;
> Or failing so, yet that I put the Moor
> At least into a jealousy so strong
> That judgment cannot cure. (2.1.295–302)

Iago deceives Othello with a combination of false descriptions and direct acquaintance with (his perception of) Cassio's possession of Desdemona's handkerchief. Othello is encouraged to conflate Cassio's possession of the handkerchief with his possession of her body, but it is not inconceivable, *pace* Russell, that Othello is more concerned about his possession of her heart. The impossibility of ocular proof would then be due to the fact that Othello can only ever know Desdemona's inner feelings by description, or by acquaintance with (his perception of) her outward behaviour. This line of interpretation is blocked by Cavell when he represents Othello's supposed lack of certainty – his lack of acquaintance with Desdemona's heart – as a mere excuse for finding her existence unbearable. For Cavell, it is not the *unknowable quality* of Desdemona's feelings but their *known reality* that troubles Othello. For Russell, by contrast, Othello's tragedy would be due to his inability to come to terms with the fact that Desdemona has an inner life with which he can never be directly acquainted. To relinquish the claim to dominion over another person is to accept this epistemic limitation. Ironically, it is Iago who alerts Othello to the impossibility of being directly acquainted with another person's soul when he observes that Othello couldn't be acquainted with Iago's thoughts even if he had his 'heart' in his 'hands' (3.3.163).[18] Immediately thereafter, Iago proceeds to make Othello believe, falsely, that he is acquiring the epistemic equivalent of such direct acquaintance. The irony of the play is that Othello's potential for doubting Desdemona's sincerity is actualised at the expense of his potential for doubting Iago's. Predictably, Russell's interpretation of Cartesian scepticism is very different from Cavell's. On Russell's interpretation, 'Descartes' "methodical doubt"' is not the sort of 'absolute scepticism' that Cavell attributes to him when he represents Descartes' hyperbolic doubt as epistemically excessive.[19] On the contrary, Descartes' step-by-step reasoning enables him to distinguish the incorrigible objects of his direct acquaintance from the corrigible objects whose existence he infers on their basis. To acknowledge the possibility of doubting the reality of corrigible objects doesn't by itself warrant the actualisation of such doubt.

Just before Othello kills Desdemona, she tries, in vain, to correct his misapprehension of the quality of her love for Cassio:

> I . . . never lov'd Cassio
> But with such general warranty of heaven
> As I might love. (5.1.58–60)

Only then does she try to correct his mistaken belief about the handkerchief, an external sign of her inscrutable love: 'I never gave him token' (5.1.60). When Emilia eventually confesses to having given the handkerchief to Iago, Othello simultaneously realises that Iago has been falsely describing his own beliefs and that Desdemona on her deathbed truthfully described the nature of her love for Cassio. This double recognition confirms rather than negates the necessity – and peril – of taking another person's descriptions on faith. Unlike Claudio and Leontes, Othello learns this lesson too late. Had his trust in Desdemona been absolute from the beginning, he would have been immune to suspicions of any sort. Indeed, he would have rejected even ocular 'proof' had he caught Desdemona and Cassio *in flagrante* and been asked by Desdemona, 'Whom are you going to believe – me or your eyes?'[20]

Of all of Shakespeare's jealous lovers, Troilus comes closest to this frame of mind when he sees Cressida give his sleeve to Diomedes. His initial response is to deny that 'his' Cressida was even there at all. Though he quickly succumbs to the realistic assessment of Ulysses, if not to the cynical assessment of Thersites, it remains a valid question as to whether Cressida actually does betray Troilus, or, for that matter, whether she herself can know. There is a touch of uncertainty in her remark: 'Troilus, farewell! One eye yet looks on thee, / But with my heart the other eye doth see' (5.2.107). Russell observes that although direct acquaintance with an object guarantees the object's existence, we become prone to error as soon as we try to describe it. Each of us is directly acquainted with our own feelings, but feelings are notoriously difficult to describe accurately, even to ourselves. Paradoxically, Cressida may not know what she knows about her feelings for Troilus and Diomedes. The problem with Troilus's initial disavowal of the evidence of his eyes – 'no, this is Diomed's Cressida' (5.2.137) – is that it doesn't take place at the right level. Instead of denying that the Cressida he saw was 'his', he should have denied that in witnessing Cressida give Diomedes his sleeve he was witnessing a betrayal of her heart. Had he really trusted her – had he truly been 'true as truth's simplicity' (3.2.169) – he would never have allowed himself to believe that he could be acquainted with such a betrayal. To a hard-nosed realist such as Ulysses (let alone Thersites or Iago), such an absolute trust or faith would be no less delusional than delusional jealousy. Yet as Kierkegaard argues in *Fear and Trembling*, it is the very nature of trust or faith to be as inscrutable as that about which it trusts.[21] The faithful lover is the one who needs to be acquainted only with his or her own love. The potential for jealousy begins when one loses that trust – when one begins to speculate or fantasise about things with which one can never be directly acquainted. From this point of view, every jealous belief could be characterised as delusional, not only because it is without warrant, but because it posits an impossible object.

Russell observes that Othello's belief that Desdemona loves Cassio poses not only an epistemological problem, but an ontological problem. If Desdemona doesn't love Cassio, then Othello's belief has no object:

> When Othello believes that Desdemona loves Cassio, he must not have before his mind a single object, 'Desdemona's love for Cassio', or 'that Desdemona loves Cassio', for that would require that there should be objective falsehoods, which subsist independently of any minds; and this, though not logically refutable, is a theory to be avoided if possible.

Russell gets around this problem by representing Othello's belief as a four-fold relation linking (in the right order) Othello, Desdemona, the universal relation of loving, and Cassio: 'the actual occurrence, at the moment when Othello is entertaining his belief, is that the relation called "believing" is knitting together into one complex whole the four terms Othello, Desdemona, loving, and Cassio'.[22] If Desdemona loves Cassio (or rather if she loves him in the way Othello fears), then over and above this four-fold relational complex there will be a three-fold relational complex linking Desdemona, loving and Cassio in the right way. If Desdemona doesn't love Cassio, then there is no such three-fold complex, but there is still the four-fold complex constituted by Othello's belief. From an ontological point of view, the advantage of this account is that it doesn't require the existence of any objects other than Othello, Desdemona, the universal relation of loving, and Cassio. As an interpretation of the play, its advantage lies in the fact that it does away not with Othello's *belief* in Desdemona's infidelity (as Cavell's interpretation effectively does) but only with the *object* of that belief.

Russell's analysis can also be related to the distinction between warranted and delusional belief. Whereas a warranted but false belief fails to refer since the object to which it purports to refer doesn't exist, a *delusional* belief fails to refer *whether the object it posits exists or not*. In other words, delusional beliefs that happen to true are no less delusional for being true, just as unwarranted beliefs that happen to be true are still without warrant. We may further suppose that any belief that purports direct acquaintance with something that can only be known by description is inherently delusional. If Othello lapses into delusional jealousy, it is by being led to conflate his acquaintance with (his perception of) Cassio's possession of Desdemona's handkerchief with Desdemona's love of Cassio. Such a conflation amounts to forgetting that Desdemona is the only person who can be directly acquainted with her own feelings. Were Othello to acknowledge that he cannot be directly acquainted with anyone else's thoughts or feelings but his own, he would be, on Russell's analysis, less, not more, self-withdrawn. Since Cavell doesn't attribute to Othello a genuine belief that Desdemona loves Cassio, he is unable to avail himself of this type of analysis. Instead of doing away with the object of Othello's belief, he does away with the belief itself, equating scepticism with disavowal. Russell's elimination of the object opens up another interpretive possibility. Since knowledge by acquaintance yields absolute certainty, beliefs that purport to know another person's heart by acquaintance will represent themselves as immune to the sort of disconfirming evidence that pertains only to knowledge by description. (Delusional believers may pretend to adduce supporting evidence *for* their beliefs, but that is no less delusional.) The difference between delusional jealousy and scepticism could be characterised as the difference between purporting to know another's heart by acquaintance and acknowledging that one can only know it by description. This, I take it, is roughly the difference between Leontes' and Claudio's states of mind. Claudio doesn't profess to be directly acquainted with Hero's heart; he thinks he knows it indirectly, through presumed acquaintance with her behaviour. By contrast, Leontes takes his acquaintance with Hermione's behaviour – tendentiously described as 'paddling palms and pinching fingers' (1.2.115) – to count as a direct revelation of heart. Once again, Othello stands between these two extremes. Like Claudio, he relies on false evidence supplied by a third party. Like Leontes – indeed, far worse than Leontes – he succumbs to a wild, murderous rage. Othello's tragedy consists in finding himself caught in a veritable antinomy between Iago's and Desdemona's respective claims to honesty, a zero sum game that he disastrously misplays.

The first half of *The Winter's Tale* is no less tragic than *Othello*, but in the second half Shakespeare manages to revive the comic potential of *Much Ado* – up to and including the resurrection of the abused beloved. In *Much Ado* we know all along that Hero isn't dead, but in *The Winter's Tale* Paulina literally does the impossible, providing ocular proof that what's done can be undone. None of these plays quite fits Cavell's conception of a 'comedy of remarriage', in which a broken marriage is repaired through conversation. Beatrice and Benedick are conversationalists, but Claudio and Hero are almost passive participants swept along to the play's happy ending. Likewise, Leontes and Hermione don't speak directly to each other at the end of *The Winter's Tale*. After so many years apart, they have to get reacquainted, and that takes time. *The Winter's Tale* might be characterised as a comedy of reacquaintance. Reacquaintance is not only a matter of getting to know someone again after a period of absence. It also involves getting reacquainted with acquaintance itself, learning anew what it is to be and not to be acquainted with another person. Othello learns this lesson too late and so succumbs to a tragedy of false acquaintance. Yet we can agree with Coleridge that it isn't his jealousy that precipitates his tragedy; it is his potential for scepticism. Coleridge's assessment of Iago's motiveless malignancy is another matter. Here we can turn back to Cavell, for it would not be far off the mark to say of Iago what Cavell says of Othello, namely, that everything he does in the play is geared towards the ultimate end of annihilating his wife. The last thing he says to Emilia, 'Filth, thou liest!' (5.2.231), is not simply the ineffective lie it appears to be: it is, *pace* Verdi, his 'Credo'.[23]

Notes

1. Shakespearean plays that deal with feminine anxiety about masculine infidelity include *The Comedy of Errors* and *Antony and Cleopatra*.
2. Samuel Taylor Coleridge, *Coleridge's Criticism of Shakespeare: A Selection*, ed. R.A. Foakes (Detroit: Wayne State University Press, 1989), p. 116.
3. All Shakespeare quotations are from *The Riverside Shakespeare*, ed. G. Blakemore Evans et al. (Boston: Houghton Mifflin Company, 1974).
4. Bernard Williams, 'Persons, Character, and Morality', in *Moral Luck: Philosophical Papers 1973–1980* (Cambridge: Cambridge University Press, 1981), p. 18.
5. Stanley Cavell, *Disowning Knowledge in Seven Plays of Shakespeare* (Cambridge: Cambridge University Press, 2003), p. 7. Elsewhere, Cavell discusses 'Othello's (other-minds) relation to Desdemona as an allegory (call it) of material-object skepticism'. See Stanley Cavell, *In Quest of the Ordinary: Lines of Skepticism and Romanticism* (Chicago: University of Chicago Press, 1988), p. 55.
6. Cavell, *Disowning Knowledge*, p. 6.
7. Ibid., p. 138.
8. Ibid., p. 133, my italics.
9. Bertrand Russell, *The Problems of Philosophy* (Oxford: Oxford University Press, 1997), p. 136.
10. Ibid., pp. 136–7.
11. Coleridge, *Coleridge's Criticism of Shakespeare*, p. 113.
12. R.B. Heilman, *Magic in the Web: Action and Language in 'Othello'*, cited in William Shakespeare, *Othello*, ed. E.A.J. Honigmann (London: Thomson Learning, 2001), p. 160.
13. Cf. the 'second maxim' of Descartes' provisional morality: 'to follow the most doubtful views, once I had decided to do so, just as steadfastly as if they were very certain'. René Descartes, *Discourse on Method and Related Writings*, trans. and ed. Desmond M. Clarke (London: Penguin, 1999), p. 20.
14. A.C. Bradley, *Shakespearean Tragedy: Lectures on Hamlet, Othello, King Lear, Macbeth* (London: Penguin, 1991), p. 11.
15. Cavell, *Disowning Knowledge*, p. 8, my italics.
16. Hegel represents the Ghost as 'an objective form of Hamlet's inner presentiment.' See G.W.F. Hegel, *Lectures on Fine Art*, trans. T.M. Knox (Oxford: Clarendon University Press, 1975), vol. 1, p. 231.
17. Sigmund Freud, 'On the Mechanism of Paranoia', in *General Psychological Theory: Papers on Metapsychology* (New York: Simon & Schuster, 1991), pp. 29–48. Cf. Martin Wangh, '*Othello*: The Tragedy of Iago', *Psychoanalytic Quarterly*, 19 (1950), pp. 201–12.
18. One suspects that Gratiano is mistaken when he predicts that 'torments' will 'ope' Iago's 'lips' (5.2.305). But even when torture succeeds in forcing people to reveal their inner thoughts it doesn't yield direct acquaintance.
19. Russell, *The Problems of Philosophy*, pp. 150–1.
20. In *Duck Soup* Chico Marx asks: 'Who are you gonna believe, me or your own eyes?' Cited in Slavoj Žižek, *The Ticklish Subject: The Absent*

Centre of Political Ontology (London and New York: Verso, 2000), p. 323.

21. Søren Kierkegaard, *Fear and Trembling / Repetition*, trans. and ed. Howard V. Hong and Edna H. Hong (Princeton: Princeton University Press, 1983).

22. Russell, *The Problems of Philosophy*, pp. 125–6.

23. Plácido Domingo, the great Otello of our day, has said that despite his late-career shift to baritone roles he could never sing Iago since doing so would 'betray Otello'. Michael Cooper, 'Domingo Undimmed: Plácido Domingo Defies the Gravity of Age', *New York Times*, 7 March 2014. Perhaps it is for a similar reason that Cavell has left it to others to apply his insights about the nature of jealousy to the character of Iago.

A different version of some material in this chapter can be found in Andrew Cutrofello, *All for Nothing: Hamlet's Negativity* (Cambridge, MA: MIT Press, 2014), Chapter 5. For helpful comments I thank Jennifer Bates, Shannon Mussett, Carlos Patarroyo, Lawrence Rhu, Dianne Rothleder, Michael Shaw, Virginia Strain and Richard Strier.

Chapter 7

Hamlet on the Edge

Edward S. Casey

> The undiscovered country from whose bourn
> No traveler returns. (*Hamlet*, 3.1.78–9)

This line from Hamlet's most famous soliloquy has haunted me for many years, and I often cite it to a friend who has just recovered from a major illness – to underline her or his good fortune: their *not* having to enter a realm from which there is no way back. But when I use it in this way, despite my good wishes, I am employing it quite reductively – not just as a mere consolation to my friend but in such a way as to imply that there is some clear-cut distinction to be made between life and death. As if this distinction could be drawn with some metrically determinable precision – as if it were, for instance, a strictly medical matter ('no longer breathing', 'brain dead', etc.).

But in taking over Hamlet's line thus, I am failing Hamlet – and myself and my friend as well. I am pretending that the line between life and death is a *border*, that is, an edge that permits, and often requires, exactitude of determination – as in the pleonastic but revealing locution 'border-line': borders, for example international borders, are conceived as linear, not just in their cartographic representations but also as ideal entities that serve to divide and distinguish that which on the ground (in the local landscape) and among peoples (and animals) is often indivisible and indistinguishable. But Hamlet knows better: by saying 'bourn', he is referring to a *boundary* – as the footnote to the Arden Shakespeare edition of *Hamlet* informs us.[1] A boundary, in contrast with a border, is a comparatively porous edge, one that lets physical things and animate beings pass through and often in two or more directions. It is permeable – if not to sight, then to motion and touch, and to feeling and thinking as well.

The distinction between 'border' and 'boundary' is mostly mine, but the argument that death is a land whose edge is boundary-like is

Hamlet's. The argument is an argument from analogy, and it runs like this: death is akin to sleeping, as when Hamlet speaks of 'the sleep of death' (3.1.65), hence to dreaming. Sleeping is notably permeable, being subject to somatic influences such as noises, uncomfortable postures of the body, etc., which can wake us out of them abruptly. Moreover, sleep is transitional in character: we pass *through* it, entering it gradually (e.g., in hypnagogic states) and often leaving it by various intermediate states (labelled 'hypnapompic'). All of these characteristics point to death as a boundary situation. If it is truly analogous to sleep, then by parity of reasoning, death is itself something porous and transitional, with many intermediaries; it, too, is a boundary state.

The same reasoning applies to death as parallel to dreaming. When Hamlet says expressly 'to do: to sleep – to sleep, perchance to dream' (3.1.63–4), he implies that in becoming dead we enter not just a quasi-comatose state of sleep but may find within such sleep a dream-like state – and more expressly a nightmarish condition:

> ay, there's the rub,
> For in that sleep of death what dreams may come
> When we have shuffled off this mortal coil
> Must give us pause . . . (3.1. 64–7)

Just as sleep comes and goes, so the dreams it makes possible are themselves vulnerable to sudden stimulations that wake us out of them; they come from we know not where – certainly not from anything like a determinate border to which they would be the strict sequel. They sweep us away – just as death does. They too are boundary-like.

The soliloquy in which these ruminations are found begins with these familiar words: 'To be, or not to be – that is the question' (3.1.54). But is it? Is it if death is more a boundary than a border, thanks to its similarity to sleeping and dreaming, both of which are more events than states? The distinction between being and not-being implies something quite distinct and highly determinable; but is death anything so definite, is it even measurable? The tradition of holding that being is determinate begins with the ancient Greeks, who on Heidegger's assessment conceived of being as determinate 'presence' (*Anwesenheit*),[2] even if Heidegger's own 'fundamental ontology' contests this determinacy of being in myriad ways.

Another aspect of the matter is this. Is not 'to be or not to be' a matter not just of dying, sleeping and dreaming, but of *being born*? The thanocentric reading of Hamlet's celebrated line is rarely questioned, given the context of his contemplated suicide. But is it not true that there is a quite decisive difference between being born and not being born? Even if not within our personal agency, birth is certainly determinative of an entire lifetime – or lack of it, if birth is aborted or fails outright. Beckoning here is the often suppressed significance of natality as first emphasised by Hannah Arendt and recently pursued trenchantly by Anne O'Byrne in her remarkable book, *Natality and Finitude*.[3] But all too often being is seen exclusively through the lens of death – its uncertain but impending finality on Heidegger's conception – rather than through the spectacles of birth. Yet can we not equally say: 'to be born or not, is that not the question'?

Whatever the outcome of these more far-ranging deliberations, in the remainder of my remarks I will focus on various ways in which this is a work on edge – a play in which boundary is very often at stake, quite beyond the immediate issues raised by Hamlet's soliloquy.

Boundary: once more, an open-ended band or zone of indetermination – vs. border, a precisely delineated division.

To take one of the leading instances of a boundary condition: Hamlet's madness. Its deeply ambiguous character is exactly what baffles so many of his entourage, though least of all the king, who sees in it the deeper thrust of rage towards himself. Certainly, it is not a clinical case of any known (or knowable) mental illness that could be neatly classified – not even in the system of unbalanced humors that was the most likely source of medical diagnosis at that time ('too much bile' and the like: late in the play, Hamlet insists that he is not 'splenative rash' [5.1.250]). Instead, any sense that Hamlet has simply transgressed the border of sanity – gone 'over the edge', as we would now say – is tempered by the presence of Hamlet's continual cleverness in dialogue with others (e.g. his talk with his mother in which he mocks her by repeating her words with a telling but sardonic twist: *Queen*: 'Hamlet, thou hast thy father much offended.' *Hamlet*: 'Mother, you have my father much offended.' *Queen*: 'Come, come, you answer with an idle tongue.' *Hamlet*: 'Go, go, you question with a wicked tongue' [3.4.8–11]). This is not to mention the brilliance of his deep insights into those around him – in which he lays bare motives they have displaced or repressed – as well as into himself: his tacit, not altogether conscious self. Nor is it to mention the sheer scintillation of his speech, which no person altogether insane could approximate. Horatio's effort to contrast reason with madness does not do justice to his friend ('Which might deprive your sovereignty of reason / And draw you into madness' [1.4.73–4]), for there is clearly reason in Hamlet's madness – in contrast with Ophelia, who appears to have gone over the deep end and who is (in the king's words) 'divided from herself and her fair judgment' (4.5.85).

Another indication that Hamlet's extraordinary state of mind is a boundary condition and no simple trespassing of a clear border of sanity is found in the performative character of his madness. From early on, he has decided to 'put an antic disposition on' (1.5.170), and this aspect of his behaviour is borne out by his felt affinity with the acting troop with whom he so eagerly seeks out collaboration. Performance is itself a boundary activity, existing as it does between (external, mundane) reality and disembodied, irreal fantasy. When Hamlet remarks that the point of theatre is 'to hold as 'twere the mirror up to Nature' (3.2.21–2), he invokes the intermediacy of mirrors, which always stand between the immediate presence of that which stands before them and the circumambient world that frames them.

Mirrors, too, provide boundaries between two orders of being: they provide 'a universal magic that converts things into spectacle, spectacle into things' in Merleau-Ponty's words.[4] If 'the play's the thing in which to catch the conscience of the King', this is because as a performance, a spectacle, it holds up a mirror to the king's carefully concealed internal world. As Winnicott has emphasised, play of every kind – not only theatrical – embodies a transitional zone between imagination and reality: a zone that is all the more effective for not having exact limits around it.[5] Indeed, any ritual, theatrical or otherwise, happens in the liminal space of a threshold between two contrary or opposed states of being. And not only space! The liminal or transitional is also temporal, requiring its own time of passage, as we see in many rituals of hospitality that are undeniably spatial and temporal at once. The failure to respect the right temporality of mourning (a boundary state if there ever was one!) surely generates Hamlet's offense at the rapidity with which his mother has remarried his uncle ('the funeral baked meats / Did coldly furnish forth the marriage table' [1.2.179–80; cf. 1.5. 75–6]) – even before he learns from his ghosted father of the regicide that preceded the hasty remarriage and forced coronation. (Other foreshortened rituals occur later: Polonius's awkward obsequies, Ophelia's 'maimed rites' [5.1.28].) All these foreclosed rituals undermine their status as bounding actions, requiring the right time and space.

And ghosts enter here as well! They, too, are betwixt and between – between heaven and hell even as they hover for a while on earth after the death that brought them into being. Even if death is 'the undiscovered country from whose bourn no traveler returns' (3.1.78–9), ghosts in many cultures are permitted to linger for a while (a week or two in older western Europe lore; forty-nine days in the Tibetan *bardo state*) so as to act as admonitory entities, or just to be bare traces of their former full-bodied existence. Like the shadows that dreams are likened to by Hamlet – dreams are 'but a shadow', he says in one variant of the text[6]

– they are demi-presences that, like visual shadows, are tethered to an actual body yet fall away from this body into a realm of their own: into a special boundary zone that is akin to a margin or fringe yet much more tenuous than either of these.

Ghosts and dreams, along with theatrical performances, belong to the domain of *seeming*, a major thematic of the play that is announced very early on. To the queen's query, 'Why seems it so particular with thee?' Hamlet responds:

> 'Seems', madam – nay it is, I know not 'seems',
> 'Tis not alone my inky cloak, cold mother,
> Nor customary suits of solemn black,
> Nor windy suspiration of forced breath,
> No, nor the fruitful river in the eye,
> Nor the dejected 'haviour of the visage,
> Together with all forms, moods, shapes of grief,
> That can denote me truly. These indeed 'seem',
> For they are actions that a man might play,
> But I have that within which passes show,
> These but the trappings and the suits of woe. (1.2.76–86)

King Hamlet's ghost, similarly, refers to the queen as 'most seeming-virtuous' (1.5.46), and Hamlet adds in reference to his uncle that 'one may smile and smile and be a villain' (1.5.197). Polonius, on the other hand, valorises seeming itself when he says that 'The apparel oft proclaims the man' (11.3.71). So does Hamlet when he is setting the trap for his uncle at the play, asking Horatio to join him in observing the king's reaction closely:

> For I mine eyes will rivet to his face
> And after we will both our judgements join
> In censure of his seeming. (3.2.81–3)

In this brief conspectus of passages, we witness the rich gamut of seemings: from pretending or faking ('acting') to revealing manifestation. Either extreme is apt, depending on the immediate context; but for all their evident differences, both designate boundary situations. How is this so?

Seeming – or 'appearing' or 'showing' – occurs either as an epiphenomenon located on the surface of things (like smiles or clothes) or it is the way in which an entire phenomenon, its whole being or becoming, comes to expression (as with telling bodily gestures). Sometimes, it is both at once: the king's facial expression at which Hamlet and Horatio intently peer is both situated on his face, *shown* there, and yet it also evinces his whole inner being, notably his guiltiness. Here, *les extrêmes se touchent*. Elsewhere, as in Hamlet's response to the queen's questioning, the showing is distinct from the being: it is a matter of 'that within which [sur]passes show', that is, of an inwardness that cannot, or will not, be captured in outward visage or gesture, that *stays back* within the psyche of the person whose overt expressions do not betray the inner self but act to cover it up.

Despite these extremities and the resulting gamut of intermediate cases that come with it, the domain of seeming has a quite coherent character when it is regarded as a species of edge: this is that of being a boundary in the mode of an intermezzo, a being of the between – where the intermediacy lies between the externally real (rugged Secondness) and the inwardly self-possessed (the sheer qualitative immediacy of feeling). Such an in-between space (or time) has the kind of breadth that calls for flanking on both sides: witness the way that seemings of every kind hover between external reality and internal cogitation. These surrounders act as margins *of the intermediate space/time*; they constitute its outer fringes, its peripheries. But it, the surrounded region, is its own area, with its own changing configurations. This is *seeming*, a boundary band that is never a strict border between the extremes of superficial showing and deep expressing.

Conceived thus, seeming also includes other boundary phenomena that we have seen to be constitutive of Hamlet – both the man and the play. For instance, performing and mirroring, dreaming and sleeping. Each of these seemingly quite different phenomena – the first two being overt activities or techniques, the last two matters of assumed passivity – are creatures of the same in-between that I am arguing is a latent structure of the drama, essential to its armature, always at stake, albeit in variations that do not resemble each other at first glance. Whether as acting in a play or 'putting on an antic disposition', performance actively inhabits this fecund middle world; mirroring is equally but differently active: it is a '*holding up* the mirror to nature', so is itself a bodily action as much as are acting or play-acting. We can say of each such case that 'it is to act, to do, to perform' (5.1.12), as the gravedigger says so forthrightly. It is a matter of active animation, of *acting out*. Sleeping and dreaming, in contrast, are instances of *acting in*: that is, of passive assumption, as when in going to sleep we assume a certain settled posture (recall Merleau-Ponty's description of going to sleep as 'imitating the breathing and posture of the sleeper',[7] or the classical description of putting yourself into the 'arms of Morpheus'); while in dreaming, I submit to the dream scene, the *Schauplatz*, I make myself the willing subject of my own dreaming activity. I inhabit a world of my own making as if I had not made it, as if it just *came to me* from elsewhere.

Whether as explicit acting-out, or in the implicit terms of acting-in, I create or enter a boundary zone that is as broad as it is deep. In that zone, my agency is itself various: as various as are mirroring, performing (whether as pretending or theatrical acting), sleeping, and dreaming from each other. But this agency is in nowise compromised by this multiplicity; on the contrary, it is energised and extended by it. Hamlet is one such agent, exemplary for the manner in which he appears in such diverse guises. Instead of this being merely cunning or confusing – as readers might be tempted to think – it manifests the layered character of the dense and richly articulated boundary zone from which all human agency stems. Hamlet lives and shows the truth of Polonius's otherwise sententious remark: 'by indirections find directions out' (2.1.63). For the locus of indirection is found in the open intermediacy of the boundaries that subtend our lives. Most of the time, we live from and in just one boundary situation at a time, ignoring the others; Hamlet thrusts a number of them forward into our faces, reminding us of the polymorphism of the several boundary states in which we are ourselves located at all times.

In this respect, death is indeed special. Here, we cannot speak of activity *or* passivity, of performing, or mirroring – and of dreaming and sleeping only by the stretch of analogy. In death, we undergo a unique form of boundary. Perhaps this is why Shakespeare chooses the word 'bourn' to describe it. A bourn is a boundary that, unlike those boundaries that are two-sided, and thus always flanked, is decidedly one-sided. It is an edge that can be traversed in one direction only: *passed into* but not *passed back across*. A one-way situation in short – even if, once on the other side, one (a strange 'one', of course: for I am then dead) can linger on this edge, though only from the far side, not the near: that is, as ghosts (assuming that our culture or our psyche permits their appearing). (As witnesses of ghosts, the still living stay on the near side.) A figure like a ghost or a demon or a fury – or a haunting memory of the departed person – lives in a boundary space and time on the very edge that is death. It populates, however transiently, 'the undiscovered country from whose bourn no traveler returns' (3.1.78–9). The ghost or memory is situated on the other side of the edge, 'over the edge' but not in the usual psychopathological sense; instead, it is a movement beyond life into a *terra incognitum* that is all too easy to enter but impossible to leave. We find this in cases of 'out-of-body' experiences in near-death experiences that constitute a boundary zone of their own which amounts to an intermediate zone of its own that remains on *this side, diesseits, en deça,* of death; whereas the ghost occupies that side, *au-delà, jenseits,* which lies beyond death as an ultimate edge. Both of these boundary sites, ghostly haunting and near-death hovering, are dis-embodied; neither lasts for very long; as transient, each transpires soon after it arises.

When truly *beyond* life's living and beyond ghosts and memories, one enters into a mute boundary domain that is open-ended on its far side. One *persists* as dead, whether as corpse, or as a soul wandering in a nether world, or as a hero who has become immortal at death (a figure invoked more than once in *Hamlet*).

The traitorous king says of Hamlet 'give him further edge' (3.1.26). This 'King is a thing' (4.2.26), but Hamlet is more than a thing even if in death he will become a thing. He is a multilayered set of interanimated boundaries. He is his own edge, and while alive he requires space and time in which to edge out of one imputed identity only into the several identities he assumes freely if not entirely knowingly. From this circumstance, there is both outgoing and coming back: two-way traffic, all enacted in the boundaries of performing and mirroring, dreaming and sleeping – and other boundaried becomings (such as almost being Ophelia's lover and husband, or almost becoming the next king of Denmark).

On the other side of every edge is an open space of indeterminacy and possibility; on the hither side, closure and actuality. Life, Hamlet's life – my life and yours too – consists in both aspects of edge. Death offers one aspect only: that of finitude, mortality, termination, end. Hamlet plays at the edge of life and death alike. In this way, he plays for us the drama of death-in-life and of life-in-death. He is not crazy, nor is he only pretending. He is enacting the asymmetry of the one-sided boundary instituted by death vis-à-vis the two-sided boundaries in which most of life consists. He moves back and forth across the edge of life and the boundary of death – until he can move no further, until 'the rest' must be 'silence'.

*

'To be or not to be – that is the question.' But *is* that the question? Is it the question we must ask? We might be driven to ask it on the brink of self-destruction – another edge but one from which we can voluntarily retreat if we decide to. And we might ask it if we are deciding to have a child: to let that now non-existent and possible future child come to birth, or not. (This is also the very question we ask when considering abortion.) But short of these extreme circumstances, we need not ask it. Indeed, we'd be better off not to ask it – at least not if 'to be' and 'not to be' are conceived as sheer opposites: that is, as differentiated by a strict division between the two states – by what I have called a 'border'. But if life and certain aspects of death have more of the character of a boundary – a permeable, non-linear band with edges like the fringes on the monochrome masses in Rothko's later paintings – then we would be far less tempted to pit being against non-being: not if this means juxtaposing a determinate presence with sheer non-presence or radical absence. For the most part, we are moving between boundary zones, which do not contradict each other but overlap in indeterminate but fecund ways. In this respect, we are 'beings of the between' who live from one intermediacy to another, all the while remaining in the *metaxu* of our life as a whole. This is a life lived primarily between and among boundaries in which the outer edges have been muted, melted down and thinned out, and the inner edges have become buried.

Instead of asking ourselves whether we want 'to be or not to be', we should wonder whether we wish to enter this particular boundary region rather than that one, including (but not limited to) whether we wish to stay in the domain of the living – alive in the very circumstance in which we currently find ourselves, with all its desperation and in the face of the winds of outrageous fortune.

Notes

1. Footnote 78 reads: '*bourn* boundary'. See Shakespeare, *Hamlet*, ed. Ann Thompson and Neil Taylor (London: Thomson Learning, 2006), p. 286. My citations from the play are taken from this edition.
2. Martin Heidegger, *Being and Time*, trans. J. MacQuarrie and E. Robinson (New York: Harper, 1962), p. 47: 'Entities are grasped in their Being as "presence".'
3. See Anne O'Bryne, *Natality and Finitude* (Bloomington: Indiana University Press, 2010).
4. See Maurice Merleau-Ponty, 'Eye and Mind', trans. C. Dallery, in G. Johnson and M.B. Smith (eds), *The Merleau-Ponty Aesthetics Reader* (Evanston: Northwestern University Press, 1994), p. 130: 'Mirrors are instruments of a universal magic that converts things into spectacle, spectacle into things, myself into another, and another into myself.'
5. Donald Winnicott, *Playing and Reality* (London and New York: Tavistock, 1971).
6. This phrase is found in a folio-only text: see *Hamlet*, app. I, p. 467: 'A dream is itself but a shadow.'
7. Maurice Merleau-Ponty, *Phenomenology of Perception*, trans. C. Smith (New York: Routledge, 2002), p. 189.

Chapter 8

Levinas and Shakespeare
Howard Caygill

At one point, well into the third of his four 1946–7 lectures on 'Time and the Other', Levinas interrupted his meditation to ask permission 'to return once again to Shakespeare, in whom I have overindulged in the course of these lectures'.[1] He continues with the observation 'But it sometimes seems to me that the whole of philosophy is only a meditation of Shakespeare.'[2] This remarkable claim bears closer examination, not only because it places philosophy within the work of Shakespeare, as a meditation of and on 'Shakespeare', but also because it identifies Shakespeare as the occasion for Levinas's putting in question 'the whole of philosophy' beginning with first philosophy or ontology. Yet after the immense importance lent to the work of Shakespeare in the immediate post-war period his significance for Levinas's thinking wanes, becoming a source for examples rather than the inspiration for a fundamental re-thinking of the premises of Western philosophy.

The role played by the work of Shakespeare – above all the tragedies *Hamlet* and *Macbeth*, but also *Romeo and Juliet* – in Levinas's revolutionary work of the immediate post-war period cannot be overestimated. The impact of Shakespeare is especially marked in the first and most difficult and enigmatic of the post-war writings, the fragment 'There Is', written during captivity in a prisoner of war camp and published in *Deucalion* in 1946 before being incorporated into *Existents and Existence*. The formulation of the *il y a* is inseparable from a meditation on Shakespeare which serves as a focus for Levinas's critique of Heidegger and Hegel. Shakespeare provides the occasion for substituting the mood of horror for Heidegger's anxiety, translating *Dasein* into the very different *il y a*, questioning the possibility of death and defending a rejection of Hegelian dialectic. Shakespeare emerges as a cipher for the critique of nothingness and the role of death in fundamental ontology, serving as the advocate for a remorseless immanence that will for Levinas mark the limit of ontology and the point from which he will move towards revelation and the ethics of the other.

Crucial testimony to the climate of captivity and deprivation from which *Time and the Other* and *Existence and Existents* emerged is provided by the *Carnets de Captivité* kept by Levinas during his internment in a camp for Jewish POWs near Magdeburg. There Levinas and his fellow prisoners were put to forced labour in the forests surrounding the camp, their lives protected by the Geneva Conventions. The latter ensured access to writing materials and books denied Jewish civilian prisoners in the concentration camp system.[3] While painfully aware of the fragile privileges guaranteed them by the Geneva Conventions, Levinas and other Jewish prisoners were also aware of being forced guests of a potentially murderous host. In Levinas's case, the National Socialist government was closely allied with the work of Heidegger, and through this – such was Levinas's uncanny and unsettling suspicion – with the tradition of Western philosophy.

In addition to plans and sketches for a novel, philosophical work on Heidegger and Hegel, observations of POW camp life and memories of the pre-war period, the notebooks also contain extended reflections on Shakespeare. These appear in the context of the retinking of *Dasein* as *il y a* and as part of the refusal to countenance any concession to negation and nothingness. Already earlier in the notebooks, the view that nothingness is an alleviation, that death is an escape, is stated unambiguously, deflating the heroism of Heideggerian resolute being-for-death or Sartre's existential confrontation with nothingness. In the bleakest moments of the notebooks, in the depths of the winter of 1941, Levinas undergoes an experience of being as deprivation: 'In the black white vision – being is black. The absence of light – being.'[4] Being as the night is aligned with the *il y a* – '*il y a* is the night of being etc.',[5] and is regarded by Levinas not only in terms of insomnia but also as the nightmare of 'night in the midst of day'.[6] Being understood as a nightmare from which it is impossible to wake reverses the value accorded to being by ontology, one in which not-being is understood as the privation of being. Being for Levinas is, on the contrary, the privation of not-being, the impossibility of not-being, the horror of captivity in being. Such reflections from the early notebooks prepare the way for the extended meditation on Shakespeare in the seventh notebook, dating from the period of the last months and weeks of the war and thereafter. There Levinas puts directly into question 'Anxiety – of death? (Heidegger)',[7] moving towards the proposition: 'Death. Not a solution in itself.' Under this heading Levinas reflects first on Macbeth and then on Hamlet. For Macbeth, the 'game is lost . . . Job curses his birth: death will not save him. All that, if death is the end of being.'[8] For the escape from being is its own loss; similarly for Hamlet, 'death is perhaps not an end (this unknown – this indeterminacy of durée – is perhaps constitutive of death)'. Levinas observes that in this case, death as an end is 'wished for, not feared', but continues that death is feared as a separation from being, but also desired as a separation. But it is also possible, and this is Hamlet's concern, that it is not an absolute end, an 'end for the body, but not for the soul'.

The discussion of the difficulty of death, the possibility that it might be impossible and that there is no escape from being, moves then towards the qualification of the concept of nothingness. For death to be possible, nothingness must be somehow lodged within being. Levinas, however, takes from Shakepeare the idea that nothingness is equivocal, illusory. For him, 'Shakespearian tragedy is above all the contact of the human with nothingness, with nothingness in its equivocal form, in its diabolical form. The lie (*King Lear*, *Othello*), the equivocation of the witches (*Macbeth*); the ghost (*Hamlet*).'[9] While philosophy, represented by Hegel and Heidegger, believes in nothingness and negation, Shakespeare shows it to be an illusion; for Levinas he is 'the fabricator of nothingness, the one who gives to nothingness the appearance of being'.[10] Hamlet, in this view, is the hero who suffers this equivocation, 'he suffers the insinuation of nothingness into being (or of being into nothingness). To be or not to be – it's all there.' Levinas prizes this insight into the ruses of being and nothingness, but especially Shakespeare's ability to hold the opposition suspended, to not move towards to a dialectical resolution.

It is this resistance to resolution that Levinas carries from Shakespeare into his philosophical reflections of the post-war period. Shakespeare showed him that there could be a movement of thought free from any dialectical implications, a thinking not confined to the opposition of being and not-being, nothingness. The outcome of this lesson is most apparent in the fragment *il y a*. This short text announces an entirely new season of thought, but one that is haunted not only by its predecessors. For at the core of the *il y a* is the condition of haunting, of the stubborn endurance of the dead who are neither there nor not there, but persist. Shakespeare serves as a means of deflating any speculative resolution, any capture of nothingness in the service of being.

The fragment opens with a reversion to nothingness, but as an act of imagination – something is left, but it is not the opening to history that Hegel (or Sartre) would see in such a reversion. What is left is an *il y a* which does not respect the movements of subject and substance mobilised by Hegel in the *Phenomenology of Spirit* or the *Logic*. The 'heavy atmosphere', the 'darkness', becomes the occasion not for a dialectical transition or a resolute leap – the philosophical options of Hegelianism and anti-Hegelianism – but for a transfixed horror: 'The rustling of the *there is* . . . is horror.' Against the anxiety of *Dasein* before death or nothingness, Levinas proposes the horror of 'the impossibility of death, the universality of existence even in its annihilation'.[11] The dead do not retreat, but persist, urge themselves forward. Clearly thinking on the victims of genocide, Levinas moves to cite Macbeth suffering the realisation that the dead do not go away: 'To kill, like to die, is to seek an escape from being, to go where freedom and negation operate. Horror is the event of being which returns in the heart of this negation as though nothing had happened.'[12] The philosophical opposition of being and nothingness and the possibility of a unidirectional transition from one to the other would guarantee that the dead remained dead; Levinas, however, finds in the Shakespearean equivocation of being and not being the possibility that the dead, the murdered, even though expelled from being, continually return. '"And that", says Macbeth, "is more strange than the crime itself".' Of this Levinas comments that 'In the nothingness which a crime creates a being is condensed to the point of suffocation, and draws consciousness out of its "retreat". A corpse is horrible; it already bears in itself its own phantom, it presages its return. The haunting spectre, the phantom, constitutes the very element of horror.'[13] The 'return of presence in negation' is not a dialectical sublation or raising up, but a deflation or check; the demanding dead not only challenge the limits of nothingness, but compromise the enjoyment of being for the still living.

For Levinas, this deflationary movement of return with its affect of horror is to be distinguished from the dialectical, cathartic movement of ancient tragedy. The clash of laws and their resolution in a higher justice that characterised ancient tragedy and served as the exemplar of dialectical thought for Hegel is succeeded by the 'fatality of irremissable being' in Shakespeare's tragedy. With this claim, Levinas is close to Walter Benjamin's view of Shakespeare's work as a *Trauerspiel* or mourning play in *The Origins of German Tragic Drama*, but his understanding of what this means is even more rigorous. For Benjamin it is possible, even necessary, for the implacable immanence of the play to be disrupted by a moment of transcendence, while for Levinas there remains only equivocation. The dead return.

Spectres, ghosts, sorceresses are not only a tribute Shakespeare pays to his time, or vestiges of the original material he composed with; they allow him to move constantly towards this limit between being and nothingness where being insinuates itself even in nothingness, like bubbles of the earth ('the earth hath bubbles'). Hamlet recoils before the 'not to be' because he has a foreboding of the return of being ('to dye, to sleep, perchance to dreame'). In Macbeth, the apparition of Banquo's ghost is also a decisive experience of the 'no exit' from existence, its phantom return through the fissures through which one has driven it.[14]

In each case the equivocation of being and nothingness is figured as the return of the dead, of bubbles or episodes of non-being spread throughout being. Horror is awareness of the place left by the dead, by the murdered. In the case of Macbeth, Levinas claims, 'It is the shadow of being that horrifies Macbeth, the profile of being takes form in nothingness.'[15] Nothingness is engrained within being, is not in opposition to or on the other side of it. From the other side of the National Socialist genocide, with a post-war reality shaped by the shadows of its victims, Levinas opposes 'the horror of the night, "the silence and horror of the shades", to Heideggerian anxiety, the fear of being to the fear of nothingness'.[16] The anxious confrontation of my death and seizure of possibility in the face of it, or its dialectical sublation, seem a luxurious option when contrasted with the fate of the survivor, who must live in a being haunted by the incomplete absence of the dead. The possibility of being is continually compromised by the haunting of the dead and their calls for remembrance and justice.

The most remarkable feature of Levinas's confrontation of Shakespeare with philosophy is the remorseless deflation of any transcendence, even that afforded by death or by being towards death. There are few intimations of the role that will be played by transendence and alterity in Levinas's ethical thought, positions already announced in the prison notebooks. In a note from 1946 he writes: 'My philosophy – is a philosophy of the face to face. Relation with the other without intermediary. That's Judaism.'[17] Shakespeare indeed served as a preparation for this position, as a questioning of the possibility of a secure contrast between being and nothingness, of the confident seizure or mastery of being. This is emphasised in *Time and the Other* where Shakespeare and in particular *Hamlet* is called to undo any and every fantasy of mastery: '*Hamlet* is precisely a lengthy testimony to this impossibility of assuming death. Nothingness is impossible. It is nothingness that would have left humankind the possibility of assuming death and snatching a supreme mastery out of the servitude of existence.'[18] The philosophically underwritten opposition of being and nothingness would permit both the mastery over and the finality of death, my own in suicide and that of the other in murder. But Shakespeare's equivocation through Hamlet undoes this certainty and opens a space for a rethinking of being, nothingness and death perhaps not even dreamt of by philosophy.

For Levinas, the only hint of transcendence to be found in Shakespeare lies in madness. For him, the 'buffoon, the fool of Shakespearian tragedy, is the one who feels and bespeaks with lucidity the unsubstantiality of the world and the absurdity of its situations . . . the fool is the opening through which this world is swept with draughts of madness'.[19] While the fool may serve as a possible mode of transcendence in Shakespeare, he does so as a limit case, at the very point of the dissolution of the distinction between being and not-being. It is at this point, however, that Levinas bids *adieu* to Shakespeare. Having faithfully served to disrupt the major philosophical and political opposition of being and nothingness, to have put into question Hegel and Heidegger, Shakespeare cannot serve Levinas in taking the further step to thinking how to live ethically in the state of constant haunting. Hamlet and Macbeth, each living their predicament in their different ways, tend towards folly, whether that of melancholy or hubris. Levinas however, will move towards the model of a fragile subjectivity who is a hostage to mourning, but he sees this step as taking us out of the world of Shakespeare and towards that of prophecy and the Judaic sources of another, ethical thought.

It is perhaps paradoxical that the Shakespearean experience of the impossibility of death, of the impossibility of an escape from being, should have provided Levinas with the means for exorcising Hegelian dialectic and Heideggerian ontology. In many ways Shakespeare served as a solvent, dissolving, inverting, deflating and exacerbating the foundational postures of ontology. In a sense Shakespeare provided the *via negationis* along which Levinas was able to pass out of ontology and to move towards an ethics as first philosophy. A spectacular example of this is the manifestation of Macbeth in Section III of *Totality and Infinity* where Levinas traverses and exceeds Hegel's dialectic of master and slave. Recognising that the struggle for recognition is the prerogative of the slave, Levinas calls upon Macbeth to figure the attempt by the 'sovereign and self-enclosed will' to struggle *against* the struggle for recognition. The act of choosing death rather than subjection to the terms of struggle set by the Other provokes the desire not only for the destruction of both self and world, but also for complete and universal non-being. Macbeth's allergy to the Other, his frail barely immunised sovereignty, drives him to the wish 'that the nothingness of death be a void as total as that which would have reigned had the world never been created'.[20] Sovereign being, in other words, the prerogative of the master, reveals itself at the limit as the desire for absolute non-being, the complete renunciation of sovereignty. The ethical relation to the Other, beyond struggle and beyond war, is an attempt to accept the exteriority of the Other. For Levinas, Shakespeare took ontology to a limit where it had to undergo a sea change and become something else, something new, showing, in the words of the late fragment 'Bad Conscience and the Inexorable' (1981): 'To be or not to be: the question *par exellence* probably does not lie therein.'[21]

It leads for Levinas to the ethical question *par excellence*, for him unasked by Shakespeare, namely that of the relation to infinity, or 'why fear God?'

Notes

1. Emmanuel Levinas, *Time and the Other*, trans. Richard Cohen (Pittsburgh: Duquesne University Press, 1987), p. 72.
2. Ibid.
3. For an extended account of the contents and the circumstances of composition of the *Carnets* see my article 'Levinas's Prison Notebooks', *Radical Philosophy*, 160 (March/April 2010), pp. 27–35.
4. Emmanuel Levinas, *Carnets de captivité et autres inedits*, ed. Rodolphe Calin and Catherine Chalier (Paris: Bernard Grasset/IMEC, 2009), p. 84.
5. Ibid., p. 103.
6. Ibid., p. 87.
7. Ibid., p. 172.
8. Ibid., p. 173.
9. Ibid., p. 174.
10. Ibid.
11. Sean Hand (ed.), *The Levinas Reader* (Oxford: Basil Blackwell, 1989), p. 33.
12. Ibid.
13. Ibid.
14. Ibid.
15. Ibid., p. 34.
16. Ibid.
17. Levinas, *Carnets de captivité*, p. 186.
18. Levinas, *Time and the Other*, p. 73.
19. Ibid., p. 59.
20. Emmanuel Levinas, *Totality and Infinity: An Essay on Exteriority*, trans. Alphonso Lingis (Pittsburgh: Duquesne University Press, 1969), p. 231.
21. Emmanuel Levinas, *Of God Who Comes to Mind*, trans. Bettina Bergo (Stanford: Stanford University Press, 1988), p. 1.

Chapter 9

Contra Schmitt:
Law, Aesthetics and Absolutism in Shakespeare's *The Winter's Tale*

Christopher Pye

I want to introduce these reflections on the relations among law, aesthetic subjectivity and Absolutism in *The Winter's Tale* by way of the figure who saw in early modernity, and in Shakespeare especially, the ideal embodiment of the political and juridical logic of the state: the conservative jurist and political theorist, Carl Schmitt. I'll focus particularly on Schmitt's claim that early modern Absolutism realises in the figure of the sovereign the identity between legislator and creator that he takes to be the founding truth of politics.[1] Schmitt's affirmation of the metaphysical force of the sovereign decision – his claim that the decision informs law as its constitutive ground and in every instance of its application – arises, in part, as a reaction against what he takes to be the signal failures of modern liberalism, the 'liberal indecisionism' of the parliamentary democracy of his own moment – Weimar Germany – and more broadly in relation to what he describes as 'liberalism's onslaught against the political'.[2] For Schmitt, that assault is a function of the normativism of the nineteenth-century 'organisational-technical' state, and is embodied particularly in the subordination of the political to the economic and the corresponding emergence of the aesthetic as the category which valorises indecision and stands as a privileged figure for the apolitical autonomy of civic formations generally.[3]

Rather than bearing it out, *The Winter's Tale* explicitly vexes such a decisionistic account of the grounds of law, not in so far as it affirms a normative view of law, but in so far as it problematises the relation between law and sovereign agency as such. Further, the drama provides an equally precise counter to Schmitt's corollary argument concerning the political and historical bearings of the aesthetic, his claim that the aesthetic appears during the nineteenth century as the embodiment of liberalism's depoliticising tendencies. In fact, the aesthetic appears earlier, not as a fully developed philosophical category, but self-consciously nonetheless from within the domain of the work, and it does so specifically in relation to the problem of sovereignty. The aesthetic is the means by which sovereign agency is sustained within the political order of early modernity, the era, that is, of autonomous law on the one hand, and the incipient citizen-subject on the other.[4] In that sense, the aesthetic is affiliated with Absolutism as a specifically modern phenomenon. Indeed, the aesthetic emerges as that which at once establishes and radically problematises the predicated conception of the relation between sovereignty and law that Schmitt takes as a given.

For recent, left-oriented political theorists, Schmitt's conservative critique of liberalism has been as animating as it has been controversial. The force and the promise of his account consist in what it suggests about the irreducibly political character of the social and juridical domains.[5] For Schmitt, the sovereign decision cannot be subsumed by the system of legal codes and norms – the grounds of the entire tradition of juristic rationalism from Locke to Rawls – precisely because it constitutes that field and determines when it does and doesn't come into play. 'Sovereign is he who decides on the exception', Schmitt famously declares, and that possibility of the exception lies at the determining core of the rule.[6] The political implications of Schmitt's decisionist argument would seem, then, to depend on whether the exceptional act need necessarily belong solely to the person of the sovereign. Decisionism, of course, doesn't necessarily mean monarchism, and Schmitt himself allows for a range of political embodiments, insisting only on the undivided character of the authority that decides the force of law, whatever that authority might be. And yet the more fundamental question, politically and philosophically, is whether the logic of the exception as Schmitt articulates it might imply just such a division of authority, and thus pose questions not just about who decides but about the nature of political agency as such.[7]

That issue of agency becomes apparent when we consider Schmitt's account of the sovereign act from the topographical perspective that underwrites it. Schmitt's argument is predicated on the recognition that, as Paul Hirst puts it, 'all legal orders have an outside' – thus Schmitt's central claim about the exceptional character of the determining act.[8] The political act as an act is premised on the possibility of such externality: that is what assures that it is not inscribed within the dimension of norms. At the same time, the political is for Schmitt that which is without exteriority. 'The political is the total, and as a result we know that any decision about whether something is *unpolitical* is always a *political* decision, irrespective of who decides.'[9] The political is illimitable, a fact all the more borne out by liberalism's efforts to bracket it. At once definitionally external and yet, because of the limitless field of its operation, incapable of assuming exteriority vis-à-vis itself – of transcending itself as an act – the political act amounts to the act that poses the problem of its own grounds.[10] Looked at 'from the perspective of the norm', Schmitt writes, 'the constitutive, specific element of the decision . . . is new and alien', it 'emanates from nothingness'.[11] The question is whether that emergence from nothing is merely an effect of the normative perspective or whether it isn't an irreducible element of the act as he conceives it.

Such questions about the status of the political act can equally be pursued from an historical perspective. It's worth asking whether Schmitt's account of the sovereign decision doesn't remain bound up with the forms of instrumental logic particular to the era of liberal individualism he repudiates. It's not a coincidence, I'd argue, that at least within the domain of English theatre, from *Gorbuduc* to *King Lear*, early modernity's most profound reflections on sovereignty gravitate towards the political act in its more opaque dimensions, that is, towards the act by which sovereign force undoes itself, as if in that self-annulling gesture something of the mysterious grounds of sovereignty came to view.[12] In *Lear*, such an act is bound up with sovereignty's self-exceeding illimitability, as well as with its *ex nihilo* character, it's unfathomable 'something out of nothing'.[13] Lear's 'darker purpose' – the act through which he divides the kingdom and no less stagily banishes his beloved child – can be read as at once the most blind and the most impossibly knowing in the play, the gesture by which in casting her beyond his own all-consuming ken he ensures not just the marriage of love for Cordelia but the entire trajectory of loss and return that marks the drama.[14] That coincidence of the monarch's inscrutable theatricality and the space of the work as such suggests how deeply if implicitly the problem of the aesthetic is related to sovereignty's own totalising character. It's worth noting the parallel between the 'purposive purposelessness' that defines Kant's account of the aesthetic and the definitionally non-instrumental character of sovereignty, it's nature as the one political form which contains its ends within itself: the aim of sovereignty is, as Foucault points out, sovereignty.[15]

But to consider the relation between the sovereign decision and the aesthetic, I want to turn, not to *King Lear*, with its backward-looking feudal preoccupations, but to *The Winter's Tale*, a play concerned with Absolutism as an emerging formation and with the explicit articulation of the aesthetic as an autonomous category. The distinction between the two plays crystallises in the differing forms their tyrants' madness take. With Lear, madness amounts to the fragmentation attending a radically totalised, organically imagined conception of the body politic, a condition in which cure is indistinguishable from disease, in which the sovereign's excision of the poisonous member reproduces the division it would resolve: 'I will punish home' (3.4.17), Lear declares, turning on his own flesh and blood and anticipating his passage into madness.

For Leontes, madness is no less reiterative and self-punitive, but derives from the recoils of delusional jealousy and mimetic desire –

> I am angling now,
> Though you perceive me not how I give line.
> Go to, go to!' (1.2.105)

– Leontes says as he sends Hermione and his twinned rival Polixenes to the garden.[16] If Leontes acts, in Camillo's words, 'as if he had been an instrument / To vice [Polixenes] to't', it's because he functions, as René Girard has argued, within the mimetic, circulatory structure in which the figure who bars desire simultaneously constitutes it (1.2.410–11). Within such a mechanism, rivalrous difference amounts to identity and identification merely reproduces desire's divisions within. In other words, we are in the space of limitless substitutability: 'Like a cipher, / Yet standing in rich place, I multiply', Polixines says, alluding to the strange, reiterative power of the empty numerical place-holder (1.2.6–7).[17] Would I 'appoint myself in vexation?', Leontes exclaims (1.2.323): he does, apparently, and his language emphasises the relation between his plight and the substitutive logic of the office holder.[18] In terms of political dispensations, we could say the play belongs less to Lear's world of hierarchisation and embodiment than to Othello's world of lateral equivalences and surrogacy – the world, that is, of the citizen subject.[19] Jealousy is a bourgeois ailment, and *The Winter's Tale* a fundamentally domestic drama.[20]

What makes it a drama of Absolutism, then? In one sense, nothing but the purity of the mimetic structure it invokes. As Girard remarks, *The Winter's Tale* is the play in which Shakespeare realises mimetic desire without causative alibi – no Iagos – which is to say it realises it as a structure that emerges, again, *ex nihilo*.[21] The play's concern with sovereignty is reflected in this preoccupation with the problem of originative grounds and derivation. In its condensation of origin and outcome, the word 'issue' becomes both the play's resolving term and its opaque point of obsession: 'I / Play . . . a part, whose / Issue will hiss me to my grave' (1.2.185–7); 'I'll not rear / Another's issue' (3.1.192–3); 'gracious be [the oracle's] issue' (3.1.22); 'This being . . . the issue / Of King Polixenes' (3.3.42–3); 'his highness' fail of issue / May drop upon his kingdom' (5.1.27–8); 'I would gladly know the issue of it' (5.2.8); 'I / . . . have preserved / Myself to see the issue' (5.3.125–8).[22] Leontes' descent into madness is bound up with that fixation on origins. 'We are / Almost as like as eggs' (1.2.128–9) he says to his son Mamillius. The phrase recurs: 'Will you take eggs for money'? (1.2.159). Leontes is absorbed with the question of the paternity of his wife's unborn child, and seeks solace in the mirror affirmation of the child he knows to be his own. But, of course, to be alike as two eggs is to be like every other egg. To stake oneself on that ground – to fix oneself at all – is to be all the more caught up within the chain of empty and limitlessly multiplying ciphers.

The often-remarked obscurity and instability of the play's language is related to the illimitability of that signifying chain. Critical discussion has focused particularly on the passage in which Leontes describes the incomprehensible *ex nihilo* of desire:

>   – can thy dam, may't be
> Affection! – thy intention stabs the centre.
> Thou dost make possible things not so held,
> Communicat'st with dreams – how can this be?
> With what's real thou coactive art,
> And fellow'st nothing. Then 'tis very credent
> Thou mayst co-join with something, and thou dost,
> And that beyond commission, and I find it,
> And that to the infection of my brains
> And hard'ning of my brows. (1.2.136–44)

Is Leontes describing Hermione's illicit affections or the workings of his own diseased imagination? Critics and editors have wondered. That ambiguity is related to another, perhaps stranger, one; to the extent that he's describing himself, Leontes seems at once to be in the throes of his delirium and to be recognising it as a delirium: 'Thou dost make possible things not so held . . . / With what's real thou coactive art, / And fellow'st nothing.' That mixture of immersion and self-reflexive knowledge is picked up more broadly in the ways Leontes seems at some level to know he is caught up in a play, even to possess an obscure foreknowledge of its imagined end:

> Go play, boy, play – thy mother plays, and I
> Play too, but so disgraced a part, whose issue
> Will hiss me to my grave. (1.2.185–7)[23]

Such boundary crossings between identities, between insides and outsides, can be understood in terms of the spiralling relation between the infinitude of the signifying chain and the demand for grounds it exacerbates. In relation to the purely differential logic of the multiplying cipher, not only will one identity stand in the place of another, but the very impulse to situate oneself outside the structure – to differentiate – reinscribes one within it.[24]

That signifying phenomenon is not exclusive to *The Winter's Tale*, of course. But its heightened presence there, as well as its explicit framing as a problem of issue and origination, is a function of the play's historical and political moment. In the play and as an historical formation, Absolutism is articulated within the horizon of a fundamentally new political/ subjective configuration – the space of illimitable equivalency – and is thus oriented around totalisation as a formal problem.[25] As the end of the play will show, with Absolutism, the contradiction between legitimacy's basis in genealogy and its basis in formal autonomy – a contradiction that in some sense had always inhabited sovereignty – assumes an outright form.[26]

What characterises the sovereign decision within such an order? The fact, I would argue, that it derives from elsewhere. Leontes' choice to invoke the judgement of the oracle at Delphos in order to determine the outcome of the public trial of Hermione might be read in terms of the proto-liberal compromises that marked Absolutism as a historical phenomenon. 'Let us be cleared / Of being tyrannous, since we so openly / Proceed in justice', Leontes proclaims (3.2.4–6). Even before the final decades of Absolutism's fragile historical interim, 'rulers were accepted only because of what they did to weaken their rule', Ivan Nagel observes.[27] We might even see an anticipation of that characteristic Enlightenment procedure by which political authority resolved its internal contradictions and legitimised itself by suspending its force in relation to supervening grace.[28] But it's not grace that is drawn down in the oracle's pronouncement: it's law and judgement. In that sense, the otherness of the oracular pronouncement should be read directly in relation to the logic of sovereignty. Within the newly infinitised signifying domain of the political, the sovereign decision can only emerge from a radical elsewhere, from out of the blue. Whatever its thematic associations with ancient social formations, the oracle figures something new and momentous.

In a sense, of course, the oracle's word is explicitly opposed to Leontes' judgement, divine truth exposing tyrannical delusion. In fact, though, the two are explicitly aligned in their effects, which is where their meaning lies. Hermione is moved less by the content of the tyrant's false judgement than the brutality of her public exposure in the court of law, a killing visibility which lays bare the spectator as well and momentarily empties out the theatrical fiction as such: My past life has been as chaste, she says,

As I am now unhappy, which is more
Than history can pattern, though devised
And played to take spectators. (3.2.34–6)

The oracle's effects are no less fatal. To recall the rapidly concatenated sequence: the judgement is opened, the message read declaring that Hermione is innocent, Leontes a jealous tyrant, and that 'the King shall live without an heir if that which is lost be not found' (3.2.130–3). When the king refuses the judgement, a messenger arrives to announce that Mamillius, 'from mere conceit of the queen's speed', has died. Declaring 'the heavens themselves / Do strike at [his] injustice', Leontes instantly forgoes his delusion (3.2.144–5).

It is, one can argue, the resistance to oracular truth that precipitates death. But the sequence feels seamless, and we know from the previous scene in which the messengers describe their visit to Delphos that the oracle's words harbour their own violence.

But of all, the burst
And the ear-deaf'ning voice o'th' oracle,
Kin to Jove's thunder, so surprised my sense
That I was nothing. (3.1.8–11)

The ground of that annihilating power is evident in the temporal character of its enactment. The oracle's pronouncement that the king shall live without an heir is fulfilled precisely in Leontes' refusal of it. Thus, even as the reply seems to be compassed in advance by oracular law, that pronouncement is only realised – only proves law – through the response it solicits. The inscribing, desubjectivising force of oracular truth consists in that elision of the distinction between law and response, between the inside and outside of the space of law.[29]

In so far as it is inscriptive and without exteriority, such a conception of law is explicitly oriented around the problem of its locus. When the oracle's words 'by Apollo's great divine sealed up' shall be broken open, 'something rare / Even then will rush to knowledge', the messenger declares (3.1.19–21). Rush to knowledge from where? The language suggests inward as much as outward revelation. That shift to the question of law's source is specific to Absolutism. When *King Lear* comes to, when he tentatively recognises Cordelia at the close, he is attempting to know what we sense he has known and not known from the outset; knowledge is sealed within the ineluctable recesses of sovereign personhood. Leontes' instantaneous coming to is a function ultimately neither of inwardness, however occulted, nor simply of external determination; it amounts instead to the annulment of the entire frame within which those structuring oppositions are sustained, which is to say, the frame within which sovereignty itself is inscribed.

Rather than implying a necessary equivalency between judicial decision and the person of the king, the play represents law as a desubjectivising effect. To return to Schmitt's terms, law, as figured in the oracle, is what undoes the distinction between constituting and constituted authority.[30] The aesthetic emerges in the play, I want to argue, specifically in relation to that problematic of law. The aesthetic functions at once as law's mirroring counter-image, the autonomy of the one reflecting the autonomy of the other, and as the necessary term for the constitution of any sort of ratio or rapport between sovereign agency and law.

The play's self-conscious turn in its second half to the category of the aesthetic is most evident, of course, in the famous statue scene at the close. But Hermione's artful return merely crystallises the larger structure through which the play itself passes into the register of the aesthetic by returning upon itself across the sixteen-year caesura at its centre. That aesthetic translation is an aspect of the late 'romances' generally, and is bound up with their tragi-comic form. It's not at all anachronistic to read Shakespeare's late plays in terms of the passage from comedy to tragedy to the reflexive return by which death is sublated and internalised as the condition of the work's status as self-reflective, self-consciously aesthetic form.[31] That formal 'solution' bears in a generalised way on the problems of autogenetic totalisation associated with sovereignty; as we will see, the thematic particulars of Leontes' reformation play themselves out within the ultimately fragile logic of the play's own aesthetic turn.[32]

That Shakespeare is conscious of the stakes of the structure is evident in the calculated tonal instabilities of the hinge scene where the play passes from tragedy to comic/romance mode. 'Thou metst with things dying, I with things newborn', the Old Shepherd declares to the pastoral clown during the scene in which he discovers the abandoned infant amidst the carnage on land and at sea – devouring bears, drowning sailors (3.3.109–10). The forced character of the turn is represented specifically as a problem of narrativisation in the clown's comically veering attempts to accommodate the grisly and disparate elements of the scene:

> I would you did but see how [the sea] chafes, how it rages, how it takes up the shore; but that's not to the point. O, the most piteous cries of the poor souls! . . . And then for the land-service, to see how the bear tore out his shoulder-bone . . . But to make an end of the ship, to see how the sea flapdragoned it; but first, how the poor souls roared . . . (3.3.85–95)

'To make an end of the ship': the complicity between the telling and the destruction it describes suggests how thoroughly violence is affiliated here with narrative mastery, all oriented around death's inassimilability.[33]

The caesura that opens the possibility of aesthetic autonomy and self-inclusiveness also brings to the fore these prospects of narrative instability, and it does so in so far as that division is shown to have a foundational rather than just a mediating relation to the work. The 'wide gap' to which the chorus makes reference, and to which Leontes will return in the final lines of the play –

> Lead us from hence, where we may leisurely
> Each one demand and answer to his part
> Performed in this wide gap of time since first
> We were dissevered. (5.2.231)

– reappears in the context of Autolycus's considerably less elevated aesthetic:

> He hath songs for man or woman of all sizes – no milliner can so fit his customers with gloves. He has the prettiest love songs for maids, so without bawdry, which is strange, with such delicate burden of dildos and fadings, 'jump her and thump her'; and where some stretch-mouthed rascal would, as it were, mean mischief, and break a foul gap into the matter, he makes the maid to answer, 'Whoop, do me no harm, good man' – pushes him off, slights him with 'whoop, do me no harm, good man'. (4.4.193–202)

To 'break a foul gap into the matter' is, according to Stephen Orgel's note, to 'interpolate something indecent into the song'. But, in the context of 'dildos' and 'fadings', the 'foul gap' carries its own sexual and misogynistic connotations. Indeed, the sexual and the interpolative are inextricable in the passage. As Orgel notes, although 'dildos and fadings' appear as empty nonce words in contemporary ballads, it is precisely the speaker's severing and isolating them from their generally bawdy context that gives them their prurient cast. Such inadvertent interpretive complicity is of a piece with the broader transferential logic of the scene. The way in which the 'stretch[ed] mouth' of the interpolating rascal mimes the 'foul gap' he would open in the matter of the song picks up on the larger uncertainty about whether the interpreter is a figure within a dialogic ballad – Orgel's reading – or an intrusive audience-member whose responses are inscribed in advance by the ditty. And that ambiguity about the interpreter within figures, in turn, the ambiguities of the playgoer's own inescapably complicit, prurient and anticipated relation to the passage. Such transferential effects arise because the interpolated, and interpellating, gap – foul or otherwise – isn't within the matter of the play or song; it *is* that matter, the constitutive division the mastering auditor can only reiterate.[34] Listening to his ballad, all, male and female alike, are gelded – 'all their other senses stuck in ears – you might have pinched a placket, it was senseless; 'twas nothing to geld a codpiece of a purse' – and what they are lost to or inscribed by is 'the nothing of it' (4.4.605–7, 609). Such is the logic of a groundless, prosthetic aesthetic that manages for that very reason to fit every customer, especially the most resistant customer, like a milliner's glove.

That Autolycus should embody such an aesthetic makes sense, given his cheerful embrace of the possibilities of self-annulment.[35] In the scene in which Autolycus snares the clown by posing as the abject victim of highwaymen, picking the rustic's pocket as he comes to his assistance – 'You ha' done me a charitable office' – and then announces he has been victimised by an 'ape-bear[ing]' rogue named Autolycus, the self-making man converts the tyrant's reflexive, self-rivening masochism into a casually self-annihilating power (4.3.76, 93). The gratuity of his gestures – no need, in fact, to name himself, no need to announce his ruses as he performs them – signals the aesthetic character of the pleasure; he stands for a self-theatricalisation more clarified than Leontes'. But that explicit passage into the register of the aesthetic allows something like the powers of sovereign self-compassment Leontes fulfilled only in the form of madness. Indeed, in his gratuitousness, Autolycus achieves something like the *ex nihilo* of sovereignty, for his aim is less the profits of his undertakings than the pleasures of speculation's potentially illimitable returns: 'if I make not this cheat bring out another, and the shearers prove sheep, let me be unrolled and my name put in the book of virtue!' (4.3.118–20).

The ease with which Autolycus empoweringly abrogates himself can be read in terms of class distinctions between the court, with its taut investment in lineal selfhood, and the more free-form, demotic culture of country and market, an ideological ranginess made possible by the capaciousness of the romance genre.[36] But it's important to recognise what nevertheless binds Autolycus's apparently unbound world. Through Autolycus, the aesthetic is affiliated with economy: it's a matter of customers and commodities. And through economy, substitutability is translated into a systematic, thus thematisable, logic of exchange, including the exchange of identities. 'Yet for the outside of thy poverty we must make an exchange; therefore discase thee instantly', Camillo says, preparing Autolycus to change forms with Florizel (4.4.627–8). 'What an exchange had this been, without boot! What a boot is here with this exchange!' Autolycus exclaims, emphasising the perfect symmetries of economy's limitless surplus value (4.4.670–72). Rather than being ontological and originative – what has already eroded identity from the outset – exchange amounts to a socioeconomic theme defined over and against 'flesh and blood', even as what comically reverses lineal derivation. The clown describes the literally 'preposterous' sequence through which he and his shepherd father are abruptly elevated at the discovery of the lost child: 'But I was a gentleman born before my father, for the King's son took me by the hand and called me brother, and then the two Kings called my father brother' (5.2.142, 134–7).[37]

The fact that Autolycus ultimately devotes his roguery to the service of the Prince he had once served, as well as the fact that he drops out of the drama before the finale, can be read in terms of the play's need to recover its aristocratic bearings and the totalising aesthetic particular to court and sovereign. At the same time, though, in its final turns, and precisely in so far as it does return to the problem of totalisation, the play engages the aesthetic beyond its stabilising affiliation with economy, and beyond the relatively manageable perils of self-fashioning. That more compassing and problematic conception of the aesthetic draws it into relation with what amounts to its counter-term in the divided structure of the play, that is, law, and particularly oracular law.

The Winter's Tale has a double resolution, and the stakes of the final scene of Hermione's return are only really apparent in relation to the immediately preceding discovery scene in which Perdita, the lost daughter, is recovered. The odd theatrical withholding of that moment of recognition – the fact that it is conveyed through a series of reports – should be seen as a visibly failed attempt to buffer the audience from a scene whose clinching resolvativeness merely reiterates the violence of the oracular pronouncement it would miraculously fulfill and allay: 'They seemed almost with staring at one another to tear the cases of their eyes', one of the reporting gentlemen says of the long-awaited reencounter (5.2.11–13). Recognition threatens to repeat the rending possessiveness which necessitated it, a violence animated now by an exacerbated desire to forcibly manage loss. Paulina 'had one eye declined for the loss of her husband, another elevated that the oracle was fulfilled. She lifted the princess from the earth, and so locks her in embracing as if she would pin her to her heart, that she might no more be in danger of losing' (5.2.73–7).

The scene's affective contradictions are bound up now with the play's larger aesthetic and epistemological demands, demands in which narrative force is equated with juridical truth. 'That which you hear you'll swear you see, there is such unity in the proofs', one of the tellers declares (5.2.31–2). Constituted through what it excludes, such a version of unity reproduces the divisions it would efface. The reports proliferate, each reiterating the violence of what it would mediate: 'I make a broken delivery of the business'; 'I never heard of such another encounter, which lames report to follow it, and undoes description to do it' (5.2.9–10, 55–7). Such violence is explicitly associated with aestheticisation's queasily forced chiastic symmetries: 'Till from one sign of dolour to another she did, with an "Alas!", I would fain say bleed tears; for I am sure my heart wept blood' (5.2.85–7).

Hermione's return, the marvel that transpires this time right before our eyes, is an explicit corrective to the fatal overproximity of the prior recognition scene. 'Good my lord, forbear', Paulina declares when Leontes moves too soon to embrace the figure (5.3.80). That vicariousness which had been a perverse effect of jealousy's possessive drive – 'go to, go to' – now becomes a function of willing deference. 'I am content to look on', Leontes remarks. 'So long could I / Stand by, a looker-on' Perdita says (5.3.92, 84–5). Even Hermione, the object of every gaze, amounts to a looker-on, merely offering back when she finally does speak her spectators' question in inverted form: 'Tell me, mine own, / Where hast *thou* been preserved?' (5.3.123–4, my italics). For the aesthetic is not simply the willing adoption of a distance towards a determined object. It's a function of the larger movement of return through which the 'wide gap' of death and loss are retained as the forming condition of subject and object alike, and thus as the groundless ground of all rapport. In the gradualness of the statue's coming to life, object and spectator are transferentially suspended in the condition of living dead, a state in which the blind masochism of tyrannical jealousy is now transformed into desire's knowingly engaged condition:

Paulina: No longer shall you gaze on't, lest your fancy
         May think anon it moves.
Leontes: Let be, let be.
         Would I were dead, but that methinks already–
         . . .
         Would you not deem it breathed?
         . . .
         No settled senses of the world can match
         The pleasure of that madness. (5.3.60–73)

The return from death, the cancelling passage from the rigours of ancient law to faith – we are clearly, as Roy Battenhouse and Julia Lupton have argued, within the ambit of a Christianising, Pauline, transformation.[38] But I want to argue that the theological reading of the close is inscribed within an aesthetic turn that is at once narrower historically and formally supervenient. The specificity of that aesthetic operation is evident in the nature of its relation to law, a relation that is something more complex than one of supercession. Like law, art is illimitable. Whatever Paulina's directorial role at the close, the mystery of Hermione's return, which figures the mystery of representational origins generally, extends beyond Paulina and beyond the explanatory horizon of the drama; with Hermione's return, the play's representational logic exceeds its narrative logic. And, like law, art inscribes – subject and object alike are constituted and sustained within the ratio and distance the aesthetic maintains.[39] Indeed, what becomes critical at the close is the mutual articulation between law and the aesthetic. 'If this be magic, let it be an art / As lawful as eating', Leontes exclaims (5.3.110–11). Even as art seeks the grounding of law, the aesthetic functions to naturalise and thus to positivise law, a transformation that recovers law as a function of sovereign agency. At once opposed and reflected in one another like the halves of the play, the infinitudes of art and law are stabilised by way of their chiasmic relation to one another.

Or almost so. It's hard not to hear something untoward in the likening of art to eating. Autolycus utters his tunes 'as he had eaten ballads', the clown declared (4.4.187). Dion, the oracle's messenger, had spoken of dangers should the king remain without issue that will descend on the kingdom and 'devour / Incertain lookers-on' (5.1.28–9). Is the prospect of aesthetic violence allayed at the close? Dion described the 'sacrifices' attending the oracle's ceremonies, and we may have reason to wonder at the close if such sacrificial violence belongs only to the domain of truth. What do we make of the unremarked disappearance of Mamillius at the close? – All members of the family return except the boy. Particularly given the unstable narcissism of Leontes' relation to the child at the opening, we can read the son's death as the offering that ensures the exogamous logic of the genealogical resolution, the breach that all the more secures patrilinealism, in this instance through the daughter.

But to understand the unacknowledged character of the child's disappearance we need to understand it in terms of the aesthetic function itself, the aesthetic now conceived in its radically autochthonous character. The title of the play derives from the story Mamillius whispers to his mother – as critics have noted, the play itself gradually converges with that tale of the supernatural.[40] We should take seriously the formal question posed by that inclusion of the title within the drama. Can the aesthetic work incorporate everything, including its ground and origin? Yes, except of course for a small remainder, the trace of the hand that recursively inscribes itself there. Egg and, as Polixines says of his own son, 'parasite', Mamillius is posited at once as source and as the sacrificial remainder that constitutes the possibility of the work as totality. The dissolution of agency implied by the figure of art as eating – art as what

devours and is simultaneously devoured – derives from the instability of
that conception of the radically self-incorporative work.

   Of course, to take the child as a figure for the aesthetic is tendentious–
a forced reading. But that's just the point. The problem of the aesthetic is
the problem of interpretive force, as the scene of Mamillius's tale-telling
suggests. Having put him aside, Hermione calls the child back –

> Come, sir, now
> I am for you again. Pray sit you by us,
> And tell's a tale. (2.1.21–3)

'I will tell it softly, / Yon crickets shall not hear it', Mamillius says, alluding to the chattering ladies in waiting. Hermione: 'Come on, then, and
give't me in mine ear' (2.1.31–2). Stanley Cavell observes the sexual res-
onances of Hermione's line, and argues that Leontes enraged entrance at
this moment to revoke the child occurs 'as if it were brought on by' the
scene of the child in his mother's lap, filling his pregnant mother's ear.[41]
In other words, it amounts to a fantasy of origins within the play. And
yet, it is the audience, not Leontes, that hears the phrase, and the question of the erotics of the passage – the question of what's there – can't
be distinguished from the question of the interpretive pressure we bring
to bear. If there are intimations of force in Hermione's words, they are
hard to separate from whatever animates our own desire to put ourselves
in the place of that scene of absolute origination, to hear what the child
whispers back into the maternal ear. Her words are our words: 'giv't me
in mine ear'. And yet, it is just that need to assert possessive force that
confirms the words are not our own, and that the sexuality of the scene
is a function of our jealous and reiterated exclusion from its unknowable
intimacy. In other words, the line has the function of a lure. Consuming
and consumed, the audience of 'incertain lookers-on' interpretively constitutes the scene – it is indeed an *ur* scene – but as one within which its
desires are from the outset already alienated and inscribed.

*

To return to Carl Schmitt's own fantasies of origination. Rather than
being decisionism's foundational scene, the representation of early
modern sovereignty brings to the fore the ungrounded, dispossessive
character of the political act. Absolutism is distinguished by the way
in which it casts that problem of grounds as an explicitly aesthetic
problem. The aesthetic appears, not as an effect of the prince's creative hand – Burkhardt's state as work of art – but as an autonomous
function within which sovereign agency and positive law are sustained;
paradoxically, in the play, it is in giving itself over to the aesthetic that

sovereignty establishes the possibility of agency vis-à-vis law.[42] And yet, that aesthetic solution merely opens a more thoroughgoing risk. Foreclosing the gap altogether, the radically incorporative, autogenetic work abolishes the very space of the interpolating subject, a dire loss of loss figured in the unmarked disappearance of the child from a scene centred on the acknowledgement of death's structuring function. In that sense, whatever its affiliations with a newly secured and domestic subjectivity, the aesthetic ultimately poses the problem of the subject at a point beyond the logic of castration and thus beyond sexuality conceived as a gendered, even an indeterminately gendered, form. That version of 'desubjectivising' extends beyond the annulments of law as we see them enacted in the play. For it amounts to the undoing of the opposition between law and art around which the play is structured. With that, law understood as a formal category based on negation and prohibition becomes indistinguishable from a more incalculable devouring in which the subject in all its phenomenological dimensions is at stake. Understood thus, the aesthetic is the site, not of a cultivated indecision as Schmitt would have it, but of the forced and radically blind decision – an unstable positing in advance of the structuring terms of negation and symbolisation.[43] In that sense, the aesthetic is where the political, understood as the domain of the act in its purely contingent character, reaches its fullest extension.

I want to conclude by reflecting on how the account I offer here bears on the modern history of the aesthetic. That history, particularly as it is has been conceived in sociological terms, is taken to begin in the seventeenth and eighteenth centuries and to be associated with the emergence of empiricism, both in so far as that philosophy served as the category against which the aesthetic defined itself, and in so far as it insisted on a degree of separation between spheres of discourse unknown to premodern culture.[44] Others argue that the notion of the autonomy of the aesthetic work, even of its ambiguously valued superfluity, coincides with early capitalism generally and the emerging consciousness of the peculiarly groundless character of exchange relations and the commodity form.[45] I've argued that the aesthetic emerges, not at the level of philosophical developments or even as a reflection of economy, but in relation to a more fundamental transformation in signifying structures, a transformation in relation to which economic exchange has a conservative, securing function; whatever 'devouring' is involved in the absolute aesthetic, it extends beyond the logic of commodity consumption, and insists that the question of the relation between aesthetics and the political be posed at a more radical phenomenological level.[46]

The aesthetic should be viewed less merely as a function of the multiplication of separate discursive spheres than as the sphere within which the very problem of autonomy and origination is posed. That association with the problem of grounds is at the core of the early-modern aesthetic's relation to the categories of sovereignty and law.[47] Paradoxically, not just the superfluity but the radical contingency of the aesthetic only becomes apparent when it is understood in its relation to its strongest totalising claims. It is at that level, too, that we can recognise the connection between *The Winter's Tale* and the problematic emergence well before Kant of something like aesthetic subjectivity.

Notes

1. See Carl Schmitt, *Political Theology: Four Chapters on the Concept of Sovereignty*, trans. George Schwab (Chicago: Chicago University Press, 1985), p. 48.
2. Ibid., pp. 26, 63, 65.
3. Ibid., pp. 34, 63–5. On Schmitt's association between the perceived abstraction of the liberal democratic political sphere and the autonomy of the aesthetic, see Victoria Kahn, 'Hamlet or Hecuba: Carl Schmitt's Decision', *Representations*, 83 (2003), p. 73. On Schmitt's analysis as a commentary on the increased subjection of life to objectivised orders such as economy and bureaucratic politics, see Slavoj Žižek, 'Carl Schmitt in the Age of Post-Politics', in Chantal Mouffe (ed.), *The Challenge of Carl Schmitt* (London and New York: Verso, 1999), p. 144.
4. On the paired relation between the emergence of formal, abstract law and the valorised private subject, see Jürgen Habermas, *The Structural Transformation of the Public Sphere*, trans. Thomas Burger (Cambridge, MA: MIT Press), p. 54.
5. See especially, Chantal Mouffe, *The Return of the Political* (London: Verso, 1993), pp. 117–33.
6. Schmitt, *Political Theology*, p. 5.
7. On the self-dividing character of the sovereign decision, see Jacques Derrida, *The Politics of Friendship* (London: Verso, 2005), pp. 68–9, and Jacques Lezra, *Wild Materialism: The Ethic of Terror and the Modern Republic* (New York: Fordham, 2010), pp. 68–9.
8. Paul Hirst, 'Carl Schmitt's Decisionism', in Mouffe (ed.), *The Challenge of Carl Schmitt*, p. 11.
9. Schmitt, *Political Theology*, p. 2.
10. Samuel Weber describes the failure of the sovereign decision – its collapse into limitless indecision – in relation to the impossibility of assuming the transcendent posture implied by Schmitt's account of the state of exception. That failure of transcendence should be understood, he argues, in terms of the fragmentary, untotalisable character of the Baroque Reformation era. See Weber, 'Taking Exception to Decision: Walter Benjamin and Carl Schmitt', *diacritics*, 22:3–4 (1992), p. 17.
11. Schmitt, *Political Theology*, pp. 31–2.

12. On abdication as an expression of sovereign will, see Franco Moretti, 'The Great Eclipse', in *Signs Taken for Wonders: Essays in the Sociology of Literary Forms*, trans. Susan Fischer, David Forgacs and David Miller (London and New York: Verso, 1988), p. 46.

13. On the *ex nihilo* character of Renaissance artistic production, see Julia Reinhard Lupton, *Afterlives of the Saints: Hagiography, Typology, and Renaissance Literature* (Stanford: Stanford University Press, 1996), pp. 67–9.

14. Such a reading is borne out by the ornate, periodic and quite controlled rhetoric of his speech in response to Cordelia's refusal of his demand for the display of love – 'For, by the sacred radiance of the sun, / The mysteries of Hecate and the night, / By all the operation of the orbs . . .' – and by the obscure, vastly overdetermined self-knowledge implied by his likening himself to the 'barbarous Scythian' 'that makes his generation his messes' (1.1.108–10, 115–16). That cannibalistic erosion of distinctions between self and other relates to the incestuous themes of the play, as well as to the vertiginous loss of boundary between the sovereign act and the space of the play itself. See Christopher Pye, *The Vanishing: Shakespeare, the Subject, and Early Modern Culture* (Durham, NC: Duke University Press, 2000), pp. 95–6.

15. Michel Foucault, 'Governmentality', in *The Foucault Effect*, ed. Graham Burchell, Colin Gorden and Peter Miller (Chicago: University of Chicago Press, 1991), p. 95.

16. Shakespeare, *The Winter's Tale*, ed. Stephen Orgel (Oxford and New York: Oxford University Press, 1996), 1.2.178–80. Subsequent references to the play will be to this edition.

17. On the phrase, 'standing in', as an allusion to Polixines' standing in Leontes' place, see Howard Felperin, '"Tongue-tied, Our Queen?": The Deconstruction of Presence in *The Winter's Tale*', in Kiernan Ryan (ed.), *Shakespeare: The Last Plays* (London and New York: Longman, 1999), p. 195.

18. On Shakespeare's Romances occupying the transition between medieval conceptions of liberties to an 'emerging identity between subjectivity and citizenship', see Simon Palfrey, *Late Shakespeare: A New World of Words* (Oxford and New York: Clarendon, 1997), p. 50. On the mixed character of Absolutism, its articulation of feudal forms in relation to fundamentally bourgeois bureaucratic transformations, see Perry Anderson, *Lineages of the Absolutist State* (London: Verso, 1974). On the relation between surrogacy and structures of office, see Julia Genster, 'Lieutenancy, Standing In, and *Othello*', *ELH*, 57 (1990), pp. 785–809. The triangulated structure of the initiating scene of desire in the play of course includes the possibilities of homoerotic affiliation: it's not a coincidence that all erupts for Leontes at the moment Polixines plans to depart. Still, to fix on homosexual identification as the scene's explanatory secret is to allay the greater threat of the radically open, dissolvative desire it represents. On the homosocial dimensions of the opening scenes, see Michael D. Bristol, 'In Search of the Bear: Spatiotemporal Form and the Heterogeneity of Economies in *The Winter's Tale*', *Shakespeare Quarterly*, 42:2 (1991), p. 155.

19. I borrow this spatial conception of citizenship from Julia Reinhard Lupton,

Citizen-Saints: Shakespeare and Political Theology (Chicago: University of Chicago Press, 2005), p. 11 and passim.

20. On Leontes as embodying the new 'self-centered, rationalist' subject of the bourgeois era – more a 'man' than a king – see William Morse, 'Metacriticism and Materiality: The Case of Shakespeare's *The Winter's Tale*', *ELH*, 58:2 (1991), pp. 291, 289.

21. Stephen Orgel implies this aspect of jealousy in the play when he associates it with the 'self-generating and autonomous nature of consciousness itself'. Introduction, *The Winter's Tale*, p. 19. Northrop Frye describes Leontes' jealousy as a 'parody of creation out of nothing'; see his *Fables of Identity: Studies in Poetic Mythology* (New York: Harcourt, 1963), p. 115.

22. Carol Thomas Neely notes the motif in the context of a reading of the play as a hard-won celebration of fertility and reproductive love; see '*The Winter's Tale*: Women and Issue', in Ryan (ed.), *Shakespeare: The Last Plays*, pp. 169–71.

23. On Leontes' unconscious meta-theatricalness, see David Young, *The Heart's Forest: A Study of Shakespeare's Pastoral Plays* (New Haven: Yale University Press, 1972), p. 124.

24. Felperin reads the passage as epitomising the play's larger preoccupation with linguistic indeterminacy and the fall from interpretive innocence ('"Tongue-tied, Our Queen?"', pp. 196–8).

25. Understood as an infinitisation of the social and symbolic order, the signifying transformation I am pointing to anticipates the process of political disincorporation that marks the advent of the modern state form. See Claude Lefort, 'The Genesis of Ideology in Modern Societies', in John Thompson (ed.), *The Political Forms of Modern Society: Bureaucracy, Democracy, Totalitarianism* (Cambridge, MA: MIT Press, 1986). That process amounts to the historical displacement of the sovereign exception by the (political) logic of the 'universal exception', the logic according to which, in Jacques Derrida's gnomic formulation, 'every other is every other': they are all equivalent, even as, precisely because of the illimitability of the structure, each one is radically other – a cipher. See Derrida, *The Gift of Death*, trans. David Wills (Chicago: University of Chicago Press, 1996), p. 87.

26. On Absolutism's preoccupation with purely formal unity – the State conceived as a system of ratios – see Jean Bodin, *The Six Bookes of a Commonweale* [1606] (Cambridge, MA: Harvard University Press, 1962), pp. 741–6, 786–94. On Bodin's emphasis on the State as 'self-originating', and his 'displacement of the center of theoretical consideration from the question of legitimacy to that of the life of the State and its sovereignty as a united body', see Michael Hardt and Antonio Negri, *Empire* (Cambridge, MA: Harvard University Press, 2000), p. 98.

27. Ivan Nagel, *Autonomy and Mercy: Reflections on Mozart's Operas*, trans. Marion Faber and Ivan Nagel (Cambridge, MA: Harvard University Press, 1991), p. 54.

28. On the Enlightenment era relation between autonomous authority and grace, see ibid., pp. 52–7, 145–8, and Slavoj Žižek, *Tarrying with the Negative: Kant, Hegel, and the Critique of Ideology* (Durham, NC: Duke University Press, 1993), pp. 169–74.

29. Read in this way, oracular law bears out Derrida's account of what

Montaigne termed the 'mystical foundation of authority'. Rather than being external to it – a matter of its enforcement – force is intrinsic to law and its performative constitution. 'The very emergence of justice and law, the founding and justifying moment that institutes law implies a performative force, which is always an interpretive force', a groundless '*coup de force . . .* that in itself is neither just nor unjust'. See Derrida, 'Force of Law: The "Mystical Foundation of Authority"', in Drucilla Cornell, Michael Rosenfield and David Carlson (eds), *Deconstruction and the Possibility of Justice* (New York and London: Routledge, 1992), p. 13.

30. On the inevitable fragility of that opposition, see ibid., pp. 38–40.

31. On the aesthetic as the privileged category of 'reflexive self-designation', see Thierry de Duve, 'Five Remarks on Aesthetic Judgment', *Umbr(a)*, 1 (1999), ed. Joan Copjec, p. 70. On the Romance genre and structures of return, see Constance Jordan, *Shakespeare's Monarchies: Ruler and Subject in the Romances* (Ithaca: Cornell University Press, 1997), p. 107, and Young, *Heart's Forest*, p. 138. On that genre's self-consciousness, see Palfrey, *Late Shakespeare*, p. 40, and Young, *Heart's Forest*, pp. 125–9. On the relexive self-consciousness of the play, and the interpretive self-awareness it prompts, see Stephen Miko, '*Winter's Tale*', *Studies in English Literature*, 29:2 (1989), pp. 259–75.

32. Hardt and Negri point to the relation between Absolutism and the new-found emphasis on the State's capacity 'to construct its own origin and structure' (*Empire*, p. 98). On self-origination and the emerging conception of the autonomy of the political domain, see also Moretti, 'Great Eclipse', pp. 45, 47. My account of the play's articulation of the State as aesthetic formation is not inconsistent with Stanley Cavell's observation that the play moves from incestuous, paternal bonds to a version of social contract. See Cavell, *Disowning Knowledge in Seven Plays of Shakespeare* (Cambridge: Cambridge University Press, 2003), p. 217.

33. Andrew Gurr sees the abruptness of the transition as a joke on Florio's literal-minded definition of tragic-comedy as 'half a tragedy and half a comedy'. Gurr, 'The Bear, the Statue, and Hysteria in *The Winter's Tale*', *Shakespeare Quarterly*, 34:4 (1988), p. 422. Shakespeare may also have in mind the opportune and oddly self-conscious conclusion of *Pandosto*, where the title character 'fell in a melancholy fit and – to close up the comedy with a tragical strategem – he slew himself' (Orgel, *The Winter's Tale*, p. 274). On the self-conscious artifice of the tragic-comic hinge scene, see C.B. Hardman, 'Theory, Form, and Meaning in Shakespeare's *The Winter's Tale*', *The Review of English Studies*, 36:142 (1985), pp. 232–3.

34. A fact intimated by the Chorus's reference to the 'growth . . . of that wide gap' rather than the growth of what occurred within that interval (4.1.6–7). On editors' bewilderment with the formulation, see Orgel's note on the line.

35. The relation between self-sufficient and self-consumption may be implied by Autolycus's name – the wolf himself, but also the auto-wolf, a turn on Erasmus's *homo homini lupus*; 'man is a wolf to man' (*Adages*, 1.1.69–70). On the character's self-createdness, see Palfrey, *Late Shakespeare*, p. 118.

36. On the class scope of the genre, see Palfrey, *Late Shakepeare*, pp. 36–9, and

David Lee Miller, *Dreams of the Burning Child: Sacrificial Sons and the Father's Witness* (Ithaca: Cornell University Press, 2003), p. 19.

37. On Autolycus's association with 'unregulated exchange' and the 'development of the placeless market', see, respectively, Miller, *Dreams of the Burning Child*, p. 127, and Bristol, 'In Search of the Bear', p. 163. On the prominence of the economic metaphor in the play generally, see Cavell, *Disowning Knowledge*, p. 200.

38. Roy Battenhouse, 'Theme and Structure in *The Winter's Tale*', *Shakespeare Survey*, 33 (1980), p. 138. Julia Lupton offers a particularly nuanced argument according to which 'the statue scene . . . stages the visual conditions of Catholic image worship', but in an iconoclastically cancelling form which nevertheless lets it retain 'vestigial thaumaturg[ical]' force (Lupton, *Afterlives of the Saints*, pp. 216, 218).

39. Note Leonard Barkan's observation that both the oracle and the statue are 'connected to resolutions in the affairs of men that seem beyond their individual actions'. Barkan, '"Living Sculptures": Ovid, Michelangelo, and *The Winter's Tale*', *ELH*, 48:4 (1981), p. 660.

40. Palfrey, *Late Shakespeare*, p. 111.

41. Cavell, *Disowning Knowledge*, p. 194. All returns to that ear in Palfrey's formulation: 'The dancing saltiers, the miraculously metamorphosing "statue" return . . . to the queen's ear wherein the tale was first whispered' (*Late Shakespeare*, p. 111).

42. Kahn similarly argues, as against Schmitt, that in Hobbes artifice functions as the ground of the sovereign decision, the basis of his *auctoritas* ('Hamlet or Hecuba', p. 70).

43. On the aesthetic in relation to the disarticulation of the structures of symbolic or tropological exchange, and the forced positing such a limit implies, see Paul de Man, *Aesthetic Ideology* (Minneapolis: University of Minnesota Press, 1996), pp. 87–90, and Andrzej Warminski, '"As the Poets Do It": On the Material Sublime', in *Material Events: Paul de Man and the Afterlife of Theory* (Minneapolis: University of Minnesota Press, 2001), pp. 28–9.

44. See Michael McKeon, 'Politics of Discourses and the Rise of the Aesthetic in Seventeenth-Century England', in Kevin Sharpe and Steven Zwicker (eds), *Politics of Discourse: The Literature and History of Seventeenth-Century England* (Berkeley: University of California Press, 1987), pp. 46–9.

45. For a persuasive analysis of such a conception of literary superfluity during the Elizabethan era and its relation to economic transformations, see Robert Matz, *Defending Literature in Early Modern England* (Cambridge: Cambridge University Press, 2000), pp. 6–24. On the claim for the analogous relation between exchange value and aesthetic value, see Michael McKeon, 'The Origins of Aesthetic Value', *Telos*, 57 (1983), p. 80.

46. On aesthetic pleasure derailing the logic of the commodity, see Jacques Lacan, *The Seminar, Book VII: The Ethics of Psychoanalysis*, trans. Dennis Porter (New York and London: Norton, 1992), pp. 218–40, and Joan Copjec, 'Pure Pleasure', *Umbr(a)*, 1 (1999), pp. 7–10.

47. For a superb account of the pertinence of the aesthetic to early modernity, a period, she argues, before the establishment of the division between

political science and aesthetics, between instrumental reason and sensibility, see Victoria Kahn, *Wayward Contracts: The Crisis of Political Obligation in England, 1640–1674* (Princeton: Princeton University Press, 2004), pp. 6–24.

Chapter 10

Arendt in Italy:
Or, the Taming of the Shrew

Julia Reinhard Lupton

Roberto Esposito is one of several contemporary Italian philosophers to pursue the politics of life in modernity and on classical and early modern scenes of thought. Locally operative in the philosophy of Aristotle, the porous, mobile membrane between *zoē* and *bios*, apprehended as interfolded, mutually implicated, often consubstantial, yet frequently antagonistic or competing forms of life, animates the critique of biopower associated with the late writings of Michel Foucault and the oeuvre of Giorgio Agamben. *Zoē* names the places, moods or zones in which at any one moment in the history of human arrangements life emerges as such, in a reduced, bare, suffering, banned, or imperfect state, whereas *bios* gathers together the kinds of public action, such as debate, deliberation, persuasion, legislation, judgement and rational speech, that distinguish humans as human in the Aristotelian tradition of civic virtue. Such a distinction does not exist *a priori* as a fact of human nature, but rather migrates and mutates in response to changes in the social landscape and in human technical capacities. The slicing of life into distinct sectors, modes, or forms both elicits and inhibits phenomenological speculation about how we live, without ever resulting in permanent solutions to the problem of who or what counts as human.

Hannah Arendt in *The Human Condition* (1958) as well as *The Origins of Totalitarianism* (1951) predates Foucault as a modern thinker who, concerned with the fortunes of both politics and life in the wake of the Second World War, tapped and reanimated Aristotle's semantic mapping of vitality in order to consider the disastrous upsurge of a bare or concentrated life as the orienting object of both cultivation and control for modern states. Contemporary Italian philosophy constitutes a particularly rich point of reception and renewal of, and in some cases resistance to, Arendt's work, a region of response distinct from the Anglo-American emphasis on Arendt's twin diagnoses of totalitarianism and the banality of evil. Following a line of thought opened by Miguel

Vatter as well as Adriana Caverero and Paul Kottman, I would like to suggest that Arendt remains a definitive interlocutor on the politics of life.[1] I would like to suggest, moreover, that the Arendtian strain in biopolitical thinking represents an especially promising resource for the reading of Shakespeare. In my book, *Thinking with Shakespeare: Essays on Politics and Life*, I argue that 'life', internally caught up among creaturely, human and political destinies, names the existential and phenomenological interests of Shakespearean drama, in so far as the plays manifest the ways in which humans appear as human to themselves and others, in tandem with other life forms. Reading Shakespeare and Arendt together, I argue, invites us to mount a biopolitical critique of liberalism in its collusion with capital, while still remaining open to aspects of the civic humanist tradition, stretching from the Greeks to the Italian communes, that are not commensurate with Marxism, and that remain vital resources for the Anglo-American political discourse that Arendt joined, and to which Shakespeare bears substantial, if not exclusive, affinities.

There are several regions of consensus between Arendt and Esposito. They generally concur that modern politics reflects an economisation of existence that reifies the needs, energy and labour of corporeal being into a thing possessed and disposed of by a rights-bearing person. For both parties, this division feeds the exploitative, concentrating, disenfranchising and often lethal administration of 'life', conceived as a biological substratum (*zoē*) that is ideationally distinct from the networks of association that gather human being up into the life of the city (*bios politikos*). Arendt and Esposito would concur that institutions of global capital as well as states deemed totalitarian by virtue of their attempt to capture and regulate life in all its instances work to conceptualise and manage populations through statistical modelling and actuarial calculation. Arendt and Esposito disagree, however, as to orientation: whereas Esposito tends to celebrate animal life over the life of the city, and to see the latter as constitutively dependent on the exclusion of the former, Arendt remained fundamentally committed to the cultivation of that part of man that is *not* animal, that is sustained by but not reducible to biological needs, and that is cultivated and transmitted through forms of deliberation, story-telling and *res gestae* that involve 'men' in their plurality and not 'Man' as species-life. Although *The Human Condition* provides intense and illuminating quasi-phenomenological descriptions of what it means to labour and to work, to meet needs and to build worlds, Arendt is centrally concerned with what makes human action (and human thought) distinctive, initiatory and self-constituting, and thus she insists on a phenomenological distinction between action and other forms of life that the Italian philosophers, including Esposito, want to de-mark rather than re-mark. For Arendt, biopower is an oxymoron or paradox, an unhappy hybrid or even a monster; for Esposito, *politics is always biopolitics*. The question for Esposito is not how to release politics from life, but rather how to configure their coupling in order to cultivate 'a politics that is no longer over life but *of* life', inhabiting, encouraging and replicating the autopoietic processes of biology in the form of new social arrangements and information ecologies.[2]

Although there are many places where one could track the exchanges between Arendt and Esposito, including their understandings of Machiavelli, Nazism and anti-Semitism, or power and potentiality, I focus in these remarks on Esposito's critique of what he calls 'the *dispositif* of the person' and then compare it to Arendt's rather different understanding of the theatrical nature of the subject who acts. I then turn to *The Taming of the Shrew* in order to stage what I understand to be the differences between their positions on personhood. In Shakespeare's play, personhood is achieved through a certain sequestering, training and shaming of animal life. Set in Italy, the birthplace of modern reflections on both civic virtue and the constituent power of the multitude, the play can be invited to broker a possible marriage between Esposito's philosophy of the impersonal as an instance of affirmative biopolitics and Arendt's recreation of the *bios politikos* as that which separates from animal life through the distinctive character of human speech. I read *The Taming of the Shrew* as a critical allegory of the domestication and disavowal, but also the brilliant retooling, retraining and regeneration of Arendtian philosophy by her Italian husband-men. I am suggesting, that is, that a certain *taming* of Arendt, at once a reduction and a reorientation, has occurred in Italian political thought, and that Shakespeare's *Taming of the Shrew* offers us dramatic and conceptual tools for understanding that process through its own probative work on the impasses of life and living. By assembling Esposito and Arendt on the Italian scene set in Shakespeare's play, we can read both Shakespeare and biopolitics for those moments in which divergent forms of life – the life of men in their plurality, of animals in the biodiversity, and of objects in both their durability and their decay – enter into world-building and future-founding relationships with each other.

Arendt in Italy

Roberto Esposito has written two substantial essays on the person, 'The Dispositif of the Person' and 'For a Philosophy of the Impersonal'. In these pieces, Esposito argues that the concept of the person is the last point of consensus among philosophers, legal scholars and critical theorists of all stripes; it is the 'philosophically correct' concept that gains the assent of all parties by granting a fundamental dignity to human being, apart from any civic or national determination, thus promising to 'reconstitute that link between body and reason that Nazism had tried to rip apart in its catastrophic attempt to reduce human life to mere biology'.[3] Yet the idea of the person, argues Esposito, is not modern but ancient, stemming from Roman law and from Christianity's simultaneous division and rebinding of the divine Person in the Incarnation and the Trinity. Moreover, the *dispositif* or conceptual apparatus of the person, far from healing the split between spirit and body, actually *installs and reinforces* that split, insuring not only the subordination of each individual's animal life to the rule of reason, but also the exclusionary scansion of human beings into various degrees of personhood and its disabilities, whose ranks include the potential person of the minor, the imperfect person of women, and the non-person of the slave, each occupying 'differential thresholds within mankind'.[4]

Personhood, then, brings with it *depersonalisation*: 'being reduced to a thing', writes Esposito, 'is implicit in the concept of person; its very definition emerges in negative fashion from the presumed difference with respect to those men and women who are not persons or who were only persons in part and temporarily; one is always exposed to the risk of falling into the domain of the thing'.[5] The person and property are of course closely linked in Roman law, and the objectification of persons, things and real estate, along with the discourse of rights and entitlements, all follow on each other. If the person is the opposite of the object, the person also finds its being doubled in the object. In the act of glorifying the human being, the *dispositif* of the person generates a whole range of reified non-persons, beginning with the bodily being of the legal person himself and radiating across a social landscape whose equalities are only apparent; thus the *dispositif* of the person spins 'an intricate web of humanization and dehumanization' that captures all of humanity in its insidiously differential grid.[6] 'No one', declares Esposito, 'is born a person. Someone may become one, but precisely by pushing those who surround him into the dimension of the thing.'[7] Reification infects not only the posture I assume towards my own body, but also my relation to the whole range of imperfect persons, objects, resources and other beings with whom I share the world.

Personhood, moreover, performs a fundamental operation on life; the attribution of personhood is 'the decisive means by which a biological material lacking in meaning becomes something intangible'.[8]

In biopolitical terms, personhood is the artificial identity created when *zoē* is subordinated to *bios*, the latter produced in its symbolic and juridical intangibility by the very act of giving a legal name to the suffering substance that it is not. *Personalisation* proceeds by way of *de-animalisation*: 'Man is a person if and only if he masters the more properly animal part of his nature.'[9] Personhood for Esposito is a fundamentally self-divided condition: 'It is thanks to the category of person that human beings are unified in the form of their separation.'[10] In the regime of personhood, the life of the creature submits to the life of the city, that is, to the society of 'persons' in their legal autonomy, formal freedom, public recognition, and theatrical self-division between self and mask (*persona*).

To the mortifying dialectic of personalisation and depersonalisation Esposito proposes a philosophy of the *impersonal*. Such a philosophy would no longer take its bearings from the integrity and inviolability of the person, but rather from 'life' as that which subsists 'before any juridical subjectivization'.[11] Following leads culled from Simone Weil (a critic of Catholic personalism after the Second World War) as well as Blanchot and Deleuze, Esposito proposes that the impersonal, far from negating the personal (which, in fact, always harbours its own negation, its own reifying, depersonalising effects), actually expands the region of individual experience by 'block[ing] the mechanism of distinction and separation with respect to those who are not persons'.[12] The impersonal, that is, avoids the constitutive divisions between quasi-persons, non-persons and potential persons (let's call them women, madmen and fools) that rule colonial programmes of exploitation and ethnic cleansing as well as debates about abortion and euthanasia. Esposito identifies this philosophy of the impersonal with Deleuze's concept of 'becoming-animal'. In this vision of a life unencumbered by what Esposito calls 'juridical subjectivization',[13] the breach between body and spirit is finally overcome, divergent forms of life become one, and being human 'no longer moves toward the thing, but ultimately . . . coincides only with itself'.[14] This is an affirmative biopolitics indeed, founded on human animality and aimed at healing the divisions, both internal and sociological, imposed by the law and theology of personhood.

In *The Human Condition*, Arendt visits similar terrain. In the section devoted to the repetitive efforts of the *animal laborans* to meet the pulsing needs of life, Arendt distinguishes the life of labour from the life of action. She cites Aristotle, for whom the *vita activa* 'is itself always full of events which ultimately can be told as a story, establish a biography; it is of this life, *bios* as distinguished from mere *zoē*, that Aristotle said that it "somehow is a kind of praxis"'.[15] *Zoē* describes life in its labouring capacity, the cyclical insistence of bodily needs both met and kept at bay by the world-building work of artisans and the domestic realm of the *oikos*, precinct of women, slaves and domesticated animals. *Bios*, on the other hand, describes the special cultivation of life by and as politics; it is life as lived among men in their capacity as civic actors, their deeds captured in the great narrative nets of epic, history, drama and biography. Although Arendt pointedly prefers *bios* to *zoē*, she nonetheless records the cost of their division: the freedom bought by the Greeks with slavery, she writes, harbours a 'violent injustice', not only to the slaves but to the citizens, who are henceforth deprived of a certain mode of living: 'the price for absolute freedom from necessity is, in a sense, life itself'.[16] Here she implicitly calls for forms of social arrangement that would allow as many people as possible to labour, work, act and think, and thus to live life in both its political and its creaturely dimensions. In passages such as these, the good life (*eu zen*) emerges in Arendt not as that which separates itself from mere living but rather as those praxes that draw forms of life together in a variegated yet coherent vitality.[17]

For Arendt, too, then, the identity of the human actor is fundamentally divided, but this split is at once less catastrophic and more revelatory than it appears in Esposito's critique of the person. In an extraordinary passage in *The Human Condition*, Arendt writes:

> In acting and speaking, men show who they are, reveal actively their unique personal identities and thus make their appearances in the human world, while their physical identities appear without any activity of their own in the unique shape of the body and sound of the voice. This disclosure of 'who' in contradistinction to 'what' somebody is – his qualities, gifts, talents, and shortcomings, which he may display or hide – is implicit in everything somebody says and does. It can be hidden only in complete silence and perfect passivity, but its disclosure can almost never be achieved as a willful purpose, as though one possessed and could dispose of this 'who' in the same manner he has and can dispose of his qualities. On the contrary, it is more likely that the 'who', which appears so clearly and unmistakably to others, remains hidden from the person himself, like the *daimōn* in Greek religion which accompanies each man throughout his life, always looking over his shoulder from behind and thus visible only to those he encounters.[18]

In action, something is revealed about the human actor – his 'whoness' – that is not reducible to a content or intent, a message or mood, but rather is more like a signature, a defining trace and trait of personhood, a subjective fingerprint revealed to the witnesses assembled on and off stage, but not to the speaking subject himself. I might intend, for example, to project an ethos of authority, but reveal instead, through the ripples and hitches in my speech as well as the inevitable run in my stocking, my tremulous vulnerability, a vulnerability that in turn might do more for my case than any rhetorical accomplishment, and yet is itself fundamentally produced and communicated by my efforts at self-mastery in public speech. This 'who' is like the person in Esposito's account in so far as it is an identity that emerges only in a public scene, as that feature of self that disengages from the body, from the 'what' of the human being, a 'who' that is largely granted the chance to appear only for those citizens free to speak in public by dint of the invisible labour of others.[19]

Arendt's distinction between the 'who' and the 'what' of the human actor renders bluntly pronominal Esposito's opposition between the subjective and the thing-like sides of the self-divided person. Moreover, Arendt's acknowledgement that the freedom of human action in the city depends on the labour of women and slaves in the *oikos* parallels Esposito's insistence that personhood not only splits the individual subject, but also distributes debilitating varieties of non-personhood throughout the population of putative persons. Arendt's concept of action, however, is more Greek than Roman, more civic and political than legal and civil. Whereas Esposito's person is above all the bearer of legal rights and the sufferer of legal disabilities in the liberal tradition, Arendt's human actor is defined more by the exercise of virtues, of capacities for excellence that can only be realised through public speech, and whose concerted practice results in *eudaimonia* (happiness) and the *eu zen* (the good life).[20] The 'who' sought by Arendt is not a legal fiction so much as an existential mode: the 'who' that appears in action is not the mask worn by an actor (*persona*), nor the office (*officium*) assumed by a magistrate in an institutional structure, but rather the involuntary manifestation of a distinctively human capacity in and for other human actors.

Arendt would agree with Esposito that the Roman juridical discourse of personhood, in league with the fundamentally economic tenets of possessive individualism, helps solidify the modern regime of politics as a form of public housekeeping whose job is to administer species-life in all of its manifestations. But she would place before and beyond such institutions of legal personhood not the Deleuzean 'becoming-animal' of 'life' 'before any juridical subjectivization',[21] but rather the possibility of human action and the who-ness that it generates in a scene constituted by the presence of other human actors. 'Plurality' for Esposito takes shape in a metamorphic environment characterised by the promiscuous cohabitation of multiple life forms: 'Contrary to the presupposed split of the dispositif of the person, the animal in man, in every man and in all men, means multiplicity, plurality, metamorphosis'.[22] For Arendt on the other hand, plurality always means the co-presence of *other people*: 'Plurality is the condition of human action because we are all the same, that is, human, in such a way that nobody is ever the same as anyone else who ever lived, lives, or will live.'[23] Plurality for Arendt always concerns speaking and acting beings, and not the interpenetration of human and non-human forms of life. The *daemon* is thus closely linked to other key Arendtian ideas, including natality, freedom, and the urge to appear, to assemble a public space by speaking in it. Esposito's legal emphasis on the person occludes what Arendt's *daemon* captures: the centrality of action and the individuating exercise of virtue to civic traditions of political thought.

And yet, in her passage on self-disclosure, Arendt speaks not of the person at all, but rather of the *daemon*, the spirit that appears behind the actor, invisible to himself but exposed to those with whom he deliberates. Born of action, the *daemon* reveals something real and true about the human actor: not a substantial, bodily or biological facticity but rather a social truth that exists only in the public sphere as the realm of specifically human appearing. Adriana Caverero writes that the whoness of the speaker remains 'as unmasterable and invisible as the *daemon* . . . Even on the active level of the properly human (or political) revelation, the meaning of the identity remains the patrimony of another.'[24] The *daemon* belongs to the human actor, yet is only visible to those who face her. Walter Burkert and John Raffan write that for the Greeks, 'There is no image of a *daimon*, and there is no cult. *Daimon* is thus the necessary complement to the Homeric view of the gods as individuals with personal characteristics; it covers that embarrassing remainder which eludes characterization and naming'; classicist Ruth Padel links the *daemon* to Greek conceptions of animal life.[25] The *daemon* crystallises the extent to which the actor-agent in the Greek world could not fully claim his act, but rather handed it over to the receiving force of history, the gods, and chance, as differently exercised and acknowledged in epic narration and tragic drama. Avatars of the *daemon* include genius, the soul, conscience and the unconscious, all names for the attempt to grasp that element of subjectivity that flares up in the human subject as both the essence and the limit of his or her willed identity and legal personhood, dividing the subject between the demonic impulses of an insurgent vitality (whether conceived as interior, anterior or posterior) and the phenomenal scene of human appearing, discourse and exchange in which such spectres of life make their astonishing exits and entrances.[26] The *daemon* bears on any Arendtian exploration of theatre, the art par excellence of human action and the forms of appearing before others that such action releases.

Whereas in Esposito's Roman discourse, the *persona* is the legal mask worn by certain hominids in order both to unify and forever divide body and reason, Arendt's Greek *daemon* emerges in the gap between the body of the actor and the role he plays in public, as something both more and other than either body or mask, an involuntary image of self released by the very freedom exercised by action. I would like to put forward this *daemon* as a way of productively linking Esposito's philosophy of the impersonal to Arendt's philosophy of action. The *daemon* manifests the phenomenal, linguistic, public and divided character of human being that Esposito wants to anneal in the philosophy of the impersonal. Yet if Arendt's *daemon* belongs to the *bios politikos*, she has recourse here to a language that is not purely human: the daemonic, both more and less than human, belongs to human being and yet is not identical with it, sporting the stamp of personality but without conferring the legal coherence and durability provided by personhood, and born of free action but itself unwilled and spontaneous. At the same time, Esposito's discourse on the impersonal and his explorations of an affirmative biopolitics invite us to link the daemonic to other forms of life, not in order to dethrone, decentre or dehumanise the human, but rather to clarify its grounds, conditions and others.

In new work on Esposito, Eric Santner reads Esposito's account of immunisation with great care and generosity, but insists on what he calls 'a compulsive, not to say demonic' remnant in human forms of life that psychoanalysis accounts for better than a biopolitical reading alone.[27] Might the *daemon* that dogs human action express a desire otherwise unavailable to me? Might the *daemon* bear the traces of creaturely life from which human action momentarily flies free? Might my *daemon* take the shape of a little bird, or cat, or falcon, dancing and shimmering behind my shoulder as not only the sign of my coming into appearance in and for the *polis* assembled by my speaking, but also as the symptom of that appearance's dependence on my own creaturely existence and on the labour of the *oikos*? In the manifestation of the *daemon*, in other words, there may also lurk an impersonalisation and a becoming-animal, though it can only appear in the forum provided by the *bios politikos*, and it remains a purely phenomenal occurrence that continues to manifest a split between forms of life rather than promising their unification.

The Taming of the Shrew

This, at any rate, is the direction in which Shakespeare's early comedy, *The Taming of the Shrew*, leads us. The play demonstrates the truth of

Esposito's critique of the person. The blustering wife-tamer Petruchio is the play's most complete person, both husband and husbandman: male mate to Katharina, and free householder who aims to 'wive and thrive' (1.2.51),[28] to marry in such a way as to increase his economic capital by advancing the domains of life over which he finds himself a most able administrator. Moreover, his masterful personhood is defined against the imperfect persons of those around him, especially the shrew Katharina, but also his abused servant Grumio, his stable of tongue-tied farm-hands, his sorry-assed horses, and the whole arsenal of thing and animal imagery that Petruchio marshals in order to retool Katharina 'from a wild Kate to a Kate / Conformable as other household Kates' (2.1.270–1). To tame Kate for personhood is to render the disabilities of female personhood ideologically transparent and immediately transferable – to other shrews in the making such as sister Bianca, for example. Moreover, as Nicole Miller has brilliantly demonstrated, Petruchio's taming programme, which includes depriving his bride of food, sleep, sex and rational discourse, is presciently biopolitical in so far as his techniques of privation directly suture the motifs of sovereignty onto the needs of life.[29] Whereas the play's foppish and instantly forgettable romantic foil Lucentio enters the play parroting the truisms of Aristotelian civic virtue, Petruchio is the brash, infinitely vital type of the possessive individual par excellence, and it is to him that the play's innovative energies belong. Petruchio is the New Prince of the biopolitical *oikos*.

And yet, as many readers of the play have pointed out, more complex mirrorings unfold between the persons of Petruchio and Kate, *each* divided between animal and rational aspects and *each* brought into dramatic focus as well as marital union by inversions of their higher and lower beings. Heath Ledger's rendition of Petruchio as a long-haired Aussie slacker in *10 Things I Hate About You* captures some of the character's originary wildness. In *Shrew*, the opening interchange between Petruchio and Katharina, alive with animal and object imagery, performs a veritable festival of *depersonalisation*, demonstrating the reifying effects of personhood. Yet it also inches towards *impersonalisation*, in so far as the two sparrers discover a common ground before such reifications through the transmogrifying energy of their insults. Finally, their exchange also produces a moment of daemonic self-disclosure, the sudden, unexpected and instantly withdrawing apparition of *a personality beyond personhood*, reflecting the object world that populates their discourse with such vigour, yet unmistakably assigned to Katharina in her capacity as speaker and thus drawing her into politics.

The scene begins with a struggle over Katharina's name:

[Enter Katharina]
Petruchio: Good morrow, Kate, for that's your name, I hear.
Katharina: Well have you heard, but something hard of hearing.
                   They call me Katharine that do talk of me.
Petruchio: You lie, in faith; for you are call'd plain Kate,
                   And bonny Kate and sometimes Kate the curst;
                   But Kate, the prettiest Kate in Christendom,
                   Kate of Kate Hall, my superdainty Kate,
                   For dainties are all Kates, and therefore, Kate,
                   Take this of me, Kate of my consolation:
                   Hearing thy mildness praised in every town,
                   Thy virtues spoke of, and thy beauty sounded,
                   Yet not so deeply as to thee belongs,
                   Myself am moved to woo thee for my wife. (2.1.178–201)

Whereas Katharina insists on the dignity of her given name ('They call me Katharine that do talk of me'), Petruchio uses the intimate diminutive 'Kate' not only to assert his marital interests but also to relegate her to the world of things: 'my superdainty Kate, / For dainties are all Kates'. The word 'cate', as Natasha Korda has brilliantly demonstrated, means cake or confection; derived from the French *achat*, purchased thing, it can extend to all commodities.[30] We might say, following Esposito, that in and through his expropriating speech we encounter 'the inert figure of the thing' (*cate*) 'silhouetted against the moving backdrop of the person' (*Kate*).[31] That Petruchio performs this operation by means of her name, primary signifier of personhood in the rule of law, indicates the intimate relation between subject and commodity in the regime of the *persona*.

In response to Petruchio's dramatically depersonalising discourse, Katharina follows suit by calling him a 'movable':

Katharina: Moved! In good time! Let him that moved you hither
                   Remove you hence: I knew you at the first
                   You were a moveable.
Petruchio: Why, what's a movable?
Katharina: A joint stool. (2.1.191–2)

'Movable' means fickle, variable (as in the famous phrase, 'La donna è mobile'), but Katharina swiftly fixes the adjective as the noun meaning furniture. As the Romance words *meubles*, *mobilia* and *muebles* indicate, furniture is defined by its status as movable property, and such movables were all the more in motion in a period when households frequently rezoned domestic spaces for different uses during the day, the week and the year.[32] To call Petruchio a joint stool is not only to call him a thing, but also to deny him even the provisional dignity of a chair, proper seat of the patriarch in housing where the homely multi-purposed stool far outnumbered the grander and less mobile chair.[33] Amenable to sitting, standing and in some instances hurling, the joint-stool is the movable par excellence; constituting the Renaissance home's most minimal piece of furnishing, it is the stool's notable ass-worthiness that affords its repurposing as an insult.

Petruchio runs with the image, finding opportunities for bawdy play that Katharina in turn deflects by animalising:

> *Petruchio*:   Thou hast hit it. Come, sit on me.
> *Katharina*:   Asses are made to bear, and so are you.
> *Petruchio*:   Women are made to bear, and so are you. (2.1.194–6)

If he must be a stool, he will happily bear her weight (disclosing a covert image of the woman on top); she in turn is quick to figure him as a mere beast of burden, whose language of 'bearing' yields further bawdy potential for Petruchio. Although objectification rules the speech – each derides the other as thing and as animal – the delirious mobility of these *mobilia* edges into what Esposito calls the impersonal, 'that which, from within the person, blocks the mechanism of distinction and separation with respect to those who are still not persons, who are no longer persons, or who have been declared persons'.[34] That is, Katharina and Petruchio cast themselves into a mobile and metamorphic environment that houses humans alongside other forms of existence, including the inanimate life of objects, the labouring life of domestic animals, and the metaphoric life of language itself, as the busy, buzzing, prolix, punning medium through which these transformations are captured, transferred and communicated.

Yet if Esposito's vision pushes towards a 'radical deconstruction of personal identity',[35] neither the legal reductions of depersonalisation nor the animal inventions of the impersonal fully describe what occurs in this revelatory interchange. The rapid movement of Petruchio and Katharina's marvellous *mobilia* shifts from the affordances shared by stools and beasts of burden to *the question of weight*, not only the weight that each partner is capable of bearing as a physical being, but also the weight each carries in his or her discourse:

> *Petruchio*:   Alas! Good Kate, I will not burden thee,
>   For, knowing thee to be but young and light.
> *Katharina*:   Too light for such a swain as you to catch;
>   And yet as heavy as my weight should be. (2.1.198–201)

'And yet as heavy as my weight should be': this weight, I'd suggest, veers closer to Arendt's *daemon* than to Esposito's impersonal, if we place the former in the precinct of the *bios politikos* and the latter in the environs of animal life. Katharina suddenly experiences her own weight, and finds that it is right, that it suits her. There is certainly something bodily about this weight. Yet it is also a weight that *only appears in discourse*, in the back and forth play between man and woman that has so far eluded Katharina in her exchanges with men; we could call it the weight of *gravitas*, associated in the rhetorical tradition with forceful and compact public speech.[36] Meeting resistance in the form of Petruchio's sparring, and pushing back in turn, she suddenly has access to her own weight, her own *gravitas* as a speaking being. There is nothing 'inert' in this weight; it is a weight that can only be measured by the movement of words in agonistic speech. This weight belongs to her; it is 'her weight', but she does not 'possess' it in the manner of a person possessing his body. Produced by discourse, it is a weight that nonetheless borrows its presence from the world of things and animals to which Katharina as shrew has been relegated, and from which Petruchio, in his own brutal way, is soliciting her to emerge. He will later figure her as his falcon, in a notorious passage in which, once more, the dialectic of personalisation (*his*) and depersonalisation (*hers*) directs both the play and its critical reception (4.2.157–8). Yet if we take the falcon as Katharina's *daemon*, as the phenomenal appearance of her subjective signature, then we can ask the play to disclose other narratives of personhood than those scripted by either the liberal tradition or its biopolitical critique.

Gravitas borders semantically on *gravidas*, not 'the human condition' but rather a *female* condition already disseminated in Petruchio's pun on 'bearing'. Images of birth populate the discourses of both Esposito and Arendt. For Esposito, abortion and euthanasia form one of the most visible battlegrounds of biopolitics, beginning with the definition of when personhood can be said to begin.[37] Esposito's book *Bios: Biopolitics and Philosophy* begins with the case of Nicolas Perruche, a baby suffering from genetic disabilities whose mother argued the case of abortion based on the child's own 'right *not* to be born'. Esposito nudges the mother's reasoning in the direction of Nazism, in so far as her ventriloquising negation of the infant institutes 'a eugenic caesura, one that is legally recognized, between a juridical life that is judged as valid and another "life unworthy of life," to use the Nazi phrase'.[38] For Arendt, too, birth is a key figure, but she lures it away from its origins in biological parturition and into the pale of action. Action, writes Arendt, 'springs from the beginning which came into the world when we were born and to which we respond by beginning something new on our own initiative'.[39] She uses the word 'natality', modelled on the word 'mortality', to capture the responsiveness of action to the fact of human birth into a preexisting world of things, narratives and relationships with which the singularity of that birth is not identical. Natality names the way in which each birth throws a human subject into the world as the chance for a fundamentally new beginning, yet the radical newness of that event, the sheer brightness of its pure futurity, also requires a world-conserving effort on the part of the guardians of public life. Natality as parturition belongs to life, yet is immediately troped by the 'second birth' of action,[40] and thus belongs to the *polis* and not to the *oikos* in Arendt's topology. Natality manifests what Miguel Vatter has called 'a way to reconcile life with politics' that avoids the ideological humanism to which Arendt's philosophy is often reduced, and whose solutions always tempted Arendt herself.[41]

Called to choose between a discourse of 'rights' and a discourse of 'life', or to cut the cards a little differently, between *gravidas* (biology) and *gravitas* (rhetoric), Esposito, I am surmising, would choose life, as more prior, more authentic, and less divided than its legal superimpositions and rhetorical re-weightings. Arendt, on the other hand, *in* her life and *as* her work, chose *gravitas* over *gravidas*, the contingencies of speech, action and thought over the exigencies of maternity, even while allowing her own femininity to draw birth into the orbit of philosophy. In any case, whereas Petruchio pushes their dialogue towards pregnancy ('Women are made to bear, and so are you'), Katharina has enough weight – enough verbal *auctoritas*, that is – to push in another direction: 'Asses are made to bear, and so are you.' The weight suddenly manifested as her own collects the semantic density of the puns that ricochet between them with such speed and punch. This weight, I am suggesting, delivered here as the non-signifying remnant of their signifying match, concretises for an instant Katharina's *daemon*, as the trace of personality inadvertently revealed through speech, an opacity animated at other moments in the play by the figures of falcon, hound and horse, not as mystified animal spirits but as elements of personality demanding public acknowledgement.

In what sense could such a scene be called political? After all, politics for Arendt, culled from the annals of Greek democracy and American revolution, gravitates around deliberative acts of public speech conducted before an audience of free men who have been released from the drudgery of household labour by the work of others. Yet a capacious reading of Arendt in search of forms of life, like those conducted by Caverero, Vatter and Kottman, would not exclude such scenes from the horizon of the political. For these readers of Arendt, the *polis* is not a fixed institution defined by laws or walls, but rather a permanent possibility, a virtuous reserve called into active duty whenever speech risks self-exposure and the adventure of contingency in the presence of others. Kottman cites Arendt: "'Wherever you go, you will be a *polis*.'"[42] What we see in the exchanges between Petruchio and Katherine is the make-shift assembly of a political scene out of and within domestic and civil ones, the momentary installation of a micro-polity, thrown together like a pup tent or a camp fire in the clearing made by action in the thicket of routine. Such a portable *polis* bears no direct relation to a larger institution, state, or community, and yet opens lines of both testing and testimony to those gathered in its circle of citizenship.[43] And drama is a peculiar form of action because it addresses those who view it not simply as passive spectators but as witnesses and jurors whose responses make a difference to the future of the drama. In the courtship scene, we are called to act as witnesses to a marriage in the making, lending our laughter, our horror, or our bafflement to the proceedings that unfold before us.

Read through Esposito and Arendt, *The Taming of the Shrew* is ulti-mately a drama not of becoming-animal but rather of becoming-person, in which both Petruchio and Kate, though in unequal measure, must pass through creaturely life on their way to the incorporated person-hood of marriage. But how do we understand the persons they have become at the end of the play? The play's brazenly bestial agenda can be read either as an instance of negative biopower, which 'subdivides the human species into an infinite series of typologies',[44] or more positively, as a groping attempt to acknowledge and subjectivise animal virtues as creative elements in an expanded scene of human personality. The latter reading, in whose compass I have staked my own wary settlement with this play, is sustained by elements in both Esposito and Arendt. Esposito helps us to calculate the several violences that attend Petruchio's styles of personhood, and also to affirm as an alternative to those styles an integrative view of politics and life in a common *Umwelt*. Arendt, however, warns us against loving life not wisely but too well, by insist-ing on the ethical priority of the *polis*, not as a place but as a possibility, as what is convened when humans appear to each other through speech and action. In the interchange staged here between Arendt and Esposito, Arendt, like Kate, can be said to *disclose her own weight*: to reveal anew both her contributions to the Italian discourse on biopower, and, in con-tinuing to push back, to distinguish those contributions from their later appropriations. It is a weight, moreover, a *specific gravitas* and not an absolute one, that can only come forward for us in the very mobility of the discourses put into play by Arendt's Italian readers.

In *Bios: Biopolitics and Philosophy*, Esposito gives the shrew her due:

Hannah Arendt was the person who understood early the modern roots of biopolitics, using an interpretive key that recasts its reason and even its semantic legitimacy. Contrary to the pervasive thesis that ties modernity to the deployment of politics, she not only refers it back to depoliticization, but ascribes the process to a crisis in the category of life in place of the Greek conception of the world held in common.[45]

Yet he goes on to establish the divergence between the Foucauldian line taken up by the Italians and Arendt's more humanistic articulation. Espousing a Greek discourse of virtues rather than a Roman discourse of law, her conclusions rest, he says, 'on the unverified premise according to which the only valid form of political activity is what is attributable to the experience of the Greek *polis*'.[46] As a consequence, politics and life in fact never meet in her thought: for Arendt, 'where there is an authentic politics, a space of meaning for the production of life cannot be opened; and where the materiality of life unfolds, something like political action can no longer emerge'.[47] I have tried to indicate to the contrary that Arendt's *daemon* issues precisely from the place where vitality and politics meet in human action. Their meeting, however, is virtual rather than real; the *daemon* in Arendt does not, that is, make life 'coincide immediately with its modes of being',[48] but rather remains an appearance, clinging to the publicity of speech. Its *gravitas* belongs to rhetoric, not biology.

Whereas Esposito posits a real relation between politics and life, or what he calls 'the vitalization of politics',[49] for Arendt, their link is always *virtual*, in the sense that it is produced by the exercise of *virtue*, a virtue conceived in the civic terms of the *vita activa* as an affair that concerns humans in their humanity. This need not prevent us from reading virtue more environmentally, as concerning the sovereignties of all animate and inanimate things – the broad sense of virtue exercised by Aristotle himself, and still visible in Shakespeare's use of the word to designate power or capacity.[50] Indeed, the *daemon* offers a living link between human virtue as civic practice and plant and animal virtues as natural potentialities or affordances; in both the civic and the natural cases, virtue requires performance in order to be actualised. Virtue traces the fold between what Arendt calls the 'whoness' and the 'whatness' of the person. Thingly virtues are ever ready to flower into use, yet themselves participate in a kind of primal dormancy that keeps its own rhythms in the order of being. If *eudaemonia* is achieved by actualising excellences, those precious *aretai* may be thingly as well as civic, demonic as well as rational, engaging the routines of daily life alongside the duties of public service. It may indeed be that we need Esposito and the discourse of biopolitics to unlock the full scope of virtue, in its human and its environmental dimensions, in both Shakespeare and Arendt. The *daemon* lies waiting to help us. The *daemon* is the involuntary trace of voluntary action. It manifests a 'whoness' not reducible to the legal person, it issues from behind the mask of the legal and theatrical *persona*, and it bears the uncanny face of the inhuman (joint stool, falcon, centaur, milch kine, to cull a few specimens from Shakespeare's vast ecology). Nevertheless the *daemon* depends absolutely for its production and appearance on the plurality constituted by the presence of other human beings, in their role as actors capable of significant speech, and as such the *daemon* inhabits and animates the political side of the biopolitical monster, even as it flies between the meadows of *zoē* and the plazas of *bios*, cross-pollinating the flowers of rhetoric and life.

The Taming of the Shrew ends with Katharina's longest and most notorious speech, in which she recites the topoi of masculine authority with a virtuosity that shocks even her animal tamer Petruchio. Demonstrating the triumph of his personhood over hers, it also shows her speaking in public; unlike the scold's bridle of village shaming rituals, Petruchio's taming program, far from silencing Katharina, has sent her off into an unprecedented flight of speech. What she says *bears weight*: if the content of her speech parrots a certain fossilised virtue discourse, the act of speaking well puts virtue into play as a distinctly public capacity that redelivers her *gravitas* in a rhetorically rounded form. Katharina's virtues are animal as well as human, since she draws on the aptitudes of the falcon and the hound in her final performance, but she does so by soliciting those animal *daimonēs* to make their appearance on the stage (the theatre of persons), and not in the circus (the theatre of beasts and freaks). For Shakespeare, to tame the shrew is not to put the woman in her animal place once and for all, but rather to invite her to run through her paces, to take flight and return, and to make something new appear in the process. Perhaps we can say the same of the dialogue I have initiated here between Arendt and Esposito. It is not a question of determining winners or losers, of either keeping Arendt firmly on the shelf of pre-theoretical intuition or celebrating her humanism, but rather of allowing her own *daimonēs*, in all of their inhuman splendour, to appear in the arena defined by biopolitical critique, with consequences not only for how we read Arendt, but also, I hope, for how we read her readers.

Notes

1. Miguel Vatter, 'Natality and Biopolitics in Hannah Arendt', *Revista de Ciencia Política*, 26:2 (2006), pp. 137–59; Adriana Caverero, *Relating*

Narratives: Storytelling and Selfhood, trans. Paul Kottman (London: Routledge, 2000); Paul Kottman, *A Politics of the Scene* (Stanford: Stanford University Press, 2008) and *Tragic Conditions in Shakespeare: Disinheriting the Globe* (Baltimore: Johns Hopkins University Press, 2009).

2. Robert Esposito, *Bios: Biopolitics and Philosophy*, trans. Timothy Campbell (Minneapolis: University of Minnesota Press, 2008), p. 11.

3. Robert Esposito, 'The Dispositif of the Person', *Law, Culture and the Humanities*, 8:17 (2012), p. 19.

4. Ibid., p. 24.

5. Robert Esposito, 'For a Philosophy of the Impersonal', *CR: The New Centennial Review*, 10:2 (2010), p. 125.

6. Esposito, 'Dispositif', p. 22.

7. Esposito, 'For a Philosophy', p. 126.

8. Ibid., p. 121.

9. Esposito, 'Dispositif', p. 22.

10. Ibid., p. 23.

11. Esposito, 'For a Philosophy', p. 132.

12. Ibid., p. 130.

13. Ibid., p. 132.

14. Ibid., p. 133.

15. Hannah Arendt, *The Human Condition* (Chicago: University of Chicago Press, 1958), p. 97.

16. Ibid., p. 120.

17. See Vatter, 'Natality and Biopolitics', on the reconciliation of life and politics in Arendt.

18. Arendt, *Human Condition*, pp. 179–80.

19. Agamben develops a similar idea in his short essay on 'Genius'. The genius, Roman heir to the Greek *daemon*, is 'that which is most impersonal in us; it is the personalization of what, in us, goes beyond and exceeds us'. Agamben associates the genius with bodily rhythms and well-being; unlike Arendt's *daemon*, it does not seem to depend so absolutely on publicity for its appearing. The Latin genius may be closer to what Arendt calls the 'whatness' of the person ('his qualities, gifts, talents, and shortcomings, which he may display or hide') than to what she culls as the *daemon* from Greek thought, though they are clearly linked genetically, and the differences say as much about the differing emphases in Agamben and Arendt as they do about the Roman and Greek views of identity. See Giorgio Agamben, *Profanations*, trans. Jeff Fort (New York: Zone Books, 2007), pp. 9–18.

20. Arendt connects *eudaimonia* to the *daemon*: Greek happiness 'has the connotation of blessedness, but without any religious overtones, and it means literally something like the well-being of the *daemon* who accompanies each man throughout life, who is his distinct identity, but appears and is visible only to others' (*Human Condition*, p. 193).

21. Esposito, 'For a Philosophy', p. 132.

22. Ibid., p. 133.

23. Arendt, *Human Condition*, p. 8.

24. Cavarero, *Relating Narratives*, p. 22.

25. Walter Burkert and John Raffan, *Greek Religion: Archaic and Classical*

(Oxford: Blackwell, 1990), p. 180. Ruth Padel, *In and Out of Mind: Greek Images of the Tragic Self* (Princeton: Princeton University Press, 1992), pp. 138–61.

26. I have learned much from two recent dissertations completed at the University of California, Irvine: Donovan Sherman, *Second Death: Theatricalities of the Soul in Shakespeare* (2011), and Rachael Hoff, *The End of What We Are: Instituting Conscience in the Work of John Milton* (2010). On the conscience and its links to the daemonic, see Ned Lukacher, *Daemonic Figures: Shakespeare and the Question of Conscience* (Ithaca: Cornell University Press, 1994).

27. Eric Santner, *The Royal Remains: The People's Two Bodies and the Endgames of Sovereignty* (Chicago: University of Chicago Press, 2011), p. 18. Santner has done more than any other critic to bring a certain biopolitical discourse (Agamben, Esposito, Schmitt) into contact with psychoanalysis (Schreber, Freud, Lacan). See his *The Psychotheology of Everyday Life* (Chicago: University of Chicago Press, 2001) and *On Creaturely Life* (Chicago: University of Chicago Press, 2006). Miguel Vatter develops the creaturely, Augustinian and political-theological dimensions of Arendt in the context of her biopolitical thought.

28. William Shakespeare, *The Taming of the Shrew: Texts and Contexts*, ed. Frances Dolan (New York: Bedford / St. Martins, 1992).

29. Nichole Miller, 'The Sexual Politics of Pain: Hannah Arendt Meets Shakespeare's *Shrew*', *The Journal for Cultural and Religious Theory*, 7:2 (2006), pp. 18–32.

30. Natasha Korda, 'Household Kates: Domesticating Commodities in *The Taming of the Shrew*', reprinted in *The Taming of the Shrew: Norton Critical Edition*, ed. Dympna Callaghan (New York: Norton, 2009), pp. 149–54.

31. Esposito, 'Dispositif', p. 13.

32. On the migration of furniture (*meubles, mobilia*) between estates for aristocrats, and within public rooms in bourgeois homes, see Witold Rybczynski, *Home: A Short History of an Idea* (London: Pocket Books, 1997), pp. 26–7.

33. On the ubiquity of stools and the paucity of chairs in the Middle Ages and Renaissance, see Florence de Dampierre, *Chairs: A History* (New York: Abrams, 2006), p. 52.

34. Esposito, 'For a Philosophy', p. 13.

35. Ibid., p. 122.

36. '"Formidable speaking", *deinotēs*, was a major style of oratory in antiquity, as Demetrius points out in the fifth section of his *On Style*'; *deinotēs* was translated as *gravitas* by the Roman rhetors. See Fredrik Ahl and Hanna M. Roisman, *The Odyssey Reformed* (Ithaca: Cornell University Press, 1996), p. 14. Although *gravitas* was generally associated with older male speakers of great dignity, Livy also attributes *gravitas* to matrons (*gravis femina, gravissima femina*). See Timothy Moore, *Artistry and Ideology: Livy's Vocabulary of Virtue* (Frankfurt am Main: Athenaüm, 1989), pp. 135–6.

37. In bioethics, 'the often bitter conflict between Catholics and secularists [*laici*] . . . turns on the exact moment when a living being is to be considered a person. For Catholics this occurs at the moment of conception, while

for secularists much later. However, both agree on the value that is to be attributed to the title of person' (Esposito, 'Dispositif', p. 18).

38. Esposito, *Bios*, pp. 3–4.
39. Arendt, *Human Condition*, p. 177.
40. Ibid., pp. 176–7.
41. Vatter, 'Natality and Biopolitics', p. 150.
42. Kottman, *A Politics of the Scene*, p. 114.
43. On circles of citizenship, see Julia Reinhard Lupton, *Citizen-Saints: Shakespeare and Political Theology* (Chicago: University of Chicago Press, 2005).
44. Esposito, 'Dispositif', p. 23.
45. Esposito, *Bios*, p. 149.
46. Ibid., p. 150.
47. Ibid.
48. Ibid., p. 152.
49. Ibid., p. 157.
50. On animal sovereignties, see Laurie Shannon, 'Poor, Bare, Forked: Animal Sovereignty, Human Negative Exceptionalism, and the Natural History of *King Lear*', *Shakespeare Quarterly*, 60:2 (2009), pp. 168–96.

Part Three
Damnable Iteration

Chapter 11

Ship of Fools:
Foucault and the Shakespeareans

Richard Wilson

O, I have suffered
With those I saw suffer! A brave vessel,
Who had, no doubt, some noble creature in her,
Dashed all to pieces! (*Tempest*, 1.2.5–8)

Half a century after Michel Foucault's career as the foremost philosopher of transgression was launched in the Anglo-Saxon world, with the first English translation of his founding work *Folie et Déraison: Histoire de la Folie à l'âge classique* as *Madness and Civilization*, his reputation amongst Shakespeare scholars appears to have sunk without trace. In particular, his claim at the start of the book that in 'Shakespeare madness occupies an extreme position' which 'opens onto a tear in the fabric of the world', because 'There is no going back to truth or reason' from Lear's lunacy or the delirium of Lady Macbeth, has been fatally discredited by its association with the image that illustrated it of the Ship of Fools, 'a strange drunken boat that wound its way down the wide, slow-moving rivers of the Rhineland and round the canals of Flanders'.[1] Nothing Foucault ever wrote has done more to wreck his reputation in Shakespeare studies than his categorical assertion that among all the legendary ships of the classical and Renaissance literary imagination, the vessels of madmen piloted by madmen immortalised in *Narrenschiff*, Sebastian Brandt's anti-Papal satire of 1494, 'alone had a genuine existence . . . these boats that drifted from one town to another with their senseless cargo'.[2] But in the 1965 translation of Foucault's book this was only the most flagrant of innumerable statements of fact that had to be taken on trust, since the French pocket edition on which it was based had been printed without scholarly apparatus, and with only a handful of the thousands of footnotes that had supposedly supported the original publication. *Madness and Civilization* did, however, benefit from the talent of an illustrious American translator, and it was

Richard Howard's prose that fuelled the fantasies of a generation of campus professors and their hallucinating students:

> Something new appears in the imaginary landscape of the Renaissance, soon it will occupy a privileged place there: the Ship of Fools, a strange 'drunken boat' that glides along the calm rivers of the Rhineland and the Flemish canals. The *Narrenschiff*, of course, is a literary composition, probably borrowed from the old Argonaut cycle, one of the great themes recently revived and rejuvenated, acquiring an institutional aspect in the Burgundian estates. Fashion favoured the composition of these Ships, whose crew of imaginary heroes, ethical models, or social types embarked on a great symbolic voyage which would bring them the figure of their destiny or their truth . . . Bosch's painting, of course, belongs to this dream fleet. But of all these romantic or satiric vessels, the *Narrenschiff* is the only one that had a real existence – for they did exist, these boats that carried their insane cargo from town to town. Madmen then led an easy wandering life.[3]

Recommended to its London publisher as not only 'brilliantly written' but also 'intellectually rigorous' by R.D. Laing, the anti-psychiatry guru who considered schizophrenics to be super sane, with its valorisation of the madman's meandering voyage as 'an absolute Passage' towards 'strange paths of knowledge', *Madness and Civilization* seemed to be offering the spaced-out 1960s Counter Culture a carnivalesque Renaissance precedent for its own Fool's Paradise of 'an easy wandering life', and Foucault's lunatic hulk would inspire scores of postmodern fictions and psychedelic artworks.[4] For the ship has been not just a means of transport, the theorist would insist, but 'from the sixteenth century up to our time the greatest reservoir' of the imagination. A sailing vessel is a 'heterotopia par excellence', he explained; meaning 'a piece of floating space' that is both inside and outside culture, a type of 'actually realized utopia in which all the other real emplacements that can be found within the culture are represented, contested, and reversed'. Self-enclosed yet 'delivered over to the boundless expanse of the ocean', the Ship of Fools was therefore a prime instance of those placeless places that are 'reserved for individuals who are in a state of crisis with respect to society'.[5] So the voyage of the 'strange drunken boat' that heralded Foucault's entry into English was not only an apt figure for the idea Shakespeare critics took from his work – that, as Stephen Greenblatt concluded in *Renaissance Self-Fashioning*, apropos his own account of 'the noble ship of Venice' (*Othello*, 2.1.22) that carries Desdemona, Othello and Iago to Cyprus, transgression is 'engendered by the very process of punishment, surveillance, discipline, and constraint' to which it is subjected[6] – the philosopher also needed the wandering bark of madmen to launch his Nietzschean theory of the 'limit experience', or 'going beyond' this impasse, which linked him with earlier thinkers of transgression such as Georges Bataille, and the paradox that it is constraint that makes resistance, and thereby freedom, possible:[7]

> Water and navigation certainly play this role. Confined on the ship, from which there is no escape, the madman is delivered to the river with its thousand arms, the sea with its thousand roads, to that great uncertainty external to everything. He is a prisoner in the midst of what is the freest, the openest of routes: bound fast at the infinite crossroads. He is the Passenger *par excellence*: that is, the prisoner of the passage.[8]

'Yes, I'm very fond of boats myself. I like the way they're – contained': one writer who seems to have read *Madness and Civilization*, and instantly applied it to Shakespeare, was Tom Stoppard, whose Guildenstern made Foucault's point about the mad-ship as a perfect image for the dialectic of fate and free will: 'You don't have to worry about which way to go, or whether to go at all – the question doesn't arise, because you're on a boat, aren't you? . . . I think I'll spend most of my life on boats.'[9] In Stoppard's 1965 play the ship taking the two spies to England is, of course, carrying them to certain death, as 'Rosencrantz and Guildenstern are dead' at the end of *Hamlet* (5.2.315), and they only enter 'real' time when they get caught up in Shakespeare's tragedy. The dramatist never lets us forget that the 'divinity that shapes' (5.2.10) their ends is literature, that there is nothing outside the text. By contrast, in Foucault's book, 'the sweet joy of Ophelia' and 'the bitter sweet dementia of *King Lear*' are said to 'bear witness' to the actual existential 'experience of madness', when the insane 'were allowed to wander in the open countryside', or float upon the current 'mermaid-like' (*Hamlet*, 5.1.147), in a 'wild state', like Millais' Ophelia, that 'can never be reconstituted'. These hyperbolic words about the 'torn presence' of 'madness itself, in all its vivacity, before it is captured by knowledge', were cut from the revised edition of 1972.[10] And after he was subjected to scathing critiques by the historian Roy Porter and others, Foucault's defenders argued that he had only ever meant the Ship of Fools 'as a striking (and rich) *symbol*' of what he called 'that inaccessible primitive purity'.[11] Yet when a complete text at last appeared in English in 2006, as the *History of Madness*, although his translators had curbed Foucault's giveaway verbal tic of 'sans doute', its veridical claims about the luxury cruises of transgression were revealed to be both literal and unambiguous:

> for they really did exist, these boats that drifted from one town to another with their senseless cargo. An itinerant existence was often the lot of the mad. It was common practice . . . The arrival in the great cities of Europe of these

ships of fools must have been quite a common sight . . . And it may be that these ships of fools, which haunted the imagination of the Early Renaissance, were in fact ships of pilgrimage, highly symbolic ships filled with the senseless in search of their reason.[12]

For fifty years Foucault's mighty tome had enjoyed a spectral existence in the minds of American and British academics, as a sort of Flying Dutchman of philosophy, the substance of which could only be guessed. His admirers always claimed he footnoted so lightly because he wished to read the past through the thinnest possible 'grid'.[13] But when the *History of Madness* finally docked on Anglo-Saxon shores, its skeletal documentation caused genuine shock, not least because its crucial assertion that the Ships of Fools 'really did exist' proved utterly unsubstantiated; and the leading article of *The Times Literary Supplement* on 23 March 2007 spoke for even erstwhile Foucauldians, with the deadly headline, 'Foucault's Fictions: Scholarship of Fools'. The 'frail foundations of Foucault's monument' were attributable to its having been researched in exile in Sweden, the spookily named Andrew Scull speculated in this devastating piece of *schadenfreude*. But 'its central image of "the ship of fools" laden with its cargo of mad souls searching for their reason, floating down the liminal spaces of feudal Europe', had been 'careless and inventive', at best, and at worst, a deliberate fabrication: 'The ship of fools was real. They existed, these boats that carried their crazed cargo from one town to another. But it wasn't; and they didn't.' *Madness and Civilization* had cast a malign spell over the psychiatric enterprise during the neoliberal assault on public services, when it became expedient to dismiss psychiatrists as 'nothing more than prison guards', Scull alleged; so the consequences of these falsifications were real for patients discharged to go their wandering ways in the great decommissioning of Western public health. Thus the real lesson of Foucault's Shakespearean foolery 'might be amusing', the review concluded, if it had 'had no effect on people's lives: the ease with which history can be distorted, facts ignored, and the claims of human reason disparaged and dismissed, by someone sufficiently cynical and shameless, and willing to trust in the ignorance and credulity of his customers'.[14]

By reviving the insinuation that the chronicler of the Ship of Fools was responsible for the bag ladies of New York, the *TLS* was stirring controversy; and Scull's polemic duly scandalised the Foucauldians, who likened its 'extreme prejudice' to the Sokal hoax that purported to explode poststructuralism, and protested that the philosopher had driven his Jaguar 'often and fast from Uppsala' to toil in the Paris archives.[15] But if the unabridged version has destroyed any lingering faith among Shakespeare critics in Foucault's volume as a serious work of Renaissance history, it merely confirms what had been made obvious decades before, when, in a famous act of parricide, Jacques Derrida punctured the hubris of the grand attempt 'to write a history of madness *itself*. *Itself*. Of madness itself. That is by letting madness speak for itself', as yet another totalitarian 'internment. A Cartesian gesture for the twentieth century.'[16] Foucault had highlighted Descartes' disavowal of madmen who fantasise that 'they are kings when they are paupers, or say they are dressed in purple when they are naked', as the instant of 'the Great Confinement', when reason excludes unreason, Erasmus's praise of folly and Montaigne's doubt are overcome, and 'A great forgetting falls on the world that was criss-crossed by the free slavery of the ship of fools', which is henceforth 'berthed at the quay. No longer a boat at all, but a hospital.'[17] But with a cruel dig at his teacher's own record of mental illness, Derrida dashed the rationality of the Cartesian subject as a mere repression of the fear of madness, when 'the reassurance given against the anguish of the fear of being mad' is 'the point of greatest proximity to madness'. Thus the pathos attending Foucault's deluded mission 'to try to capture, in history, this degree zero of madness, when it was undifferentiated experience', was that of an emperor without clothes, the irreverent pupil hinted, since the *folie de grandeur* of such a megalomaniac historicism was symptomatic of 'this crisis in which reason is madder than madness'.[18] Foucault had performed his own thesis, it was wickedly insinuated, for this colossal construct of His Majesty the Ego was *itself* a gigantic fool's errand:

> It is only by virtue of this oppression of madness that finite-thought, that is to say, history, can reign . . . one could say that the reign of finite thought can be established only on the basis of the more or less disguised internment, humiliation, fettering and mockery of the madman within us, of the madman who can only be the fool of a logos which is father, master, and king.[19]

Derrida's iconoclastic deconstruction of the *History of Madness*, as a certifiable specimen of a historicism haunted by the 'terror of going mad',[20] accounts for the ferocity of Foucault's notorious response, when the book was reissued in 1972, that such textualisation was itself 'a historically well-determined little pedagogy . . . which teaches the student that there is nothing outside the text . . . a pedagogy that gives to the voice of the master that unlimited sovereignty that allows it to indefinitely re-say the text'.[21] The ensuing schism in French theory would resemble nothing so much as the lunatic scene aboard the Ship of Fools in *The Tempest*, when, as the vessel founders, Shakespeare's voyagers fight over who and where is the master (1.1). But Foucault grasped well enough that what was at stake in this graceless altercation was whether it was 'possible that there might be something anterior or exterior to philosophical discourse. Could it have its condition in an exclusion, a refusal?'[22] The answer to his question seemed to have been, no, for after Derrida's sabotage Foucault systematically abandoned the concept of unmediated 'experience'.[23] As Ian Hacking points out in the Foreword, successive rewritings of the *History of Madness* therefore reveal its author turning himself inside-out, as the Foucault who valorised the 'romantic fantasy' of 'the dream of madness in the wild', and 'the purity of the possessed, those who speak the truth in paradox, like the fools in Shakespeare', disappears, until nothing remains of this archaeologist of 'unreason' but the grin, like that of Alice's Cheshire Cat, of the gene-alogist who in the *History of Sexuality* argues, *contra* his own earlier 'repressive hypothesis', that power is productive and inclusive, rather than deductive and exclusive, and thereby does indeed embrace the 'madman within':[24] 'We pass from a technology of power that drives out, excludes, banishes, marginalizes, and represses, to a fundamentally positive power that fashions, observes, knows, and multiplies itself on the basis of its own effects.'[25]

The translation of the *History of Madness* has been relished by Foucault's Anglo-Saxon detractors as an embarrassment comparable to that of Althusser's *The Future Last a Long Time*, the memoir in which the Marxist theoretician claimed to have read barely a word of Marx.[26] But the fact that this work is now discredited as history, for relying on literary and artistic sources such as Bosch's *Ship of Fools* or Cervantes' *Don Quixote*, makes it all the more vital to reconsider what Foucault might yet contribute as a reader of Shakespeare. What can be salvaged for literary criticism from the great wreck of this Ship of Fools? For whatever the evidence for 'the ritual embarkation' of the insane, Foucault had asserted, 'one thing is certain: the link between water and madness is deeply rooted in the dream of Western man'.[27] More specifi-cally, in his study 'Staying Afloat', Bernhard Klein has commented that 'only a cultural imagination that still encoded the sea as the morally transgressive and inherently repulsive realm of formless and unfinished matter was amenable to such a literary conceit' as this ghostly galleon that sails the seas without destination, given that 'No greater conceptual difference from the spirit of Columbus's enterprise can be imagined than the lack of purpose that defines Brandt's mad voyage.'[28] So, that Foucault was on to something, with his reverence for Shakespeare as the poet of the unfathomable 'dark backward and abyss' (*Tempest*, 1.2.50) of death and madness, dreams and night, is a powerful under-current of Steve Mentz's *At the Bottom of Shakespeare's Ocean*, which riffs upon the *topos* of the capsizing 'ship boring the moon with her main mast'

(*Winter's*, 3.3.92) to float the thesis of a new 'blue cultural studies': that 'Shakespeare asks us to read for salt . . . as if certain narratives can help us embrace and endure ocean-driven disorder.'[29] In our latest fanciful Shakespeare phenomenology, therefore, it seems that Foucault returns, but as himself a poet and fabulist rather than historian, whose importance was indeed to have recognised in these liminal dramas the rites of passage that define the threshold of the modern:

> The madness to be found in the works of Shakespeare leads to death and murder . . . [Thus] they in all probability still bear witness to the tragic experience of madness born in the fifteenth century more than they reflect the critical or moral experience of unreason that is nonetheless a product of their era. Through time, they connect with a kind of madness that is in the process of disappearing, and which will live on only under the cover of darkness.[30]

In his very first publication, his 1954 essay *Dream and Existence*, Foucault saluted Shakespeare as a laureate of the 'dark space' of night, whose texts were among the last to figure the irrational not as a reflection of reality, but as 'something of great constancy' (*Dream*, 5.1.26), truer than the waking world.[31] As I proposed in *Shakespeare in French Theory*, by enthroning the Bard as a 'king of shadows' (3.2.348) in this rapturous way, the philosopher was interpreting the plays within a French Romantic tradition that valorised them as 'the Gothic ruins of the Dark Ages'.[32] Hence, after Shakespeare, the *History of Madness* related, the 'dark power' of resistance to the therapeutic society 'begins to lose its violence', as 'that darkness into which man stared and made out impossible forms slowly begins to retreat'. The surprise turn that Derrida's acid critique of this 'romantic illusion' of exclusion prompted, however, was to reread Shakespeare not as a staging of the triumphant 'cortège of reason', but as a commemoration of the incorrigible 'madman within' the disciplinary order.[33] Thus, throughout his courses at the Collège de France in the 1970s and '80s, Foucault kept raiding the plays for traces of the insidious irrationality at the heart of the modern regime of 'biopolitics' that was his theme. And tellingly, the madman who came back in these Shakespeare citations was no longer an ostracised scapegoat on the margins of modernity, one of those 'outsiders-who-make-the-insiders-insiders',[34] but a psychopathic maniac in the seat of power, with the grotesque body yet exalted office of the king. For long before Alan Bennett wove *The Madness of King George III* around scenes from *King Lear*, what was Shakespearean theatre, Foucault asked repeatedly in these talks, but 'a sort of ceremony, or rememorialization of public right', in face of the mad arbitrariness, indeed criminal illegitimacy, of sovereign power?[35] Thus, Shakespeare appealed to the late

Foucault as a precursor of Absurdism, who had installed the grinning 'antic' on the throne, 'within the hollow crown / That rounds the mortal temple of a king' (*Richard II*, 3.2.156–9), and thereby exposed the *grotesque* unworthiness of rule:

> I am calling 'grotesque' the fact that . . . a discourse or an individual can have effects of power that their intrinsic qualities should disqualify them from having. The grotesque or, if your prefer, the 'Ubu-esque', is not just a term of abuse . . . I think there is a precise category of historico-political analysis, that would be the category of Ubu-esque terror, grotesque sovereignty, or, in starker terms, the maximization of effects of power on the basis of the disqualification of the one who produces them . . . The problem of the infamy of sovereignty, of the discredited sovereign, is, after all, Shakespeare's problem.[36]

In a recent article, Zita Turi demonstrates how, despite the popularity of Alexander's Barclay's 1509 translation of Brandt's *Narrenschiff*, in Tudor England 'the critical aim of *The Ship of Fools*' was steadily focused upon the licensed role of the court jester.[37] Critics have, of course, long identified in the cap and bauble of Shakespeare's Fool the signifiers of phallic privilege that Foucault also understood, when he told a conference in Japan that in a tragedy such as *King Lear* the lunatic spoke the truth to power, 'for he saw what the other characters did not see, and he revealed the ending of the plot . . . the madman is a character who expresses with his body the truth that the other actors and spectators are not aware of'.[38] The idiot rides alongside Caesar, and strikes him, from time to time, to remind the victor of mortality. As Shakespeare's Countess says, 'There is no slander' in such 'an allowed fool' (*Twelfth*, 1.5.80). But what Foucault noticed in the monstrous Richard III, or even the charmer Henry V, was something darker about the grotesque Ubu-like buffoonery of power, which was the cunning with which sovereignty intrudes itself as 'odious, despicable, or ridiculous'. No wonder Alfred Jarry based his preposterous tyrant on the infantile Macbeth. For Shakespeare was a genius, on this view, in the representation of 'vile sovereignty': the aberration whereby its self-portrayal as 'abject, despicable, Ubu-esque', far from curtailing its effects, instantiates 'the unavoidability, the inevitability of power, which can function in its full rigour and at the extreme point of its rationality even when in the hands of someone who is effectively discredited'. Thus, all the 'mediocre, useless, imbecilic, superficial, worn-out', reviled and sordid functionaries of the modern bureaucratic machine, as depicted by Dostoyevsky or Kafka, are prefigured, according to the later Foucault, when Shakespeare's madcap prince presents himself to us, warts and all, as the wisest fool, who has 'sounded the very base-string of humility', to make himself as much beloved by 'all the good lads in Eastcheap' (*1 Henry IV*, 2.5. 5–13), who he will betray, as he is despised by us for his own callous and casual criminality.[39]

'Theatre is not set over against power, but is one of power's essential modes': the lesson Greenblatt and New Historicism learned from Foucault was the old one that power uses circuses, that the king will 'play bo-peep / And go the fools among' (*Lear*, 1.4.154–5) the clowns, so that 'in the perfectness of time' he can 'Cast off his followers ... Turning past evils to advantages' (*2 Henry IV*, 4.3.67–78).[40] Much of the debate in Shakespeare studies during the Foucault years was therefore about the degree to which this immunological trick to –

> imitate the sun,
> Who doth permit the base contagious clouds
> To smother up his beauty from the world. (*1 Henry IV*, 1.2.175–7)

– operated as *containment*, or whether the plays demonstrated how these 'filthy rites' of abjection were vulnerable to more radical *subversion*.[41] If transgression was a strategic ruse, a 'bourgeois bohemia', was Shakespearean theatre itself a mimetic *staging* of repressed desire, as Mikhail Bakhtin had shown Carnival to be a periodic fit of madness, the 'temporary liberation from the prevailing truth of the established order',[42] or did it, as Peter Stallybrass and Allon White countered in *The Politics and Poetics of Transgression*, effectuate 'a strange carnivalesque diaspora' that carried the heresy of a world turned upside-down beyond the mere interrogation of boundaries and towards a transformational politics?[43] Greenblatt's Kafkaesque answer, that there is 'subversion, no end of subversion, but not for us',[44] took its cue from Foucault's dispiriting pronouncement, in his 'Preface to Transgression', his homage to Bataille, that if transgression is 'for our culture' what dialectic was for Sartre's, its meaning lies 'almost entirely in the future'.[45] But the critique of Shakespeare outlined in the lectures at the Collège de France was altogether more engaged, indeed enraged, about the idiocy of power and the madman in the palace:

> Ubu the 'pen-pusher' is a functional component of modern administration ... just as in the grotesque character of someone like Mussolini power provided itself with an image in which power derived from someone who was theatrically got up and depicted as a clown or a buffoon ... This is precisely the problem posed by Shakespeare in the royal tragedies, without, it seems to me, the sovereign's infamy ever having been theorized. But from Nero down to the little man with trembling hands crowned with forty million deaths who, from deep in his bunker, asks only for two things, that everything about him be destroyed and that he be given chocolate cakes until he bursts, you have the whole outrageous functioning of the despicable sovereign.[46]

Grimacing 'man, proud man, / Dressed in a little brief authority . . . Plays such fantastic tricks before high heaven / As makes the angels weep' (*Measure*, 2.2.120–5): the Chaplinesque Shakespeare Foucault quoted in his lectures stood out among the lickspittles by his refusal to sing 'power's ode to itself'. At a time when historicists like Thomas Hobbes were struggling to 'get around the terrible problem of the Conquest', the ineffaceable aporia that the English state had been founded by violent usurpation, Shakespeare, according to this account, instead revelled in the bastardy and madness of the monarchy.[47] Foucault's grasp of English history was shaky, and he seems to have thought Monmouth's Rebellion of 1685 was a Saxon rising against the Normans, led by the medieval chronicler Geoffrey of Monmouth, a howler that remained uncorrected in 2006![48] But in his reading of these dramas as 'one of the great ritual forms in which public right was displayed and its problems discussed' by ceaselessly revisiting the primal scene of founding violence, he unerringly foretold current thinking about Shakespeare as a witness to 'the uncanny proximity' of the sovereign and the beast.[49]

Despite disastrously hailing the return of the Ayatollah as the restoration of a 'political spirituality' that had been forgotten in the West since the Renaissance, Foucault never used the term 'political theology', and had presumably never heard of Carl Schmitt.[50] But he organised his most political work, *Discipline and Punish*, around the theological nostrum he derived from Ernst Kantorowicz and *The King's Two Bodies*, that 'In the darkest region of the political field' the condemned criminal 'represents the symmetrical, inverted figure of the king'.[51] And in Richard III's anachronising self-realisation as 'Deformed, unfinished, sent before my time' (*Richard III*, 1.1.20), he identified a Shakespearean premonition of the theme of 'the link between the sovereign above the law and the criminal beneath' which he developed in these lectures: the homology that 'the first moral monster is the political monster . . . The first monster is the king . . . Kings are nothing else but tigers.'[52] Like Ubu, Shakespeare's 'king of shreds and patches' is 'A cutpurse of the empire and the rule' (*Hamlet*, 3.4.89–92); and what that means for Foucault is that this sovereign lawbreaker 'is he who decides on the exception':[53]

Shakespeare's 'historical' tragedies are tragedies about right centered on the problem of the usurper and dethronement, of the murder of kings and the birth of the new being who is constituted by the coronation of a king. How can an individual use violence, intrigue, murder, and war to acquire a public might that can bring about the reign of order? How can illegitimacy produce law? At a time when the theory and history of right are trying to weave the unbroken continuity of public might, Shakespearean tragedy, in contrast, dwells on the wound, on the repeated injury that is inflicted on the body of the kingdom when kings die violent deaths and illegitimate sovereigns come to the throne.[54]

'We touch here on an apparently marginal problem that I think is important', Foucault explained to bemused listeners at the Collège, when he swerved from his subject of 'governmentality' to Shakespeare, 'and this is the problem of theatrical practice in politics, or the theatrical practice of *raison d'État*'.[55] For unlike recent American critics who present the plays as propagandist fanfares for the political theology of divine right, and follow Greenblatt in viewing Shakespearean theatre as one of sacred kingship's 'essential modes', an idealisation of 'high Christian royalism' and the mysterious ways of the executive decision, in these lectures the French theorist never lost sight of drama as performance.[56] Such dramatisation might well be 'a mode of manifestation of the sovereign as holder of state power', he conceded. But he had grasped Kantorowicz's point about the difference between the fiction and the man enough to insist on the 'contrast and opposition' between the 'traditional ceremonies in which royalty wanted to be shown', those displays which, 'from anointment to coronation up to the entry into towns or the funerals of sovereigns, marked the religious character' of monarchy, and 'this modern kind of theatre' in which the scenario was always the exception, the emergency of the *'coup d'Etat* carried out by the sovereign himself'.[57] Theatre, on this view, was indeed set over against power, which it depicted as operating in 'a wilderness of tigers' (*Titus*, 3.1.54), for Shakespeare's significance was to have demonstrated how *raison d'État* was not *rational* at all. Thus, just as the Kantorowicz of *The King's Two Bodies* crowned Dante over his erstwhile *Fuhrer*-type Frederick II, on the grounds that while the emperor stood for 'the manipulation of myth, the *Commedia* (like *Richard II*) stands for the fiction that knows itself as such',[58] so the Foucault of these lectures advanced Shakespeare above the maniacal monarchs he served, in awed appreciation of how the plays stage the clownish irrationality of power, and over and again confront the Pascalian Catch 22 that prefaces the *History of Madness*, that 'Men are so necessarily mad, that not being mad would be being mad through another trick that madness played':[59]

Shakespeare's historical drama really is the drama of the *coup d'État* . . . Just as in politics *raison d'État* manifests itself in theatricality, so this theater is organized around the representation of this *raison d'État* in its dramatic, intense, and violent form of the *coup d'État* . . . State, necessity, and risky *coups d'État* will form the new tragic horizon of history. At the same time as the birth of *raison d'État*, I think a certain tragic sense of history is born . . . in this theatrical and violent form . . . something that quite remarkably makes one think of Hitlerian nights, of the night of the long knives.[60]

'Why was he sent into England? Why, because he was mad. A shall recover his wits there; or if a do not, 'tis no great matter ... 'Twill not be seen in him there. There the men are as mad as he' (*Hamlet*, 5.1.138–42): with his Ship of Fools bound for England, Foucault's Shakespeare is the undeceived servant, in these lectures, of the Ubuesque 'Wisest Fool in Christendom', a writer who through the performances he plots for a mad and murderous monarchy 'represents the state to itself'.[61] Thus his Prince of Denmark is truly 'mad north-north-west' (*Hamlet*, 2.2.361), if we follow this logic, in aspiring to the kind of foolish sovereignty that was personified by the King of Scots, or his brother-in-law Christian, the actual Danish prince, who before his coronation in 1596 was carted by actors from London on a ship of fools dressed up as the pope, and on his return from the ceremony robed as a whore.[62] Nothing more is heard about the 'author function', as a means to insure 'the possibility of transgression attached to the act of writing',[63] in Foucault's praise of the playwright as the author whose function was to 'hold as 'twere the mirror up' (*Hamlet*, 3.2.20) to such moral and juridical monstrosity, and reveal how 'The grotesque is one of the essential processes of arbitrary sovereignty.' Instead, the philosopher whose history of madness had been trashed for confusing fact and fiction, Renaissance experience and Shakespearean literature, rejoices in the uninhibited transgressiveness of dramas that represent 'the person who possesses power' as, 'in his costume, his gestures, his body, his sexuality, and his way of life, a despicable grotesque, and ridiculous individual'.[64] 'The limit and transgression depend on each other', Foucault had written in his 'Preface to Transgression'; but in Shakespeare, where the Ship of Fools became the ship of state, it seems he found at last a form of symbolic transgression that was itself 'as mad as the vexed sea, singing aloud' (*Lear*, 4.3.2).

Notes

1. Michel Foucault, *History of Madness*, trans. Jonathan Murphy and Jean Khalfa (London: Routledge, 2006), pp. 8 and 38.
2. Ibid., p. 9.
3. Michel Foucault, *Madness and Civilization: A History of Insanity in the Age of Reason*, trans. Richard Howard (New York: Pantheon, 1965; London: Tavistock, 1967), pp. 7–8.
4. Ibid., pp. 11 and 25.
5. Michel Foucault, 'Different Spaces', trans. Robert Hurley, in Michel Foucault, *Essential Works of Foucault: 1954–1984, III: Aesthetics, Method, and Epistemology*, ed. James D. Faubion (London: Allen Lane, 1998), pp. 179 and 184–5; originally published in *Architecture, Mouvement, Continueté*, 5 (October 1984), pp. 46–9.

6. Stephen Greenblatt, *Renaissance Self-Fashioning: From More to Shakespeare* (Chicago: Chicago University Press, 1980), p. 80.
7. For Foucault's debt to Bataille, see Frank Pearce, 'Foucault and the "Hydra-Headed Monster": The *Collège de Sociologie* and the two *Acéphales*', in Alain Beaulieu and David Gabbard (eds), *Michel Foucault and Power Today* (Lanham: Lexington Books, 2006), pp. 115–37.
8. Foucault, *Madness and Civilization*, p. 11.
9. Tom Stoppard, *Rosencrantz and Guildenstern are Dead* (London: Methuen, 1965), pp. 3 and 55.
10. Foucault, *History of Madness*, pp. xxxii–iii and 37–8.
11. Ibid., p. 164; Gary Gutting, 'Foucault and the History of Madness', *The Cambridge Companion to Foucault* (Cambridge: Cambridge University Press, 2005), p. 72, n. 21. For the refutation of Foucault's history of madness, see, in particular, Roy Porter, 'Foucault's Great Confinement', in *Rewriting the History of Madness: Studies in Foucault's 'Histoire de la folie'*, ed. Arthur Still and Irving Velodie (London: Routledge, 1992), pp. 119–25; and Lawrence Stone, 'Madness', *The New York Review of Books*, 16 December 1982, pp. 28–36. Other important interventions include H.C. Erik Midelfort, 'Madness and Civilisation in Early Modern Europe: A Reappraisal of Michel Foucault', in Barbara C. Malament (ed.), *After the Reformation* (Philadelphia: University of Pennsylvania Press, 1980), pp. 247–65; Peter Sedgwick, *Psycho Politics* (London: Pluto Press, 1982); José Merquior, *Foucault* (London: Fontana, 1985), Chapter 2; Colin Gordon, '*Histoire de la folie*: An Unknown Book by Michel Foucault', *History of the Human Sciences*, 3:1 (1990), pp. 3–26; Andrew Scull, 'Michel Foucault's History of Madness', *History of the Human Sciences*, 3:1 (1990), pp. 57–67; Colin Gordon, 'History, Madness and Other Errors: A Response', *History of the Human Sciences*, 3:3 (1990), 381–96; and Elisabeth Roudinesco et al., *Penser la folie* (Paris: Galilée, 1992). For a recent overview, see Alain Beaulieu and Réal Fillion, 'Review Essay: Michel Foucault, *History of Madness*', *Foucault Studies*, 5 (2008), pp. 74–89.
12. Foucault, *History of Madness*, pp. 9–10.
13. Valerio Marchetti and Antonella Salomoni, 'Course Context', in Michel Foucault, *Abnormal: Lectures at the Collège de France, 1974–1975*, ed. Valerio Marchetti and Antonella Salomoni, trans. Graham Burchill (New York: Picador, 2003), p. 348.
14. Andrew Scull, 'Scholarship of Fools: The Frail Foundations of Foucault's Monument', *Times Literary Supplement*, 23 March 2007, pp. 3–4. For Foucault's alleged culpability in the release of mental patients onto the streets of New York, see Gerald Weissmann, 'Foucault and the Bag Lady', *Hospital Practice* (August 1982), pp. 28–39.
15. Colin Gordon, 'Extreme Prejudice: Notes on Andrew Scull's *TLS* review of Foucault's *The History of Madness*', *Foucault Blog*, 20 May 2007; see also *Times Literary Supplement*, 'Letters', 6 April and 20 April 2007.
16. Jacques Derrida, 'Cogito and the History of Madness', in *Writing and Difference*, trans. Alan Bass (London: Routledge & Kegan Paul, 1978), pp. 31–63, here pp. 33 and 55.
17. Foucault, *History of Madness*, pp. 41 and 44–5.

18. Foucault, 'Preface to the 1961 Edition', ibid., p. xvii; Derrida, 'Cogito and the History of Madness', p. 61.
19. Ibid.
20. Ibid., p. 62.
21. Michel Foucault, 'My Body, This Paper, This Fire: Appendix to the 1972 Edition', in Foucault, *History of Madness*, pp. 550–74, here p. 573.
22. Ibid., p. 552.
23. See Eric Paras, *Foucault 2.0* (New York: Other Press, 2006), pp. 121–2 and 142–4.
24. Ian Hacking, 'Foreword', in Foucault, *History of Madness*, pp. ix–xi.
25. Foucault, *Abnormal*, p. 48.
26. Louis Althusser, *The Future Lasts a Long Time*, trans. Richard Veasey (London: Chatto & Windus, 1993).
27. Foucault, *History of Madness*, p. 11.
28. Bernhard Klein, 'Staying Afloat: Shipboard Encounters from Columbus to Equiano', in Bernhard Klein and Gesa Mackenthun (eds), *Sea Changes: Historicizing the Ocean* (London: Routledge, 2004), p. 94.
29. Steve Metz, *At the Bottom of Shakespeare's Ocean* (London: Continuum, 2009), p. 99.
30. Foucault, *History of Madness*, p. 37.
31. Michel Foucault, *Dream and Existence: Michel Foucault and Ludwig Binswanger*, trans. Forrest Williams, ed. Keith Hoeller (Atlantic Highlands, NJ: Humanities Press, 1993), pp. 54–5.
32. Richard Wilson, *Shakespeare in French Theory: King of Shadows* (London: Routledge, 2007), p. 75.
33. Foucault, *History of Madness*, p. 41.
34. Peter Stallybrass and Allon White, *The Politics and Poetics of Transgression* (London: Methuen, 1986), p. 22.
35. Michel Foucault, *Society Must Be Defended: Lectures at the Collège de France, 1975–1976*, trans. David Macey (London: Allen Lane, 2003), pp. 174–5.
36. Foucault, *Abnormal*, pp. 11–13.
37. Zita Tura, '"Border Liners": The Ship of Fools Tradition in Sixteenth-Century England', *Trans: Revue de littérature générale et comparée*, 10 (2010), unpaginated.
38. Foucault, 'Madness and Society', in *Essential Works of Foucault: 1954–1984, III*, p. 340.
39. Foucault, *Abnormal*, pp. 11–13.
40. Stephen Greenblatt, 'Invisible Bullets', in *Shakespearean Negotiations: The Circulation of Social Energy in Renaissance England* (Oxford: Oxford University Press, 1988), p. 46.
41. Stephen Greenblatt, 'Filthy Rites', in *Learning to Curse: Essays in Early Modern Culture* (London: Routledge, 1990), pp. 59–79.
42. Mikhail Bakhtin, *Rabelais and his World*, trans. H. Iswolsky (Cambridge, MA: MIT Press, 1968), p. 109.
43. Stallybrass and White, *The Politics and Poetics of Transgression*, pp. 190–201.
44. Greenblatt, 'Invisible Bullets', p. 65.
45. Michel Foucault, 'Preface to Transgression', in *Language/Counter-Memory/*

Practice, trans. D. Bouchard and S. Simon (Ithaca: Cornell University Press, 1977), p. 33.

46. Foucault, *Abnormal*, p. 13.
47. Foucault, *Society Must Be Defended*, pp. 110 and 174.
48. Ibid., p. 101.
49. Eric Santner, *The Royal Remains: The People's Two Bodies and the Endgames of Sovereignty* (Chicago: Chicago University Press, 2011), p. 47.
50. Michel Foucault, 'A Quoi rêvent les Iraniens?', *Le Nouvel Observateur*, 16 October 1978, 48–9.
51. Michel Foucault, *Discipline and Punish: The Birth of the Prison*, trans. Alan Sheridan (Harmondsworth: Penguin, 1977), p. 29; Ernst Kantorowicz, *The King's Two Bodies: A Study in Medieval Political Theology* (Princeton: Princeton University Press, 1997).
52. Foucault, *Abnormal*, pp. 92, 94 and 97.
53. Carl Schmitt, 'Sovereign is he Who Decides', in *Political Theology: Four Chapters on the Concept of Sovereignty*, trans. George Schwab (Chicago: University of Chicago Press, 2005), pp. 5 and 33.
54. Foucault, *Society Must Be Defended*, p. 174.
55. Michel Foucault, *Security, Territory, Population: Lectures at the Collège de France, 1977–1978*, trans. Graham Burchell (Basingstoke: Palgrave, 2007), p. 265.
56. Debora Shuger, *Political Theologies in Shakespeare's England: The Sacred and the State in 'Measure for Measure'* (Basingstoke: Palgrave, 2001), p. 56 and passim.
57. Foucault, *Security, Territory, Population*, p. 265.
58. Victoria Kahn, 'Political Theology and Fiction in *The King's Two Bodies*', *Representations*, 106 (2009), pp. 77–101, here pp. 95–6; cf. Alain Boureau, *Kantorowicz: Stories of a Historian*, trans. Stephen Nichols and Gabrielle Spiegel (Baltimore: Johns Hopkins University Press, 2001), p. 106: 'Kantorowicz inverted Schmitt's understanding of political theology. Political theology did not furnish an authoritarian arm to secular sovereigns because they possessed it already. Political theology used the moment of the Incarnation as the model . . . to create fictions that remove man from the direct pressures of nature, power, and the group.'
59. Blaise Pascal, *Pensées*, 414; quoted Foucault, 'Preface to the 1961 Edition', *Madness and Civilization*, p. xxvii.
60. Foucault, *Security, Territory, Population*, pp. 265–6.
61. Ibid., p. 266.
62. See Mara Wade, 'The Coronation of Christian IV', in James Ronald Mulryne, Helen Watanabe-O'Kelly and Margaret Shewring (eds), *Europa Triumphans: Court and Civic Festivals in Early Modern Europe, Volume 2* (Aldershot: Ashgate, 2004), pp. 245–69.
63. Foucault, 'What is an Author?', trans. Josué Harari, in Foucault, *Essential Works of Foucault: 1954–1984, III*, p. 205.
64. Foucault, *Abnormal*, p. 12.

Chapter 12

Antinomies of Desire: Lacanian Psychoanalysis and the Sonnets

Catherine Belsey

To desire in Shakespeare's Sonnets is also to fight. Whatever we set out to find in these poems – the inscription of love, a historical narrative, or a sexual identity – antagonism clearly inhabits the passion they portray. Projected outwards, this hostility is variously directed at time, death, nature, and a rival poet, but its objects also include the addressees, as well as poetry itself. The antipathy that accompanies the love these poems declare would come as no surprise to psychoanalysis. Sigmund Freud noted a similar pattern among his analysands, and the imbrication of love and hate is well documented in his work. *Beyond the Pleasure Principle*, for example, does its best to hold apart the life-giving sexual drive and the death drive projected outwards as aggression but ends with the speculation that the perhaps the two are after all in alliance.[1] Julia Kristeva goes on to read *Romeo and Juliet* as an account of 'love-hatred' in the couple.[2] Jacques Lacan, meanwhile, has developed the psychoanalytic account in *Seminar 7: The Ethics of Psychoanalysis*, where Freud's apparently antithetical drives are decisively rolled into one. It might be rash to assume that we can find perfect continuity in Lacan's work, since it spanned nearly fifty years. While there are recurring preoccupations, *Seminar 7* was in some ways transitional: Lacan would not reiterate every proposition he put forward there. But the seminar of 1959–60 can be read as taking psychoanalysis in a direction that illuminates Shakespeare's fascinating, enigmatic, elusive sequence of poems.[3]

If love repeatedly manifests itself as ambivalent there, very little else about the Sonnets is as clear-cut. Individually, they are admired as if their meanings were self-evident: specific sonnets have been variously anthologised, declaimed at weddings, recited in *Shakespeare in Love* and quoted in *Doctor Who*.[4] Read consecutively, on the other hand, they withhold almost as much as they deliver. There is no way to be sure whether they form a sequence addressed to two people, a fair young man and a dark woman, or a collection, written at intervals to various people and not bound together until their publication in 1609.[5] The order and numbering cannot confidently be ascribed to the author. Were they composed mainly in the 1590s, at the height of the sonnet vogue in England, or later, to rewrite with a difference the conventions that vogue might be thought to have exhausted? Are they fact, based on personal experience, or fiction, an exploration by a dramatist of new possibilities for an old genre? And does that distinction between fact and fiction hold when it comes to love? Doesn't any sexual relationship exist as much in the distinct imaginations of each lover as in the exchanges of the couple?

Critics have been eager to provide answers to many of these questions, supplying conjectural addressees, dates of composition, and sexualities. But perhaps we do the Sonnets a disservice when we come up with solutions to the puzzles they present. Although he was presumably in a position to do so, there is no evidence that Shakespeare himself made any effort to issue corrections or clarifications, to confirm occasions, or name names. Without appealing to the author as the final authority, it can be argued that criticism strips the texts of their subtlety when it resolves what they leave inconclusive. Any univocal explanation of the Sonnets necessarily diminishes them – and reduces, in the end, our motive for reading them.

Their thematic undecidability owes much to their ambivalence, since animosity repeatedly intrudes into the love they depict. Antagonism appears in a variety of contexts, but most obviously in the group concerning the so-called 'Dark Lady'. The term is a Victorian misnomer: whoever she is, the addressee of these twenty-six sonnets is no lady. Sonnets 127–52 seem to be about a woman, or possibly more than one.[6] Six of them dwell on the discrepancy between their addressee's dark colouring and the 'fair' beauty that convention endorses, and two of these associate her 'blackness' directly with moral disgrace (Sonnets 131, 147). Since the moral disgrace is affirmed elsewhere, and since this group seems consistently to concern a relentlessly physical passion and a corresponding self-reproach, I take the line of least resistance and follow convention in treating them as a sub-sequence. Seen, then, as a single figure, the dark woman is deceitful, promiscuous, treacherous, sexually voracious, and probably diseased.

For all their shared antipathy to these qualities, however, the register of this group of sonnets is elusive. Are they best read with compassion, as the record of despair at love's falsehood, or enjoyed as an exercise in wit at the expense of its waywardness? If we see these poems as telling a story, the tale is a bleak one; at the same time, the manner is intelligible as mischievous, caustic, or outrageous. Many of them mock the Petrarchan conventions: 'My mistress' eyes are nothing like the sun', Sonnet 130 insists, while others seem to parody the whole idealising tradition by addressing sonnets to a whore.[7] The dark woman may share her black eyes with Berowne's Rosalind and Sidney's Stella,[8] but in other respects she represents the exact antithesis of the beauty, virtue and constancy valued by Petrarch and his successors. Even so, she remains desirable: 'And yet, by heaven, I think my love as rare', Sonnet 130 concludes, 'As any she belied with false compare'. But what exactly is being affirmed here? That, equally *exceptional* in her own way, she deserves to be loved as well as any Petrarchan lady? That the poet, depicted ironically as blinded by passion, mistakenly *thinks* her equally worthy of devotion? Or that the conventional Petrarchan *comparisons* falsify both love itself and the nature of women? Perhaps all three.

Under the influence of New Historicism, much attention was devoted in the 1980s and beyond to the sonnet tradition as a place of self-fashioning.[9] The self Shakespeare fashions as the first-person protagonist of the dark woman sonnets seems puzzled by love's contradictions; at the same time, the writing self who puts this bewilderment on display appears shrewd, witty and self-deprecating. Although in 1598 Francis Meres applauded 'mellifluous & hony-tongued *Shakespeare*' for 'his sugred Sonnets among his private friends',[10] it is not clear which, if any of those that survive, he might have had in mind. Sonnet 138, however, is one of two published in slightly different form in *The Passionate Pilgrim* a year after his comment appeared in print: 'When my love swears that she is made of truth, / I do believe her, though I know she lies'. References here to the poet's 'vain' desire to be thought young give this text enough specificity to send the biographers off in search of women under thirty-five in 1599, which does not narrow the field greatly, but the sonnet can also be read as a general observation on love's propensity to deception and self-deception. Its account of the lovers' reciprocal flatteries leads neatly to the couplet's sexual pun, at once surprising and inevitable: 'Therefore I lie with her, and she with me'.[11] 'Sugared' seems hardly the word to describe such clever, worldly wisdom, and yet 'the sweete wittie soule of *Ovid*' that Meres also found in Shakespeare brings with it a knowing scepticism concerning the art of love. If the private friends who read Shakespeare's sonnets included some of the young men about town who so enjoyed *Venus and Adonis*, they must have relished the cynicism and the sheer effrontery of his appropriation of a predominantly spiritu-alising convention for such a purpose, delighting in the carnival of sexual puns, including those on the poet's own name (Sonnets 135, 136).

There were anti-Petrarchan precedents, of course, in which another's object of desire was depicted as ill-natured or unchaste, and the blazon of conventional beauty was absurdly reordered to deplore eyes like pearls and sapphire lips.[12] Such parodies throw into relief the element of excess and, indeed, repetition in the Petrarchan comparisons themselves. Shakespeare's anti-Petrarchan sonnets, witty as they are, distinguish themselves from these earlier instances by the close attention they pay to the paradoxes of love. Cupid is conventionally blind, but this is not mere blindness (Sonnet 141): the poet judges truly, but then ignores his own judgement (Sonnet 137). This love, unlike Petrarch's, is indifferent to faults; indeed, delinquency excites desire.

'Two loves I have, of comfort and despair', Sonnet 144 asserts. In the miniature moral play the poem records, 'The better angel is a man right fair; / The worser spirit a woman coloured ill'. This contrast between male virtue and female evil has been ascribed to misogyny pure and simple,[13] but misogyny, as Oscar Wilde might have agreed, is rarely pure and never simple. Instead, the texts themselves confront a puzzle. How is it that, when there seems nothing about her to admire or to like, when no aspect even of her body seems calculated to seduce (Sonnets 137, 141), the dark woman's very inadequacy remains so compelling? 'O, from what power hast thou this powerful might / With insufficiency my heart to sway?' (Sonnet 150).

A moralising tradition has come to insist that love belongs with virtue, recuperating passion for the superego. Thus domesticated, sexual desire joins the list of civic and social proprieties as the motive for the public, institutional and regulated partnership that grounds and reproduces family values. In the interests of this development, heroes and heroines who opt for unworthy objects of desire have progressively been seen as either deluded, mistaking charm for virtue, or at the mercy of counterfeit attachments, named infatuation or lust. There is already plenty of moral condemnation in the dark woman sonnets of the 'expense of spirit in a waste of shame' that constitutes 'lust in action', as the superego turns the death-drive against the ego in self-loathing. Sonnet 129 could hardly state the case against desire more sharply or more fervently: the condition is 'Mad in pursuit, and in possession so, / Had, having, and in quest to have, extreme'.[14] Puns here explicitly define lust in action as at once a moral problem and a sexual event. The expense of 'spirit' (mind and semen) takes place in a 'waste' (and waist) of shame. This leads to 'hell', which means vagina, as well as the wages of sin (Sonnet 144). It is the receptacle implied by waist and hell that causes the poet's flesh to 'rise and fall' (Sonnet 151), while it also imperils his soul (Sonnet 146).

But the self is by no means the only target. Successive sonnets dwell on the dark woman's 'will', slang term for the sexual organs of both men and women and for desire itself. 'Large and spacious' as it is (Sonnet 135), 'the wide world's common place', 'the bay', indeed, 'where all men ride' (Sonnet 137), her 'will' comes close to naming the emptiness constructed at the heart of all this witty excoriation. Ultimately, so much ado is about, in early modern English, 'nothing'. This recognition ends not in reform, however, but in the paradox that truth does not dispel desire. Clear sight is no cure: 'All this the world well knows, yet none knows well / To shun the heaven that leads men to this hell' (Sonnet 129). 'Whence', the poet continues to wonder, 'hast thou this becoming of things ill?' 'Who taught thee how to make me love thee more, / The more I hear and see just cause of hate?' (Sonnet 150).

Freud locates hostility at the beginnings of culture in the story of little Ernst, who adopted a wooden reel as a stand-in for his mother. This good boy, deeply attached to his mother, hated her absences when she was obliged to attend to other matters for a few hours. The child didn't cry, however. Instead, he played a game that involved throwing a wooden reel out of his curtained cot so that it became invisible. '*Fort*', he exclaimed, 'gone'. Although the part of the game that involved pulling the object back was more pleasurable ('*da*', 'there'), it was the act of throwing it away that was most frequently repeated. The satisfaction gained, Freud construes, derived from exercising mastery over the situation in the impulse to revenge: Ernst was punishing his mother.[15]

To put it in Lacanian terms, the little boy had found in the differentiating signifier a way to take possession of his own destiny, but that destiny would not erase the alternation of love and hate that defined his first relationship. Instead, the ambivalence repeated on the plane of language offers a certain satisfaction. In *Seminar 7* Lacan rewrites Freud to treat love as an instance of sublimation, where what is sublimated to form culture is not sex itself, as in Freud, but the drive and its impossible object. Lacanian love is at least as ambivalent as Freud's. Here the beloved, or successive objects of desire, are no more than stand-ins for the archaic, maternal target of the drive, the lost object, the inaccessible and dangerous Thing (*das Ding*), which simultaneously promises *jouissance* and threatens to engulf the subject. The Thing constitutes itself as filling the gap created by the loss of the real, when the little human animal accedes to the symbolic order of language and subjectivity. Access to the symbolic order separates the subject from the organic being it cannot discard, and for the adult organism-in-culture there continues to reside beyond the immediate object of desire the magnetic, inhuman, terrifying Thing. Since it is outside the symbolic order, the Thing cannot be represented, except by emptiness. Sublimation takes place in the symbolic, at the level of the signifier, and it gives pleasure – the pleasure, for example, offered by a Petrarchan sonnet sequence. But sublimation does not erase the Thing. Instead, while pleasurable signifiers encircle it, fence it off and prevent it from devouring the subject, representation marks the place of the Thing by an absence, emptiness, vacancy, nothing.

The sonnet, invented in thirteenth-century Italy,[16] shares a line of descent with the troubadour poems of courtly love. Among the texts of this civilising, idealising tradition, addressed to arbitrary and unattainable mistresses so remote that they appear curiously depersonalised, Lacan finds a unique example of a scatological poem that seems to contradict every rule they otherwise observe. It concerns a lady who, to the poet's disgust, insists that her knight must put his mouth to her 'trumpet', where he will find all kinds of noxious odours and repellent substances. There is no serious equivocation here: the image is explicitly anal and remarkably specific. Lacan comments, 'This quite extraordinary document opens a strange perspective on the deep ambiguity of the sublimating imagination.' The lady, he goes on, suddenly finds herself 'brutally positing, in a place knowingly constructed out of the most refined of signifiers, the emptiness of a thing in all its crudity', a thing that reveals itself to be the Thing, the nothing that is all we know of the object of the drive.[17]

Allusion to the Thing is not reducible to physiology, but a bodily cavity may figure the void that is as close as we come to its representation. An orifice that gives onto vacancy is oddly interchangeable with the emptiness of the lady idealised out of substantial existence, and either image, for Lacan, alludes to the unrepresentable Thing. In the psychoanalytic account, the Thing is both life-giving and deadly. Lacan's single drive impels the speaking being towards both life and death. It follows that the Thing, as the object-cause of desire, motivates both love and hate, adulation and antagonism, sometimes in equal proportions, sometimes in ways that make the two hard to distinguish from one another.

If psychoanalysis is right about this ambivalence, the poet's animosity towards the dark woman is no obstacle to desire; on the contrary, hostility is a likely component of love. This is neither a wholly new discovery nor one confined to an ex-centric work by a single troubadour. In one sense, Shakespeare's Sonnets do no more than reverse the weight of the existing Petrarchan paradoxes. Tradition identifies the lady as the 'cruel fair' who 'wounds' with her disdain; this virtuous tyrant is conventionally the lover's 'sweet foe'. But beauty, virtue and sweetness are her prevailing characteristics: her cruelty consists above all in refusing to pity her lover. Shakespeare's dark woman, by contrast, is more cruel than fair, more tyrannical than virtuous, and the poet's complaint is that, when it comes to others, she is not disdainful *enough*.

Even Thomas Wyatt's love poetry, where a latent antagonism turns to full-blown hostility in threats of vengeance,[18] does not depict a figure whose defects are themselves the cause of passion. Catullus, among Latin models for early modern lyric verse, recognised a relationship between love and hate;[19] only Shakespeare, however, turns Petrarchism inside out to produce in the genre itself an ironic confrontation with the antinomies of desire.

*

'Two loves I have, of comfort and despair'. At first glance, Sonnet 144 seems to set up an antithesis between the 'man right fair' and the 'woman coloured ill', the one offering contentment and repose, while the other turns love into torment. It is widely agreed, if only for want of counter-arguments, that the first 126 poems constitute a sub-sequence addressed to a fair young man. In practice, only about one-fifth of these poems make clear that their subject is male. That many of the others could equally concern a woman, however, may only go to confirm the ambiguity of the master-mistress and the passion he elicits. The last of them certainly marks a distinct break. Where Sonnet 126 seems to bring to an inconclusive end the sub-sequence, if that is what it is, concerning the young man, the following sonnet explicitly introduces the new topic of the dark woman:

> In the old age black was not counted fair,
> Or if it were it bore not beauty's name;
> But now is black beauty's successive heir,
> And beauty slandered with a bastard shame.

Placed as it is, Sonnet 127 seems to derive its contrast between past and present not only from comparison with a traditional world of blond beauty, but also with the epoch of the preceding poems. And indeed, it is as if this text rewrites the opening terms of Sonnet 1:

> From fairest creatures we desire increase,
> That thereby beauty's rose might never die,
> But as the riper should by time decease,
> His tender heir might bear his memory.

Where Sonnet 1 confirms the association of beauty with fairness, Sonnet 127 records a startling reversal of this convention. Where Sonnet 1 proposes the preservation of such beauty by legitimate succession, Sonnet 127 laments a fall from the proper processes of inheritance; and where the general proposition of Sonnet 1 flows smoothly and lyrically from its apparently non-controversial and timeless premise, Sonnet 127 goes on to enlist the reader in a complex and difficult set of paradoxes concerning the decay that characterises the present moment.

Similar pairings across the two groups initially seem to confirm the contrast between two kinds of love. 'Shall I compare thee to a summer's day?' Sonnet 18 asks the young man. 'Thou art more lovely and more temperate'. 'I have sworn thee fair, and thought thee bright', counters Sonnet 147 to the dark woman, 'Who art as black as hell, as dark as night'. Most obviously, the generalisations of Sonnet 129 concerning 'lust in action' stand in direct opposition to those of Sonnet 116 about 'the marriage of true minds'. Nowhere in the first 126 poems, at least on the surface, is there explicit and contemptuous reference to sexual acts; there is no evidence of physiological disgust with the object of desire; nor is there anything comparable to the self-reproach and self-loathing that pervade the dark woman sonnets. Perhaps the 'one thing' that defines the young man sexually, because it is 'nothing' to the poet's purpose (Sonnet 20), bars allusion to that other and more dangerous nothing that evokes the enticing and forbidden Thing, the object-cause of hate, as well as love?

But the antithesis between fair young man and dark woman is not so straightforward. In the first place, the poet's 'purpose' as defined in Sonnet 20 is as strongly disputed as any other aspect of the collection. And second, the *psychomachia* recorded in Sonnet 144 does not go quite according to convention. In a move unprecedented in the morality tradition, the bad angel trains her seductive powers on the good angel himself, leaving the poet to suspect a sexual outcome: 'I guess one angel in another's hell'. This practical instance of deconstruction *avant la lettre* indicates that the other may literally and materially have been invaded by the selfsame. Binary oppositions, Jacques Derrida repeatedly points out, do not hold; as a theoretical necessity, the meaning of the term that defines another by antithesis penetrates in that very process the term it defines. Sonnet 144 registers an extreme case of linguistic theory put into bodily practice. Although Sonnets 1–126 may not always assert the fact with the same intensity, in its own way the young man's thing is also capable, evidently, of disturbing the poet's peace of mind.

It comes as no surprise, then, that antagonism inhabits the first group, as well as the second. Many of the vices attributed to the mistress are also ascribed in due course to the friend. In some instances, his 'fault' (Sonnet 96) is a not very clearly specified 'disgrace' (Sonnets 33, 34) or a 'trespass' (Sonnet 35). Elsewhere, it is gregariousness (Sonnet 61) or susceptibility to praise (Sonnet 84). But Sonnets 40–42 name promiscuity as treachery. Indeed, Sonnet 41 might rank as a companion piece to Sonnet 144, telling the same story from another point of view and in another key: the young man's inconstancies are 'pretty wrongs'; temptation is inevitable; his beauty will inevitably be assailed. But then the sestet marks a new turn: 'Ay me, but yet thou might'st my seat forbear'. The friend's infidelity to the poet with the poet's mistress betrays 'a two-fold truth', his own and hers. With its imagery of temptation and falsehood, Sonnet 41, like Sonnet 144, also records a *psychomachia*. Indeed, this poem even includes its own miniature moral play: the young man is urged on by beauty and 'thy straying youth, / Who lead thee in their riot'. These personifications evoke the popular *Interlude of Youth*, where the young hero, proud of his handsome and vigorous body, falls into the clutches of Riot, who introduces him to Lechery.[20] The poet's prevailing impulse is to make excuses for the friend's faults. So lovely does the young man make his own shame that the poet 'Cannot dispraise, but in a kind of praise' (Sonnet 95). Even so, the lover registers a puzzled ambivalence, represented in one near-oxymoron after another: the young man is a 'gentle thief', 'Lascivious grace, in whom all ill well shows' (Sonnet 40), 'Most worthy comfort, now my greatest grief' (Sonnet 48). The contradictions are explained by the antinomies of desire itself: 'Such civil war is in my love and hate' (Sonnet 35).

The manner of Sonnet 41, at least at first, is resigned, not angry, but the vocabulary of the sonnets to the friend is not always so temperate. Sonnet 69 accuses its addressee of hypocrisy. There are those, it alleges, who, looking behind appearances, 'To thy fair flower add the rank smell of weeds'. 'But why thy odour matcheth not thy show', the sonnet concludes, 'The soil is this, that thou dost common grow'. 'Soil' is a conjectural emendation: the quarto text, the only one published in Shakespeare's lifetime, gives 'solye', which makes no sense. If 'soil' is right, it not only indicates a 'ground' for the general opinion and fits in, however loosely, with the metaphor of growing things: it also brings with it associations of dirt, and perhaps especially sexual contamination.[21] Here the young man's fault is that he grows 'common'. John Kerrigan glosses this as 'vulgar, commonplace, cheap', and adds, 'With a quibble on "public pasture, unenclosed field"'.[22] This is not far, surely, from 'the wide world's common place', or that other figurative account of the dark woman as 'the bay where all men ride' (Sonnet 137).

The contrast between flower and weed recurs in Sonnet 94, and here the culminating moment of the poem, while not as sexually outspoken, seems to me as brutal and as bitter as any of the accusations addressed to the dark woman.

The summer's flower is to the summer sweet,
Though to itself it only live and die,
But if that flower with base infection meet,
The basest weed outbraves his dignity:
　　For sweetest things turn sourest by their deeds;
　　Lilies that fester smell far worse than weeds.

The poem apparently concerns a generalised 'They', but this comparison gathers up all that has gone before of roses and summer's days and, if we link it back to the procreation sonnets, now concedes the relative legitimacy of self-containment and self-sufficiency. Meanwhile, 'infection' points to parallel indications in the dark woman sonnets of sexually transmitted disease, while remaining intelligible here as a moral metaphor. 'Lilies that fester', however, is shocking. Festering is a function of bodies, not plants; the metaphor breaks the limits of lyric vocabulary as suppurating flesh abruptly intrudes into the conventional flower imagery. Lilies, we know, are white, pure, scented. That they were also thought in the period to smell bad when they decomposed does not diminish the incongruity of 'fester', which takes 'infection' to its literal and logical outcome in a world that knew nothing of antibiotics.

Roland Barthes, most Lacanian of literary critics, discusses a comparable moment in *A Lover's Discourse: Fragments*. This quintessentially modernist text resembles Shakespeare's Sonnets in unexpected ways. Now narrative, now reflective, each of its eighty sections stands more or less alone, and each can be read as an episode in a story or stories that are never consecutively assembled or connected. Overtly intertextual and at the same time original, *A Lover's Discourse*, like the Sonnets, isolates the momentary triumphs and the disproportionate anxieties of passion. One fragment, 'Alteration', centres on the linguistic consequences of finding a flaw in the object of desire:

> In the other's perfect and 'embalmed' figure (for this is the degree to which it fascinates me) I perceive suddenly a speck of corruption. This speck is a tiny one: a gesture, a word, an object, a garment, something unexpected which appears (which dawns) from a region I had never even suspected, and suddenly attaches the loved object to a *commonplace* world. Could the other be vulgar, whose elegance and originality I had so religiously hymned? Here is a gesture by which is revealed a being of another race. I am *flabbergasted*.

Stupefaction arises from the discrepancy between the ideal image of the other, sanctified by the lover's overvaluation, and the new vision that overturns that ideal. The object of veneration is for a moment – unbearably – banal, 'paltry', and it hardly matters that the corruption in question is only a speck. This altered perception modifies the vocabulary that defines the beloved:

> The lover's discourse is usually a smooth envelope which encases the Image, a very gentle glove around the loved being. It is a devout, orthodox discourse. When the Image alters, the envelope of devotion rips apart; a shock capsizes my own language.

Though Barthes cites a number of authorities here, including Goethe and Proust, he could have found no better instance than Sonnet 94. 'Lilies that fester' rips apart the smooth envelope of Petrarchan verse and momentarily capsizes the genre, to reveal the unbridgeable gap between idealisation and an equally extreme revulsion. One way or the other, as we know from Sonnet 129, desire is 'perjured', 'extreme' and 'not to trust'. When the Sonnets leave unoccupied the gap between idolatry and disgust, making a no man's land in the place of ordinary graduated reaction, they mask – or fail to mask – a void that incorporates into the desire they record an allusion to the creating, annihilating Thing.

'Horrible ebb of the Image', Barthes adds. And then he comments, '(The horror of spoiling is even stronger than the anxiety of losing)'.[23] But in the Sonnets what spoils the friend is not always a speck of corruption: on the contrary, despoliation does not wait for a perceived modification of his image. Instead, 'All in war with Time for love of you' (Sonnet 15), the poet imagines that alteration in advance:

> When forty winters shall besiege thy brow,
> And dig deep trenches in thy beauty's field,
> Thy youth's proud livery so gazed on now
> Will be a tattered weed of small worth held. (Sonnet 2)

Time is the youth's enemy here, and yet from the perspective of an addressee, it is as if the poet writes on Time's behalf – 'in war *with* Time' against the friend, as well as 'for love of' him. True, the poem appropriates the *carpe diem* tradition to urge the young man towards fathering a child while time allows, but the threat far outweighs the promise as the sonnet dwells on the ravages of age.

Perhaps the *carpe diem* motif was always aggressive, demanding love with menaces. Even in the first sonnet, where lyricism apparently predominates over threat, 'beauty's [quintessentially fragile] rose' is no match for the vocabulary of mortality: 'die', 'decease', 'famine', 'grave'. Indeed, the rose is the supreme traditional figure of mutability, along with the 'spring' and 'bud' that are related analogues for the friend in Sonnet 1. Time, the opponent of loveliness, is integral to beauty's representation in these early sonnets; perfection and its loss are coupled inseparably; antagonism inhabits adulation. Moreover, the proposed remedies are to a degree spurious, since what survives is always something *else*: children, perfume, poetry. Sonnet after sonnet relentlessly holds up to the young man a mirror showing his appearance in ruins (Sonnets 5, 12, 63). 'The wrinkles which thy glass will truly show', Sonnet 77 insists, 'Of mouthed graves will give thee memory'. Sonnet 104 seems at first to take the opposite line: 'To me, fair friend, you never can be old'. Three years have passed and no change in his appearance is detectable. But the sestet takes back most of what the octave seems to have given: beauty steals away so imperceptibly that 'mine eye may be deceived'. The couplet ends the poem with a compliment that is nothing if not minatory: 'For fear of which, hear this thou age unbred: / Ere you were born was beauty's summer dead'.

There are not always compensations, even false ones, for the threatened decay and death. The final sonnet of this sub-sequence leaves the issue unresolved. Beginning with praise for the 'lovely boy', who stays young while his lovers age, it goes on to remind him that Nature cannot prevail over Time for ever. In the end, she must give up her 'treasure' to death: 'Her audit (though delayed) answered must be, / And her quietus is to render thee'. Sonnet 126 has only twelve lines. These are followed, whether on the initiative of the author or the printer there is no way to tell, by a space for the missing couplet, indicated by two sets of empty brackets. What might have filled them? An epigrammatic reinforcement of the threat? Another promise of immortality in verse, or in the poet's heart? But there is nothing there, only punctuation marks enclosing a void.

Unlike the dark woman's, the young man's beauty is never in question, and yet it becomes a target for aggression of another kind. 'Extreme' in this respect too, the poems acknowledge no space between present perfection and inevitable perdition, as 'never-resting Time leads summer on / To hideous winter, and confounds him there' (Sonnet 5). The negation of the gradual process that divides these opposites has the effect of foregrounding the contrary impulses that structure desire. Those sonnets that affirm the friend's beauty also lay siege to it in the construction of the panegyric itself, as if the poet cannot praise but in a kind of dispraise, and the brutality is the more pronounced in that this beauty which is simultaneously endorsed and destroyed is the young man's defining mark. We know almost nothing else about him. There are indications of high rank, but virtually no personal characteristics. ''Gainst death, and all oblivious enmity / Shall you pace forth', asserts Sonnet 55; 'your praise shall still find room, / Even in the eyes of all posterity'. So far the claim has been borne out in its most literal sense: the praise survives; but of its subject we know, despite the best efforts of the biographers, nothing certain. 'Your name from hence immortal life shall have', Sonnet 81 confidently affirms. A great deal of scholarly energy might have been saved if it had.

Moreover, when it comes to representation, beauty itself, ironically, empties its bearer of substance. Barthes draws attention to this paradox in *S/Z*. 'Beauty', he notes, '(unlike ugliness) cannot really be explained.'[24] 'Like a god (and as empty) it can only say: *I am what I am.*' Beauty cannot be satisfactorily described, but only invoked by comparison with what is already known to be beautiful (flowers, summer, works of art). In that sense, beauty is always *citational*. '*Lovely as Venus?*', Barthes suggests. 'But Venus lovely as what?'[25] Beauty's material embodiment is rendered invisible by representation, disappearing into an infinite regress of citations. 'What is your substance, whereof you are made', wonders Sonnet 53, 'That millions of strange shadows on you tend?' Adonis, Helen, the spring, all are 'poorly imitated after you'. If Shakespeare here inverts the citational process, making the young man the ultimate standard to which all other beauties refer, he does not thereby succeed in making him present. On the contrary, whatever physical specificity he possesses only recedes behind his named copies, vanishing among these strange, unnumbered shadows.

Never did the subject of a series of love poems so palpably stand in for the lost object of the drive. There is at the centre of the fair young man's representation in these texts nothing that does not waver, shift, cancel itself out, except a beauty that is affirmed most powerfully in its own threatened destruction. And yet the signifiers that encircle what is missing are among the most seductive in the English language, enticing, perhaps, not least on account of what they do not tell.

*

The dark woman and the fair young man are not the poet's only antagonists in the Sonnets. Perhaps, indeed, they are not even the primary objects of his love and hate. It is at least arguable that the true topic of these poems is the poetry of their inscription. At intervals, this is invincible. If Time wins out over Nature, verse will triumph, the Sonnets repeatedly assert, over Time:

>   thy eternal summer shall not fade,
> Nor lose possession of that fair thou ow'st;
> Nor shall Death brag thou wand'rest in his shade,
> When in eternal lines to time thou grow'st.
>   So long as men can breathe or eyes can see,
>   So long lives *this*, and *this* gives life to thee.
> (Sonnet 18, my emphasis)

Both Ovid and Horace assert their own immortality in their poetry. Following Petrarch, however, Shakespeare appropriates that claim for the theme of the Sonnets, the friend, his source and inspiration, a tenth muse (Sonnet 38), who cannot die until Doomsday, which is to say while the poetry he occasions survives: 'So, till the [J]udgement that yourself arise, / You live in this, and dwell in lover's eyes' (Sonnet 55).

The Sonnets are oddly specific in their reference to the materials (frail, it might be thought) that will create works to outlast tombs and monuments: yellowing 'papers' (Sonnet 17), 'my pen' (Sonnet 81), 'black lines' (Sonnet 63), 'black ink' (Sonnet 65). But to transcend their own fragile materiality, the texts lavish on their subject every kind of figure and wordplay, demonstrating the poet's mastery of the sonnet form. The discipline imposed by the genre is a severe one.[26] Shakespeare's rhyme scheme, though not the most difficult of the available possibilities, is unrelenting none the less. Meanwhile, the fourteen-line limit, too long for a single *aperçu* but too short to develop a narrative, both encourages depth and demands precision.[27] Often, a quatrain constitutes the inscription of a completed thought, while the sestet marks a turn in the argument. The concluding couplet, meanwhile, commonly epigrammatic, represents a witty summary or an unexpected twist. Though the sonnet could not compete with epic for esteem in its day, it is notable that many serious poets of the period opted to take up its challenge and struggle with and against its constraints.

Conflict, in other words, is not confined to love. Jean-François Lyotard, most Lacanian of philosophers, points out that 'to speak is to fight', and 'speech acts fall within the domain of a general agonistics'. His point in the context is that dialogue is a power game. He adds, however, that the opponent is not always another person and the project may not be to secure victory:

> This does not necessarily mean that one plays in order to win. A move can be made for the sheer pleasure of its invention: what else is involved in that labor of language harassment undertaken by popular speech and by literature? Great joy is had in the endless invention of turns of phrase, of words and meanings . . . But undoubtedly even this pleasure depends on a feeling of success won at the expense of an adversary – at least one adversary, and a formidable one: the accepted language, or connotation.[28]

The rhetorical mode of the Sonnets is agonistic. Whether in fact or fiction, they mostly set out to convince, and etymology defines conviction as conquest. The project is to coax the dark woman to yield, or the young man to have children, pay attention, behave better, or simply to return the poet's love, and the inventiveness of the poems is designed in the first place to overcome opposition. Elsewhere, the opponent may be time, or nature, or another poet. But the ultimate antagonist is the poetry itself, the exacting process of representation.

In this contest, however, the poet does not always win. The ringing confidence of the affirmations of immortality alternates with doubt. In an incitement to procreate, Sonnet 17 tells a different story:

> Who will believe my verse in time to come
> If it were filled with your most high deserts?
> Though yet, heaven knows, it is but as a tomb
> Which hides your life, and shows not half your parts.
> If I could write the beauty of your eyes,
> And in fresh numbers number all your graces,
> The age to come would say 'This poet lies:
> Such heavenly touches ne'er touched earthly faces.'
> So should my papers (yellowed with their age)
> Be scorned, like old men of less truth than tongue,
> And your true rights be termed a poet's rage,
> And stretchèd metre of an antique song.

Here the poem, itself at time's mercy, is no more than a monument concealing the beauty it commemorates, since the poet distrusts his own power to depict the friend's qualities. And even if he could do justice to so high a theme, the future would surely treat his account like the stories told by of old men of their lost youth, more heroic than true.

The problem here, as elsewhere, is that the object of desire exceeds any praise the poet can confer (Sonnets 83, 103, 106). Metaphor only distances its theme, doubly deferring by a figure the thing itself. Moreover, the conventional similes for beauty are by definition 'false compare', too remote to tell the human truth (Sonnet 130). Who can trust a poetry of inflated analogy, or a poet who 'heaven itself for ornament doth use, / And every fair with his fair doth rehearse' (Sonnet 21)? To invoke Adonis and Helen, in other words, is to lose touch with the incomparable immediacy of this individual, to banish him among the millions of shadows that attend him.

Instead,

> O let me, true in love, but truly write,
> And then, believe me, my love is as fair
> As any mother's child, though not so bright
> As those gold candles fixed in heaven's air. (Sonnet 21)

The proposition seems irresistible. 'True in love', which is to say truly in love, faithful in love, and truthful in love, the poet has only to record what he knows, without reference to the stars, for the beloved's brightness to be made plain. But how? Quite apart from the fact that it has already become a conventional poetic move to reject poetic convention (Astrophil deploys it to good effect in several of his sonnets to Stella[29]), how can the unvarnished truth be told? By what means, in other words, can the inevitable gap between things and their representation be bridged?

Rivalry with another poet brings the matter to a head (Sonnets 78–86) and Sonnet 84 draws the logical conclusion: 'he that writes of you, if he can tell / That you are you, so dignifies his story'. 'You alone are you' is the proposition here, and it is the only possible affirmation if the young man is to be represented 'In true, plain words, by thy true-telling friend' (Sonnet 82). Barthes arrives at a similar paradox in *A Lover's Discourse*: 'What is characteristic of desire, proper to desire, can only produce an impropriety of the utterance.' Words are always other, *beside* the sameness of the selfsame: 'From word to word, I struggle to put "into other words" the ipseity of my Image, to express improperly the propriety of my desire: a journey at whose end my final philosophy can only be to recognize – and to practice – tautology. The adorable is what is adorable . . . I love you because I love you.'[30]

But in the Sonnets this strategy does not meet the case, either: instead, it simply reiterates the familiar story in a poetry 'barren of new pride', 'dressing old words new, / Spending again what is already spent' (Sonnet 76). The third option, however, is silence:

> My tongue-tied Muse in manners holds her still,
> While comments of your praise, richly compiled,
> Reserve their character with golden quill
> And precious phrase by all the Muses filed.
> I think good thoughts, whilst others write good words,
> And like unlettered clerk still cry 'Amen'
> To every hymn that able spirit affords,
> In polished form of well-refinèd pen.
> Hearing you praised, I say ''Tis so, 'tis true',
> And to the most of praise add something more,
> But that is in my thought, whose love to you
> (Though words come hindmost) holds his rank before.
> Then others for the breath of words respect;
> Me for my dumb thoughts, speaking in effect. (Sonnet 85)

This is more than a sulk occasioned by conflict with a rival poet. The concessions to the other writer's skill may be ironic, but they confirm the problem implied by the unsatisfactory alternatives of ornament and tautology: neither does full justice to love since, while actions may speak, words come hindmost and thoughts are dumb. Like Cordelia, the poet is not able to heave his heart into his mouth, not out of perversity or peevishness in either case, but because it cannot be done. Love, which reaches for the signifier in poems and songs and stories, cannot in the end be made present in the signifier itself – not even by the most eloquent, the most inventive of poets. Truth, which is what we *tell*, remains itself an object of desire, forever lost between the symbolic and the real.

The Sonnets mark by truth's ultimate unattainability the unbridgeable gap that in Lacanian terms divides demand from desire. Do they win by this concession their struggle with and against their symbolic antagonist, the poetry of love's inscription? No one finally conquers language, if conquest means bringing it into line with the world it only seems to name. Lyotard's point, however, was not that the game had to issue in outright victory, but only that pleasure depended on a feeling of success acquired at the expense of the adversary. Shakespeare, I can't help thinking, was entitled to some of that pleasure. Meanwhile, as bystanders, we are free to relish the contest without deliberating too precisely on the final score.

*

But are we no more than bystanders? The history of criticism indicates that the Sonnets commonly enlist the desire of the reader – with all the ambivalence that entails. Interpretation, it seems, seeks mastery, which itself never entirely escapes aggression. The poems are admired, loved and celebrated; at the same time, frustrated by their textual difficulty, critics constitute themselves as rival poets, rewriting Shakespeare's texts in a way that gratifies their own projects.[31] To do so, however, is implicitly to find fault with the poems themselves, to declare them inadequate: out of love, the critic takes up a position of antagonism. To interpret, in that instance, is also to fight. Evidently, the Sonnets tempt commentators to supply what is missing, compose a narrative, replace textual undecidability with definitive choices, and delineate their own substitute for the object beyond representation. But if we succumb to that temptation we betray, I believe, a twofold truth – to the poems and to the desire they inscribe.

Paradoxically, the Sonnets themselves invite such attention. Ostensibly so personal and yet so direct, they appear to confide in us, creating the illusion of an intimate relationship between reader and poet. Unlike drama, which addresses an audience in the first instance, the Sonnets seem designed to be read in solitude. The world they generate remains self-contained: we are never addressed directly. Instead, the poems position the reader in different ways. Sometimes it is as if we have access to a private journal, where the poet reflects on the situation, while the object of desire is identified in the third person: 'Ruin hath taught me thus to ruminate, / That Time will come and take my love away' (Sonnet 64); 'And yet, by heaven, I think my love as rare / As any she belied with false compare' (Sonnet 130). More often, the reader stands in for the addressee, occupying the second-person place of the beloved, so that it is as if we take the full force of the text's distinct pleas, complaints or accusations, though without ever mistaking ourselves for their object: 'O learn to read what silent love hath writ' (Sonnet 23); 'In nothing art thou black save in thy deeds' (Sonnet 131). At other times it is as if the poet begins by communing with himself, and then turns his attention to the beloved, placing the reader as privy to a written message to the addressee, which is the text itself:

> When to the sessions of sweet silent thought
> I summon up remembrance of things past,
> I sigh . . .
> But if the while I think on thee (dear friend)
> All losses are restored, and sorrows end. (Sonnet 30)

By this means, even while the details remain elusive, the Sonnets create the impression of figures so palpable that they must be real. Drawing especially on strategies developed in *Astrophil and Stella*, Shakespeare the dramatist constructs the illusion of dialogue, though he rarely reproduces it in his sonnets in the manner of Sidney. Instead, any number of the poems begin in the middle of the story, seeming to refer back to an incident or an utterance that poet and addressee can be expected to remember: 'No more be grieved at that which thou hast done' (Sonnet 35); 'Alas 'tis true, I have gone here and there' (Sonnet 110); 'O call not me to justify the wrong / That thy unkindness lays upon my heart' (Sonnet 139). In this way the Sonnets gesture towards an apparently known and therefore seemingly knowable context, shared between the characters they depict.

But the circumstances are very rarely specified,[32] and this is part of the tease that enlists the reader's desire in the production of a narrative that would hold together the individual lyrics. Sonnet 36 reluctantly concedes that the lovers must separate, lest the poet's guilt should shame the beloved. What is this guilt and why would its disclosure entail dishonour? The situation the poem invokes is not made clear; nor is it intelligible by reference to the existing conventions.[33] In consequence, the knowledge that the text does not provide seems to solicit the invention of a story to explain the allusion. In some versions this traces a consistent psychological development in the relationships; in others it means naming the historical protagonists. Either way, narrative comes to stand in for the missing content.

A certain circularity emerges here, however: the conjectural stories interpretation invokes depend on interpretation in the first instance. When Sonnet 58 begins, 'That god forbid, that made me first your slave, / I should in thought control your times of pleasure', is this an acknowledgement of total submission in the manner of the courtly lover, a due recognition of a difference in rank between the public play-wright and his aristocratic friend, or a sarcastic retort in the course of a lovers' quarrel?[34] Different readers form different opinions, construct-ing distinct narratives on the basis of their readings. These stories in turn affect the interpretation of other poems. The next sonnet discusses whether former ages could have known an image to equal the friend's. It concludes, 'O, sure I am the wits of former days / To subjects worse have given admiring praise' (Sonnet 59). In isolation, this seems to say that ancient panegyrics never depicted the young man's equal. Depending on how they interpret Sonnet 58, however, some commen-tators prefer the opposite meaning: 'I am sure they praised (even) worse people.'[35] The narrative critics produce influences their reading of each sonnet; at the same time, one sonnet bleeds into another, so that an assumption about its place in the sequence affects the understanding of its ambiguities.

If, as I have suggested, the Sonnets defer the addressees they simul-taneously do so much to make present, and at the same time withhold the immediate contexts they seem to take for granted, they also tantalise with their own linguistic opacity. Even discounting the problems of punctuation and the editorial questions prompted by the quarto text of 1609, the Sonnets are hard to read: densely argued, polysemous and unpredictable, at times they all but defeat the ingenuity of successive commentators. Any amount of analysis has been brought to bear on Sonnet 94 ('They that have power to hurt') but without, as far as I can see, resolving its difficulties.[36] Sonnet 116, by contrast, appears trans-parent: 'Let me not to the marriage of true minds / Admit impediments'. But what exactly is the force of 'admit' here? Coming at the beginning of the second line, the word seems to attract attention, not least because it does not appear in the marriage service that is so clearly cited. Does the poem say, 'Let me not concede that there are any obstacles', or 'Let me not acknowledge the obstacles that exist'? On the first reading, the rest of the sonnet celebrates love's constancy; on the second, the affirmations of eternal fidelity are overtly utopian, pious hopes rather than convictions. Perhaps only a nuance separates the two versions, but the first interpretation picks out love's triumph over change, while the second dwells on the impediments to constancy: 'alteration', removal, 'tempests', time's 'bending sickle'. Ironically, the following sonnet does admit to all the alterations Sonnet 116 condemns and in precisely the terms the previous poem denies.[37] Even Sonnet 144, where the contrast between two loves seems so straightforward, can be read in radically different ways.[38] In these instances one reading may seem more plausible than another, but alternatives cannot be ruled out entirely.

Meanwhile, in the wake of queer theory, the most disputed text has surely been Sonnet 20, addressed to the 'master mistress'. Nature, the conceit declares, intended the young man to be a woman but, falling (homoerotically) in love with her own creation, she cheated the poet of his 'love's use':

> And by addition me of thee defeated,
> By adding one thing to my purpose nothing.
> But since she pricked thee out for women's pleasure,
> Mine be thy love, and thy love's use their treasure.

Does this mean what it seems to say, that the relationship with the young man is not a sexual one? Helen Vendler thinks so.[39] Or should we follow Bruce Smith in speculating that the apparent denial of sexual interest might actually be an avowal of it? If the prick is not to the poet's purpose, 'Does he find other parts of the beloved's anatomy more commodious?', Smith wonders.[40] Stephen Orgel ingeniously proposes that 'women's pleasure' could mean an 'ability to take pleasure as women do', if the 'But' of the couplet is seen as reversing the previous argument.[41] Katherine Duncan-Jones, meanwhile, following Eve Kosofsky Sedgwick, proffers the possibility that, since 'nothing' means vagina, the one thing that Nature added is precisely 'to my purpose' as equivalent to female genitalia. She suggests that, while the sonnet can be read as renouncing sex, it might equally imply the exact opposite, on the grounds that 'its naivety is too simple to be believed'.[42] To all this several editors add that 'use' as usury is elsewhere associated specifically with breeding since it can mean the interest generated by capital.[43] Love's use, allotted to women, might then be read as the production of children, with no commitment either way as to the practice of the love the poet desires for his own.

More elaborate queer readings of the first 126 sonnets depend heavily on the identification of double entendres.[44] The majority of these were very thoroughly uncovered in the last days of New Criticism by Stephen Booth, whose edition finds sex whenever it looks closely – which is most of the time. Booth is inclined to see the sexual meanings as 'latent' and does not commit himself on the question of their implications for the nature of the relationship. Later commentators have been less reluctant to draw inferences. But puns are elusive quantities. When is a homonym an innuendo, and when does an innuendo reveal the *un*equivocal truth? 'Prick' in Sonnet 20, for example, evidently has two meanings: to select from a list and to equip with a penis. But is 'nothing' really a pun, as

Sedgwick suggests it might be? And is 'use' another, as some conjecture it could be? More important, if we select an alternative meaning *at the expense of* the obvious one, are we not precisely denying the double entendre its doubleness? If we are right to find what Roman Jakobson called 'the co-presence of a sublime and a crude meaning within the same words', surely we are not at the same time right to opt for the crude meaning as the true one, to the exclusion of the first? Such a critical practice treats poems as cryptograms and criticism as code-breaking.[45] In the case of 'prick' the two meanings converge: Nature, the word indicates, selected you for the addition of one thing, and that thing was a penis. Since 'thing' already carries this meaning in the period, interpretation does not require us to choose the sexual meaning at the cost of the other. But 'nothing', to revert to that example for the sake of argument, disperses meaning in opposite directions: *either* the additional thing is irrelevant to my purposes, *or* the additional thing, as equivalent to the vagina, is exactly what I want. To opt for one of these meanings is to exclude the other.

My own view is that here too the issue is undecidable. In other words, Sonnet 20 does not reveal what some of its readers most want to know. Instead, it wittily equivocates, and the answer to the question whether we are to understand that a homoerotic partnership is or would eventually be sexually consummated joins the list of deferred meanings that make of the Sonnets such an object of desire for their readers. In *Figuring Sex between Men* Paul Hammond gives a brilliant account of the way the texts invite sexual interpretations while at the same time placing them under erasure, so that 'a term is written and then cancelled, but remains legible through the cancellation'.[46] The Sonnets, he demonstrates, suggest, revise, modify, redescribe and reverse what they seem to have proposed, often within the same fourteen-line space. Figures of desire and possession repeatedly run counter to the poem's argument in ways that tease us into conclusions contradicted elsewhere. Although in the end Hammond's case is that equivocation serves to ward off disapproval of a same-sex relationship, he also maintains that 'Indirections and refusals to disclose are intrinsic to the mode of the *Sonnets*, and it would be a fundamental misreading to impose a clarity on the careful obscurities of Shakespeare's text'.[47]

In the event, however, such fundamental misreading evidently remains all but irresistible. Again and again, critics have rewritten the Sonnets in the image of their own desire: for a love story, to identify the characters as historical figures, to unmask misogyny or vindicate homosexuality. And at every stage of this process, critical mastery entails an act of aggression in terms of a decision at the expense of the undecidability that prompted it. For love of the texts, readers long to resolve the uncertainties the Sonnets seductively offer, but we enter into competition with the poems themselves, betraying antagonism whenever we supply what they withhold, correct and complete them, filling their interstices with definitive meanings, and writing in what they leave unwritten.

In other words, we do violence to the texts when commentary banishes enigma to secure victory for the critic. In their reticence Shakespeare's Sonnets inscribe yet another paradox. They need us as their guarantee of immortality: 'Your monument shall be my gentle verse, / Which eyes not yet created shall o'er-read' (Sonnet 81); 'So long as men can breathe or eyes can see, / So long lives this, and this gives life to thee' (Sonnet 18). At the same time, they keep us at bay, fend off in the last instance the curiosity they do so much to enlist. Their equivocation is not wilful, nor, in my view, is it wholly attributable to a judicious self-censorship. On the contrary, love is not only personal, intimate and private; its antinomies are also ultimately beyond the reach of the signifier. Moreover, at the heart of these texts there resides a necessary absence, an enigma that marks the place of the lost object beyond the individual beloved, and this mystery, as the cause of their textual desirability, brings readers back to the Sonnets again and again.

Perhaps, indeed, this single feature is the best guarantee of immortality they could possibly offer.

Notes

1. See Sigmund Freud, 'Instincts and their Vicissitudes' and *Beyond the Pleasure Principle*, in *On Metapsychology: The Theory of Psychoanalysis*, ed. Angela Richards (Harmondsworth: Penguin, 1984), pp. 105–38, 269–338. The superego turns the death drive against the self in *Civilization and its Discontents*, trans. David McLintock (London: Penguin, 2002).
2. Julia Kristeva, '*Romeo and Juliet*: Love-Hatred in the Couple', in *Tales of Love*, trans. Leon S. Roudiez (New York: Columbia University Press, 1987), pp. 209–33.
3. Jacques Lacan, *The Ethics of Psychoanalysis, 1959–60 (Seminar 7)*, trans. Dennis Porter (London: Tavistock/Routledge, 1992).
4. *Shakespeare in Love*, dir. John Madden, 1998; *Doctor Who: The Shakespeare Code*, dir. Charles Palmer, BBC 1, 7 April 2007.
5. Christopher Warley points out that 'sonnet sequence' is a nineteenth-century category; in the sixteenth century the genre was not sharply defined or regulated and the relation between lyric and narrative not given. See Christopher Warley, *Sonnet Sequences and Social Distinction in Renaissance England* (Cambridge: Cambridge University Press, 2005), pp. 2–3, 10, 19.
6. Sonnet 145 is so odd that commentators conventionally assign it to a much

earlier epoch. Others are very generalised: Sonnet 128 reproduces a familiar conceit; Sonnet 143 comically develops a near-epic simile in which the beloved pursues a chicken round the farmyard, neglecting the poet, who features as her baby; Sonnet 129 condemns all passion as shameful, while acknowledging its continuing power.

7. I have quoted from Colin Burrow's edition of the text (William Shakespeare, *The Complete Sonnets and Poems* [Oxford: Oxford University Press, 2002]), but I am also indebted to John Kerrigan (ed.), *The Sonnets and A Lover's Complaint* (London: Penguin, 1995); G. Blakemore Evans (ed.), *The Sonnets* (Cambridge: Cambridge University Press, 1996); Katherine Duncan-Jones (ed.), *Shakespeare's Sonnets* (London: Thomson, 1997); as well as Stephen Booth (ed.), *Shakespeare's Sonnets* (New Haven: Yale University Press, 1977), which also includes a facsimile of the quarto text of 1609.

8. John Kerrigan speculates that tastes may have changed in the course of the 1590s: 'Daniel's Delia is fair in 1592, dark in the revised edition of 1601' (*The Sonnets and A Lover's Complaint*, p. 59).

9. See, for example, Anne Ferry, *The 'Inward' Language: Sonnets of Wyatt, Sidney, Shakespeare, Donne* (Chicago: University of Chicago Press, 1983), especially pp. 170–214; Joel Fineman, *Shakespeare's Perjured Eye: The Invention of Poetic Subjectivity in the Sonnets* (Berkeley: University of California Press, 1986); Michael R.G. Spiller, *The Development of the Sonnet: An Introduction* (London: Routledge, 1992), pp. 150–75.

10. G. Blakemore Evans et al. (eds), *The Riverside Shakespeare* (Boston: Houghton Mifflin, 1997), p. 1970.

11. 'Therefore I'le lye with Love, and love with me' in 1599. This may be an early version or imperfectly remembered (Booth, *Shakespeare's Sonnets*, pp. 477, 481).

12. See, for instance, Mopsa in *The Old Arcadia* (William A. Ringler [ed.], *The Poems of Sir Philip Sidney* [Oxford: Clarendon Press, 1962], p. 12). Heather Dubrow discusses the tradition in *Echoes of Desire: English Petrarchism and its Counterdiscourses* (Ithaca: Cornell University Press, 1995), pp. 163–201.

13. See, for example, Eve Kosofsky Sedgwick, *Between Men: English Literature and Male Homosocial Desire* (New York: Columbia University Press, 1985), pp. 28–48; Valerie Traub, 'Sex Without Issue: Sodomy, Reproduction, and Signification in Shakespeare's Sonnets', in James Schiffer (ed.), *Shakespeare's Sonnets: Critical Essays* (New York: Garland, 1999), pp. 431–53.

14. Sonnet 129 is the more subtle in that 'lust' is not yet fully synonymous with lechery. Instead, its primary association is pleasure (see my essay, 'Love as Trompe-l'oeil: Taxonomies of Desire in *Venus and Adonis*', *Shakespeare Quarterly*, 46 (1995), pp. 257–76). The poem therefore begins as paradox, not moral rant.

15. Freud, *Beyond the Pleasure Principle*, pp. 283–6.

16. For an excellent history of the form see Spiller, *The Development of the Sonnet*.

17. Lacan, *Ethics of Psychoanalysis*, pp. 161–3. Richard Halpern also discusses with great subtlety Lacan's account of this poem in relation to the Sonnets, though his emphasis is different from mine. See Richard Halpern,

Shakespeare's Perfume: Sodomy and Sublimity in the Sonnets, Wilde, Freud, and Lacan (Philadelphia: University of Pennsylvania Press, 2002), pp. 86–101.

18. Michael McCanles, 'Love and Power in the Poetry of Sir Thomas Wyatt', *Modern Language Quarterly*, 29 (1968), pp. 145–60.

19. Carmen 85 confines itself to this topic: 'Odi et amo. quare id faciam, fortasse requiris. / nescio, sed fieri sentio et excrucior' ('I hate and love. Why do I do this, perhaps you ask. I don't know, but I feel it and am tormented' [my translation]). In carmen 72 the injury she has done him lessens his friendly feelings towards Lesbia – but promotes his desire. Its closest Shakespearean analogue, Sonnet 150, is in no sense a translation. As evidence of the widespread influence of Catullus, carmen 5, for instance, was translated by Thomas Campion, Ben Jonson, and William Drummond of Hawthornden, among others. See Eleanor Shipley Duckett, *Catullus in English Poetry* (Northampton, MA: Smith College Classical Studies, 1925), pp. 31–4.

20. Peter Happé (ed.), *Tudor Interludes* (Harmondsworth: Penguin, 1972), pp. 113–38, lines 39–58, 362–95. *The Interlude of Youth* belongs to the early years of the sixteenth century but it remained remarkably popular. Shakespeare also invokes it in *Lucrece*, where Tarquin rejects the virtues that counsel him against rape: 'My part is youth and beats these from the stage' (line 278). The interlude also helps to structure Prince Hal's story in *1 Henry IV* (see especially 1.1.84–5).

21. Burrow compares *Measure for Measure*, 5.1.140–1 (*Complete Sonnets and Poems*, p. 518).

22. Kerrigan (ed.), *The Sonnets and A Lover's Complaint*, p. 261.

23. Roland Barthes, *A Lover's Discourse: Fragments*, trans. Richard Howard (London: Cape, 1979), pp. 25–8.

24. *S'expliquer* is stronger than the translation implies: it means something more like 'make itself clear', or even 'give an account of itself'. Roland Barthes, *S/Z* (Paris: Seuil, 1970), p. 36; trans. Richard Miller (London: Cape, 1975), p. 33.

25. Barthes, *S/Z*, trans. Miller, pp. 33–4.

26. See Roman Jakobson and Lawrence G. Jones, *Shakespeare's Verbal Art in Th'expence of Spirit* (The Hague: Mouton, 1970).

27. Spiller, *Development of the Sonnet*, pp. 4, 96, 125.

28. Jean-François Lyotard, *The Postmodern Condition: A Report on Knowledge*, trans. Geoff Bennington and Brian Massumi (Manchester: Manchester University Press, 1984), p. 10. Cf. '*The beyond of the couple is a beyond of the mother. Those who believe they have reached it do not cease violating her in the language: they are creators of style, of music . . .*' (Kristeva, *Tales of Love*, p. 228).

29. See especially Sonnets 1, 3, 15, 55, 74 (Ringler [ed.], *Poems of Sir Philip Sidney*, pp. 163–237).

30. Barthes, *A Lover's Discourse*, pp. 20–1.

31. Heather Dubrow, '"Incertainties Now Crown themselves Assur'd": The Politics of Plotting Shakespeare's Sonnets', in Schiffer (ed.), *Shakespeare's Sonnets: Critical Essays*, pp. 113–33, p. 129.

32. Spiller, *Development of the Sonnet*, pp. 153–4.

33. According to Anne Ferry, this construction of an undisclosed context is specific to Sidney and Shakespeare (*The 'Inward' Language*, pp. 26–7). She compares Shakespeare's Sonnets 86, 111 and 117–20.

34. 'The poem clearly asks to be read as one party's retort in a lovers' tiff.' David Schalkwyk, 'Love and Service in *Twelfth Night* and the Sonnets', *Shakespeare Quarterly*, 56 (2005), pp. 76–100, p. 84.

35. Booth reads the couplet as (faint) praise (*Shakespeare's Sonnets*, p. 239); Duncan-Jones sees the first reading as 'undercut' by the second (*Shakespeare's Sonnets*, p. 228); Burrow combines Booth's account with a 'hint' of the second (*Complete Sonnets and Poems*, p. 498).

36. See, most notably, William Empson, *Some Versions of Pastoral* (Harmondsworth: Penguin, 1966), pp. 75–96; also J.H. Prynne, *They that Have Powre to Hurt: A Specimen of a Commentary on* Shake-speares Sonnets, 94 (Cambridge, 2001). (I owe this reference to Neil Reeve.)

37. In Sonnet 116 love is 'the star to every wandering barque'; in Sonnet 117 the poet has 'hoisted sail to all the winds'. Sonnet 116 insists, 'If this be error and upon me proved, / I never writ'; Sonnet 117 concedes 'just proof' of the poet's 'errors' (and concludes that he was just testing).

38. Paul Hammond points to the ambiguities concerning which love is which. 'Does the boy provide affectionate comfort, while the woman makes the poet despair because of his sexual attraction to her? Or does the boy generate despair by refusing to sleep with the poet, while the woman comforts him by taking him into her bed? Or does the boy comfort the poet sexually? Or do both his lovers provide comfort and despair?' Paul Hammond, *Figuring Sex between Men from Shakespeare to Rochester* (Oxford: Clarendon Press, 2002), p. 68.

39. Helen Vendler, *The Art of Shakespeare's Sonnets* (Cambridge, MA: Harvard University Press, 1997), p. 129. Evans thinks so too (*The Sonnets*, p. 134).

40. Bruce R. Smith, *Homosexual Desire in Shakespeare's England: A Cultural Poetics* (Chicago: Chicago University Press, 1991), p. 250.

41. Stephen Orgel, *Impersonations: The Performance of Gender in Shakespeare's England* (Cambridge: Cambridge University Press, 1996), p. 57.

42. Sedgwick, *Between Men*, pp. 34–5; Duncan-Jones (ed.), *Shakespeare's Sonnets*, pp. 150–1. Hammond follows her reading (*Figuring Sex between Men*, pp. 16, 83).

43. Booth (ed.), *Shakespeare's Sonnets*, p. 165; Evans (ed.), *The Sonnets*, p. 134. Burrow (ed.), *Complete Sonnets and Poems*, p. 421.

44. See especially Joseph Pequigney, *Such is my Love: A Study of Shakespeare's Sonnets* (Chicago: Chicago University Press, 1985).

45. Jakobson and Jones, *Shakespeare's Verbal Art*, p. 14. We are invited 'to decode puns and so make ourselves privy to secrets – secrets that are specifically sexual' (Smith, *Homosexual Desire*, p. 254). Although it is not one I finally share, Richard Halpern offers a sophisticated reading of the puns: 'The sublimating rhetoric of the sonnets separates out an impeccably refined and aestheticized form of desire from a sodomitical discourse that is then abjected as fecal remainder. This remainder is not, however, expelled to a space outside the poems, but is rather relegated to a nonspace *within* the poems. That is to say, it abides in the half-light of wordplay, implication,

and insinuation. Sodomy subsists as the speaking of the unspeakable' (*Shakespeare's Perfume*, p. 21).

46. Hammond, *Figuring Sex between Men*, p. 70.
47. Ibid., p. 63. Booth notes 'Shakespeare's delight in words and phrases that support a particular response and simultaneously confound it' (*Shakespeare's Sonnets*, p. 209).

Chapter 13

'No' as Affirmation: A Continental-Philosophical Reading of *Coriolanus*

Bernard Freydberg

In a recent essay concerning the significance of the classics for us today, Mary Beard makes the following thoughtful observation:

> To put this as crisply as I can, the study of the classics is the study of what happens in the gap between antiquity and us. It is not only the dialogue that we have with the culture of the classical world; it is also the dialogue that we have with those who have gone before us who were themselves in dialogue with the classical world (whether Dante, Raphael, William Shakespeare, Edward Gibbon, Pablo Picasso, Eugene O'Neill, or Terence Rattigan).[1]

The case of Coriolanus provides both challenges and opportunities that Beard's insight provokes. She goes on to make two suggestions that flow from this insight: 1) 'we should be much more alert than we often are to the claims we make about the classical world – or, at least, we should be more strategically aware of whose claims they are', and 2) she offers what might seem like a truism, affirming 'the inextricable embeddedness of the classical tradition within Western culture'.[2] Taken together, these suggestions point to a tantalising elusiveness of what we clumsily call 'the classics'.

In this chapter, I will attempt to reveal aspects of Shakespeare's *Coriolanus* that escape most if not all scholarly readings of the play, and to illuminate the far-reaching significance of a major character who is relegated to the most minor status almost as a matter of course. Virgilia, wife of Coriolanus, speaks only twenty-eight lines in which no 'speeches' occur. The military courage and aptitude of her husband, his brusque treatment of the plebeians at the outset and his disgust at the Romans who banish him, and his much-acknowledged pride assure that the eponymous hero will receive ample attention. Volumnia, his mother, is herself such an outsized and voluble personage that it is easy to miss who displays the greater power in their exchanges. When these matters are placed in their proper perspective, once again we find 'the inextricable embeddedness of the classical tradition' as still quite alive within ours.

The material of which Shakespeare availed himself for his play derived from Plutarch's *Life of Coriolanus*, which was written in 75 CE. The chronological gap between the writing of the play and the biography was more than 1,500 years. Looking back, Plutarch wrote this account after a gap of 500 years, that is, he wrote it long after Coriolanus lived. However, another gap of a quite different nature has arisen in the historical scholarship: there never was a figure named Coriolanus. Rather, the name 'Coriolanus' is said to refer to a pastiche of qualities, some real and others imagined, of Roman military men of his time. 'German critical historians in the nineteenth century from Barthold Niebuhr to Theodor Mommsen have irrefutably proved that there never was a Coriolanus in Roman history, that the character about whom Shakespeare had read in Plutarch and Livy was a fiction concocted from legendary materials.'[3]

Although this would be the case under any circumstances, the above considerations definitively establish the status of Shakespeare's *Coriolanus* as pure *poetry*, however its author, or the eponymous hero's putative biographer, or the historians who dispute his actual existence regard him. A poem and a philosophical text require different interpretive strategies, although the chronological gap might be similar. While philosophical texts often reveal aspects of thought that have been sedimented during centuries of having been buried under presuppositions and doctrines that have overlaid their originary insight and power, poetical texts often present another challenge, namely that of an oversupply of more or less manifest materials. For example, Heidegger's excavation of imagination in *Kant and the Problem of Metaphysics* has precipitated new and fruitful directions in Kant scholarship, in philosophy of imagination, and in philosophy of art. However, the figure of Hamlet, for example, seems so exceptional, displays so many various qualities and behaviours, that the problem is to locate a core. For such reasons and other, more aesthetic ones, T.S. Eliot has famously called *Hamlet* a 'failure' that he remarkably ascribes to a weakness in Shakespeare himself.[4]

Eliot's derisive comment that more people have thought Hamlet to be a work of art because they found it interesting than found it interesting because it was a work of art provides special provocation on account of his ascription of assured success to the supposedly less interesting *Coriolanus*. I would rather say, in the case of *Coriolanus*, that its 'success' resides not only in those impersonal qualities (metrical consistency and interest, objective correlates for the emotions and actions of the characters, especially the hero), but as much or more in the way that the play itself functions as an act of excess that spills over into other regions that crash against the nature of our humanity.

In this chapter, I will venture an interpretation that follows an untrodden path in hopes of refreshing Shakespeare's *Coriolanus* for us. As noted, Virgilia, wife of Caius Marcius,[5] has very few lines, merely twenty-eight. She has no speeches through which the complexities of her thought can be revealed. Yet both her presence and her bearing carve out a figure around which the action and the sense of the play can shine forth in a surprising way. Virgilia herself appears on first glance to be a sort of gap, a more or less empty vessel into which well-worn female stereotypes seem to fit nicely. However, this view cannot hold under more sustained attention, which will show her as both more powerful and more paradigmatic.

*

In the most straightforward sense, Shakespeare's *Coriolanus* projects magnitude, i.e., sheer magnitude in so far as the latter can present itself in human terms. The eponymous hero earns his place by virtue of his physical martial prowess, which no single man or group of men can defeat or even equal. The '*Über*' in *Übermensch* makes itself manifest in every aspect of his character. His contempt for the plebes does not merely derive from his patrician status, if indeed it does so at all. Rather, inconstancy marks their character, as opposed to the steadfastness of the noble soul that stands firm throughout all of life's vicissitudes.

Further, Caius Marcius' sense of noble decorum would never permit him to display his wounds in order to win the favour of his larger community, as was typically done. After his virtually single-handed rescue of Rome from the Aufidius-led Volscan invasion during which he suffered many injuries, he not only denied that his actions were extraordinary but fairly spat at the suggestion that he should display the scars of war in order to win a much-deserved seat on the Council.

Given his mother Volumnia, one need not wonder how such a figure emerged. Her fondest wish for her son consisted of his dying in battle and so repeating the fate of her husband, his father. This view, so different from even the most scarcely sentimental picture of mother-son love, must be seen – I suggest – as a love that exceeds rather than diminishes the normal measure. For Volumnia, the question as to whether such a love might be inappropriate in light of the human limits and frailties to which we are all given over does not seem to occur for her.

Thus, one does not wonder at all that Caius Marcius embodies the Socratic saying from the *Apology* according to which fear of death is disgraceful. But Caius Marcius misinterprets the second part of Socrates' saying (that we should fear doing injustice since we know that injustice is always wrong); he misinterprets it because he is a lover of honour, so he fears only dishonour. This fear precipitates the most wrenching self-cleaving. As the saviour of Rome and the most noble and most loyal of the Romans, his honour consists precisely in these qualities. But as his friend Menenius Agrippa declares: 'His nature is too noble for the world . . .' (3.1.252).

However, his wife Virgilia may seem to embody a warmer side. Her mere presence is capable of softening his heart. His tender concern for her is reciprocal. She may seem especially out of place in the triangle that includes Volumnia, whose normal manner of speech is strident bombast. Virgilia's love for her husband – unlike that of her mother-in-law's for her son – is a human size love. In terms of magnitude, it will show itself to be both other and greater than Volumnia's. Its very unobtrusiveness stands as a renunciation of a transcendent ideal. On the other hand, it elevates the sacred promise of the marital vow and bond above all other claims. It is tempting to regard the difference between Volumnia and Virgilia as stark and as virtually absolute. I dispute this view. I also claim that Virgilia's love of honour equals that of her husband's.

To demonstrate this requires a reversal of the usual ways of analysis. *Coriolanus* seems to fit very well indeed into the notion of tragedy that has been handed down from Aristotle's *Poetics*. It fits the definition entirely: 'A tragedy, then, is the imitation of an action that is serious and also, as having magnitude, complete in itself; in language with pleasurable accessories, each kind brought in separately in the parts of the work; in a dramatic, not in a narrative form; with incidents arousing pity and fear, wherewith to accomplish its catharsis of such emotions.'[6] The hero is a 'great man' with a 'flaw': Marcius, it seems, could not conform to this account any more than he does. His flaw is pride, excessive self-regard.

A prominent psychiatrist who contributed an essay to a collection titled *Twentieth Century Interpretations of Coriolanus* includes the following clinical diagnosis of its hero: 'the category into which Coriolanus most nearly fits is that of the phallic-narcissistic character, as originally delineated by Reich'.[7] The physician correctly lists several positive characteristics of persons to whom such a diagnosis applies, including strong personal loyalties and undaunted courage. I shall consider other remarks of the good doctor that merit attention later in this chapter, but the juncture presents a splendid occasion to present the reversal that I mentioned above. The twentieth-century analysis, after all, says nothing essentially different from the much less scientist classical determination.

When engaging with a great work of art, the task does not involve *our* taking *its* measure; it is not a matter of *our* judging *it*. Rather, the task – more difficult and quite other – is letting the work take *our* measure, that is, determining where we stand in relation to the work, to what the work presents. To give a playful/serious example of this reversal, what would be the diagnosis of the distinguished psychiatrist Dr Hofling, should he find himself (or have found himself) in danger from a military attack waged by a furious, vicious enemy determined to lay waste to him, his loved ones, his neighbours and his land? If a Coriolanus-like warrior stood between such devastation and safety, I wager that the 'diagnosis' would be set aside for another, less clinical one: saviour, even 'friend'.

A more suitable interpretation responds in kind to its artistic original, in this case a twentieth-century American poet's creative appropriation.[8] In Delmore Schwartz's magisterial poem 'Coriolanus and his Mother',[9] the poet imagines a performance of the play in which Aristotle, Beethoven, Freud and Marx look on as audience members and offer frequent comments, while the poetic interlocutor expounds with playful seriousness between the acts. Each of the distinguished spectators holds forth upon the hero's shaping influences. The poet has Aristotle sing:

> 'By six', the father of Nichomachus
> Murmurs to me, 'by six the man is made,
> Habitus, virtue, and his lasting shade.'[10]

Marx intones the overwhelming power of social status as Coriolanus departs, infuriated, from his Roman aristocracy:

> 'O as disease indeed!' Marx intervenes,
> 'See what a fracture such uniqueness means!
> He who would rend himself from his own class
> Shall feel himself ragged as broken glass.'[11]

Freud answers Marx with a rhyme of his own:

> 'His mother's breast', intrudes the Viennese,
> 'Delighted him too much, fixed his disease.
> The child misunderstood, blind animal:
> Dark Id rules all, and though impersonal,
> Fixed to the womb, this individual . . .'[12]

But the musician's merely musical answer may well possess the most appropriate response of those gathered. No words attach to it. We are merely told that:

> The orchestra resumes, Beethoven blows
> The raw emotion through the passive air

As through the body's darkness. Well he knows
(And well the violins are sworded there)
Responsive anger savage in the head,
Hammered and stammered till its fist is fed.[13]

Between the third and fourth acts, the interlocutor sings of the
freedom that remained latent but unexpressed in the discourses of the
four consequential spectators:

> I gave you each part of your being, or you took that part from me. The word
> of your tongue is mine. Your effort to depart from me is your pain, your evil.
> I am your mother or Rome. I am Volumnia or Rome.
>   But I am yours. You are your own; lips, face, hair, look, your own, your
> property. This is your freedom. You are free, self-choosing, a king. Your
> words are yours, although they are mine . . . Nothing compels you, no imper-
> ative dictates to you, the actuality of your choice is what it is for you . . .[14]

Recalling Beard's recommendation that we be mindful of whose
claims are being made concerning classical matters, the discourse of the
interlocutor is unmistakably *ours*. Schwartz's poem is indeed an inspired
work, but its inspiration is drawn from modern and contemporary concerns more than it is from classical ones. A remarkable poetic appeal to
Kant bears this out:

> 'O tell me, tell me, O Immanuel Kant,'
> I said when they were silent, frenzied then,
> 'You who diminished knowledge, inverted hope,
> Divided day from night, assigned the night
> The avid dreams of the practical heart.'[15]

As readers of the much more prosaic *Critique of Pure Reason* and
Critique of Practical Reason are aware, freedom can only arise 1) out of
the insoluble conundrum of the Third Antinomy, where it can receive
only the status of logical possibility alongside natural necessity; and 2)
as an *assertion* of pure practical reason, from which it ascends to the
apex of the system of reason. Thus, the system of reason itself emerges
only from darkness, or 'the night'. Another gap makes itself manifest,
the gap that begins where knowledge leaves off, the one concerning
which Kant himself regarded as incomprehensible.

*

While the question of human character animates both the poem and
its distinguished spectators (including an unnamed fifth), the poet
(Schwartz) gives Virgilia surprisingly short shrift given his regard for
details that might otherwise escape notice. To her, he ascribes the
epithet 'meek'. 'Meek girl' she is called, also 'meek mother'.[16] In the

poem, Freud notes that some early historians called Volumnia, rather than Virgilia, Caius Marcius' wife.[17] The critic John Middleton Murry has written: 'Of all the characters in Coriolanus one alone can be said to be truly congenial; and she is the least substantial of them all.'[18] In a singularly inept interpretation, Michael Long goes so far as to call her 'wretched' and to speak of 'the sense of frigidity which surrounds the marriage of Marcius and Virgilia'.[19] The gladness and delight of the hero in his wife is interpreted by Murry as indicating 'a woman whose delicate nature stood apart, untouched by the broils and furies of her lord's incessant battling'.[20] However, Virgilia's posture contradicts this view.

Act I, Scene III presents the first meeting between Volumnia and Virgilia to which we are privy. The scene begins with Volumnia as what we today might call the mother-in-law from hell, who insults her daughter-in-law for the latter's failure to rejoice in the news of her husband's war wounds:

> *Vir*: His bloody brow? O Jupiter, no blood!
> *Vol*: Away, you fool. It more becomes a man
>   Than gilt his trophy. The breasts of Hecuba
>   When she did suckle Hector, look'd not lovelier
>   Than Hector's forehead when it spit forth blood
>   At Grecian sword contemning . . . (38–43)

However, Virgilia soon displays her mettle. After the frequently cited passage that celebrates young Marcius' innocent and undisguised cruelty to a butterfly (leading Valeria, its narrator, to exclaim: 'Oh, I warrant how he mammocked it'[21] [65]),Virgilia interjects a firm, terse, sarcastic rejoinder: 'A crack, madam' (68). In contemporary usage, we would hear this as sharply ironic, indicating that such unfeelingness is hardly charming at all. (In another irony, the same Murry who saw only insubstantial sweetness in Virgilia is credited with ascribing a meaning like this one, 'a deprecatory check to Volumnia'.[22])

Further opposition to Volumnia's domineering stand is not long in coming. During the previous exchange, Virgilia sews. Volumnia issues a command: '*Come, lay aside* your stitchery, *I must have you* / play the idle huswife with me this afternoon' (69–70; the emphasis on the three imperatives within so brief a speech are mine). In a few words that resound with infinitely more power than even the very forceful demand of her imperious mother-in-law, Virgilia rejoins: 'No, good madam, I will not out of doors' (71). Virgilia's 'No' cannot be regarded as reactive, although the placement after Volumnia's command might seem to indicate this. To the contrary, Virgilia's 'No' is affirmative in every essential sense.

Her 'No' proclaims her independence from the influence of those who would usurp her prerogative within her own home. Further, her 'No' signals her fearlessness and steadfastness in the face of ridicule even as she worries about the well-being of her husband. Her 'No' enables her to remain true to her own nature just as her husband, in his fashion, remains true to his when he trumpets his enraged 'No' to the Rome that he saved but that banished him. Finally, I interpret her 'No' as *pure positivity* in this sense, that in her position as a woman who has married into an aristocratic family and as the mother of the only child of the warrior-hero it is the only means of self-assertion available to her.

After Valeria asks incredulously, 'Not out of doors?' (72), Volumnia persists in her command, this time in response to Valeria: 'She shall, she shall' (73). But Virgilia refuses adamantly: 'Indeed, no, by your patience; I'll not over the threshold till my lord returns from the wars' (74–5). Even in this early part of this initial exchange, it is plain that the qualities that best describe Virgilia are her firm constancy and her adherence to the code she has freely chosen. The mutual attraction between Caius Marcius and Virgilia consisted of an affinity of two souls, different in accord with the role of each but akin in their resolute natures.

By contrast, Volumnia and Valeria soon show themselves to be inconsistent, even flighty. Volumnia likens her daughter-in-law to Penelope, whose spinning of yarn while waiting for her husband's return she finds laughable: 'they say, all the yarn she spun in Ulysses' absence did but fill Ithaca full of moths . . .' (82–4). The capriciousness beneath the surface of Volumnia's unyielding persona makes itself manifest towards the end of Act I, Scene III, where she urges Valeria to cease insisting that Virgilia join them since her daughter-in-law 'will but disease our better mirth' (103–4). This early glimpse of inconstancy foreshadows her later encounter with her son after his crowning military feat and before he is to stand before the people in order to request his deserved honours.

It grows clear in the latter exchange that such outward, external honours are the ones prized by Volumnia. These are the engines of her astonishing vainglory. The argument between Volumnia and Coriolanus in Act II, Scene II amounts to nothing more interesting than an average mother exhorting her talented son to compromise his principles in order to receive a prestigious award about which she could crow. In the same way, she boasts at every opportunity of her husband's sacrifice of his life in battle. However, in this instance she does not know her son as well as she supposes. The required political ritual of showing his wounds to the populace, and his giving of a humble speech that indicates the pleasure of his being a Roman subject, proves to be a more daunting task to Coriolanus than the most dangerous military assignment.

Volumnia's appeals to her son to hide his true nature come to less than nothing. When, during his speech in the square, Coriolanus is accused by the astute demagoguery of Sicinius and Brutus, the Tribunes, the warrior cannot restrain himself; as the crowd banishes Coriolanus from Rome, Coriolanus banishes Rome from himself:

> You common cry of curs whose very breath I hate
> As reek o' th' rotten fens, whose loves I prize
> As the dead carcasses of unburied men
> That do corrupt my air: I banish you! (120–3)

For the sake of this chapter, the plot until the final act requires little rehearsing. The exiled Roman hero joins forces with Aufidius, his former most hated enemy, and the two lead the Volscan forces towards Rome, which has no chance of defending itself against the onslaught.

Act V, Scene III provides the ultimate disclosure of the nature of power in this work that has so often been characterised as primarily concerned with the display of Roman military characteristic qualities. To no avail whatsoever, Cominius and Menenius beg their former friend and colleague to spare his former city. Enter, then, the women and child. Stunned, Coriolanus exclaims:

> My wife comes foremost; then the honour'd mould
> Wherein this trunk was fram'd, and in her hand
> The grandchild to her blood. But out, affection!
> All bond of nature and privilege break! (22–5)

Just as she led the procession, Virgilia initiates the first and most crucial exchange; it determines the atmosphere of all that follows:

> *Vir.*   My lord and husband!
> *Cor.*   Those eyes are not the same I wore in Rome.
> *Vir.*   The sorrow that delivers us thus chang'd
>   Makes you think so.
> *Cor.*   Like a dull actor now
>   I have forgot my part and I am out,
>   Even to a full disgrace . . . (36–42)

I do not wish to overinterpret the role of Virgilia in the play, and perhaps the weight I shall place upon their next brief exchange is too much for it. However, it provides the transition to Volumnia's final and successful petition to her son to spare Rome, and (I suggest cautiously) exercises a strong influence upon its success, if not a decisive one. The hero's wife gestures towards her womb:

> *Vir.*   That brought you forth this boy to keep your name
>   Living through time.

Boy.   A shall not tread on me.
   I'll run away till I am bigger, then I'll fight. (127–8)

Only after the above exchange can Volumnia persuade her son not to lay waste to her city and to the city of his wife and child. The remainder of the act consists of the moving exchange between Volumnia and Coriolanus, in which the most uncharacteristically kneeling mother entreats her son to spare Rome, and Coriolanus recognises that his decision to acquiesce exposes him to the greatest peril. While it is impossible to determine the degree to which the sight of his wife and son (and the hearing of his son's voice reflecting his own manner!) prepared the way for Coriolanus' fateful decision, it is indeed probable that it had considerably more significance than is usually ascribed to it.

In this telling moment, Virgilia finds herself confronted with a predicament very much like that of her husband when confronted with the choice between his steadfast stance and the need for compromise – of softening, perhaps – in the city. He could not choose both; he could only choose his constant nature. Analogously if not similarly, Virgilia found herself confronted between two irreconcilable options: her duty as a wife to be with her husband under all circumstances, and a duty to nurture and protect his child and his name. That she chose the latter did not trouble Coriolanus at all. I venture to say – bearing in mind Mary Beard's scruple that one attend to who is making a claim about the classics and, I would add, when – he *understood*.

It seems to me that, perhaps oddly, the most compelling, most revelatory and significant appearance of Virgilia occurs in Act II, Scene I. Volumnia asks:

Vol. What is it? – Coriolanus must I call thee
  But oh, thy wife –
Cor.   My gracious silence, hail!
  Wouldst thou have laugh'd had I come coffin'd home? (173–5)

Virgilia utters not a single word. A greater contrast to the garrulity of her mother-in-law cannot be imagined, nor could there be a more eloquent attestation of her human-sized love, which is returned in kind by her playfully responsive husband.

When we read this play through the lens provided by Virgilia, we move into a gap here guided by one of our own ways of orientation, provided by continental philosophy, and by one of our own issues, gender relations, and by our own questions concerning ourselves in this very perplexing era. In this chapter, which highlights Virgilia and her relationship with her husband, the other supposedly more prominent matters recede. The play becomes illuminated both differently and freshly. Virgilia is both strong and authentic. She is a match in every way for her husband, and he is a match for her. Out of this venture into this gap, a concealed and now perhaps untimely theme of *Coriolanus* emerges: the awesome power of human marital love.

Notes

1. Mary Beard, 'Do the Classics Have a Future?', *New York Review of Books*, LIX:1, 12 January 2012, p. 54.
2. Ibid.
3. Maria del Sapio Barbero, *Identity, Otherness and Empire in Shakespeare's Rome* (London: Ashgate Publishing, 2009), p. 46.
4. T.S. Eliot, '*Hamlet*' (1919), in *The Selected Prose of T.S. Eliot*, ed. Frank Kermode (San Diego, New York, and London: Harcourt Brace & Company, 1975), pp. 47–9.
5. This is Coriolanus' name before he received his new name.
6. *The Complete Works of Aristotle*, Vols I–II, ed. Jonathan Barnes (Princeton: Princeton University Press, 1984), p. 2330.
7. Charles K. Hofling, M.D., 'An Interpretation of Shakespeare's *Coriolanus*, in James E. Phillips (ed.), *Twentieth Century Interpretations of Coriolanus* (Englewood Cliffs, NJ: Prentice-Hall, 1970), p. 84. Reprinted from *American Imago*, 14 (Spring 1957).
8. Harold Bloom, *Shakespeare: The Invention of the Human* (New York: Riverhead Books, 1999), p. 580.
9. In Delmore Schwartz, *Selected Poems: Summer Knowledge* (New York: New Directions, 1959), pp. 79–142.
10. Ibid., p. 99.
11. Ibid., p. 110.
12. Ibid.
13. Ibid., p. 109.
14. Ibid., p. 124.
15. Ibid., p. 102.
16. Ibid., pp. 86 and 98.
17. Ibid., p. 97.
18. John Middleton Murry, 'VIRGILIA: Coriolanus', in Phillips (ed.), *Twentieth Century Interpretations of Coriolanus*, p. 111.
19. Michael Long, *The Unnatural Scene* (London: Methuen & Co. Ltd., 1976), p. 67. This is a very disappointing book, as it attempts to read Shakespeare's tragedies through Nietzsche's *The Birth of Tragedy*, a most promising premise. However, this author is determined to read virtually every phenomenon in *Coriolanus* as the effect of Rome in crushing the natural human spirit. This is a determinism that Nietzsche certainly could not sustain.
20. Ibid., p. 112.
21. That is, he tore it to pieces.
22. See *The Arden Edition of the Works of William Shakespeare: Coriolanus*, ed. Philip Brockbank (London, 2006), p. 124 n.

Chapter 14

Provoking Philosophy: Shakespeare, Johnson, Wittgenstein, Derrida

Christopher Norris

When Keats famously remarked of Shakespeare that he possessed the attribute of 'negative capability' – as opposed to the *echt*-Wordsworthian 'egotistical sublime' – he very clearly meant it as a compliment (to Shakespeare, not Wordsworth) and also perhaps, in mock-modest style, as a piece of implicit self-description.[1] There has been a good deal of critical debate as to just what he might have meant by that cryptic phrase and I shall draw on it here by way of suggesting that the description applies just as well, albeit in a somewhat different way, to certain prominent features of Jacques Derrida's writing. Another way of approaching this topic is the *via negativa* of asking what it might be that Shakespeare and Derrida have in common and that some philosophers find unsettling, offensive, or downright rebarbative.[2] In fact each of Keats's reasons for admiring Shakespeare's peculiarly 'negative' genius has a counterpart in one or other of the arguments advanced (whether by philosophers or a minority of literary critics) for thinking Shakespeare to be grossly over-rated. Moreover each finds a near equivalent in one or other of the reasons often put forward by those in the mainly analytic camp for treating Derrida as a latter-day sophist – or mere charlatan – whose admirers (wouldn't you know?) hail mostly from departments of literature or, just as bad, from departments of philosophy bitten by the dread 'continental' bug. So what I aim to do here is take the negative route by way of these familiar objections and use them as a kind of litmus-test for those shared Shakespearean-Derridean traits that have tended to create such an adverse response among readers wedded to a certain conception of linguistic, conceptual and ethical propriety.

Of course Shakespeare has had plenty of admirers in the broadly philosophical community, past and present, and so few detractors as to make my case seem flimsy at best and at worst just an instance of that typically Derridean desire to subvert all the standards of rational debate. Thus it might well be said that the only noted philosopher of recent times who has registered genuine doubts on this score – who indeed seems utterly baffled by the fact that Shakespeare has enjoyed such widespread acclaim – is Ludwig Wittgenstein in the various wondering, incredulous or downright scandalised *obiter dicta* published or reported by friends and disciples after his death.[3] And again, in more positive terms, there are some who have expressed not only a keen admiration for Shakespeare as poet and dramatist but also a conviction that one – perhaps the best – way of raising central issues about language, ethics and human relationship (or the sometimes tragic failures thereof) is through a close and sensitive reading of Shakespeare. Such reading may be part of a larger project, like that of Martha Nussbaum, to wean philosophy away from its attachment to overly abstract or generalised (e.g., Kantian) conceptions of ethics and bring it down to earth – to the messy contingencies of situated human conduct and choice – through immersion in the kinds of moral dilemma most vividly enacted in literary works.[4] Or it may take the form, as with Stanley Cavell, of a sustained and intensive brooding on certain key Shakespearean themes – in particular themes of solitude, doubt, mistrust, self-deception, and the craving for a perfect (impossible) union of minds – which can be seen to dramatise various issues in current philosophical thought.[5] At any rate there is little enough in common – or so it might appear – between the high esteem in which Shakespeare is held by those who have written about him from a broadly philosophic standpoint and the sorts of attack launched against Derrida by mainstream analytic philosophers in whom the fierceness of denunciatory zeal very often seems to vary inversely with the depth or extent of their acquaintance with his work.[6]

Thus it is fair to say that Wittgenstein is out on a limb amongst his fellow philosophers when he expresses a strongly negative view of Shakespeare's plays on account of what he thinks their verbal self-indulgence, their formal shortcomings, their frequent lapses of motivational or psychological plausibility, and – above all – their lack of a firm moral compass that would properly apportion weal or woe to the kinds and degrees of human virtue or vice. The following passage from *Culture and Value* catches precisely the curious mixture of puzzlement, misgiving, renewed confidence in his own judgement and sheer exasperation with the judgement of others that typifies Wittgenstein's remarks.

> When, for instance, I hear the expression of admiration for Shakespeare by distinguished men in the course of several centuries, I can never rid myself of the suspicion that praising him has been the conventional thing to do; though

I have to tell myself that this is not how it is. It takes the authority of a Milton really to convince me. I take it for granted that he was incorruptible. – But I don't of course mean by this that I don't believe an enormous amount of praise to have been, and still to be, lavished on Shakespeare without understanding and for the wrong reasons by a thousand professors of literature.[7]

To this extent he comes out pretty much in agreement with those well-known critics of Shakespeare such as Dr Johnson, Tolstoy and Shaw who have drawn up a strikingly similar charge-sheet but done so from the standpoint of creative/imaginative writers with their own very definite axes to grind.[8] Thus they were either (like Johnson) measuring their distance from Shakespeare in historical-political and cultural-ideological terms, or setting up as self-declared rivals to him like Shaw, or else – like the aging Tolstoy with his aspirations to sainthood – writing from a standpoint that required Shakespeare as a suitable foil to his own grand gesture of ascetic renunciation. That is to say, Shakespeare figured for Shaw as a brilliantly gifted but ultimately trifling dramatist who had squandered his talent on plays which, unlike Shaw's, had nothing of a serious, morally improving or politically progressive nature to impart. For Johnson, Tolstoy and Wittgenstein, on the other hand, he figured as the powerful disturbing embodiment of various possibilities – political and social as well as creative or linguistic – which for various reasons these thinkers had come to mistrust, disown or reject. In Johnson's case, as emerges very clearly in his writing on other early (i.e., pre-Civil War) seventeenth-century poets such as Donne, what triggered this response was a dread of some further such outbreak of political and religious strife, along with a sense of that conflict's having been prefigured, even somehow brought about, by the kinds of verbal licence – especially the flights of multiplied metaphor and far-fetched metaphysical conceit – that typified the poetry of Shakespeare and Donne.[9] In Tolstoy it was more a case of the desire for ascetic self-denial with regard to all worldly pleasures (among them the pleasures of creative self-fulfillment through literature) coming up against the single most exuberant instance of just such unbuttoned creativity deployed in ways that he, like Shaw, found morally repugnant.

However it is with Wittgenstein that the issues become more sharply focused and, I would suggest, more directly relevant to the question not only of Derrida's relationship to Shakespeare but also of how that relationship bears on the reception-history of Derrida's work at the hands of (some, not all) academic philosophers. For what Wittgenstein found so rebarbative about Shakespeare – especially (here in agreement with Johnson) the poet's deplorable lack of restraint in allowing language such a free rein against all the sanctions of social, communal or literary custom – is also what philosophers have often adduced as good enough reason to count Derrida an anti-philosopher, a latter-day sophist, or (worse still) a literary critic with misplaced philosophical pretensions.[10] More precisely: what they often object to (perhaps because it challenges an ancient and still disputed line of demarcation) is Derrida's way of thinking in and through a language that is often deployed at full crea-tive-exploratory stretch but also with the highest degree of conceptual and analytic rigour. That is to say, it is a mode of philosophising that shares something of the later Wittgenstein's famous aptitude for hitting on metaphors, similes and highly evocative turns of phrase in order to convey what would otherwise lack any adequate or sufficiently strik-ing means of expression. Yet in Wittgenstein this goes along with the idea – witness his response to Shakespeare – that really such linguistic indulgences should have no place in philosophical work since the proper (indeed, the sole legitimate) purpose of such work is to talk us down from the giddy heights of metaphysico-linguistic delusion to a restored sense of how our various language-games are normally, typically, or properly played as components of some given communal practice or cultural 'form of life'.[11]

Thus one finds Wittgenstein on occasion lamenting his own proclivi-ties in this regard – his proneness to substitute image or simile for the hard business of thinking constructively without falling back on such devices – and moreover, in a curious twist of redoubled self-criticism, confessing that he lacks the native genius to produce really strong, origi-nal, creative, or (one is tempted to suggest) Shakespearean metaphors. Indeed there are passages where he goes so far towards qualifying his negative evaluation as to say that Shakespeare simply cannot be judged by normal literary-critical standards, that his plays are more like forces of nature than products of human contrivance, and that the only fit state of mind in which to appreciate their imaginative power is one that regards them as one might an overwhelming manifestation of nature's sublime (and potentially destructive) power. Indeed 'it may be that the essential thing with Shakespeare is his ease and authority and that you just have to accept him as he is if you are going to be able to admire him properly, in the way you accept nature, a piece of scenery for example, just as it is'.[12] And again:

His pieces give me the impression of enormous 'sketches' rather than paint-ings; as though they had been 'dashed off' by someone who can permit himself 'anything', so to speak. And I can understand how someone can admire that and call it 'supreme' art, but I don't like it. – So if anyone stands in front of these pieces speechless, I can understand him; but anyone who admires them as one admires, say, Beethoven, seems to me to misunderstand Shakespeare.[13]

Moreover it is through comparisons of just this sort – clearly with their source in a certain, distinctively German-romantic conception of creative genius – that Wittgenstein tends to disparage or devalue his own (as he thinks it) essentially derivative and second-rate talent. What he is good at, so this gloomy self-assessment runs, is producing 'similes' that manage successfully to hit off some philosophic point or other. What he cannot create are the sorts of vital or visionary metaphor that extend beyond localised passages to entire works, and which bring about the kinds of revelatory or world-transformative experience that Wittgenstein famously gestured towards in the cryptic final passages of his early *Tractatus Logico-Philosophicus*.[14] That is to say, it is a question of meanings or insights that may be 'shown' through some manner of oblique, suggestive or analogical expression but which cannot be 'said' – laid out in the form of articulate, coherent, logically concatenated statements or propositions – since their import intrinsically eludes or transcends any such means of conveyance.

*

So there is a tension, even a flat contradiction at the heart of Wittgenstein's philosophy, and one that is brought home with particular force when he confronts the problem of Shakespearean language in relation to the claims of 'ordinary language' or the needs of practical-communicative discourse. For of course it was precisely in order to acknowledge those claims – to coax philosophy down from its delusions of metaphysical grandeur and put it back in touch with our everyday language-games or cultural 'forms of life' – that Wittgenstein developed his later ideas about the open-ended multiplicity of ways in which our signifying practices made sense from one such context to another. This development is most often portrayed as a drastic mid-career turning away from the austerely logical-atomist programme set out in the *Tractatus* with its numbered propositions and denial that statements could be meaningful unless they were either empirically verifiable or self-evidently valid (hence vacuous or tautologous) in virtue of their logical form. Thus the 'old' (roughly up to 1990) view, not without strong support from Wittgenstein's text, has him utterly repudiate the Tractarian concept of language as aspiring to a state of crystalline logical perfection and replace it with the communitarian view, i.e., that the standards of intelligibility are as many and various as the social practices or shared ways in life in which they play a role. For proponents of the 'new' Wittgenstein, conversely, there is no such radical mid-career break but rather – in the writings of his later period – a shift towards making more explicit what was always there to be gleaned from the *Tractatus* by those sympathetic readers, fit though few, who could grasp the purport of its last few cryptic remarks.[15] On this view, his sole purpose in composing what went before – the entire elaborate structure of numbered propositions ordered *more geometrico*, that is, in a quasi-mathematical or axiomatic-deductive mode – was to offer a kind of exemplary failure, an object-lesson in the impossibility that any such logical-atomist approach could begin to make sense of language or the most important issues for human existence like those of ethics, aesthetics and religious belief.

At any rate both parties, old and new, are agreed that 'late' Wittgenstein was out to discredit any version of the logical-positivist project that he – along with Russell and members of the 1920s Vienna Circle – had thought of as a veritable new instauration or turning-point in philosophic history. Where the revisionists demur from the orthodox account is merely in giving Wittgenstein greater credit for having shrewdly preempted the naive misreading of his work by those, like Russell, who first hailed it as a striking – if somewhat obscure – manifesto for their own set of doctrines. However my main interest here is not so much in these often rather tedious wranglings amongst the Wittgensteinian faithful but rather in what they may have to reveal about Derrida's and Wittgenstein's respective (very different) relationships to Shakespeare. This connects in turn with the wider issue regarding philosophy's ambivalent and at times highly charged relationship to a certain idea of the poetic which finds its most prominent example in Shakespeare, or in a certain idea of Shakespeare as the writer who exhibits these qualities in the highest possible degree.

So when Derrida's detractors (mostly speaking from a mainstream-analytic standpoint) describe him as a 'literary' thinker, one whose work belongs more to the province of literary criticism than philosophy, it is a safe bet that the characterisation is not meant as any kind of compliment. Still less should one take it to express the idea that Derrida's writing on philosophic themes has about it something of Shakespeare's capacity to raise the most complex and challenging philosophic issues through language of a likewise complex and intensely creative-exploratory kind. On the contrary, what these critics most often have in mind is the received 'analytic' image of Derrida as a latter-day sophist, a gadfly rhetorician or game-playing 'textualist' perverter of truth whose seeming ability to run rings around earnest or literal-minded opponents like John Searle is in fact just a sign of his refusal to engage the substantive philosophical issues. The same case was put by Jürgen Habermas when he accused Derrida of seeking to annul the genre-distinction between philosophy and literature, and thereby revoke the hard-won gains of an enlightenment discourse whose 'unfinished' character (or failure so far to realise its various emancipatory aims) was no good reason to renounce or betray the critical distinctions upon which its project had crucially depended.[16]

*

This is why, as I have said, there are some texts of Derrida (such as the 'Envois' section of *La carte postale*, some lengthy stretches of his commentary on Hegel in *Glas*, and a great many passages in his later writing) which do seem to come out strongly on the side of a 'literary' language that explores – indeed exploits – the maximum range of metaphorical, fictive or other such departures from what is normally taken (at least on analytic terms) to constitute the proper philosophical-linguistic norm.[17] Yet it remains the case – indisputably so for those who have read his work with anything like the requisite care – that Derrida has also produced many texts, starting out with that lengthy and meticulously argued essay on Husserl's philosophy of mathematics, that could be refused the title 'analytic' only on an understanding of that term which confined it to a merely parochial or honorific usage. Moreover, there are instances such as his writing on Austinian speech-act theory where one would (or should) hesitate to venture any such confident classification since the texts in question exhibit a high degree of linguistic inventiveness or conceptual creativity while none the less arguing their philosophic case with impressive vigour and force.[18]

Indeed that very 'phrase 'conceptual creativity' might stand here as a kind of shibboleth in so far as it offers what a good many continental philosophers – Derrida among them – would happily accept as an accurate characterisation of one major aspect of their work, while to many trained up on the norms and protocols of analytic discourse it will strike an oddly discordant, even vaguely oxymoronic note. It is here, I believe, that we can find the chief source of that deep-laid, almost reflex hostility that has so typified (at times so disfigured) the analytic reception of Derrida's work, as well as a reason for Wittgenstein's mistrust of metaphorical or 'literary' language, whether in his own or others' writing. Moreover it provides a likely explanation for the fact that Wittgenstein's stock has continued to ride so much higher than Derrida's amongst analytic philosophers. Finally, it offers a suggestive clue not only to Wittgenstein's thoughts about Shakespeare with their mixture of well-nigh contemptuous dismissal and well-nigh mystical regard but also to that wider philosophical unease as concerns any writing that stretches the bounds of linguistic discipline, decorum or propriety beyond what is required by a decent regard for the needs of straightforward communicative discourse.

Those bounds have been policed in different ways and with different looming perils in view by rationalists, empiricists, logicists, positivists and other linguistic-reformist types as well as by those – like the ordinary-language philosophers and current neo-pragmatists – who would seek to bring about a complete reversal of roles and thereby turn the gamekeepers into poachers. What these all have in common is a strongly marked sense of the dangers attendant on any too drastic departure from, or infraction of, the various linguistic-conceptual norms that are taken to inform the business of serious, good-faith, competent debate in a well-regulated philosophic or wider intellectual and cultural community. To repeat: Derrida is very far from rejecting those norms and is indeed more than capable of turning the tables to convincing effect on any hostile commentator – such as Searle – who thinks to catch him out in logical blunders or blind-spots of presupposition.[19] However he is just as far from accepting *either* the *echt*-analytic idea that linguistic creativity of, say, the Shakespearean-Joycean order has no place in philosophical debate *or* the Wittgensteinian approach that in principle allows all manner of language-games their role as parts of some given, communally warranted form of life but which in practice draws the line pretty firmly at some such games and the life-forms involved. These latter include, above all, the sorts of expression that Wittgenstein regarded as ill-begotten products of the typically philosophic urge to use language in abstract, specialised, technical or otherwise deviant ways for which it is simply not suited – not having evolved or developed for such purposes – and through which it exerts a malign propensity for creating philosophical and other kinds of bewilderment. Yet they also include, less emphatically, those various figural or 'literary' modes that he seems to have regarded as all very well in their place – that is say, when bearing the generic markers 'poetry', 'fiction' or (at a stretch) 'religious, hence analogical' – but as liable to cause great harm elsewhere by encouraging language to 'go on holiday' or to 'idle' like an engine detached from its machine or a philosopher content with mere gratuitous word-spinning.[20]

Of course Shakespeare's plays come tagged with a whole range of such markers – tragic, comic, tragi-comic, poetic (or mixed verse-and-prose) drama, and 'Renaissance' as a complex temporal descriptor with numerous cultural values attached – that must be supposed to have informed Wittgenstein's response as a highly cultivated reader with wide literary interests. Besides, there is long tradition of proprietary attitudes towards Shakespeare among German (or German-speaking) literary critics, philosophers and others who sometimes go so far as to state their preference for the Schlegel/Tieck translation over the English original, or again – with slightly less chutzpah – to claim that only German thinkers after Kant have possessed the kind of philosophic insight or profundity required to take full measure of Shakespeare's achievement.[21] My point is that Wittgenstein came to Shakespeare with a good deal of cultural baggage whose effect might well have been to predispose him in a certain admiring, reverential, even bardolatrous direction. Signs of this do occasionally show through in those quasi-mystical passages where Wittgenstein indulges an inherited taste for the rhetoric of sublimity and the idea of creative genius as more like a force of nature than a humanly cultivated gift or capacity. On balance, however, his exposure to this notion seems to have had just the opposite effect, that is, to have focused his attention (like Johnson's and Tolstoy's before him) on the moral aspect of Shakespearean drama as distinct from – or indeed as grounds for ignoring or condemning – its creative-linguistic qualities. It strikes me that Wittgenstein's moral sensibility was most keenly offended by the specific combination – one that Shakespearean drama exemplifies in the highest degree – of extreme verbal inventiveness with a tendency (as in *King Lear*) to push far beyond tolerable limits with the tragic assault on all accepted or normative ideas of just desert. Thus in Wittgenstein, as in Johnson, there is a strong sense that the objection to Shakespeare's 'weakness' for multiplied metaphors, puns, ambiguities and other such forms of linguistic self-indulgence goes along with a stern disapproval of the dramatist's failure in this latter, i.e., moral regard.

There are echoes of the same joint response in those critics of Derrida who seem to suppose that a highly developed, even preternatural capacity for verbal inventiveness is sure to be a mark of philosophical frivolity at best and at worst a malevolent drive to subvert all the norms of rational, good-faith, ethically responsible discourse. More than that: what seems to trigger this response in a particularly sharp, at times quite virulent form is the contra-Wittgensteinian idea – apt to be prompted by a close-reading of Shakespeare and Derrida alike – that language does most to advance and refine our powers of intellectual, moral and communicative grasp when it manifests a power to break with the currency of this or that language-game or cultural form of life. That is to say, there is ultimately no distinguishing those aspects of verbal creativity that are most prominent when viewed in a 'literary' perspective from those other aspects – of subtlety, acuity, range and depth of analytic grasp – that tend to rate higher on the philosophic scale of significance or value. It seems to me that the chief result of Wittgenstein's influence on Anglophone philosophy of language over the past four decades has been to close many minds to this very possibility by reinforcing a strongly communitarian – and to this extent strongly conservative – idea of the scope and limits of linguistic and cultural intelligibility.[22] Thus it has tended to foreclose the idea of philosophy as a genuine adventure in thought, one that is able (like the best of Derrida's writing) to reconcile the need for conceptual clarity and logical rigour with a remarkable gift for the invention of new linguistic resources whereby (or wherein) to test and refine its analytic powers.

One might also hazard the conjecture – borne out by many hostile responses to Derrida's work – that this particular way of doing philosophy goes very much against the grain of certain currently deep-laid philosophical (mainly analytic) habits of thought. What so irks these respondents is, I suggest, something very like the unusual combination of qualities that struck such a dissonant chord with Dr Johnson in his reading of Shakespeare and the metaphysical poets, and which likewise stretched Wittgenstein's patience to the point of his declaring Shakespeare in some way a nonpareil genius but Shakespeare's admirers just a bunch of charlatans or fools. In short, it is the highly unusual (and at times highly disconcerting) combination of a singular power of linguistic creativity – what Johnson famously deplored in Donne as 'heterogeneous ideas linked violently together' – with a likewise singular power to tax the best efforts of conceptual and analytic thought. For Johnson, famously, the reading of *Lear* was painful almost beyond endurance, so that having read it a second time by way of editorial obligation he hoped very much that he would never be compelled to take it up again.[23] However, just as painful – though for different reasons – was the experience of reading (and, worse still, of having to edit) language that was so 'inextricably perplexed' or so tied up into knots of figural and logico-semantic complication as to render his task well-nigh unendurable.

Thus:

> not that always where the language is intricate the thought is subtle, or the image always great where the line is bulky; the equality of words to things is very often neglected, and trivial sentiments and vulgar ideas disappoint the attention, to which they are recommended by sonorous epithets and swelling figures.[24]

Nevertheless, as with Locke and other empirically minded mistrusters of figural language, it is instructive to observe how Johnson finds himself embroiled in thickets of multiplied metaphor – in talk of 'fatal Cleopatras', of 'malignant powers' and 'luminous vapours' that lead the unwary traveler off his path – in the very act of denouncing Shakespeare's proclivities in that regard.[25] So likewise Wittgenstein repeatedly expresses a deep unease about what is likely to result when language metaphorically 'goes on holiday' even though there is nothing more characteristic of his thought – and nothing that has contributed more to its extraordinary impact and influence – than his remarkable capacity for striking out suggestive metaphors whose very suggestiveness has since given rise to endless debate around just the sorts of problem (or pseudo-problem) for which he believed those writings to have offered a cure.

*

What these reactions have in common despite issuing from sharply opposed evaluative standpoints is a keen sense of the way that such writing cuts across some of the most problematic and sensitive distinctions in present-day philosophy of language. What they are reacting to, in Derrida as in Shakespeare, is not – or not only – the stylistic brio, the extraordinary power of metaphoric suggestion, or the way that its logico-semantic complexities exceed the furthest bounds of straightforward explication or plain-prose paraphrase. Rather it is a question of the conflict induced between a mindset responsive to those commonly acknowledged features of 'literary' (especially poetic) language and a mindset schooled in the primary 'philosophic' virtues of conceptual precision, logical rigour, and – supposedly prerequisite to those – univocal or unambiguous sense. This goes some way towards explaining the signs of acute cognitive dissonance that have periodically surfaced in the annals of Shakespeare criticism from Johnson to Wittgenstein and have also been such a marked feature of the strong, sometimes febrile resistance to Derrida's work amongst analytic philosophers. Hence, I would suggest, the striking resemblance between their respective receptionhistories and the pattern of extreme antithetical response – of fiercely opposed valuations 'for' and 'against' – which seems to have its source in something other and more than a difference of attitude concerning issues of linguistic or stylistic propriety. So likewise, when Johnson registers his sense of unease with regard to Shakespeare, Donne and other representatives of the seventeenth-century 'conceited' style this doesn't have to do merely with localised instances of multiple meaning such as puns, ambiguities or other forms of semantic over-determination. It is also – and I think more crucially – concerned with the challenge so insistently posed by a language that presses these departures from the norm of straightforward, literal sense to the point where any adequate analysis will have to take account of the way they function in a larger context of logically co-implicated uses or occurrences.

Thus what Johnson perceives as a threat to the stable economy of usage and representation is not so much Shakespeare's endemic weakness for 'quibbles' – though he certainly considers that a fault – but more the kinds of intricate logico-syntactic complication that are often manifest in just such instances of localised wordplay but can also be seen to involve much deeper and longer-range conflicts of sense. This helps to explain Johnson's rueful account of his editorial work on Shakespeare as having frequently required such a strenuous effort of reconstruction as to make the business of textual scholarship an almost superhuman undertaking. 'Where any passage appeared inextricably perplexed', he writes, 'I have endeavoured to discover how it may be recalled to sense with least violence.'[26] Such a task indeed 'demands more than humanity possesses', so that 'he who exercises it with most praise has very frequent need of indulgence', and may reasonably join Johnson in protesting: 'Let us be told no more of the dull duty of an editor.' What exacerbates the problem for Johnson is also what provokes the curious mixture of hostility and fascination amongst those of Derrida's analytically minded detractors who have at least made some attempt to engage with his work, rather than dismissing or denouncing it outright on the strength of second-hand (often grossly inaccurate) report.[27] Once again it is that truly remarkable power of creative-exploratory thinking in and through language whose demands upon the reader go well beyond anything that philosophers (or textual editors) are accustomed to confront in their normal line of work.

Moreover, as Johnson plaintively admits, this aspect of Shakespearean language tends to exert a seductive spell over those – the hapless textual editors – whose business it is to rectify errors of transmission, to select among variant or disputed readings, and to strive with least 'violence' (his own term) to make rational sense of corrupt, confused or impossibly convoluted passages. On the one hand he comes out firmly against that free-for-all attitude of hermeneutic licence that had led some previous editors of Shakespeare into regions of self-indulgent creative 'emendation' far in excess of what their task required or indeed what their strictly subordinate role properly allowed. Such excesses must lead to an 'unhappy state' wherein 'pleasure is hid under danger' since they leave the editor hopelessly stranded in a fantasy-land of unsupported conjecture where his obtrusive revisions become a kind of ersatz poetry or inferior substitute for the real Shakespearean thing. Even so, Johnson acknowledges, 'the allurements of emendation are scarcely resistible', since 'conjecture has all the joy and all the pride of invention, and he who has once started a happy change is too much delighted to consider what objections may rise against it'.[28] Thus the scholar's predicament is strangely akin to that of Shakespeare himself for whom, we recall, a pun or other such verbal excrescence 'is what luminous vapours are to the traveler; he follows it at all adventures, it is sure to lead him out of his way . . . It has some malignant power over his mind, and its fascinations are irresistible . . . A quibble was to him the fatal *Cleopatra* for which he lost the world, and was content to lose it.'[29] Where of course their situations differ is with respect to the far greater licence that poetry enjoys in comparison to textual scholarship or literary criticism, even according to Johnson and despite his strictures on Shakespeare in that regard. To be sure, he finds much to deprecate in Shakespeare and, more generally, in the poetry of a period – the early seventeenth century – that he sees as having led up to the English Civil war, for Johnson (like most of his contemporaries) a dreadful recollection and one which he seems to have associated with the kinds of intellectual and cultural disorder manifest in this sort of language. Still he cannot conceal his intense admiration for Shakespeare, especially in the face of classically minded French objectors such as Voltaire.

On occasion this produces a downright conflict between Johnson's sense of the dangers presented by unbridled figuration and his desire to celebrate Shakespeare as a native genius simply not subject to all those crampingly abstract classical rules. Thus 'he who has mazed his imagination in following the phantoms which other writers raise up before him, may here be cured of his delirious ecstasies by reading human sentiments in human language'.[30] The former, strongly negative assessment on grounds of linguistic impropriety or stylistic self-indulgence is one that finds any number of echoes in the hostile commentaries on Derrida – or, one might say, on a certain idea of what Derrida stands for – by analytic philosophers. The latter, just as strongly appreciative remark has no such direct resonance in terms of Derrida's reception-history since, after all, his most fervent admirers would scarcely claim that his work has the chief merit of leading us back (as Johnson and Wittgenstein would wish) to a restored sense of being properly at home in the language and culture to which we belong. On the contrary: the likeliest effect of Derrida's writing – on receptive and antipathetic readers alike – is to bring about a sharpened sense of the ways in which language can sometimes throw into question all our self-assured ideas of propriety, intention, communicative purpose and cultural-linguistic 'at-homeness' generally. When he traces out those various deviant logics of 'supplementarity' in Rousseau, 'iterability' in Austin, 'parergonality' in Kant, *différance* in Husserl, the *pharmakon* in Plato, and so forth, the result is to raise serious doubt as to whether – in Paul de Man's more dramatic phrasing – 'it is *a priori* certain that language is in any way human'.[31]

Although he shares this doubt at least up to a point and very often finds texts turning out to mean something other (and more) than the author could conceivably have had it in mind to convey, still it is safe to say that Derrida would never make the case in such starkly uncompromising terms. Thus he typically concedes that authorial intentions have a real though limited role to play as an 'indispensable guardrail', that is to say, as imposing some needful restraint on the range of plausible interpretations but not excluding those most likely unintended complexities of sense and logic that a deconstructive reading brings to light.[32] Still this has the consequence – objectionable to some – that language must be thought of as belonging rather less to the sphere of purposeful and shared (since mutually accessible) meaning and more to a complex interplay of codes, structures, logical entailments and always defeasible expectations that cannot be equated *tout court* with even the most liberal or elastic conception of utterer's intent. Indeed, the whole project of deconstruction can be seen to require the possibility – the necessary possibility, as Derrida insists in one of his many excursions into the realm of modal logic – that intentions may indeed miscarry or be subject to changes of context so far beyond the subject's foreknowledge as to create large problems for any approach (whether in philosophy of language or ethics) premised on a straightforward intentionalist approach.[33]

*

It is not hard to see why this aspect of Derrida's work has tended to generate a hostile response amongst philosophers belonging to each of the two main categories that William James distinguished in his own time. On the one hand are those 'tough-minded' analytic types, like Searle, for whom Derrida's (to them) highly irregular procedures and even more heterodox conclusions can only be evidence that he is either deliberately flouting the basic conditions for logical argument or failing to grasp those conditions. On the other are those 'tender-minded' thinkers whose chief desire is to conserve the intimate and, as they believe, properly indissoluble tie between language and the various human contexts – social, interpersonal, above all intentional – that constitute the very element or condition of possibility for meaningful language. From both points of view – dividing as they do pretty much along the line that currently distinguishes hardcore analytic from this or that variety of 'ordinary language' philosophy – there is something about Derrida's writing that constitutes a standing provocation or downright affront. So I should not wish to press too hard on the comparison between Derrida's and Shakespeare's reception-histories, partly because the two cases involve such grossly disparate time-spans but also because there is no plausible equivalent, on Derrida's side, to the idea expressed by Johnson (along with many others) that Shakespeare, despite his verbal excesses, none the less stands out as a true representative of natural feelings naturally expressed. That is to say, his writings and the kinds of response they evoke (or provoke) are about as far as possible from the Wittgensteinian idea of philosophy as a form of linguistic therapy – a non-Freudian 'talking cure' – designed to grant readers a welcome release from the toils of obsessive philosophic enquiry or metaphysical 'bewitchment by language'.

Here again one can see how Derrida and Wittgenstein both occupy a fiercely contested zone in terms of this 'ancient quarrel' (as Plato already described it) between philosophy and poetry, concept and metaphor, or reason and rhetoric. However they occupy that zone in very different ways and with very different kinds of impact on the thinking of those who have been influenced by them. In Wittgenstein's case, it has led to a curious situation where some of the most intensive consequent debate often gives the distinct impression of having been pre-programmed by metaphors or idiosyncratic turns of thought in Wittgenstein's writing which have just the opposite of their intended (therapeutic or problem-solving) effect. If anything this tendency has been reinforced by his insistence, faithfully echoed in the orthodox camp, that philosophy should not be in the business of propounding doctrines, theories, hypotheses, or (least of all) Russell-Frege style projects for correcting or reforming – even seeking to clarify – our everyday forms of communicative utterance. For very often the main result of this self-denying ordinance has been to block just the kind of keenly analytic self-awareness with regard to its own and other thinkers' linguistic practices that has typified alternative, more heterodox modes (hardly 'schools') of Wittgenstein commentary. Among the latter, as I have said, are hermeneutically adventurous readings that draw upon Derrida's work as a means of opening up Wittgenstein's text, so to speak, by performative example or else by way of deconstructing those various metaphors that can be shown to have exerted a powerful grip on his own thought, as likewise on that of his more fideist or literal-minded interpreters.

In Derrida's case, conversely, what we find is a remarkable, at times well-nigh Shakespearean degree of verbal creativity joined to a level of self-conscious linguistic as well as conceptual-analytic awareness that again has a markedly divisive effect on the commentators although not in quite the same way. On the one side are those – like his earliest admirers in the 'literary' camp, such as Geoffrey Hartman, not to mention 'post'-philosophers like Rorty – who gently deplore or just ignore what they see as Derrida's residual attachment to certain philosophical ways of thought and instead play up his extraordinary gifts as a stylist or imaginative writer.[34] On the other are those, like myself and Rodolphe

Gasché, who make the case for his continued (however heterodox) engagement with distinctively philosophic issues.[35] However it is fair to say that both parties, whatever their sharp and much-debated differences of view, would at any rate be able to reach broad agreement on two major claims. Thus they could each without loss of face assent to the thesis that Derrida's philosophical investigations are conducted in and through what Hartman once termed an 'answerable style', that is, a language that answers in the highest degree to the demands placed on it by sustained reflection on the nature and scope of human linguistic creativity.[36] At the same time – and by no means incompatibly with this – it should be evident (anti-philosophical prejudice aside) that such reflection requires a degree of critical acumen that goes well beyond the kinds of free-associative verbal gymnastics that some of those early commentators took to be Derrida's greatest gift not only to literary criticism but also to philosophy and the human sciences in general. Few writers have managed to offer so distinctive and creative a slant on our everyday or specialised (e.g., philosophical) modes of talk while none the less maintaining an acute awareness – an acutely *analytical* awareness, in the non-proprietary sense of that term – of what is going on in the production and reception of just such utterly singular yet utterly commonplace linguistic events.

It is here that Derrida's texts invite comparison with Shakespeare despite belonging to a genre of discourse that cannot be reduced – *pace* admirers like Rorty and also those, like Habermas, who criticise Derrida on the same putative grounds – to yet another 'kind of writing' fully on a par with poetry, fiction, literary criticism, or any other genre you care to name so long as it finds room for creativity of Derrida's kind.[37] Moreover it is here that one can best make a start in explaining why they have met with a degree of resistance, hostility and resolute misreading unequalled except in the case of those philosophers – Epicurus, Hume, Spinoza and Sartre among them – who have been exposed to such treatment largely on account of their heterodox religious or political views. In the context of present-day analytic (or 'post-analytic') philosophy there are still clear signs of that conflict – nowadays more of an uneasy truce – that Rorty wrote about in 1967 when assembling the various essays for his edited volume *The Linguistic Turn*.[38] It is a context in which there can be seen to exist certain strongly marked generic expectations, among them that any philosophical text belonging to that same (albeit very broad) tradition will own allegiance to one or other of its two main sub-genres. That is to say, there should be some indication – explicit or otherwise – of its alignment either with that *echt*-analytic mode of thought descending from Russell and Frege which grants logic pride of place over natural ('ordinary') language or else with that other, Wittgenstein- or Austin-influenced mode that endorses the reverse, i.e., 'language-first' order of priority. When the signal is absent, as so often in Derrida's analytically acute yet hermeneutically ultra-responsive investigations, then there tends to develop just the kind of resistance for which psychoanalysts could no doubt produce any number of plausible explanations but which are better accounted for in terms of this clash between opposing philosophical viewpoints. For again it is among the most notable (and also most suggestively Shakespearean) aspects of Derrida's writing that he manages so often to combine an extraordinary power of metaphorical or figural expressiveness with an equally remark-able power of self-reflexive conceptual and critical analysis.

Indeed, one effect of reading his work upon any but the most diehard opponent must be to raise large questions concerning the very idea of 'ordinary' language given how many and varied are the ways in which language typically (not exceptionally) proves to outrun the utmost resources of any such normalising approach. Even then – as Derrida brings out to such striking (and for some, like Searle, such disquieting) effect – there is a further important distinction to be drawn between that approach in its orthodox Wittgensteinian or 'therapeutic' guise and Austin's keenly self-critical, at times ironically self-subverting sense of linguistic possibility. It seems to me that what has prevented many Anglophone philosophers from taking adequate stock of Derrida's work is also what might yet enable that work to exercise a highly beneficial effect on the impasse that Rorty was among the first to diagnose and which still leaves its mark on the various debates that occupy present-day philosophy of language. In brief, it is the capacity – shared by Austin and Derrida – to see some way around the communicative block that typically results when the analytic drive for logical rigour or conceptual precision comes up against the contrary emphasis (most often with its source in late Wittgenstein) on the sheer multiplicity of language-games or cultural life-forms along with their equally diverse range of context-specific criteria.

*

One version of the story, recounted on both sides but mostly by those of an analytic mind, prefers to tell it in terms of the rift between Anglophone and 'continental' (i.e., post-Kantian mainland-European) philosophy. What this version manages to keep from view – whether or not by conscious design – is the extent to which late Wittgenstein, despite his recruitment as an honorary member of the former camp, in fact stands squarely and avowedly askew to every chief tenet of mainstream analytic thought. After all, this was just the purport of his celebrated mid-career switch of priorities from logical analysis to a wise acceptance of the wisdom enshrined in ordinary language, thereby demoting logic (along with mathematics and philosophy of science) from any kind of privileged status vis-à-vis our everyday-communicative modes of linguistic exchange. However – as I have argued – the effect of Wittgenstein's therapeutic ministrations has been not so much to help philosophy get over its various needless (since self-inflicted) problems and dilemmas but rather to reinforce them by encouraging the view that analysis somehow excludes or debars an adequate respect for the subtleties, nuances and depths of implication conveyed by such everyday usage. Moreover this idea of a basically antagonistic relation between language as deployed in its 'normal' kinds of expressive or communicative context and language as a proper subject or topic of conceptual analysis is one that runs deep in Wittgenstein's thinking and which emerges with particular force in his remarks about Shakespeare's deplorable lapses of style and taste.

Such negative responses have a long pre-history in Shakespeare criticism and – as the example of Johnson very pointedly shows – are by no means confined to rabid detractors or those (like Tolstoy and Shaw) with their own doctrinal or in some way self-interested axe to grind. Rather it seems to be a matter of resistance to that highly specific combination in Shakespeare – as likewise in Derrida's most complex and philosophically challenging texts – of performative inventiveness or creativity with a power and depth of analytical thought that often over-taxes the best efforts of plain-prose commentary. For if there is one characteristic that Shakespeare possesses in the highest degree and that is brought out by his best, most perceptive and rewarding exegetes it is just this capacity to stretch and redefine what counts as an adequate (that is, a duly appreciative but also a sufficiently thought-out or analytically cogent) response. In this chapter I have focused mainly on critics, from Johnson to Wittgenstein, in whom the experience of reading Shakespeare and the effort to achieve that response have somehow been thwarted or thrown off track by an unresolved conflict between those apparently opposite and mutually exclusive poles. That is to say, the business of conceptual analysis has typically been seen as posing a threat to any mode of 'appreciative' response that would claim to value the poetry for what it is – or what it holds out to the sympathetic reader – quite apart from such alien since overly rationalist and hence *ipso facto* un-poetic (or anti-poetic) intrusions.

This pattern of response goes back to the earliest debates within Western literary criticism, such as Socrates' exchanges with the rhapsodes and other purveyors of (as he thought it) a false and beguiling poetic pseudo-wisdom which collapsed into manifest incoherence at the least touch of rational or philosophic thought. Since then it has rumbled on at intervals, especially during the Renaissance and whenever the claims of poetry seemed set to encroach upon the philosophers' domain or vice versa. This 'ancient quarrel' acquired a yet more strident and defensive edge in the face of those modern developments – spectacularly heralded by William Empson's 1930 book *Seven Types of Ambiguity* – which made a virtue of hard-pressed verbal analysis and therefore tended to place highest value on the most (to them) rewardingly complex kinds of literary language.[39] Thus Empson went out of his way to anticipate the objections of 'appreciative' critics who – sure enough – lined up to denounce his tough-minded rationalist approach as at best a tedious distraction from the poetry and at worst a threat to the sources of any genuine, i.e., sensitive and deeply attuned, poetic response. Moreover, this concern to keep analysis (or a certain kinds of analysis) safely apart from the business of literary criticism is evident not only amongst the apostles of pure, unaided intuition but also in other, more robustly unsentimental critics whenever issues of 'theory' loom into view. Thus it is often prominent in the work of those – like F.R. Leavis – who stress the importance of textual close-reading but who focus on the typically 'Shakespearean' aspects of poetic language (imagery, metaphor, sensuous 'enactment', the subtle heightening of dramatic tension through a complex interplay of speech-rhythm and metre) as distinct from the sorts of logico-semantic complication that so preoccupy a critic like Empson.[40]

The *locus classicus* here is Leavis's largely dismissive, even scornful response to René Wellek's well-meant request that he offer some explicit 'philosophical' account of the aims, priorities and modes of evaluative judgement that lay behind his various readings of poetry and the firm declarations of comparative worth that always issued from them. To which Leavis just as firmly replied by rejecting Wellek's invitation and denying *tout court* that 'philosophy' – or theory – could or should have anything whatever to do with the process of responding as intently as possible to the poem in hand and thereby arriving at a properly discriminate, critically (rather than theoretically) informed evaluation.[41] In short, this idea of a 'Shakespearean' use of language does triple duty as a compact statement of critical belief, a touchstone by which other poets may be judged or ranked, and – not least – a means of signaling Leavis's downright opposition to any idea that literary criticism might stand to benefit (i.e., to improve or refine that process) by some advance in its powers of theoretical grasp.

Along with it goes the kindred idea that too much analysis, especially when focused on the logical (or logico-semantic) structures of language, is sure to have a deleterious effect by diverting attention from those other, more authentically 'Shakespearean' attributes that call upon the reader's capacity to realise their vividly enacted sensuous, i.e., visual or tactile, character. Here, as so often, the term 'analytic' tends to hide a significant difference of views since in Leavis's case the analysis of language very markedly observes certain limits on its range or scope of application. They have to do with what he – like T.S. Eliot before him – considers the high-point or *echt*-Shakespearean moment in English poetic tradition where the perfect fusion of intellect and feeling or thought and emotion that typified the poetry of the early seventeenth century gave way to a subsequent 'dissociation of sensibility' and a constant pendulum-swing between periods of overly cerebral, emotionally under-charged versifying and periods of intense but intellectually vapid (e.g., romantic) self-indulgence.[42] This is not the place for an extended commentary on the gaps, elisions and distortions involved in the Eliot-Leavis historical purview and its highly selective account of that canonical or critically sanctioned line of descent.[43] More to the point is its way of encoding that anti-theoretical or anti-philosophic bias through a largely mythic but none the less effective historical and cultural narrative. This in turn derives much of its persuasive force – for those of a likewise sceptical mind concerning the claims of analysis – from its invocation of the various dualisms (as between thought and feeling or theory and experience) which are then taken to show just how far we have travelled from the kind of complex yet unimpeded response that Shakespeare both embodies in the highest degree and requires of the fit reader.

On the contrary, I would argue: the best modern critics of Shakespeare are those like Empson who have shown the most sensitive attunement to nuances of verbal implication while also – quite compatibly with this – providing some account of the linguistic structures (in Empson's case, the logico-semantic 'machinery') without which those subtleties would fail to register. Indeed, the main line of development in Empson's thought is precisely an advance from the brilliant though somewhat ad hoc and intuitive approach of *Seven Types of Ambiguity* to the kinds of philosophically informed (that is to say, conceptually precise and logically articulated) reading that typify his essays on Shakespeare, Pope, Wordsworth, Jane Austen and other writers in *The Structure of Complex Words*.[44] Above all it is the chapters on Shakespeare – on the semantics of 'sense' in *Measure for Measure*, of 'dog' in *Timon of Athens*, and (most impressively) of 'fool' in *King Lear* – that show Empson exploring this ground between the normative constraints of 'ordinary language' and the limits to which language may at times be forced under pressure of extreme expressive, dramatic, or indeed 'ordinary' (everyday-practical) circumstance. I have put the case here that analytic philosophy – whether in the Frege-Russell or the late-Wittgensteinian line of descent – has shown itself peculiarly prone to the sorts of dilemma that typically arise when these two dimensions are allowed to come apart, or so far apart that any attempt at mediation is apt to appear misguided or forlorn. Indeed one could claim without serious over-statement that its history has been slung between these rival conceptions (most strikingly embodied in Wittgenstein's mid-career change of mind) and moreover that it is through their kindred resistance to this drastically compartmentalised mode of thought that Shakespeare and Derrida have come to represent so potent or pro-vocative a challenge. Hence the striking resemblance between their two reception-histories, at least in so far as they have both attracted criticism – or downright hostility – on account of their proneness (so the charge-sheet runs) to let language run amok in figural excesses or metaphoric deviations from the normative standards of straightfor-ward communicative discourse. In more positive terms, what they both have to offer is a striking example of the way that language can trans-gress those standards – as for instance through the kinds of 'deviant' performative that Derrida enacts as well as describes in his work on Austin – while none the less maintaining an acutely analytical aware-ness with regard to just such inherent possibilities of divergence from the everyday or commonplace expressive norm.

Notes

1. John Keats, *The Letters of John Keats: A Selection*, ed. Robert Gittings (Oxford: Oxford University Press, 1970), p. 43
2. For a survey and critique of various hostile or uncomprehending responses to Derrida, see Christopher Norris, 'Of an Apoplectic Tone Recently Adopted in Philosophy', in Norris, *Reclaiming Truth: Contribution to a Critique of Cultural Relativism* (London: Lawrence & Wishart, 1996), pp. 222–53; also Maurice Charney (ed.), *'Bad' Shakespeare: Revaluations of the Shakespeare Canon* (London and Toronto: Associated University Presses, 1988).
3. See especially the various references to Shakespeare in Ludwig Wittgenstein, *Culture and Value* (2nd edn), ed. G.H. von Wright, trans. Peter Winch (Oxford: Blackwell, 1980); also Norris, 'Extraordinary Language: Why Wittgenstein Didn't Like Shakespeare', in *Fiction, Philosophy and Literary Theory: Will the Real Saul Kripke Please Stand Up?* (London: Continuum, 2007), pp. 159–211.

4. See especially Martha Nussbaum, *Love's Knowledge: Essays on Philosophy and Literature* (New York: Oxford University Press, 1990).
5. See for instance Stanley Cavell, *Disowning Knowledge in Seven Plays of Shakespeare*, 2nd edn (Cambridge: Cambridge University Press, 2003).
6. See note 2, above; also Derrida, 'Afterword: Toward an Ethic of Conversation', in Gerald Graff (ed.), *Limited Inc* (Evanston: Northwestern University Press, 1989), pp. 111–54.
7. Wittgenstein, *Culture and Value*, p. 48e.
8. See George Bernard Shaw, *Shaw on Shakespeare*, ed. Edwin Wilson (Harmondsworth: Penguin, 1968) and Leo Tolstoy, *What is Art?*, trans. Almyer Maude (New York: Macmillan, 1960).
9. Samuel Johnson, 'Preface to the Plays of William Shakespeare', in *Dr Johnson on Shakespeare*, ed. W.K. Wimsatt (Harmondsworth: Penguin, 1969); also Johnson, *The Lives of the Most Eminent English Poets: With Critical Observations on Their Works*, ed. Roger Lonsdale, 4 vols (Oxford: Oxford University Press, 2006).
10. See notes 2 and 6, above; also John Searle, 'Reiterating the Differences', *Glyph*, Vol. 1 (Baltimore: Johns Hopkins University Press, 1975), pp. 198–208 and Bernard Harrison, 'White Mythology Revisited: Derrida and his Critics on Reason and Rhetoric', *Critical Inquiry*, 25:3 (1999), pp. 505–34.
11. See especially Ludwig Wittgenstein, *Philosophical Investigations*, trans. G.E.M. Anscombe (Oxford: Blackwell, 1953) and *On Certainty*, ed. and trans. G.E.M. Anscombe and G.H. von Wright (Oxford: Blackwell, 1969); also – for some highly illuminating commentary – Stanley Cavell, *Must We Mean What We Say?* (New York: Oxford University Press, 1969) and *Philosophical Passages: Wittgenstein, Emerson, Austin, Derrida* (Oxford: Blackwell, 1994).
12. Wittgenstein, *Culture and Value*, p. 49e.
13. Ibid., p. 83e.
14. Wittgenstein, *Tractatus Logico-Philosophicus*, trans. D.F. Pears and B.F. McGuiness (London: Routledge & Kegan Paul, 1961).
15. See especially Alice Crary and Rupert Read (eds), *The New Wittgenstein* (London: Routledge, 2000); also James Conant, 'Putting Two and Two Together: Kierkegaard, Wittgenstein and the Point of View for Their Work as Authors', in Timothy Tessin and Mario von der Ruhr (eds), *Philosophy and the Grammar of Religious Belief* (Basingstoke: Macmillan, 1995), pp. 248–331.
16. Jürgen Habermas, 'Excursus on Levelling the Genre-Distinction Between Philosophy and Literature', in *The Philosophical Discourse of Modernity: Twelve Lectures*, trans. Frederick Lawrence (Cambridge: Polity Press, 1987), pp. 185–210; also Norris, 'Deconstruction, Postmodernsm and Philosophy: Habermas on Derrida', in *What's Wrong with Postmodernism* (Hemel Hempstead: Harvester-Wheatsheaf, 1990), pp. 49–76.
17. Derrida, *Glas*, trans. John P. Leavey and Richard Rand (Lincoln: University of Nebraska Press, 1986) and *The Post Card: From Socrates to Freud and Beyond*, trans. Alan Bass (Chicago: University of Chicago Press, 1987).
18. See notes 2 and 6, above; also Derrida, 'Limited Inc abc', *Glyph*, Vol. 2 (Baltimore: Johns Hopkins University Press, 1977), pp. 75–176.

19. See notes 2, 6 and 18.

20. Wittgenstein, *Philosophical Investigations*.

21. For some interesting background information and commentary see Ken Larson, '"The Classical German Shakespeare" as Emblem of Germany as "Geistige Weltmacht": Validating National Power Through Cultural Prefiguration', available at <http://aurora.wells.edu/~klarson/papers/mla91.htm> and 'Did Shakespeare Really Write in German? Or: How the Bard Became *ein Klassiker*', available at <http://aurora.wells.edu/~klarson/papers/facclub1.htm>. See also Terence Hawkes, *Meaning By Shakespeare* (London: Routledge, 1992).

22. Norris, 'Extraordinary Language'; also 'The Limits of *Whose* Language?: Wittgenstein on Logic, Science and Mathematics', in *Language, Logic and Epistemology* (London: Macmillan, 2005), pp. 66–110, and 'Kripkenstein's Monsters: Anti-realism, Scepticism, and the Rule-following Debate', in *On Truth and Meaning: Language, Logic and the Grounds of Belief* (London: Continuum, 2006), pp. 155–202.

23. Johnson, 'Preface to the Plays of William Shakespeare'.

24. Ibid., pp. 67–8.

25. Ibid., p. 68.

26. Ibid., p. 93.

27. See for instance Simon Glendinning (ed.), *Arguing with Derrida* (Oxford: Blackwell, 2001); also Reed Way Dasenbrock (ed.), *Re-Drawing the Lines: Analytic Philosophy, Deconstruction, and Literary Theory* (Minneapolis: University of Minnesota Press, 1989); Newton Garver and Seung-Chong Lee, *Derrida and Wittgenstein* (Philadelphia: Temple University Press, 1994); Christopher Norris and David Roden (eds), *Jacques Derrida* (4 vols, London: Sage, 2002); Samuel Wheeler, *Deconstruction as Analytic Philosophy* (Stanford: Stanford University Press, 2000).

28. Johnson, 'Preface to the Plays of William Shakespeare', p. 96.

29. Ibid., p. 68.

30. Ibid., p. 61.

31. Paul de Man, 'The Resistance to Theory', in *The Resistance to Theory* (Manchester: Manchester University Press, 1986), pp. 3–20; p. 17.

32. Jacques Derrida, *Of Grammatology*, trans. Gayatri C. Spivak (Baltimore: Johns Hopkins University Press, 1976), p. 158.

33. For an earlier (and more extreme) variety of anti-intentionalist doctrine, see Cleanth Brooks, *The Well Wrought Urn: Studies in the Structure of Poetry* (New York: Harcourt Brace, 1947) and W.K. Wimsatt, *The Verbal Icon: Studies in the Meaning of Poetry* (Lexington: University of Kentucky Press, 1954).

34. See for instance Geoffrey Hartman, *Saving the Text: Literature, Derrida, Philosophy* (Baltimore: Johns Hopkins University Press, 1981) and Richard Rorty, 'Philosophy as a Kind of Writing', in *Conequences of Pragmatism* (Minneapolis: University of Minnesota Press, 1982), pp. 89–109.

35. See Christopher Norris, *Derrida* (London: Collins/Fontana, 1987) and 'Derrida on Rousseau: Deconstruction as Philosophy of Logic', in *Language, Logic and Epistemology*, pp. 16-65; also Rodolphe Gasché, *The Tain of the Mirror: Derrida and the Philosophy of Reflection* (Cambridge, MA: Harvard University Press, 1986).

36. See note 34, above; also G. Douglas Atkins, *Geoffrey Hartman: Criticism as Answerable Style* (London: Routledge, 1990).

37. See notes 16, 27 and 35, above.

38. Richard Rorty (ed.), *The Linguistic Turn: Essays in Philosophical Method* (Chicago: University of Chicago Press, 1967).

39. William Empson, *Seven Types of Ambiguity*, 2nd edn (London: Chatto & Windus, 1953).

40. See especially F.R. Leavis, *The Living Principle: 'English' as a Discipline of Thought* (London: Chatto and Windus, 1975) and *Valuation in Criticism and Other Essays*, ed. G. Singh (Cambridge: Cambridge University Press, 1986).

41. F.R. Leavis, 'Literary Criticism and Philosophy: A Reply', in *The Importance of Scrutiny*, ed. Eric Bentley (New York: New York University Press, 1964), pp. 30–40.

42. T.S. Eliot, 'Tradition and the Individual Talent', in *Selected Essays* (London: Faber, 1964), pp. 3–11.

43. On this topic, see various contributions to Norris and Richard Machin (eds), *Post-Structuralist Readings of English Poetry* (Cambridge: Cambridge University Press, 1987).

44. William Empson, *The Structure of Complex Words*, 2nd edn (London: Chatto & Windus, 1961).

Chapter 15

Miracle Play

Nicholas Royle

– Unbelievable, Shakespeare, if I'm perfectly frank.[1]

– We were up in Stratford, a few moons ago now it was, saw *Henry IV* the so-called Part 1 one night, the so-called Part 2 the next. First days of August 2007 if I recall aright, the Avon still very high after the flooding from the previous couple of weeks, afternoon of the second day it absolutely tipped down, we parked just outside the church and waited for it to subside a bit. Great puddles, splashing our way down the tree-lined churchyard path as the sunshine started breaking through. Two pounds now, can you credit it, used to cost nothing, give it time and it'll be a thousand, to get access to the chancel and set eyes on the family gathering, William and widow and all, and the bust to the left of the altar, put up in her lifetime, as the bumph stresses. 'Good friend for Jesus sake forbeare, / To dig the dust enclosed here. / Blessed be the man that spares these stones, / And cursed be he that moves my bones.' Unbelievable. You were there.

– Me? Where?

– You were standing on the right side, close to the 1605 Geneva Bible they have on display, the one from which he would have heard readings during his visits to church in the last few years of his life, as the bumph stresses. There's a door, to the right, in front of the altar, and sunlight was streaming in through a gap. A single padlock securing the thing. And you were thinking, God knows why, but people do, about what would be required in order to break in at night, lift the stone (it's not clear why it says 'stones', except for the rhyme, there's just the one slab, isn't there, but I suppose he wasn't to know), dig the dust and get some DNA – the deserts, the forests, the gypsies –

– You're mental, you are.

– We're both mental, you fool. Personally I was struck by the prosopo-poeia, the voice-from-beyond-the-grave, the way I was being addressed as 'dear friend'. Shakespeare's a miracle.

– What do you mean? What is a miracle? And when? You remind me of something the bizarre narrator of Henry James's *The Sacred Fount* comes out with: 'I don't insist on the name. Nothing is, I admit, a miracle from the moment one's on the track of the cause, which was the scent we were following. Call the thing simply my fact.'[2]

– Your fact? Is that with an 'a' or a 'u'?

– I want to say –

– Tush, never tell me.

– I want –

– You're going to have to be quiet. You'll already have annoyed enough people as it is. You cannot write Shakespeare criticism in or for more than one voice: it's against all the monological, monophonocentric rules of scholarship and academic decorum.

– I –

– No more. Never never never never never. Remember what a certain philosopher says.

– Jesus wept. He groaned in the spirit. Anyway, who said this was 'Shakespeare criticism'?

– Precisely apropos Shakespeare, he says: 'There has never been a scholar who really, and as scholar, deals with ghosts. A traditional scholar does not believe in ghosts – nor in all that could be called the virtual space of spectrality.'[3] He is meditating on Marcellus' plea in the face of the Ghost – 'Thou art a scholar, speak to it Horatio' (1.1.42). It's a question of the kinds of writing, thinking and life (yes, living, learning to live, living on) that follow the knowledge that 'address[ing oneself] to spirits . . . is not only possible, but . . . will have at all times conditioned, as such, address in general' (SM, p. 12). To be a philosopher worthy of the name, in this context, is to be someone 'mad enough to hope to *unlock* [open up or unbolt: *déverrouiller*] the possibility of such an address' (p. 12/34).

– So the voice from beyond the grave –

– I told you to shut it.

– You just told me to open up.

– Incredible, Derrida. Yes, mad enough to hope. I could imagine someone writing at great length about hope in the work of this mad philosopher, the madness to hope, the madness of hope, a figure that he connects with Heidegger, for example, in the relatively early essay 'Différance',[4] but that plays a perhaps somewhat subterranean role in so many other texts.

– Can you just clarify – am I to infer that I am dead? . . . I see . . . Not a mouse stirring . . . I see . . . In any case, I think first of all you need to be concerned about the word 'miracle'. You said it in the context of Shakespeare: I wasn't sure if you meant his work or his life, his having lived, or again his epitaph, his tomb and monument at Stratford, the force of prosopopoeia, in other words his living on. It made me uneasy. I'm not at all sure whether the word 'miracle' is prudent. And then for a split-second I had the distinct feeling you were going to make a similar pronouncement about Jacques Derrida.

– Absolutely, you must have been reading my mind. But I'll say it anyway, for the benefit of the audience who otherwise might not believe it: *Derrida's a miracle.*

– I find all of this quite troubling. To say that someone or – more precisely, I suppose – someone's writing is a miracle is surely to subscribe to a religious and more narrowly perhaps a Christian kind of discourse . . .

– It depends. There is miracle and miracle. Miracle play, dear friend. That is where we have to begin.

– Where we have to begin? That sounds like an allusion to the mad philosopher's answer to the question, in the form of that emphatic and extraordinary sentence: 'Wherever we are: in a text already where we believe ourselves to be [Quelque part où nous sommes: *en un texte déjà où nous croyons être*].'[5] Rodolphe Gasché quotes this sentence from *Of*

Grammatology in a recent essay on Derrida and wonder. (Perhaps you were citing him? Or perhaps you haven't read it? If not, I recommend it.) Gasché considers the ways in which wonder lies at the origin of philosophy, whether for Plato in the *Theaetetus* or Aristotle in his *Metaphysics*.[6] No philosophy without *thaumazein*. And yet, as Gasché goes on to say, despite its significance throughout the history of philosophy, up to and including the writings of Husserl and Heidegger, 'explicit reference to the problematic of philosophical wonder is oddly absent from Derrida's work' (p. 332). Gasché suggests that one reason for this is that '*thaumazein* as the origin of philosophical thought contains . . . the outlines of a metaphysics of the subject, the conception of an anthropology, as well as the elementary features of humanism' (p. 332). The point then, he says, is that, 'as an integral part of the whole of philosophy, wonder cannot . . . escape deconstructive vigilance' (p. 337). Derrida's writings entail a thinking of wonder otherwise, as without single origin. Wonder itself will have been supplemented, overtaken, surprised. Gasché illustrates this by reference to that statement about having to begin 'in a text already where we believe ourselves to be'. Alluding to Derrida's emphasis (in the same section of *Of Grammatology* [pp. 157–8/226–7]) on the way in which language takes us by surprise, Gasché writes:

> thinking, philosophical thinking, for example, is always necessarily 'held within' [*prise*] and 'overtaken' [*surprise*] by a language and a logic constituting a system which cannot be dominated by thinking: this system has always 'sufficiently *surprising* resources' to which discourse whatever is said is always otherwise than what is intended. The wonder that causes thinking, would thus be nothing less than an awareness of being overtaken by the resources of that in which one is caught. (p. 338)

Language always takes first prize. Indeed there's no competition. As Sarah Wood once remarked, it's a matter of trying 'to undo the magic isolation of surprise as the property of somebody, or as an aesthetic effect which merely blinds and binds the movement of writing'.[7] Gasché's essay 'Thinking, Without Wonder' focuses on philosophy, on what he calls 'a certain irreducibility of the philosophical' (p. 333), and on the ways in which deconstructive thinking necessarily dislocates the philosophical. Gasché doesn't say anything as such about religion or literature. It's no wonder, you might think, he doesn't talk about miracle.

– Nor, if I may get a word in edgeways, would it be any wonder that Derrida doesn't much trouble himself to write about miracles. So far as I am aware, the word 'miracle' appears only rarely in his work.

– I'm not so sure about that.[8] And of course it depends also what you mean by 'appear'. Miracles would always have to do with some kind of verbal apparitioning, wouldn't they?

– Anyway, I was saying . . . The funny thing is that the word does indeed crop up just when he is discussing that formulation, first published in *Of Grammatology* in 1967, about where we have to begin, viz. '*Wherever we are*: in a text already where we believe ourselves to be [*Quelque part où nous sommes: en un texte déjà où nous croyons être*].' It's thirty years later, in *Counterpath*, in some reflections addressed to Catherine Malabou, on 25 November 1997. Derrida writes:

> I wonder whether today, at the end of a long road, I wouldn't make the word 'believe [*croyons*]' carry the whole weight of it. In the polysemy, indeed the homonymy of the verbs *croire* (*believe that* this can happen, *believe* someone's word, *believe in* someone, so many different things, but most often *possible*, likely, thus credible, and hence independent of *pure* belief [*la pure croyance*]), I would insist on that *other* belief, the credence par excellence – which is possible only by *believing in the impossible*. A miracle is in the realm of the ordinary for *pure* belief [*Le miracle serait l'ordinaire de la pure croyance*]. And the 'text where we believe ourselves to be', another name for this place, place in general, interests me only where the impossible, that is to say the incredible, encircles and harries it, making my head turn, leaving an illegible trace within the taking-place, there, in the vertigo, 'where we believe ourselves to be' . . . [*sic*] Place is always unbelievable to me, as is orientation.[9]

Miracle would be the ordinary of *pure* belief. 'Place is always unbelievable to me': it's making my head turn, it's vertiginous. This interest in the impossible, in the play of place and the theatre of the impossible, is what you find, for example, in his reading of Shakespeare's *Romeo and Juliet*. It's a question of how, in Shakespeare, '*the impossible happens*'.[10]

– Ah, Shakespeare: I was beginning to wonder . . . So what are you saying exactly?

– I'm saying that miracle, in Derrida, has to do with writing, with a sense of place, with an experience of the impossible in the text wherever we are. Literature, in this context, has special significance as the space in which the dead return, where ghosts speak, where resurrection happens, but also where the most unbelievable things occur, the most miraculous coincidences, miraculous recoveries and miraculous escapes. Here, in a sense, the miraculous is the ordinary or everyday of literature. And when 'the impossible happens', as Derrida stresses in 'Aphorism Countertime', this has nothing to do with '"objective reality"' (as he calls it, in scare quotes: AC, p. 422). It is about Shakespeare's 'theatre of the impossible' (p. 422). At the same time, however, miracle would also be, in a differently exemplary fashion, the ordinary of deconstruction, if there is any. That's why, in the piece on *Romeo and Juliet*, Derrida goes on to declare, nevertheless, that 'The impossible . . . also tells the truth' (p. 422). If miracle is a question of text, writing or inscription, in the generalised sense in which Derrida has elaborated these terms (a situation, such as being in church, is a text; DNA is a text; etc), it is also about iterability.

– Hang on, I'm losing you.

– Come back. Come to. Be astonished. Miracles today – as if everything were absolutely new. Remember that strange verbless, perhaps subjectless sentence in Derrida's 1963 essay 'Force and Signification': 'Astonishment . . . by language as the origin of history [*Étonnement . . . par le langage comme origine de l'histoire*].'[11] OK, listen. Here are a few prompts or stage directions regarding the miracle or miraculous in Derrida and Shakespeare:

1. Iterability. Discussing that aphoristic text about *Romeo and Juliet*, the 'tiny little text [*un tout petit texte*]' called 'Aphorism Countertime', the mad philosopher stresses that one must 'reconstitute in the most informed and intelligible way, if necessary against the usual history of the historians, the historical element in a play . . . not just the historicity of its composition by Shakespeare, its inscription in a chain of works, etc., . . . but also what is historical in the play itself . . . This has to do with the structure of a text, with . . . its iterability, which both puts down roots in the unity of a context and immediately opens this non-saturable context onto a recontextualization. All this is historical through and through. The iterability of the trace (unicity, identification, and alteration in repetition) is the condition of historicity.'[12] My reading of the so-called first part of *Henry IV* (I will rename it shortly) is guided by this question of iteration and iterability. *Henry IV* has a unique position in the Shakespearean oeuvre for the analytical, theatrical and poetic stress it gives to what Falstaff calls 'iteration'. Iterability, that strange logic that binds repetition and alterity, is traced in Shakespeare's 'iteration'; but iterability, like the trace, is not and cannot become an object of thought. Rather it entails what Rodolphe Gasché calls 'a non-thinkable tear within what is' (TWW, p. 334). If Derrida's writing performs trapeze-artist effects, generates uncanny feelings or perceptions resembling the miraculous, transforming the scene of reading in

ways that might seem magical (Plato's *pharmakon* never the same again after Derrida, for example, likewise Rousseau's 'supplement', likewise Freud's 'telepathy', and so on), if (as Frank Kermode once remarked) Derrida can leave us with a sense that what he does is beyond the human or that what he requires of us 'may not be humanly supportable', as though indeed Derrida were not 'of the same species' as the rest of us,[13] if Derrida does something with 'life', living on and spectrality that is new or unprecedented in the history of writing (this would be the Derrida that Hélène Cixous describes as 'a buried-alive supernatural, who gets wind of a new definition of immortality through the magic of writing': he 'writes as he posthumes. The writing is his survivor, she [*l'écriture, f.*] survives him'),[14] and if (as various commentators have observed) Derrida's innumerable accounts of the trace, text, supplement, spectre and others in that long-established 'non-synonymic chain of substitutions' can themselves arouse feelings of wonder or astonishment, all of this must be tempered in effect by the humility of the ordinary, the miracle as the ordinary.

2. Lazarus –

– Enough! I can do this just as well or badly as you. I'm doing Number 2. It's the number of the ghost. Number is the ghost, after all, as Derrida also suggests.[15]

2. *Lazarus, come forth.* That's what literature is about, according to Maurice Blanchot. In 'Literature and the Right to Death' he writes: 'Take the trouble to listen to a single word: in that word, nothingness is struggling and toiling away, it digs tirelessly, doing its utmost to find a way out, nullifying what encloses it – it is infinite disquiet, formless and nameless vigilance.'[16] Literature, Blanchot suggests, has to do with the '*Lazare, veni foras* [which] summon[s] the dark, cadaverous reality from its primordial depths' (p. 326). At the same time, however, necessarily placing its hope in 'the materiality of language, in the fact that words are things, too', literature is also 'a search for this moment which precedes literature', it is concerned with 'the abyss, Lazarus in the tomb and not Lazarus brought back into the daylight, the one who already smells bad, who is Evil, Lazarus lost and not Lazarus saved and brought back to life' (p. 327). Blanchot's account of literature might serve as a sort of cautionary prompt to any quick-fix impulse simply to characterise literature as the space of miracle: if the literary work produces resurrectional effects, driven by the passion to let us hear the 'infinite disquiet' of 'a single word' (for example, 'miracle' or 'iteration'), it is also what encrypts itself, what

wants to bury itself or be buried, buried alive, *before* the miracle, before 'Lazarus saved and brought back to life'. Blanchot's figure of Lazarus alerts us to the deep strangeness of literary language as well as to the complexity of a miracle motif that runs through all of Shakespeare's work, namely coming back or being brought back from the dead: literature as Lazarature. Jesus wept. He groaned in the spirit. If you were to let me have a little more time here I would like to elaborate further on the story of Lazarus, especially in terms of Freud, telepathy and what is called magical thinking. You see, for me, it starts with that strange sense of voice and place, that disorienting of what is called narrative voice or point of view, in the story of Lazarus: 'Jesus wept. He groaned in the spirit.' In grief at the death of his friend, Jesus 'groaned in the spirit'. What is that groan? Can a groan 'in the spirit' be heard? Where, whose or what is this quasi-telepathic voice that apparently knows and tells us that Jesus groaned *in the spirit*? At issue here is the great question of magical thinking in the Bible. If you turn to Freud . . .

– I'm sorry. Not now. Number 3. Hélène Cixous. As I was suggesting, Jacques Derrida's writings contain little explicit or sustained reference to miracles or the miraculous. I know you wanted to quibble about that, but there is one particular author in relation to whose work he talks about the miraculous, namely Cixous, above all in his remarkable book *H.C. for Life, That Is to Say . . .*[17] Here the notion of the miracle is, I think, surprisingly insistent. I will recall just four of the most striking examples.

The first concerns his discussion of how, quite differently from him, she 'writes by dream' (*HCFL*, p. 75). Derrida writes, he says, at the end of the night, 'when [his] awakening . . . begins by turning off the current of the phantasm and putting an end to the night' (p. 76). Cixous, on the other hand, writes 'by drawing energy as well as the figures of her writing from a phantasmoneiric flux that – and this is its miracle and its magic – is not interrupted by awakening' (p. 75). This 'phantasmoneiric flux' marks out her work, in Derrida's view, from all other work, at least from other writing in the twentieth (or twenty-first) century (see *HCFL*, pp. 12–13). He remarks: 'I do not know any other example of such a miraculous alliance between day and night, between the mad turbulence of the dream and the calculating culture of the literal and literary realization' (p. 76). And he adds, as a sort of blinding proviso to this apprehension of the miraculous, that he 'believe[s his] eyes all the less, in front of this miracle', since he himself 'work[s] on the contrary by dream's interruption' (p. 76), by the light of day.

The second example has to do with Derrida's analysis of 'the mighty power of the *might*' in her writing, the way in which it sings, like a wire that would be as much a telepathic or telephonic thread as a telegraph wire, the way it connects what he calls 'the thought of magic' with 'life' and above all with the imperative 'Live [*vis*]'. This 'might' has to do with 'the magic of what, by a stroke of writing, does the impossible' (p. 107). Derrida declares:

> the mighty power of the *might* of which we are speaking, as of Hélène Cixous's poetics in fact, is the enchantment, the arrival as if by an enchantment, where the poetic song, the charm, the *Carmen*, and magical power are allied to *kommen lassen*, make come in letting come . . . [this is the] formula of the miracle of a chant of enchantment, which is also a song of songs. (*HCFL*, p. 79)[18]

– Ah, the song of songs! –

– Not groaning but singing now, are you? Backing vocal, back on the song or track of the Bible, let me guess, you'd like to juxtapose, compare and contrast this miraculous song of 'making come in letting come' (this force of 'Live', *vis* of *vis* or live-force, this 'would that you might live' [*HCFL*, p. 77]), with Blanchot's markedly more sombre and deathly *Lazarus, come forth*.

– 'The voice of my beloved! behold, he cometh leaping upon the mountains, skipping upon the hills . . .'[19]

– The third occasion concerning the miraculous in Cixous is where Derrida speaks of the 'oceanic mood' he experiences when confronted with her writing. It's like a miraculous catch of fish. He says:

> the oceanic mood I feel in front of this work is also reminiscent of what one feels about a miraculous catch. Magical, miraculous, and mystical: why? I ask myself why because, as a man of the Enlightenment, I would still like to give an account and reason for this miraculous, mystical magic – which must not be an act of witchcraft. An inexhaustible magic, however . . . [These] shimmering fish are not caught by her net. The mighty fish are born from the *net* in which they are caught. That is what I call the poetics of the event. It produces magically, miraculously, and quasi-mystically the very thing it nominates. It brings about what it catches. (*HCFL*, p. 97)

Here, perhaps more explicitly than anywhere else in the book, Derrida insists on this figure of the miraculous while also emphatically distinguishing it from any sort of witchcraft or supernaturalism. At issue in Cixous's work, rather, is a new 'poetics of the event' for which it would be necessary, as he says, to elaborate a new understanding of what is meant by 'magic', 'the soul or spirit of animism', 'telepathy', 'telephony', 'phantasm', 'omnipotence' or 'incantation' (p. 76).

The final instance is specifically about the instance, the instant or instantaneity, the bounding miraculous speed of Cixous's writing, in particular thanks to substitution. Derrida thus speaks of 'the infinite play of substitution of letters that Hélène Cixous's opus operates, she who knows how to replace everything, at full speed, including time and death, by the bond of an immortality'. He goes on:

> Substitution is her top game, the power and magic of this writing, of what happens or takes place, miraculously through the mighty power of substitution, but of a substitution that leaves the living itself [*vivant singulier*] in place. Thus the latter is kept alive or given back to life through the grace of a bound. At an infinite speed, on the instant, in a single bound. (*HCFL*, p. 131)

It is in this context that Derrida speaks about 'a speed of displacement in writing' (p. 73), 'a speed that, playing with time, outplays time' (pp. 61–2).

Now I would like to say first of all that with these cases or instances that Derrida talks about – the 'miraculous alliance between day and night', between 'dream' and 'literal and literary realization', in short the 'phantasmoneiric flux'; the miracle of the chant of enchantment and 'the mighty power of the *might*'; the miraculous *catch* of the 'poetics of the event' which 'brings about what it catches'; and the miraculous speed of substitution, a substitutability always affirming the living singular, living itself [*vivant singulier*], even as it 'outplays time' – with all of this that shimmers up before us in the book *H.C. for Life, That Is to Say . . .*, we are given an extraordinary account of the work of Hélène Cixous, a reading or countersigning of Cixous that is itself, it seems to me, in its own singular and singularly enlightening fashion, miraculous. To adapt a formulation suggested a little earlier, Cixous's work might never be the same again. At the same time, however, and indeed in accordance with the mighty powers of literature and substitution about which Derrida writes and which he reads in her work and draws on for the energy of his own writing, everything that he says about the miraculous in Cixous might, with appropriate regard to the irreplaceable that is replaced on the spot, be transposed to a reading of Shakespeare.[20]

I will try to sketch at least the beginning of such a reading, focusing on a few appearances of the word 'miracle' or 'miraculous' itself, in

particular with regard to *Henry IV*, though I do also want to say something about *Hamlet*, before concluding with . . . Are you back again?

– Yes, I haven't been anywhere. You're the one who drifted away.
That's where we have to begin, I've been saying, 'miracle play' – first of
all perhaps as a sort of *hysteron proteron*: you have to reckon with the
place of play, play's displacing, 'play' before 'miracle', where *play* – or
at any rate 'play in a radical way', as Derrida says – has to do with a
kind of thinking that goes 'beyond the activity of a subject manipulating
objects according to or against the rules, et cetera'.[21] It is a matter of
thinking play in ways that are not 'dominated by meaning' or by 'finality', play as something no longer simply 'in the world' or the 'activity'
of someone. As Derrida notes: 'Philosophy has always made play into
an activity, the activity of a subject manipulating objects.'[22] To *miracle
play*, you have to dream, cast off into the phantasmoneiric flux, think
play anew. It has to do with the organisation and disorganisation of
dreams and letters. This is one of the discoveries or conceptual break-
throughs that Derrida attributes to Freud, thanks to the 'polycentrism
of dream representation'.[23] I am citing his essay 'Freud and the Scene of
Writing', which focuses on that tiny but fascinating Freud text 'Notiz
Über den "Wunderblock"', usually referred to in English as 'A Note
Upon The "Mystic Writing-Pad"', though you might like to imagine it
as the note on the miracle pad, the miracle block or miracle book.[24] 'We
must be several in order to write, and even to "perceive"' (FSW, p. 226),
the mad philosopher says.[25] 'The *sociality* of writing as *drama* requires
an entirely different discipline' (FSW, p. 227). That's why drama, and
Shakespeare above all, is so crucial to understanding what deconstruction, if there is any, is about. Deconstruction is inventive or it is nothing
at all, as Derrida has remarked: invention happens, if it happens, only
in multiple voices.[26]

– OK, that wasn't what I was saying, but I think I'm with you. 'Miracle
play': among other things, then, it's a question of trying to read or think
backwards, preposterously as Puck would say. (You recall his words in *A
Midsummer Night's Dream*: 'And those things do best please me / That
befall prepost'rously' [3.2.120–1].) Isn't that also what Shakespeare's
plays are, things that work backwards, animal-machines that see their
own futures? It's the very fabric of a play like *A Midsummer Night's
Dream*, but it's also what makes the so-called history plays historical,
even when they break with the usual historical account and invent (as in
the case of Falstaff or more accurately perhaps, Falstaff and the other,
all the others, a motley crew of hundreds including Prince Hal, the king

in waiting). As the crazy 'I' narrating *The Sacred Fount* intimates, there's always something preposterous about a miracle, in the sense that 'one's on the track of the cause' as soon as the word 'miracle' is in front of you: you're already behind.

– Back, as you've been saying, back to backing and backtracking vocals, in a background that's right in front of us. You have to catch up. That's what is always going on with Shakespeare. As Harold Bloom says: 'As we read Shakespeare, we are always engaged in catching up.'[27] But let's recall the initial promise of the title for a moment: 'a title is always a promise', as Derrida stresses.[28] After all, for all the preposterousness of 'play' preceding or being the scene or staging of 'miracle', surely the phrase 'miracle play' will have been taken as primarily referring to 'A dramatization based on events in the life of Jesus or the legends of the saints, popular in the Middle Ages' (to give it in the words of the *OED*)?

– Yes, I imagine that may have led a few people astray, at least provisionally. And there are of course numerous links between *Henry IV* and medieval miracle, mystery or morality plays. There is the correspondence, for example, between Falstaff and the figure of Vice, an identification of admittedly limited value, and then there is the enigmatic place of a certain Nicholas as evoked by Gadshill (see 2.1.59), St Nicholas or Nick, patron saint of children, scholars and robbers, who in at least one version of a medieval play 'miraculously restores to life three slain clerics'.[29] But for me it's a question of a sort of palaeonymic deployment of the phrase: 'miracle play', in other words, *after Derrida*. Shakespeare's writings, all of their poematic theatre, irreducibly plural, together or alone, instantiate *miracle play*.

– In fact, you know, the term 'miracle play' does not appear as such until 1602.[30] It is as if anachrony were written into the term. And there is something funny going on, in any case, already with this word 'miracle' (and its cognates, including the adjective 'miraculous'), something to which Shakespeare's writing bears witness, while also in singular fashion meddling with it. There is a sort of dehiscence within the history of the word, where the religious signification sheers off, and 'miracle' appears simply as a word for . . .

– Simply? Did you say 'simply'?

– Yes, the order of the day here is simply 'simple'. The *Oxford English Dictionary*, under the entry for 'miracle', starts off with the quite charming, comical phrase 'simple uses'. 'Miracle', we read: 'I. Simple uses. **1. a.** A marvellous event not ascribable to human power or the operation of any natural force and therefore attributed to supernatural, esp. divine, agency; *esp.* an act (e.g. of healing) demonstrating control over nature and serving as evidence that the agent is either divine or divinely favoured.' The earliest recorded appearance of the word in this 'simple' sense, according to the *OED*, is around 1160. Then, under sense 4, there is this other 'simple use' of 'miracle' (it is difficult, I confess, to refrain from slipping away here into a revery on this venerable diction-ary's use of 'use', at once solemn and hilarious, the seemingly unmen-tionable use of 'use' as distinct from 'mention', the funny time one might have with undoing, precisely in the spirit of Shakespeare or Cixous, the demented instrumentalism of the dictionary and of all the institutions correspondingly believed to function on the basis of such instrumental-ism, 'believed', what a word, no place apparently for that here, like a ghost, yes, it is to come back). 'Miracle', 'simple uses' number 4: 'A remarkable, wonderful, or (in weakened sense) very surprising phenom-enon or event; an achievement or occurrence seemingly beyond human power; an outstanding achievement.' Now this sense of 'miracle', which crosses and crosses with the 'use' of sense 1a, doubles or iterates it, making it different from itself, above all in the veering off from the attribution to 'supernatural, esp. divine, agency' towards something less clearly or explicitly religious, marked by the word 'seemingly' ('seem-ingly beyond human power'), this 'miracle' (and I will come back to that phrase, *this miracle*, it in turn is already a citation or iteration), the phenomenon or event of 'miracle' in this sense, according to the *OED*, dates back to 1586. The dehiscence, the doubling or we might even say the counterfeiting of 'miracle' in this context is also evident in the *use*, as they say, of the adjective 'miraculous'. Traced back to the mid-fifteenth century, and defined as 'Of the nature of a miracle; produced or effected by a miracle; not explicable by natural laws; supernatural' (sense 1a), 'miraculous' is subjected, in the later sixteenth century, to a discernible shift. It takes on a more ambiguous, less markedly religious sense, defined in the *OED* as 'Resembling a miracle; so extraordinary as to appear supernatural; remarkable, astonishing' (sense 2). The earli-est recorded instance of 'miraculous' in this sense is Edward Fenton's *Certaine Secrete Wonders of Nature* in 1569: 'It may seeme miraculous & almost incredible, that fishes do flye.' These fish, one might be led to imagine, fly for more than four hundred years, all the way into the writings of Cixous and Derrida. More generally, it could be said, what happens to 'miracle' and the 'miraculous' in the late sixteenth century strangely prefigures what is at issue in the emergence of the space of the 'uncanny' ('uncanny' as having to do with what resembles or is seemingly or apparently supernatural) some two hundred years later.

– Don't get started on the uncanny. We'd be here all night. Stay focused. As for that shift in the sense of 'miracle', Shakespeare, of course, is onto it, mixed up in it, from the beginning. For one of the earliest instances of 'miracle' in the sense of remarkable, wonderful, very surprising, seemingly or apparently supernatural, the *OED* cites *The Merry Wives of Windsor*. It is when Falstaff tells Ford, disguised as Master Brook, about how he 'suffered the pangs of three several deaths', the last of which was 'to be stopped in like a strong distillation with stinking clothes that fretted in their own grease': 'It was a miracle to 'scape suffocation', Falstaff says (see 3.5.86–94). The *OED* might just as well, however, or still more appositely have cited the so-called first part of *Henry IV*. But let's stop calling it by this name, let's follow Harold Bloom's suggestion and call it *Falstaff's Wake*.[31] Either that or *Falstaff's Miracle*. The *OED*, I was saying, could just as well have cited Falstaff, yes, him again. As if he might lay claim to some patent on the thing, 'miracle' in this sense is Falstaff's: 'miracle' is Falstaffian. So much takes off from him, the one whom Bloom, in the course of a thirty-five page eulogy, more than once calls precisely 'a miracle'.[32] Falstaff, writes Bloom, 'is a miracle in the creation of personality' (p. 313): he is 'the signature of Shakespeare's originality, of his breakthrough into an art more nearly his own' (p. 278). With Falstaff, as a little later with Hamlet, Shakespeare creates an unprecedentedly powerful 'illusion' ('if you want to call it "illusion"', says Bloom) of 'being a real person'. Falstaff, like Hamlet, is a 'miracle' (p. 287). This miracle, for Bloom, has to do with Shakespeare's 'astonishing ability to represent change' (p. 280): 'Falstaff, like Hamlet, is always transforming himself, always thinking, speaking, and overhearing himself in a quicksilver metamorphosis' (p. 281).

– That's good, if I may say so, *overhearing himself in a quicksilver metamorphosis*. But it's not just a matter of that, of 'self-overhearing' as Bloom calls it.[33] There's the mercurial magic of telepathic writing, a shivering of voice, irreducible play of voices in the voice, dissemination of character, vertigo of place, time out of joint.

– Catching up with Shakespeare is about the future as much as the past. Bloom seems to touch on that when he makes the apparently straightforward observation: 'we want to hear what Falstaff will say next' (p. 314). He stresses Falstaff's satirical power, his irrepressible wit, as well as the sense that (in William Empson's phrase) 'Falstaff is the first major joke by the English against their class system' (in Bloom, p. 293). Bloom admiringly recalls A.C. Bradley's view that the 'essence of Falstaff' consists in 'the bliss of freedom gained in humour'; Falstaff, says Bradley, 'lifts us into the atmosphere of perfect freedom' (cited in Bloom, pp. 296–7).

– If I can just butt in for a second: at the back of your mind, I know, you're feeling strongly tempted to pick up here also on the characterisation of Falstaff as a rogue, and to link it with Derrida's discussion of the English and especially Shakespearean senses of the word 'rogue', in *Rogues: Two Essays on Reason*: Falstaff, in other words, *as* rogue state.[34] Everything you are in the process of trying to formulate regarding 'miracle' is also evident in that meddling imp of a word, 'rogue'. It too bears a kind of Falstaffian mark or signature. I imagine you might start by working backwards from that marvellous four-word sentence he comes out with in *The Merry Wives of Windsor*: 'Reason, you rogue, reason' (2.2.12). Derrida cites the OED on 'rogue' but, a shade roguishly, neglects to say, chooses to hold back on the 'playful' sense, in which 'rogue' is 'a term of endearment'.[35] This is 'rogue' as 'One who is of a mischievous disposition': 'Common as a playful term of reproof or reproach, and frequently used as a term of endearment by 17th century dramatists' (OED, sense 3). Again, the word is identified with Falstaff in its first recorded usage in this sense. The OED quotes Doll Tearsheet in *The Second Part of Henry IV* addressing him: 'Ah, you sweet little rogue, you! . . . Ah, rogue, i'faith, I love thee' (2.4.213–16).

– Speak for yourself. For Harold Bloom, as I was saying, Falstaff is above all 'a teacher': he is 'the Socrates of Eastcheap' (p. 275): he 'instructs us in freedom – not a freedom *in* society, but *from* society' (p. 276). This freedom Bloom also characterises as the miraculous 'blessing' which is encapsulated, for him, in the great Falstaffian phrase: 'more life' (p. 313). 'Falstaff teaches us *not to moralize*' (p. 297). He is 'neither immoral nor amoral but of another realm, the order of play' (p. 298). And this, concludes Bloom, is 'the essence of Shakespeare's dramatic art: the principle of play' (p. 299).

– I would subscribe to all of that, but would like to complicate and, I hope, enrich this reading. Bloom's account is character-based or, we might say, in a bloated neologism that perhaps does not deserve to survive beyond the end of this sentence, characterologicocentric. It is not only a question of Falstaff as 'a miracle in the creation of personality' or as an embodiment of 'the order of play', but also of trying to reckon with a thinking of play that goes beyond the subject, of play as play of dreams and letters, a sort of polycentric thinking of the mighty power of the *might* that might entail, in an instant, at any instant, a miraculous catch. One way of trying to do this might be in terms of the play of the word 'miracle' itself, of what this little changeling of a word is doing in Shakespeare's play. For it seems to me that it merits another reading, it summons up a strange supplementary dimension, a third sense to mingle and meddle irrevocably with those we have so far tracked through the *OED*. 'Miracle', in this other sense, has to do with a kind of laying on of hands, in particular the writing hand or hands of Shakespeare, where 'miracle' signifies the very phenomenon of play, the magical shimmery surface-depth of drama, in which we, as readers or spectators, know *more than* Falstaff, and this on account of the structure of the text, its dramatic irony, its preposterousness, its exposition of magical thinking, its radical elaboration of 'iteration' and play within and beyond the play. 'Miracle' in Shakespeare is always already caught up in the poetic event that is itself, the net that is (in Derrida's terms) the nomination of itself.[36]

– How would the *Oxford English Dictionary* deal with that?

– I know. It's a funny thought, isn't it? To define 'miracle', the *OED* would need to set out its play *within* the play or plays of Shakespeare, 'miracle' as self-remarking, irreducibly plural scenography that stages, in the same instant, the very ground of the authority of a definition, of any and every definition in the dictionary.

– Before coming to the moment in question, then, the place where Falstaff says (or Shakespeare writes) *miracle*, we need to track the context of this 'iteration'.

– You're about to nick my idea, I see. Bloom calls it *Falstaff's Wake*; you call it *Falstaff's Miracle*; I call it *The First Part of Henry IV*. In *The First Part of Henry IV* Shakespeare seems to me to make a kind of breakthrough not just with the miraculous 'creation of personality', but with the strange nature of 'iteration' as such. *The First Part of Henry IV* contains not only the remarkable instance of 'iteration' that I know you're about to quote, but also the first recorded instance in English of the word 'cital' (5.2.61), meaning 'citation' or 'calling of oneself to account', as well as the first recorded instance in English, and the only instance anywhere in Shakespeare, of the word 'misquote' (5.2.13).[37] The play is deeply preoccupied with the meddling, comical, magical, not to mention roguish or indeed devilish strangeness of iteration. Think of those references to the starling (1.3.223) and the parrot (2.4.97), Prince Henry's parroting of 'Percy's mind' (2.4.99–105) and all of that extended, rather brutal, comical but demented play on the word 'anon' as the Prince and Poins get the tapster Francis to repeat, over and over: 'Anon, anon, sir' (2.4.35ff). I am onto something with all of this, I am on, I'm sure: anon, anon.

– No, this was my idea in the first place. Anyway the two things belong together, that's the point. The breakthrough in creating or counterfeiting what Bloom calls 'a real person' is indissociably entwined, entwinned, spinning out of the more narrowly textual or writerly sort of breakthrough you just evoked concerning the parrot.

– Did I say that?

– 'Damnable iteration': that's a key to *Falstaff's Miracle*. It's one of the innumerable treasures that the mad philosopher lets you into: 'everything is in Shakespeare', as he says, but also anything in Shakespeare leads to everything, anything can be a key, starting with iteration or iterability which of course has already started.[38] That is the ordinary miracle of place. To iterate: that is, 'to say, mention, or assert again or repeatedly; to repeat' (*OED*, sense 2). Damnable iteration: for better for worse, there's always more than one voice in the voice and no saying where it starts.

– Just ask yourself: What is going on in Shakespeare's iteration of Biblical sayings? Who is iterating? Who is it iterated?

– I'm sorry. Did you say rated or iterated?

> *Falstaff.* . . . An old lord of the Council rated me the other day in the street about you, sir, but I marked him not; and yet he talked very wisely, but I regarded him not; and yet he talked wisely, and in the street too.
> *Prince Henry.* Thou didst well, for wisdom cries out in the streets and no man regards it.
> *Falstaff.* O, thou hast damnable iteration, and art indeed able to corrupt a saint. Thou hast done much harm upon me, Hal, God forgive thee for it. Before I knew thee, Hal, I knew nothing; and now am I, if a man should speak truly, little better than one of the wicked. I must give over this life, and I will give it over. By the Lord, an I do not, I am a villain. I'll be damned for never a king's son in Christendom.
> *Prince Henry.* Where shall we take a purse tomorrow, Jack?
> (1.2.80–95)

The Bishop's Bible, not the one he's later to listen to sitting in the church at Stratford, with only a little time to go (perhaps in a dream thinking back to Hotspur near the end of the play, presented with some letters to read, sighing 'I cannot read them now /. . . the time of life is short' [5.2.80–1]: as Derrida stresses in that truly crazily recessive future anterior, *life will have been so short*[39]) – but let's leave aside the question of iteration between Bibles, rating Bibles iterating or rating one another – the Bishop's Bible, the one scholars suppose Shakespeare is recalling here, at Proverbs 1: 20, reads as follows: 'Wisdom crieth without, and putteth forth her voice in the streets'; and verse 24: 'Because I have called, and ye refused, I have stretched out my hand, and no man regarded.'[40] Where does the iteration begin? Is it with Hal as he iterates Jack who recalls being rated in the street without apparently realising that he is iterating, or in effect being iterated by, the Bible? Or is it with Jack as he iterates, indulging in that 'parody of religious cant', the 'tedious and inane repetition' (as David Bevington puts it) of *homiologia*?[41] Is there a subject of 'damnable iteration'? Who is who here, in these words, and where? 'Thou hast done much harm upon me, Hal, God forgive thee for it. Before I knew thee, Hal, I knew nothing': supplementing the strange meddling of voice, this apparent inversion of character and narrative, history and identity (Hal teaching Jack, rather than vice versa), would participate in the logic of what you have elsewhere called the 'iteraphonic', what you propose as a 'term without term' for 'iterability in the voice', a kind of magical thinking in writing that goes 'faster than time' (*HCFL*, p. 63), to recall a phrase from the mad philosopher. It is a matter of what you call 'the meddling imps of words shared, inhabiting and traversing, as if magically or demonically'.[42] Iteration, iterability, iteraphonia: they jump borders, they move faster than time, not only between one character and another (without knowledge), or between one scene and another, but also between one play and another, in the instant of the poematic.

– OK, I'll do my damnedest not to repeat myself. Let's cut and thrust to Falstaff's 'miracle'. He's recounting what happened to him after he and three others stole 'money of the King's coming down the hill' (2.2.50–1), only to have it stolen from them in turn, moments later, without any fight, by others (in other words by Prince Hal and Poins who, speeding ahead, back to the tavern in Eastcheap, have been playing their game of 'anon' with the unsuspecting Francis). From one game of 'anon' to another. It is already, then, a play within the play, the Prince and Poins in their own little theatre within the theatre, having played their several parts all the way from London to Kent and back (see, in particular, 1.2.173ff). This is where we encounter both the 'rogue' and the 'miracle'. The Prince asks him where the 'thousand pound' is.

> *Prince Henry.* Where is it, Jack, where is it?
> *Falstaff.* Where is it? Taken from us it is. A hundred upon poor four of us.
> *Prince Henry.* What, a hundred, man?
> *Falstaff.* I am a rogue if I were not at half-sword with a dozen of them two hours together. I have scaped by miracle. I am eight times thrust through the doublet, four through the hose, my buckler cut through and through, my sword hacked like a handsaw – *ecce signum*! I never dealt better since I was a man. All would not do. A plague of all cowards! Let them speak. If they speak more or less than truth, they are villains and the sons of darkness.
> (2.4.154–65)

Ecce signum! Behold the sign. Falstaff's iteration of the Catholic Mass points at once to the singularity of the 'miracle' to which it would purportedly bear witness and into the phantasmoneiric flux of Shakespeare's writing, here the dreamy but miraculous displacement in particular perhaps of *hacking* into *hawking*, of Falstaff's 'hacked like a handsaw' into Hamlet's claiming to know 'a hawk from a handsaw' (*Hamlet*, 2.2.374), or of 'ta[king] a thousand pound' (2.4.153) while being asked to take Falstaff's word (else 'they are villains and the sons of darkness') into 'tak[ing] the ghost's word for a thousand pound' (*Hamlet*, 3.2.270–1). 'I have scaped by miracle', says Falstaff: behold the sign of this sword 'hacked like a handsaw'. This is a kind of 'damnable iteration' of 'miracle', a *miracle* play that meddles with the sense of 'miracle' at once as a 'marvellous event . . . attributed to supernatural, esp. divine, agency; *esp.* an act . . . serving as evidence that the agent is either divine or divinely favoured' *and* as a 'remarkable, wonderful, or (in weakened sense) very surprising phenomenon or event; an achievement or occurrence seemingly beyond human power; an outstanding achievement'. For the iteration goes beyond that: the miracle play of 'miracle' here also and above all includes the *ecce signum* of the play itself. The 'miracle' is self-remarking, already marked as play, *in* a play, counterfeited, in a play within a play. Prince Henry and Poins know, and we know that they know, that Falstaff's 'miracle' is a fiction and that it is the effect of that play-within-the-play which Poins and the Prince have been at once directing and acting in. Falstaff's 'miracle' is always already ironic, preposterous, not his or anyone else's, a thing of the play in which the play's the thing.

– I know why you have been quoting *Hamlet* apropos this inscribing of 'miracle' in the play and of the play in 'miracle', thus of a play over and beyond any neatly enclosed 'play within the play', play no longer limited by the activities, language or representation of a subject but caught up already, in advance, in the nets of a kind of telephonic or telepathic scenario as a new thinking of the 'poetics of the event'. It is because of the way, as if by chance, that Hamlet, in soliloquy, draws on the word 'miraculous' (one of only three appearances of this word in Shakespeare's work[43]):

> . . . About, my brains. Hum, I have heard
> That guilty creatures sitting at a play
> Have by the very cunning of the scene
> Been struck so to the soul, that presently
> They have proclaimed their malefactions;
> For murder, though it have no tongue, will speak
> With most miraculous organ. I'll have these players
> Play something like the murder of my father
> Before mine uncle. (2.2.541–9)

The play within the play in *Hamlet* is in effect already being specified here as the 'miraculous organ'. But of course we only know this on account of Shakespeare's dramaturgic consorting with telepathic or magical thinking, with the form of soliloquy as 'miraculous organ' in turn. It is not just self-overhearing (as Harold Bloom has it), it is a strangely private-public theatre, a sort of interior magic show that passes show, the exposure or exscription of a character's otherwise secret and unknown thoughts and feelings.

– I appreciate that you must feel as if you've been doing most of the talking, but I would like to say something – by way of finishing off – about Falstaff's death, or at any event about Prince Henry's epitaph and Falstaff's –

– Finishing off, who's talking about finishing off? Cixous remarks and Derrida recalls: 'No dead person has ever said their last word.'[44] That's what makes drama the very counterfeit of life: no one in Shakespeare has said their last word, least of all Falstaff.

– Yes, this is why Bloom wants to call the play *Falstaff's Wake*. He talks about it as 'the most joyous representation of secular resurrection ever staged' (p. 305). Derrida's interest in *Romeo and Juliet* has to do with what he calls 'the theatre of the impossible', with the power of 'the simulacrum' (or the dramatic 'counterfeit', we might say) to reveal 'the theatre of the impossible' in which 'two people each outlive each other' (AC, p. 422). You have gone on elsewhere about Shakespeare's (and Derrida's) evident fascination with this miracle of double survival, in particular with regard to what W.H. Auden once called the greatest love poem in the English language, *Antony and Cleopatra*. But the figure of coming back from the dead, miraculous recovery or escape, is of course everywhere in Shakespeare. It's not just in *Romeo and Juliet* or *Antony and Cleopatra* or even in those final plays such as *Pericles*, *Cymbeline* and *The Winter's Tale* that are specifically designated as 'miracle plays', for example, by H.W. Fawkner.[45] When '*Falstaff riseth up*' (as the stage direction puts it: see 5.4.109), it is doubtless a parody of that coming back from the dead that is characteristic of medieval miracle plays, the sort of parody that is subject to attack in the celebrated Lollard polemic 'A Tretis of Miraclis Pleyinge', an attack doubtless impelled by what T.G. Bishop calls 'fear of blurred boundaries between authoritative and parasitic signs'.[46] But it is also immeasurably more and other than this. As Bishop observes:

> Shakespeare's poetry does what medieval drama always threatened to do, what Aquinas indicated was always implied by the logic of a sacramental semiosis: it unbinds itself and its shaping power from the Church. At the heart of Shakespeare's drama is a power confident that words can incarnate lives before the eyes of an audience without the institutional apparatus of the Church to guarantee their orthodoxy, and without a structure of dogma external to the dramatic occasion.[47]

What Shakespeare spirits up in *Henry IV* is a new kind of 'scaping by miracle', a new writing of miracle play.

– Why don't you try to read this final passage then? Prince Henry addresses the dead Hotspur, whom he has slain, then notices 'poor Jack'. You can be the Prince, I'll be Falstaff.

Prince Henry.   Thy ignominy sleep with thee in the grave,
But not remembered in thy epitaph!
He spieth Falstaff on the ground
What, old acquaintance, could not all this flesh
Keep in a little life? Poor Jack, farewell!
I could have better spared a better man.
O, I should have a heavy miss of thee
If I were much in love with vanity.
Death hath not struck so fat a deer today,
Though many dearer, in this bloody fray.
Embowelled will I see thee by and by.
Till then, in blood by noble Percy lie.   *Exit*

Falstaff riseth up

Falstaff. Embowelled! If thou embowel me today, I'll give you leave to powder me and eat me too tomorrow. 'Sblood, 'twas time to counterfeit, or that hot termagant Scot had paid me, scot and lot too. Counterfeit? I lie, I am no counterfeit. To die is to be a counterfeit, for he is but the counterfeit of a man who hath not the life of a man; but to counterfeit dying, when a man thereby liveth, is to be no counterfeit, but the true and perfect image of life indeed. The better part of valour is discretion, in the which better part I have saved my life. (5.4.99–119)

– So much for dear friends. It's all about the strangeness of soliloquy –

– I beg your pardon?

– I said the strangeness of soliloquy –

– In which Falstaff apparently returns from the dead (as Prince Henry says, in astonishment, on seeing him again a few lines later: 'Art thou alive? / Or is it fantasy that plays upon our eyesight?' [5.4.131–2]). This speech (as if by 'miraculous organ'), witnessed by no one *in* the play, also plays on the fantasy of *our* eyesight, on a phantasmoneiric fiction that we are *not* witnesses ourselves ('Nothing confutes me but eyes and nobody sees me', as Falstaff goes on to say [5.4.124–5]). It veers at such incredible speed and in so many directions at once. Try to track and read, for example, the weird repetition of 'counterfeit' here, a word that appears repeatedly in reference to the king, just a little earlier (5.4.27, 34), but when Falstaff is not present, and that at the same prefigures the counterfeit 'death' of Henry IV in the so-called second part of *Henry IV*. Or try to trace the iteraphonic force of 'life' here (recall Falstaff's great motto: 'Give me life' [5.3.59]), 'life' injecting itself after life, all the way up to and into the collected writings of Hélène Cixous. Or think on how this 'wake' is hauntingly inscribed in the '[scape] by miracle' encountered earlier. It is what everything in the play will have been leading up to. Preposterous and magical, this is *miracle* strangely deferred, miracle iterated, miracle iterable. *Tableau.*   [*Exit*]

– Hang on. Where did you go? There was something else I had to say. A brief epilogue, that's all. But you're gone. How did that happen? You're impossible. No one now but me . . . Talk about bad timing . . . You mentioned *Antony and Cleopatra* as a love poem. Cixous also speaks of it, I seem to remember, as a miracle. Yes: the 'miracle' of Antony and Cleopatra, she says, 'is to have captured death at last, to have appropriated the enemy, to have put death into their enchanted bed . . . to have substituted forever for the unlivable absence an absolute embrace'.[48] And then in 'Aphorism Countertime', when Derrida speaks about the theatre of the impossible telling the truth, it has to do with love, with the way in which any two lovers pledge to keep the other, interiorise the other, beyond death. As he remarks: 'This double interiorization would be possible neither in monadic interiority nor in the logic of "objective" time and space. It takes place nevertheless every time I love' (AC, p. 422). It makes me think of that line near the end of *The Taming of the Shrew*: 'Love wrought these miracles' (5.1.112). And then there is a certain sonnet, which links love, the name of love, the act of nomination, with the miracle of writing, 'this miracle'. This is the *might* of miracle play, as if it had already dreamt while dreaming itself up for 'the mighty power of the *might*' of which Derrida writes and which he finds in Cixous:

Since brass, nor stone, nor earth, nor boundless sea,
But sad mortality o'ersways their power,
How with this rage shall beauty hold a plea,
Whose action is no stronger than a flower?
O how shall summer's honey breath hold out
Against the wrackful siege of batt'ring days,
When rocks impregnable are not so stout,
Nor gates of steel so strong but time decays?
O fearful meditation; where, alack,
Shall time's best jewel from time's chest lie hid?
Or what strong hand can hold his swift foot back?
Or who his spoil or beauty can forbid?
   O none, unless this miracle have might
   That in black ink my love may still shine bright.[49]

Notes

1. References to Shakespeare are based on the following editions: *Henry IV Part One*, ed. David Bevington (Oxford: Oxford University Press, 1987); *Henry IV Part Two*, ed. René Weis (Oxford: Oxford University Press, 1997); *A Midsummer Night's Dream*, ed. Harold F. Brooks (London: Routledge, 1979); *The Merry Wives of Windsor*, ed. David Crane (Cambridge: Cambridge University Press, 1997); *Hamlet*, ed. Philip Edwards (Cambridge: Cambridge University Press, 2003); *Macbeth*, ed. A.R. Braunmuller (Cambridge: Cambridge University Press, 1997); *The Tempest*, ed. David Lindley (Cambridge: Cambridge University Press, 2002); *The Taming of the Shrew*, ed. H. J. Oliver (Oxford: Oxford University Press, 1982); *Shakespeare's Sonnets*, ed. with an analytic commentary by Stephen Booth (New Haven: Yale University Press, 1977).
2. Henry James, *The Sacred Fount* (New York: New Directions, 1983), p. 187.
3. Jacques Derrida, *Specters of Marx: The State of the Debt, the Work of Mourning, and the New International*, trans. Peggy Kamuf (London: Routledge, 1994). Further page references are given parenthetically in the

main body of the text, preceded by 'SM' where appropriate. References to the original French text, *Spectres de Marx: L'État de la dette, le travail du deuil et la nouvelle Internationale* (Paris: Galilée, 1993), are given parenthetically, where appropriate, following a slash.

4. Jacques Derrida, 'Différance', in *Margins of Philosophy*, trans. Alan Bass (Chicago: Chicago University Press, 1982), p. 27.

5. Jacques Derrida, *Of Grammatology*, trans. Gayatri Chakravorty Spivak (Baltimore: Johns Hopkins University Press, 1976), p. 162; *De la grammatologie* (Paris: Les Éditions de Minuit, 1967), p. 233. Further page references are given parenthetically in the main body of the text.

6. Rodolphe Gasché, 'Thinking, Without Wonder', *Epoché*, 10:2 (2006), pp. 327–40, here, in particular, p. 328. Further page references to this chapter are given parenthetically in the main body of the text, preceded by 'TWW' where appropriate.

7. See Sarah Wood, 'Surprise in Literature', *Angelaki* 1:1 (1993), pp. 58–68, here p. 60.

8. It is one of our concerns here, indeed, to suggest how numerous and significant the miraculous 'pockets' in Derrida are. Besides *H.C. for Life, That is To Say . . .* and other texts we go on to cite here, we might note at least the following additional references: *Given Time: I. Counterfeit Money*, trans. Peggy Kamuf (London: Chicago University Press, 1992), p. 123; *Monolingualism of the Other; or, The Prosthesis of Origin*, trans. Patrick Mensah (Stanford: Stanford University Press, 1998), pp. 20, 23, 72, 93; 'Faith and Knowledge: The Two Sources of "Religion" at the Limits of Reason Alone', trans. Sam Weber, in *Religion*, ed. Jacques Derrida and Gianni Vattimo (Cambridge: Polity Press, 1998), pp. 63–4; *Demeure: Fiction and Testimony* (with Maurice Blanchot's *The Instant of My Death*), trans. Elizabeth Rottenberg (Stanford: Stanford University Press, 2000), p. 75; '"Above All, No Journalists!"', trans. Samuel Weber, in *Religion and Media*, ed. Hent de Vries and Samuel Weber (Stanford: Stanford University Press, 2001), p. 76; and *Echographies of Television: Filmed Interviews* (Jacques Derrida with Bernard Stiegler), trans. Jennifer Bajorek (Cambridge: Polity, 2002), p. 117. In happy corroboration of our concerns here, see also Michael Naas's brilliant study, *Miracle and Machine: Jacques Derrida and the Two Sources of Religion, Science, and the Media* (New York: Fordham University Press, 2012), a copy of which reached us, as if by what Mark Twain calls mental telegraphy, just as this chapter was completed. In answer to the question of how to understand the word *miracle* in Derrida's work, Naas observes: 'As is always the case with Derrida's terminology, it must be read both in relationship to its traditional meaning and as a radical interruption of that meaning' (p. 97).

9. Jacques Derrida, in Catherine Malabou and Jacques Derrida, *Counterpath: Traveling with Jacques Derrida*, trans. David Wills (Stanford: Stanford University Press, 2004), p. 147 (trans. slightly modified); *Jacques Derrida, La Contre-allée* (Paris: La Quinzaine Littéraire – Louis Vitton, 1999), p. 147.

10. Jacques Derrida, 'Aphorism Countertime', trans. Nicholas Royle, in *Acts of Literature*, ed. Derek Attridge (London and New York: Routledge, 1992), pp. 414–33, here p. 422. Further page references are given parenthetically in the main body of the text, preceded by 'AC' where appropriate.

11. Jacques Derrida, 'Force and Signification', in *Writing and Difference*, trans. Alan Bass (London: Routledge & Kegan Paul, 1978), p. 4; 'Force et significa-tion', *L'écriture et la difference* (Paris: Éditions du Seuil, 1967), p. 10.

12. Jacques Derrida, 'This Strange Institution Called Literature', trans. Geoffrey Bennington and Rachel Bowlby, in *Acts of Literature*, p. 63.

13. See Frank Kermode, 'Endings, Continued', in Sanford Budick and Wolfgang Iser (eds), *Languages of the Unsayable: The Play of Negativity in Literature and Literary Theory* (New York: Columbia University Press, 1989), p. 73.

14. Hélène Cixous, *Portrait of Jacques Derrida as a Young Jewish Saint*, trans. Beverley Bie Brahic (New York: Columbia University Press, 2004), pp. 58–9; *Portrait de Jacques Derrida en Jeune Saint Juif* (Paris: Galilée, 2001), pp. 56–7.

15. 'One can neither classify nor count the ghost, it is number itself, it is numerous, innumerable as number, one can neither count on it nor with it' (Derrida, *Specters of Marx*, p. 138).

16. Maurice Blanchot, 'Literature and the Right to Death', in *The Work of Fire*, trans. Charlotte Mandell (Stanford: Stanford University Press, 1995), pp. 300–44, here p. 326. Further page references are given parenthetically in the main body of the text.

17. Jacques Derrida, *H.C. for Life, That Is to Say . . .*, trans. Laurent Milesi and Stefan Herbrechter (Stanford: Stanford University Press, 2000). Further page references are given parenthetically in the main body of the text, pre-ceded by 'HCFL' where appropriate. References to the original French text, *H.C pour la vie, c'est à dire . . .* (Paris: Galilée, 2002), are given parentheti-cally, where appropriate, following a slash.

18. For a recent critical exposition of this 'might', see Mark Dawson, 'Of Force and the Future – Hélène Cixous's Poematic "Might"', *Oxford Literary Review*, 33:2 (2011), pp. 151–65.

19. The Song of Solomon, 2:8.

20. As Derrida puts it: 'The example is not substitutable; but at the same time the same aporia always remains: this irreplaceability must be exemplary, that is, replaceable. The irreplaceable must allow itself to be replaced on the spot' (*Demeure: Fiction and Testimony*, p. 41).

21. Jacques Derrida, *The Ear of the Other: Otobiography, Transference, Translation*, trans. Peggy Kamuf, ed. Christie V. McDonald (New York: Schocken Books, 1985), p. 69.

22. See ibid., p. 69, and cf. Derrida's remarks about play regarding *Romeo and Juliet* in 'This Strange Institution Called Literature', p. 64.

23. See Jacques Derrida, 'Freud and the Scene of Writing', in *Writing and Difference*, trans. Alan Bass (London: Routledge & Kegan Paul, 1978), pp. 196–231, here p. 217. Further page references are given parenthetically in the main body of the text, preceded by 'FSW' where appropriate.

24. Sigmund Freud, 'A Note Upon The "Mystic Writing-Pad"', *The Standard Edition of the Complete Psychological Works*, trans. James Strachey (London: Vintage/Hogarth Press, 2001), vol. 19, pp. 225–32.

25. Concerning 'the fundamental property of writing', that is to say *spacing*, Derrida writes: 'diastem and time becoming space; an unfolding as well, on an original site, of meanings which irreversible, linear consecution, moving from present point to present point, could only tend to repress, and (to a

certain extent) could only fail to repress. In particular in so-called phonetic writing. The latter's complicity with logos (or the time of logic), which is dominated by the principle of non-contradiction, the cornerstone of all metaphysics of presence, is profound. Now in every silent or not wholly phonic spacing out of meaning, concatenations are possible which no longer obey the linearity of logical time, the time of consciousness or pre-consciousness, the time of "verbal representations". The border between the non-phonetic space of writing (even "phonetic" writing) and the space of the stage (*scène*) of dreams is uncertain . . . A certain polycentrism of dream representation is irreconcilable with the apparently linear unfolding of pure verbal representations' (FSW, p. 217).

26. See Jacques Derrida, 'Psyche: Invention of the Other', trans. Catherine Porter, in *Psyche: Inventions of the Other*, ed. Peggy Kamuf and Elizabeth Rottenberg (Stanford: Stanford University Press, 2007), vol. 1, 1–47, here, pp. 23, 47.

27. Harold Bloom, *Shakespeare: The Invention of the Human* (London: Fourth Estate, 1999), p. 271.

28. See, for example, Derrida, *Mémoires: for Paul de Man*, trans. Cecile Lindsay, Jonathan Culler and Eduardo Cadava (New York: Columbia University Press, 1986), p. 115.

29. See Bevington (ed.), *Henry IV Part One*, p. 163, n.

30. The *OED* cites Robert Carew's *Survey of Cornwall*: 'The Guary miracle, in English, a miracle-play, is a kinde of Enterlude, compiled in Cornish out of some scripture history, with that grossenes, which accompanied the Romanes *vetus Comedia*.'

31. Bloom, *Shakespeare: The Invention of the Human*, p. 305.

32. See Bloom's chapters on *Henry IV* and *The Merry Wives of Windsor*, in ibid., pp. 271–318. Further page references are given parenthetically in the main body of the text.

33. Elsewhere in *Shakespeare: The Invention of the Human*, for example, Bloom asserts that '*overhearing [one]self speak* . . . is not just a question of rhetoricity or word consciousness; it is the essence of Shakespeare's greatest originalities in the representation of character, of thinking, and of person-ality' (p. 423). His wording here seems at once to assume and underscore thinking *as* character-based or personality-centred. The interest of 'Miracle Play' is rather in figures and ways of thinking that catch up, exceed or fall short of 'self', reinscribing 'self-overhearing' in a Shakespearean practice of telepathic writing.

34. For Derrida's discussion of the senses of 'rogue' see his *Rogues: Two Essays on Reason*, trans. Pascale-Anne Brault and Michael Naas (Stanford: Stanford University Press, 2005), p. 93.

35. In correspondence at any rate with this usage of 'rogue' in English, of the French 'voyou' (rogue, rascal) he remarks, at the beginning of section 8 of 'The Reason of the Strongest (Are There Rogue States?)': '"Voyou!" . . ., I neglected to say, can be turned with the right intonation into something tender, affectionate, maternal (when I was little, my maternal grandmother would sometimes say, pretending to be angry with me, "Voyou, va!" [You little rascal!])' (ibid., p. 76).

36. See, in particular, *H.C. for Life*, p. 97.

37. For the first recorded use of 'misquotation', *OED* cites Thomas Heywood, in his *Apology for Actors* in 1612, writing about 'Infinite faults', such as 'misquotations, mistaking of sillables, misplacing half lines, coining of strange and neuer heard of words'.

38. See Derrida, 'This Strange Institution Called Literature', p. 67.

39. See Jacques Derrida, *Aporias: Dying – awaiting (one another at) the 'limits of truth'*, trans. Thomas Dutoit (Stanford: Stanford University Press, 1993), p. 49; 'A Silkworm of One's Own', in Hélène Cixous and Jacques Derrida, *Veils*, trans. Geoffrey Bennington (Stanford: Stanford University Press 2001), p. 33; and passim.

40. Quoted in Bevington (ed.), *Henry IV Part One*, p. 138.

41. See ibid.

42. We have been unable to establish satisfactorily the exact provenance of this quotation.

43. The word 'miraculous' also occurs in a passage in *Macbeth*, Act 4 scene 3, concerning the King's Evil: in lines that are quite possibly not Shakespeare's, Malcolm refers to 'A most miraculous work in this good king, / Which often since my here-remain in England / I have seen him do' (4.3.149–51); and in *The Tempest*, Antonio says of Gonzalo: 'His word is more than the miraculous harp' (2.1.82), i.e. what he says is better than the mythical harp of Amphion which was said to have built the walls of Thebes. Gonzalo can make 'impossible matter . . . easy' (2.1.84), Antonio goes on to observe.

44. Hélène Cixous, *OR, les letters de mon père* (Paris: Des Femmes, 1997), p. 25. Cited by Derrida in *H.C. for Life*, p. 124.

45. See H.W. Fawkner, *Shakespeare's Miracle Plays: Pericles, Cymbeline and The Winter's Tale* (London: Associated University Presses, 1992).

46. 'A Tretis of Miraclis Pleyinge', in *Medieval Drama: An Anthology*, ed. Greg Walker (Oxford: Blackwell, 2000), pp. 196–202; T.G. Bishop, *Shakespeare and the Theatre of Wonder* (Cambridge: Cambridge University Press, 1996), p. 45.

47. Bishop, *Shakespeare and the Theatre of Wonder*, pp. 87–8.

48. Hélène Cixous, 'Sorties: Out and Out: Attacks/Ways Out/Forays', in Hélène Cixous and Catherine Clément, *The Newly Born Woman*, trans. Betsy Wing (Manchester: Manchester University Press, 1986), p. 125.

49. Sonnet 65, in Booth, *Shakespeare's Sonnets*, pp. 58–9. Booth is one of the few commentators to note the suggestion of play in 'might' here. His gloss is worth citing in full: '*might* [:] power, efficacy (the strength of the word is appropriate to the metaphors of violent attack in the preceding lines, but *might* is idiomatically ill-suited to its clause; the usefulness of *might* as a rhyme presumably recommended it, and so, perhaps, did its homonym, the verb 'might', which enables the line to embody the shadow of an alternate construction: "except if this miracle might occur": note the presence of *may* in line 14)' (p. 247).

Index

Main entries are in **bold**.